Resignation and Ecstasy

Studies in Critical Social Sciences Book Series

Haymarket Books is proud to be working with Brill Academic Publishers (www.brill.nl) to republish the *Studies in Critical Social Sciences* book series in paperback editions. This peer-reviewed book series offers insights into our current reality by exploring the content and consequences of power relationships under capitalism, and by considering the spaces of opposition and resistance to these changes that have been defining our new age. Our full catalog of *SCSS* volumes can be viewed at https://www.haymarketbooks.org/series_collections/4-studies-in-critical-social-sciences.

Series Editor
David Fasenfest (Wayne State University)

Editorial Board
Eduardo Bonilla-Silva (Duke University)
Chris Chase-Dunn (University of California–Riverside)
William Carroll (University of Victoria)
Raewyn Connell (University of Sydney)
Kimberlé W. Crenshaw (University of California–LA and Columbia University)
Heidi Gottfried (Wayne State University)
Karin Gottschall (University of Bremen)
Alfredo Saad Filho (King's College London)
Chizuko Ueno (University of Tokyo)
Sylvia Walby (Lancaster University)
Raju Das (York University)

Resignation and Ecstasy

The Moral Geometry of Collective Self-Destruction

Mark P. Worrell

Haymarket Books
Chicago, IL

First published in 2020 by Brill Academic Publishers, The Netherlands
© 2020 Koninklijke Brill NV, Leiden, The Netherlands

Published in paperback in 2021 by
Haymarket Books
P.O. Box 180165
Chicago, IL 60618
773-583-7884
www.haymarketbooks.org

ISBN: 978-1-64259-609-0

Distributed to the trade in the US through Consortium Book Sales and Distribution (www.cbsd.com) and internationally through Ingram Publisher Services International (www.ingramcontent.com).

This book was published with the generous support of Lannan Foundation and Wallace Action Fund.

Special discounts are available for bulk purchases by organizations and institutions. Please call 773-583-7884 or email info@haymarketbooks.org for more information.

Cover design by Jamie Kerry and Ragina Johnson.

Printed in the United States.

10 9 8 7 6 5 4 3 2 1

Library of Congress Cataloging-in-Publication data is available.

Thank you, Diane. You are my best friend and my greatest love.

Contents

Preface IX
Acknowledgements XII
List of Figures XIII
Abbreviations XIV

Introduction: the Beatings Will Continue until Morale Improves 1
1   The Negative Absolute 1
2   Anti-reason 5
3   Good and Evil 6
4   Necessity and Reductionism 7
5   Social Facts 10
6   Suicide 13
7   Absolute Psychology 14
8   Sacrifice and the Concept 16

1 **The Whirlpool of the Negative Absolute** 20
1   The Ghost of Solidarity 21
2   The Bert and Ernie Dialectic 27
3   The Void 46
4   Infinity and Taboo 61
5   Autonomy and Heteronomy 64
6   Rights, Inevitability, and Necessity 73
7   Nihilism and Skepticism 78
8   *Ekstasis* and Resignation 87
9   *Piacula* and Asceticism 94
10 The Savage Child: Infantilism and Primitivism 108
11 Heterarchy and Autothematicism 110
12 Compound Alienation 116
13 Bombers, Shooters, and Drones 127
14 The Grimace of the Vortex 145

2 **A Formal Condensation of Moral Geometry** 150

Conclusion: the Beginning of the End 155

Appendix: Energy, Form, and Concept   157
1   The Spirit of Obsolescence   158
2   The Consciousness of the Whole   161
3   Realism, Nominalism, Idealism, and Materialism   164
4   Representations   171
5   The Post-Kantians   173
6   Split Reasoning   177
7   Hegel   184
8   Dialectical Materialism   186
9   Universals and Individuals   191
10   Rationalism and Empiricism   195
11   Viewpoints and Perspectives   198
12   Sharks and Moderate Realism   200
13   Social Realism and Social Constructionism   205
14   The Return of Subjectivist Understandings   210
15   Methodological Individualism   217
16   The Really Real   223

Bibliography   229
Index   271

Preface

Toward the end of 2019, I received a call for papers regarding a special journal issue dedicated to problems facing contemporary critical theory. The proposed topics covered gender, feminism, communications and recognition theory, psychoanalysis, capitalist pathologies, alienation, ideologies, mass culture, power, democracy, and emancipation. The 'call' indicated that social research should be directed at *the* problem, inherited from Hegel and Marx, of realizing historical reason via critique. Of course, the rubrics were broad enough to cover just about anything, I suppose, but it is revealing that 'revolution' was all but forgotten, presumably subsumable under the notion of 'emancipation.' But more conspicuously absent were the commodity form, the proletariat, class, unions, party, socialism, communism, and so on. Presumably, a lot can be jammed into the "capitalist pathologies" box.

Naturally, we should not expect much from an academic vitae-stuffing exercise but what these abstract indicators veil is the background problem of a vacuum of critical research on what might be called the 'engines' of social effervescence and the sacred energies that can animate the critical spirit, and the renewal of democratic social organization. But where critical academics are gathered we should not expect sustained concern for 'the sacred' or, really, even a concern for genuine social solidarity. I discovered years ago, to my own satisfaction, that 'critical' academics are among the least-solidified people on earth. The resignation baked into the special issue is, one has to admit, probably realistic and therefore warranted since we gave up on the proletariat by the middle of the 20th Century as a mass of ignorant reactionaries; where one has capitulated to the positivity of "capitalist society" (blissfully unaware of the contradiction built into such a phrase) we should infer that the game is truly up. Where there had been a faith in revolution[1] (for a while it was even *inevitable*) we now have the revolving door of academic conferences and journal symposiums. I guess it was inevitable.

The current global turmoil is being driven not by the classical 'proletariat' but by the aspiring, petit bourgeoise urban middle classes in opposition to rural and suburban authoritarian populists, and there is no real indication that a genuine socialism holds any special charm for these liberal aspirants over the prospects of a freshly-regulated free-market consumer utopia and the kinds

---

[1] In the syllogism of society, individual love manifests itself as a universal faith only through mediating secondary associations and institutions. Lacking those middle fortifications, faith and love are essentially hopeless.

of representation the Democratic party, a cornucopia of pressure groups, and some hashtags can provide. However, it is necessary to grasp that 'resignation' is dialectically identical with a *negative ecstasy* (just as ecstasy signifies a *positive resignation*). Within the detailed division of labor, academics will be academics, and the hermetic seal between private critiques and collective praxis is seldom perforated but, presumably, at some point in time, in a wish to grasp the sense of the whole, reflection will turn its light on the voids and lacunae in the sociological tradition and rediscover new sources of energy and enrichment.

Resignation and Ecstasy represents the third volume of *Sacrifice and Self-Defeat*, a project which has three broad goals: to articulate the terms and conditions (Volume One)[2] under which we may explicate the moral geometry[3] of collective consciousness (combined here with the second volume, *Disintegration*)[4] in a social system dominated by the commodity (the final phase of the project). Presently, as with *Disintegration*, we are interested in the antinomies of the moral economy of neoliberalism, but we are equally interested in the deep structures that persist across time and space as a run-up to

---

2 *The Sociogony* (Volume 128 in the *Studies in Critical Social Sciences* series, Brill, 2019).

3 By 'geometry' I am playing off the original meaning of the word: the measuring and surveying of a ground with an eye toward pulling various, disconnected determinations into formal relations with one another. Where there is rationalism and universal thought there is a "geometry" even though it remains, "simple," abstract and untrue (Durkheim 1961: 279). There is a danger in associating this 'geometry' with the "abstract sensuousness" of materialism: "In its further development materialism became one-sided. *Hobbes* was the one who *systematized Bacon's* materialism. Sensuousness lost its bloom and became the abstract sensuousness of the *geometrician. Physical* motion was sacrificed to the *mechanical* or *mathematical, geometry* was proclaimed the principal science. Materialism became *hostile to humanity.* In order to overcome the *anti-human incorporeal* spirit in its own field, materialism itself was obliged to mortify its flesh and become an *ascetic*. It appeared as a *being of reason,* but it also developed the implacable logic of reason" (Marx and Engels 2008: 66). For us, 'geometry' is the teleological work of the concept in giving a form or shape to things such that they stand out as moments within an integrated constellation of synthetic *a priori* judgments. Further, whenever we are in the presence of the untrue representations of the sacred we are also encounter geometry: lines, circles, spirals, cubes, and so on (Durkheim [1912] 1915: 148–49). The bare minimum seems to be the straight line (e.g., the gospels of the New Testament). Galileo is famous for making geometry a prerequisite for comprehending the universe (see Hodgkin 2005: 133) but the triangle, for example, is a concept projected into nature, not nature directly imposing itself upon the intellect. Moreover, we follow Durkheim's sense of 'organicism' as an organicism of ideas, representations, and concepts in opposition to classical organicism. Treated 'geometrically' things "cannot be treated *biologically*" (McGilvery 1898: 238).

4 *Disintegration: Bad Love, Collective Suicide, and the Idols of Imperial Twilight* (Volume 163 in the *Studies in Critical Social Sciences* series, Brill, 2020).

the concluding volume that examines the puritanical logic of ascetic labor in a calling as a "vanishing medium" (Karl Rosenkranz, in Hegel 2002: 264), opening the way for the modern epoch. Volume Four will extend the concept of a moral geometry in an effort to reconstruct and expand Marx's general formula for capital.

Acknowledgements

Thanks to my family and to Chris Altamura, Robert J. Antonio, David Arditi, Harry Dahms, David Fasenfest, Tony Feldmann, Dan Krier, David Norman Smith, Tony Smith, and all the participants of The Symposium for New Directions in Critical Social Theory at Iowa State University.

Figures

1. The Bert and Ernie dialectic   43
2. The social octahedron   49
3. The autothematic-Rabelaisian expansion   115
4. Compound alienation   118
5. The primordial assemblage square   151
6. The monster   152
A. The spiral of political economy   175

Abbreviations

A number of sources have been referenced so frequently that abbreviations are relied upon for the sake of tidiness. I have also abbreviated some reference works such as encyclopedias and dictionaries the details of which are listed below.

AJ	*Ancient Judaism*, Max Weber (1952).
C	*Capital*, Karl Marx. Vol. 1 ([1867] 1976); C, 2: Vol. 2 ([1884] 1978); C, 3: Vol. 3 ([1894] 1981). A reference to page 150 in Volume 3, for example, would appear as: (C, 3: 150).
C, 2	See above.
C, 3	See above.
CPE	*A Contribution to the Critique of Political Economy*, Karl Marx ([1859] 1970).
DOL	*The Division of Labor in Society*, Emile Durkheim ([1893] 1984).
EFRL	*The Elementary Forms of Religious Life*, Emile Durkheim, translated by K. Fields ([1912] 1995).
EP	*Encyclopedia of Philosophy*, (1967). A reference to page 150 in Volume 3, for example, would appear as: (EP, 3: 150).
ES	*Economy and Society*, Vol. 1, Max Weber, (1978); ES, 2: Vol. 2. A reference to page 150 in Volume 2, for example, would appear as: (ES, 2: 150).
ESS	*Encyclopedia of the Social Sciences*, edited by Edwin R.A. Seligman ([1930–1934] 1933–1937). A reference to page 150 in Volume 3, for example, would appear as: (ESS, 3: 150).
FMW	*From Max Weber*, edited by Hans H. Gerth and C. Wright Mills (1946).
G	*Grundrisse*, Karl Marx ([1857] 1973).
MECW	*Collected Works of Marx and Engels*, Karl Marx and Friedrich Engels ([1835–1895] 1975–2004). A reference to page 150 in Volume 44, for example, would appear as: (MECW, 44: 150).
PESC	*The Protestant Ethic and the Spirit of Capitalism*, Max Weber (1930).
PM	*The Economic and Philosophical Manuscripts of 1844*, Karl Marx ([1844] 1964).
PR	*Elements of the Philosophy of Right*, G.W.F. Hegel ([1821] 1991).
PS	*Phenomenology of Spirit*, G.W.F. Hegel ([1807] 1977).
RC	*The Religion of China*, Max Weber (1951).
RSM	*The Rules of Sociological Method*, Emile Durkheim (1982).
S	*Suicide*, Emile Durkheim ([1897] 1951).
SGS	*The Sociology of Georg Simmel* (1950).
SL	*Science of Logic*, G.W.F. Hegel ([1812] 1969).

Introduction: the Beatings Will Continue until Morale Improves

The sociological absolute is society in general, but the problem of absolute sociology is society's concept of itself, i.e., the dialectic of dialectics, the syllogism of syllogisms, the consciousness of consciousnesses, or the "triangle of triangles" (Rosenkranz [1844] 2002). The universal point of view toward facts and things is no longer fashionable but, as H.G. Wells says, "it is no more pretentious to work upon the whole of life than upon parts and aspects..." (1928: 7). Wells is also correct that, in itself, no idea is inherently more valuable than any other; just as there is no such thing as value *per se* (Adorno [1975] 2000: 41), and just as things in themselves are not *actually* capital (C: 975), it is not until ideas and energies are related (positively or negatively) that a sense of scale and value are registered within the social system.

1   **The Negative Absolute**

To speak of the 'Idea' of something in the Hegelian sense presumes a victory of sorts (or at least the anticipation of a universal achievement) but society is never an *empirically* unified thing, and, if anything, it appears to be continuously sliding into a vortex of misery. But integration and wholeness are meaningless without corresponding disintegrations and partitions. Society, by its very nature, is a moral *being*[1] with its own autonomy apart from the lives of individuals. Society "cannot be assembled all the time" and it mostly exists as a memory in a dispersed state of semi-profanity (Durkheim [1912] 1915: 391). Because the current phase of universal profanation, alternating or existing alongside impure bewitchments seems interminable, pessimists would be justified in assuming that teleological activity, if there ever was such a thing, has fallen short of its terminus. Society is definitely not as it should be, and the persistent defects and backslidings have left many writers today unsure whether 'society' is anything more than an empty signifier. Some professional negationists have even joined the ranks of the intellectually departed via regression into some form of crude reductionism or 'moderate realism' of the Aristotelian variety.

---

1   Our society as a *being* is a conscious conceptual actuality with a real personality. This being abides (it is an 'abode') in the sense of endurance, expectation, continuation, and dwelling. It waits and tolerates us as we await and bear it.

The hottest trends in social ontology (replete with magicians, disembodied minds, enchanted objects, and archaic forces) are symptomatic of intellectual suicide. But the negation of society only amounts to a capitulation to bourgeois nominalism and assists in keeping repressed that which has sunken into unconsciousness (cf. Durkheim [1912] 1915: 387).[2]

We know for a fact that *the negative absolute of capitalism exists as an autonomous and determining necessity, otherwise commodities could not even circulate* (C: 146). Indeed, Marxism has clung fervently to the negative absolute in the automatism of 'gravedigger' production concomitant with production for exchange. We also know that the social domain is one of moral *polarities* and where there is a negativity there must necessarily exist a corresponding positivity. The profane is diametrically opposed, even absolutely, to the sacred but the sacred is characterized, in itself, by the polar opposition of purity and impurity. For this reason, Moret and Davy say that not every "sacred principle is a social principle" ([1926] 1970: 52). Some sacred principles (the impure or negative) are essentially *anti-social* (e.g., magic). Therefore, if the negative absolute exists, as it obviously and necessarily does, the positive absolute also *necessarily* exists, sunken in the spiritual underground where concepts have their relations dissolved. We even find empirical verification of this phantom positivity, the 'Eros' of things, in the reconciliation of the 'gravediggers' to the cemetery itself. Disintegration is meaningless without the concept of regeneration. The Absolute "wants to realize itself" but "sees its self-actualization destroyed by interests that have now become explicitly free in the real world and are directed only on what is accidental and subjective, then the presence and agency of the Absolute no longer appears positively unified with the characters and aims of the real world but asserts itself only in the negative form of cancelling everything not correspondent with it…" (Hegel 1975b: 1236). The 'Absolute' is not just another word like 'Progress' that functions as a substitute for god.[3] For us, the absolute is a way of thinking about rational *social organization*.

As a negative absolute, the capitalist 'superstructure' is a nebula of sacred powers even as the system is populated, seemingly, by "'Specialists without

---

[2] One can write a very good book on the problem of science-denial and the fatal lure of magical thinking in contemporary society, but, lacking a direct and sustained attack on the perversion of science by capital and the profit motive, the critique is blunted (e.g., Crease 2019). Nine out of ten dentists recommend a critique of capital in order to preserve scientific integrity.

[3] "With the decline of divine sanctions some influential thinkers for a time tried to substitute collective reifications with a teleological twist, such as Natural Law, History, and Progress. These, too, failed to provide an objective standard for moral approval and condemnation" (Moore 1978: 434).

spirit'" (PESC: 124).⁴ These sacred forces are, however, *anti*-social in nature (per Moret and Davy); the Reason deployed by capital is not merely a 'technical rationality' or negative rationality (ES, 2: 545)⁵ but an actual anti-reason. Where capitalist rationality is pushed to the point of purity we find "the *battle of man with man*" (ES, 1: 93). The war of all against all is not a feature of concrete Reason.⁶ "For example, the sense in which the capitalist is said to be 'rational' is not the sense attributable to a socialist" (Chattopadhyaya 1987: 152). We know anti-reason as hyper-rationality, e.g., antisemitic conspiracies and mythologies that fetishize and preserve the rule of capital (Sartre, in Wilson 1982: 604; see

---

4   Again, it is crucial to recall that the 'individual' (undivided) is always a non-sacred 'moment' distinguishable from the mediated personality and genuine social individuality. This is why Weber could simultaneously embrace the notion of the disenchanting power of reason over superstition while also embracing the *necessity* of a devotion to a calling. "We shall set to work and meet the 'demands of the day,' in human relations as well as in our vocation. This, however, is plain and simple, if each finds and obeys the demon who holds the fibers of his very life" (FMW: 156). Recall, "The Puritan wanted to work in a calling" whereas "we are forced to do so" (PESC: 123). The demon is the (Occidental and puritanical) calling itself. Clearly, the vocation of the Puritan differs from the calling of the banker and the scientist, etc., yet they are called, and we have not, despite the notion of 'disenchantment,' moved to a social ground devoid of 'demons' and Spirit. Weber's allusion to 'disenchantment' is not the world regulated by Reason but only "the return and ascendance of a plurality of old gods, who once again renew their eternal struggle with one another" (Garcia 2011: 268). Charisma, grace, mana, orenda, and even big-V Value, are not universals but historical individuals. The charisma of Jesus works only for believers and salvation is for but a few (Weber [1922] 1991: 271–72) and the "mortal enemy" of miracles is the unbelief of "wits and scoffers" (MECW, 11: 158). Even though a church may set itself up as a universal it can never actually live up to that aspiration. Even money, the thing that Marx thought was becoming the singular global power, the new global divinity, is still lacking planet-conquering authority. Only reason is the universal power that can resolve sundry values and forces into a substantive, translucent, conceptual unity. Why, then, are we constantly disappointed with reason? Examined through the actions and thoughts of individuals, reason seems to lack even the capacity for distinguishing between good and bad (Williams 1993: 100). But reason is not something 'in' the abstract individual (ES, 1: 245). Reason is a synthesizing power emergent in some social relations (here crystallized and 'transcendental,' there fluid, practical, and transactional). For sure, some individuals are more reasonable than others, even in isolation, but this is, as Marx would have say, because they have "absorbed" the principle, or, as Durkheim would say, they have been absorbed *by* the principle. But even the 'reason-able' person will lose their reasoning abilities once they fall out of a social matrix that cultivates and sustains reason. In other words, the person possessed of reason will 'devolve' into, at best, a merely *intelligent* individual, i.e., in possession of discernment and understanding (cf. Fromm 1981: 10–11).
5   Negative rationalization is the *instrumentalization* of rationality toward any goal, including any irrational end whatsoever (ES, 2: 545).
6   This is despite the fact that reason involves a kind of violence, as Aquinas indicates (1993: 173).

also Massing 1949: 13; Worrell 2008; Worrell 2017)[7] as well as the hypo-rationality of the abstract schematics of garden-variety prejudice, common sense, and folk wisdom, etc. Within the negativity of anti-reason separating and breaking relations (e.g., keeping white free of brown contamination), there is a 'positivity' that seeks to recombine elements in perverse forms (e.g., everything enveloped by the signifier of 'the Jew' in deranged conspiracy theories).[8] The value dimension under capital suffers twists and turns just as any other moral substance does.

One could argue that exchange-value is not directly the enemy of society and is not necessarily an abuse of reason, but the drive for the accumulation of surplus value (grounded in excess labor) is the negation of rational (substantive) human values. The drive for accumulating surplus value harbors a self-defeating logic of self-delusion, hauntings, and concrete liquidations (Szrot 2019; Worrell 2009). If money is dead people, i.e., the crystallized remains of abstracted human life, the imperative to make and accumulate as much as possible (the capitalist ideal) is necrophilia in almost ideal-typical purity. The billionaire stands atop a mountain of corpses. The pursuit of surplus value, or 'Value' (as if there is now only one worthy of such a lofty designation) devalues the remainder of ideals and what should be a system of self-limiting and self-containing forces devolves into an energetic but morbid whirlpool of destruction (Durkheim [1912] 1915: 233). But if the negative seems to have the upper hand, surrounded as we are on all sides by death and disintegration, it might very well be that the enemies of society are unintentionally engaged in actions that raise positivity into the sphere of conscious reflection. The bad and the wrong keep us in chains, but the effects of terror and repression are also simultaneously productive of energies that mobilize populations around the values of positive freedom, the general welfare, social democracy, and universal peace.

---

7 See Eco's (2011: 79) important contribution to what amounts to a universal conspiracy form in the vein of Marx's analysis of the value phenomenology and Hegel's dialectics such that we could construct an historical matrix of Individual conspiracies that are functionally Particularized under the hegemony of a revealed Universal.

8 In modern antisemitic conspiracies, 'the Jew' is the attempt to personify the negative (diabolical) absolute of capital. Political economy represents a constellation of taboo concepts for subjects under the reign of capital, so reactions draw upon race, faith, gender, and other identity-based conflicts as source materials. Americans do not talk about 'capitalism' because it works pretty well for some and, for those on the losing end of the stick, they take their frustrations out in the terms of Jesus, gays, snowflakes, and free-riding immigrants, etc.

2   Anti-reason

It is often the case that the enemy of X (let us call it the -X) is itself negated by the compression effect that arises from its own propagation and multiplications. This presupposes that the negative cannot only negate itself but that it contains some positive element, and this is difficult to swallow after the horrors of the last one hundred years. It seems impossible that a nightmare can embody reason. Where is the reason, for example, in the Holocaust or the Sandy Hook massacre? The slaughter of children and the concept of 'reason' cannot make contact without eliciting absolute disgust. The common solution is not to search for the reason 'in' a thing but, rather, the reason 'for' a thing. But Hegel says that a real dialectical method develops the reason *within* the thing, not by attributing an external, subjective reason to it, but developing the actual, inner kernel residing within it (PR: 60). It might have been realizations such as this that drove Reich insane: "There is a truth and a rationale in everything irrational that happens, in every murder, rape, war suicide…" (1953: 115). But this inner kernel is not reason in its positive mode. We arrive at the realization that the negative and positive absolutes are not two separate things but two dimensions of one mysterious thing. For example, anti-authoritarianism is not necessarily the negation of authoritarianism but, as we have seen in the previous two volumes, the negation of *authority*.[9] Anti-authoritarianism, compared to *non*-authoritarianism, can be another polar form of authoritarianism. In the same way, anti-hierarchy does not negate hierarchy[10] and anti-magic does not necessarily destroy magic (Radkau 2009: 560). Consider bureaucracy: as the routinization of charisma bureaucracy does not actually eliminate charisma from the world but, in a way, exists as a nearly indestructible form of

---

[9]   To recapitulate our previous position, leftist hyper-critique leads into a corner with two suicidal escape routes: the regression to instinct theory or moral anarchism. As Wolff says, "The primary obligation of man is autonomy, the refusal to be ruled … and philosophical anarchism would seem to be the only reasonable political belief for an enlightened man" (1970: 18–19). Since we do not have instincts and can only evade authority *philosophically*, this leaves one pining for a utopian democratic no-place.

[10] Materialism insists that the human brain is structured hierarchically, that the 'work' of evolution has delivered us to hierarchic thought, and that to reason is to think hierarchically (see LeDoux 2019: 372ff.). Sociology, on the other hand, insists that it is the hierarchies of social organization that are reflected in the structures of thought. Either way, hierarchy prevails as a fact, natural or social. We may reason our way to an anti-hierarchical form of thinking and social organization, but, either way, we have still not negated hierarchy itself but merely changed the dialectical (syllogistic) values and weights of our 'moments.'

anti-charisma.[11] We can extrapolate that Reason is evil (by virtue of also 'containing' a full share of anti-Reason) and where the actualization of the Idea has been perverted we are led to the conclusion that the beatings will continue until morale improves. Reason and evil are inseparable; one need only read Goethe's *Faust* to see that the only character in the story with reason on their side is Mephistopheles (Dahms 2019). The figure of the devil in *Faust* is not only the spirit of negation but also the voice of reason.[12] The good is not the absence of evil, we will never be free of evil, but merely the daily struggle against it, and there really is no greater miracle than the apparently humdrum concept of regulation that, until the day it is sublated and internalized, must exist (tragically) as a restraining externality.[13]

It is possible to fight fire with fire, bullets with bullets, and demons with demons, but once these dynamics get wound up, they know few limits and can lead to widespread destruction. That leaves us with the struggle over the negative with the positive and that means knowing the positive within the negative, which seems impossible, though we are all too familiar with the inversion. The negative freedom of individuals under the reign of capital "is the freedom of the void" that, when it becomes active, manifests itself as fanatical destruction, fury, suicide, murder, and terror (PR: 38–39). These phenomena fall *within* the odyssey of the Concept, not exterior to it, and we will make no headway until we embark on discovering the veiled reasons for which people are killing and dying (PR: 102).

3   Good and Evil

The easiest rationalization to make for any social pathology is the one that individuates the problem, avoiding the social causes altogether, through psychological reductions. Every day, at least one mass shooting is sloughed off with the magic phrase "mental health issues." With Durkheim, the solution lies in the direction of grasping that what is abnormal and morbid are only *exaggerations* of what is considered normal and healthy. This insight is the most difficult

---

11   Anyone who perceives mana or its various analogs operating in the modern world (e.g., 'the mana of mass society') is lacking a theory of *routinization* and forms.

12   Klinkenborg observes that for Twain (*Letters from the Earth*) "Satan is the Connecticut Yankee *in extremis*, a rational being in an irrational world" (2019). The Christian devil can be cast as an angle and even a gentleman if one's conception of god is one of a wrathful and uncaring monster (Maurier [1894] 1998: 183).

13   "Inward liberty and external necessity are the two poles of the tragic world" (Schelling, in Hedge 1847: 429).

to hold consistently: the virtuous and the vicious are not compartmentally sealed off from one another but exist along a continuum and separated analytically by degrees. As Leonard Nelson once said, "good is the evil we choose to ignore" ([1917] 1957: 90)[14] and, by extension, the evil is merely the good we cannot get enough of.[15] In no way is this congruous with the kind of simple relativism or subjectivization of values wept over by the likes of Bloom (1987: 142). Where there is good, its double or other half is also necessarily present (Plato, in Hegel [1840] 1995a: 32). Disease is inseparable from health and life is meaningless without death. However, those that would promote the health of society over egoism and greed themselves prohibit the critique of the sacred principle of the modern system by normalizing the predication of capitalism with the sign of 'society.' We know from Hegel that the predicate provides what is essential in the relation between two self-subsisting totalities (SL: 624–25) and that capitalism is essentially anti-social. Anti-capitalism seems like the way back toward real society but the unpleasant truth about American politics is that it is defined and wholly dominated by a one-party system consisting of two wings or personalities, both purely capitalistic, and while Red and Blue politicians may personally dislike one another they are nonetheless partners, and their collaborations are, if filled with animosities, still necessary (from a capitalistic standpoint) and destructive to democracy; the entire establishment setup is designed to frustrate democracy rather than make it flourish. Whatever "progressive" elements one might find in the party system are easily contained by capital and exhausted in populist miasmas. What is necessary always contends with other necessities.

4   Necessity and Reductionism

Dialectical necessity has been penetrated by a more powerful necessity of a different species, from another domain of life, that has diverted the course of

---

14   "Good or evil lived in the same country, spoke the same language, came together like old friends, feeling the same completion, touching hands beside the iron bedstead" (Greene [1938] 2004: 135).

15   The etymology of 'evil' indicates that it comes from the Proto-Indo-European *upélos*, from *upo*, up, *eup*, down, up, over, for the exceeding of approved limits. 'Evil' is a permanent condition, especially among those who turn their rage against fresh waves of humanity that keep a civilization vibrant and supple: "Once customs are established and prejudices rooted, reform is a dangerous and fruitless enterprise; a people cannot bear to see its evils touched, even if only to be eradicated; it is like a stupid, pusillanimous invalid who trembles at the sight of a physician" (Rousseau [1762] 1968: 88–89).

Spirit away from the goal of conceptual, rational unification. Concreteness is misplaced, and mimesis devolves from complex social emulations into simple imitations (Bechtold 2019). For this reason, it appears that necessity has given way to pure contingency, but where we can still speak of causes and effects there is still the inevitable and the predetermined, at least in a 'subterranean' sense. Where there should be society and Reason, what Durkheim calls the "consciousness of the whole" (1961: 277), we instead have capitalism (anti-society), bits and pieces, and an instrumental rationality (Bechtold 2019) that breaks the whole down into a negative mechanical totality of disjointed abstractions. Yet, even though the positive concrete universal has never realized itself in a permanent condition, it nonetheless exists at least as a concept in a kind of 'fourth spatial dimension' (to appropriate a metaphor from Mauss).[16] All the same, even anti-society is, in its own way, still a social form in the same way that anti-capitalism has so far and paradoxically inclined towards capitalism. It should come as no surprise when altruism turns into egoism, yesterday's communists are today's investors, critical academics keep an eye on equity prices, good becomes evil, or magenta chaos delivers us to the threshold of umber fate. These kinds of transpositions are really inevitable in a world of moral polarities. Still, if anti-society is a kind of society (defective, abstract, and 'evil') it nonetheless possesses all the resources needed to resume its odyssey. We do not have to wait for something external to the system or add an extra, missing supplement in order to reorganize the thing. The point is not simply to reject the existent *in toto* but to reevaluate the hitherto "highly esteemed" aspects, reject "much" of that, and alter and reorganize relations and functions of the materials.

> If the building of a new city in a waste land is attended with difficulties, yet there is no shortage of materials; but the abundance of materials presents all the more obstacles of another kind when the task is to remodel an ancient city, solidly built, and maintained in continuous possession and occupation. Among other things one must resolve to make no use at all of much material that has hitherto been highly esteemed (SL: 575).[17]

---

16   Not to be confused with Zöllner's "'fourth dimension'" (MECW, 25: 352).
17   Admittedly, the facts of bourgeois society have not precluded the enjoyment of genuine, creative individuality and concrete personality for some, even as most are reduced to one-sided beings (subjects) pushed around by impersonal forces and alien desires; the reigning spirit of individualism leads people away from actual individuality and into the waiting arms of heteronomy.

And what are our most valuable 'materials' if not our concepts and ideals? "Much" will have to go but not all.

The fact that society is a conceptual being (Durkheim [1912] 1915: 386; see also Harms 1981) has been lost to generations of sociologists who have for the most part abandoned or misinterpreted their classical roots (Smith 2019). Most self-professed 'dialectical materialists' oscillate between ordinary materialism and transcendental idealism of one form or another. Sociologists have renounced concepts for variables, have given up explaining the complex through the complex (Durkheim 1974: 29), and chased titles and prizes by emulating the methods of the physical sciences. The techniques seem objective, but the results are purely subjective (Adorno 1976: 72). Instead of relations and dialectical matrices, we see only individuals, brains, descriptions, and the dipping of sticks into prejudice.[18] *Ipso facto*, it is refreshing to see the old concept of alienation approached in a new way, i.e., from the standpoint of the logical moments of the syllogism (Altamura 2019), which might sound quaint, but what this really means is that dialectics possess a unified method and a precise structure beyond jargon.

It is certainly true that the only active elements in society are *individuals* (S: 310; Durkheim [1912] 1915: 386; Hegel [1807] 1967: 160). In fact, everything is an individual (even the last of the Scholastics were forced to admit as much) but the decisive fact is how individuals *relate* to one another as well as their institutional *functions*. An 'individual' is an abstraction, is alienated, and stands in marked contrast to a concrete *singularity*, i.e., an individual that has been swept up in the dialectical process of self-relation and has "absorbed ... dynamic social forces" (CPE: 189). Genuine human individuality (personality) is the product of society (CPE: 189; see also PS: 235; RSM: 128; S: 126; SGS: 255). Even an individual work of art that is self-contained, closed, and inseparable from its cultural horizon (Bechtold 2019) expresses potential functions both particular and universal, and, in relation to the psyche, as Altamura (2019) reinforces, it is social organization and collective consciousness that determine the structure and the disposition of the individual mind. Anywhere we find an actual individual of sociological importance we are interested in its *singularity* rather than its subjective infinity, which is of no interest to sociology.

---

18 Prejudice *per se* is irrelevant apart from psychology whereas the self-defense mechanisms employed to defend them against reflection are of sociological significance: "If your judgment is moved to protest against ... prejudices, your neighbors ... scream 'impiety' and frighten you" (Voltaire 1962: 432). The real problem of prejudice resides in the logic and construction of things taboo (negatively sacrosanct).

5 Social Facts

The 'singular' is not what it is commonly imagined to be but the moment where a plenitude has been sacrificed (and simultaneously preserved in its transformation) for the sake of a social function, or, lacking subordination to a concrete universal, submission to the facts of the master (Cassano 2019). Put simply, piety is rewarded, and voluntary integration is a sign of credibility (Smith 2019). Being a 'function' lacks the kind of glamour we seek in the bourgeois hologram (Bageant 2007) but being a function also means being a fact (Worrell 2018) and while social facts in our world are not as they should be, fraught with contradictions, they are nonetheless essential moments of teleological activity—as such, if one fantasizes about Radical Transformation™ without going through the facts, i.e., sublation, one will be forever disappointed. The road to heaven runs through hell and we will need facts in the future even as we are restrained by them—this is especially pertinent when one dreams of the authority of democracy or the authority of positive freedom. There is no such thing as society without the facticity of the social (Feldmann 2019). If we ever arrive at a world of universal democratic freedom, we would want to not only preserve the facticity and authority of that condition but make it absolute and inviolable (positively sacred).[19] The only alternatives are, on the one hand, the triumph of the Idea, and, on the other, anarchy, but to actually work at a universal scale anarchy would have to rest on a philosophical anthropology that includes instinctual behavior rather than ethical conduct. As we saw in *The Sociogony*, instinct theory is not only a sociological non-starter but one of the contradictions that subverted Marx's theory of revolution and communism.

Apropos the process of mono-valuation and the drive for infinite accumulation, people are invited to imbibe in the spirits of limitlessness and hyper-individualism, compressed into the negative unity of infinity disease (S: 287; see also Altamura 2019; Worrell 2015; 2018; 2019). When one stops to question the wisdom of blindly pursuing an alien goal the subject is beset with guilt for lack of faith (Szrot 2019). Insofar as the invitations are accepted, society, like any 'being,' begins to question the value of existence: to be, or not to be, that

---

19   If society were adequately comprehended in the Concept the 'facticity' of the social would be sublated into the Idea of society (cf. RSM: 35–36). In other words, social facts would dissolve into reason, i.e., we would be 'governed' by the Concept. However, I am going out on a limb and assuming that, people being people, the allure of the Concept would be underwhelming for most. "To put the matter ... generally, not every rational form of authority can possibly suit everybody. There has to be an element of compulsion" (Moore 1978: 442).

really is the question. The negative absolute of the modern world is an autonomous subject that bends the wills of individuals to suit its own fancy; it even pleasures itself for no other reason than for its own self-enjoyment (EFRL: 385). Just as positive society lives on sacrifices, negative society runs on deaths, partial and mass (e.g., war, suicides, murder, accidental overdoses, being struck down by gainful employment, and so on). We have lost sight of the fact that *collective* representations, in contrast to the ordinary or the individual, are born from ritual ecstasy and the frenzied mayhem of self-destructive acts that often teeter on the edge of death (Krier 2019). Collective representations are generated in blood, fire, beatings, lacerations, and excruciating pain that mundane life does not engender.

For this reason, Marxism unhitched from the effervescence of revolution is impotent and falters on the substitution of collective representations with the representations of the understanding which are connected to routine 'practical activity' (cf. Marx's eighth thesis on Feuerbach) or "dynamic-practical behavior" (Scheler 1973: 318). The notion of eradicating hyper-praxis or surplus production, religious ceremonies, and so forth, is absurd. Our 'species being' is inherently excessive so long as we remain assembled. 'Regulation' (in its myriad conceptual and normative forms) sounds boring and obviously counter-revolutionary but surplus activity linked to a rationalized *Nomos* is more feasible than the impossibility of extinguishing the fires of surplus itself. "The creation of surplus does not necessarily require appropriation by individuals leading to the kind of concentrated wealth and poverty if social institutions and economic activities are not designed for the perpetuation and reproduction of capitalist social relations, as outlined by Marx" (Fasenfest 2018: 852).[20]

With rites and fury in mind, from our standpoint, an orthodox labor ontology is the path to nowhere. As we saw in the "Formal Intermezzo" in *The Sociogony*, hyper-praxis produces material abundance beyond need but these surpluses are swept up into the circuits of *Nomos* and shift from use-values to being carriers of an exchange principle to being poetic instruments. "The essential character of poiesis was not its aspect as a practical and voluntary process but ... a mode of truth understood as unveiling.... And it was precisely because of this essential proximity to truth that Aristotle, who repeatedly theorizes this distinction within man's 'doing,' tended to assign a higher position to poiesis than to praxis. According to Aristotle, the roots of praxis lay in the very condition of man as an animal, a living being: these roots were constituted by the very principle of motion (will, understood as the basic unit of craving,

---

20   "In and by itself the extraction of a surplus does not prove the existence of predatory rule" (Moore 1978: 445).

desire, and volition) that characterizes life" (Agamben 1999: 69). It would be technically inaccurate, then, to refer to something like "sacred praxis." The sacred and praxis belong to opposed domains. "Ritual acts," says Mauss, "are eminently effective; they are creative; they do things…. However, human skill can also be creative and the actions of craftsmen are known to be effective. From this point of view the greater part of the human race has always had difficulty in distinguishing techniques from rites" (1972: 19).

Magic was used by people to aid in hunting or fishing whereas some crafts, such as medicine, are "entirely swamped by magic" (Ibid.). However, "there has always been an intangible difference in method between the two activities" (Ibid: 20). It is crucial to recall that in order to deploy magical rites as part of mundane activities like hunting, a society would first of all had to have *already* passed through the outrageous and blood-curdling developments of religion as a precondition before magic could develop and then be extended into what is basically ordinary praxis, punctuated as it is, with bursts of energy.[21]

Every explosive but futile act of destruction is, in a way, an attempt to recreate the fury of the rite that generates the energy of the objective social phantom but, ironically, functions to preserve the abstractions and dysfunctions of the prevailing negativity.[22] Žižek would have us believe that explosions of terror are desperate attempts to mask the *absence* of some big Other but the sociology of the aftermath reveals the opposite: the product of terror is not reducible to the number of corpses or assigning monetary figures to events, but also the generation of what we might call a counter-terror sentiment and a collective will for rational regulation. As capitalism 'works' for fewer and fewer people, with whole classes falling under the wheels of the planetary juggernaut, the estranged and the deranged act out. Their acting out is inspired by the very thing that hates them and that directs their animosity toward substitutes and scapegoats. It is true that a push for "universal background checks" is a far cry from what is necessary but the precondition for every worthy goal is a collection of insufficiencies.

Every moment of every single day, subjects are communicated to in positive and negative tones from 'on high' (Durkheim [1912] 1915: 242). Demands are conveyed through averted eyes, slammed doors, dismissals, rejections, slights, insults, silence, broken promises, the lure of fame, the promise of wealth, the

---

21 It is decisive to always keep magic connected to egoism, the profane, and the abstract.
22 When we hear right-wingers jabbering on in a Trump-like fashion, parroting the rhetoric they hear on Fox News, we have to perceive the babble as ritual incantations or invocations. When some enraged granny goes on and on about "fake news" (etc.) it is out of a desire to keep the rallying going. These people are not 'brainwashed' but participants in a never-ending, virtual political rally.

generation of impossible dreams, the suffering of insatiable desires and unrestrained fantasies, holy allegiances, sanguine passions, revenge, a hail of bullets, blocked endeavors, the impenetrable wall of destiny, and 1001 other things. In the ups and downs, augmentations and negations of emotional life, most people (more or less) manage to actively (Feldmann 2019) harmonize the pluses and minuses and keep their chins up as they navigate their daily routines. They suffer the divisions of alienation but enjoy the reflected multiplications, summon enough courage to temper their self-destructive impulses, and accept the claim on the part of their superiors that to succeed they should model their thoughts and actions on those that have preceded them through dedication and hard work, i.e., they should identify with their betters and desire what is in reality a constellation of alien desires (Cassano 2019; Worrell 2009c).[23] Never mind that 'dedication' and 'hard work' are all too frequently mere euphemisms for luck and random connections. But the moral and immoral athletes among us cannot be fooled. They take things from another point of view and to extremes.

6 Suicide

When we look back on 2019 we will find that something like 1.5 million people in America will have attempted suicide and that, give or take, 50,000 people will succeed in taking their own lives. The individuals themselves are not predestined to destroy themselves but the fact that more than one million people will try is predestined (S: 325). Suicide is a conscious act, of that, there is little doubt but the social causes that drive individuals to dispose of themselves operate in an almost completely unconscious way. Social forces are not nonconscious but invisible to the mind. People do not know what forces are and, with a nod to Confucius, do not know what they do not know (Thoreau [1854] 1960: 12). Suicide notes are notorious for occluding true motives because the subjects themselves are unaware of the underlying reasons for their symptomatic expressions. But just as consciousness is more complex and multidimensional than mainstream psychology leads us to believe, the unconscious is also more complex. Freud assures us that there is no such thing as a collective unconscious, not because it is not real, but because the phrase is redundant. "It is not easy to translate the concepts of individual psychology into mass psychology," says Freud, "and I do not think that much is to be gained by introducing

---

23 Although, contra Žižek, e.g., a theory of subjective desire is no substitute for a theory of authority.

the concept of a 'collective' unconscious—the content of the unconscious is collective anyhow, a general possession of mankind" (1939: 170). In short, the unconscious is social from the very beginning (Fromm 1981: 36–37).[24] As Fromm says, "the contents of the social unconscious vary depending on the many forms of social structure: aggressiveness, rebelliousness, dependency, loneliness, unhappiness, boredom, to mention only a few" (Ibid: 36). Paradoxically, the repression that is necessary for association and solidarity also invades language and practices with a disorienting effect on individuals, but traditional psychologies have not had a mass de-reification effect of any kind on those suffering from the myriad pathologies that fall under the banner of 'psychology.'

7   Absolute Psychology

Given the somewhat impoverished state of psychological understanding in critical philosophy and political economy, I think it is important to draw out what goes presupposed in Freud. For example, if one slogs through any of the top-flight analyses of Marx's theory of the commodity as a value-bearing object, one quickly realizes that even the best writers are utterly lacking in what is meant by the ideal, the mental, and consciousness as these concepts pertain to exchange-value. They would do well to revisit Freud but also Hegel and, perish the thought, seriously consider Durkheim's theory of sacred forces[25]

---

24   The unconscious, like the underworld and the chthonic, is a place not only of repressed traumas but also of valued treasures. "Into the underland we have long placed that which we fear and wish to lose, and that which we love and wish to save" (Macfarlane 2019: 8).

25   In both *The Sociogony* and *Disintegration* I stressed, following Durkheim, that the *forces* of nature are unconsciously modelled on social forces and reflect the possibilities and limitations of social organization; social organization is the ground of mental and spiritual organization (see Durkheim and Mauss [1903] 1963: 82). As Harrison says, "*Themis was the mother of Dike*; the social conscience, the social structure, gave birth, not of course to the order of nature, but to man's conception, his representation, of that order" (1962: 533). CNN reports that Hungarian physicists are hot on the heels of a fifth natural force that might connect the world of the visible to the realm of dark matter. "Jonathan Feng, a professor of physics and astronomy at the University of California, Irvine, told CNN he's been following the Hungarian team's work for years, and believes their research is shaping up to be a game changer…. 'There's no reason to stop at the fifth,' Feng said. 'There could be a sixth, seventh, and eighth force'" (Prior 2019). Rest assured, there will a fifth, sixth, seventh, and an eighth force! Our conceptions, classifications, and our capacity to comprehend relations are "rigorously determined by social conditions" and "social facts" (Rivers 1914: 3). People who propose living in a world free from "social facts" actually propose suicide, and, since social facts are constructions, a life free of social facts would

(*Nitimur in vetitum semper cupimusque negata*).²⁶ This theoretical synthesis, let us call it the Marxheimian, or better, perhaps, the *absolute* strain,²⁷ embodies an eight-sided psychological matrix: (1) individual / personal; (2) particular / mass / intra-group; (3) universal / social / inter-group; (4) profane / linear understandings; (5) sacred pure / positive; (6) sacred impure / negative; (7) consciousness; and (8) unconsciousness. An absolute psychology would be attuned to the multifaceted nature of Spirit.

It is not possible to grasp the logic of capital and theoretically negate the accumulation of surplus value until critique situates Value within the realm of the sacred, as it refracts through the various dimensions and spheres of the absolute 'psychic' matrix. Value is not a category of the understanding restricted to, or comprehended by, the domain of political economy but is an ultramundane or 'otherworldly' principle (Smith 1988).²⁸ If 'the economy' was a rational system restricted to the production and distribution of goods and services, we could get out of it what we put into it. Further, if class exploitation were merely a problem of simple domination it could never sustain itself continuously. It is a fact that the rewards that accrue to sellers of labor power, in general, are inferior to the quantum of energy expended in the labor process so this inferiority must appear, at least in part, to be valid and fits with the logic of "sacrificial tribute" whereby "they give to the sacred beings a little of what they receive from them, and they receive from them all that they give" (Durkheim [1912] 1915: 383). These "sacred beings" are the avatars or personifications of capital (positive and negative). Marx is correct that *having a job means paying to work* but modern workers are not just 'talking tools' and do not like to think of themselves much in the degrading terms of 'laborers' or 'workers' and they certainly do not hate the positive personifications of capital. They may hate the signified substance, but they have not connected the signifiers to that element and, consequently, are of two minds or ambivalent toward the problem of wealth distribution.²⁹

---

    reduce us to nothing but subjects of natural necessity, i.e., we would be reduced to nothing but inhuman things. We will either be the makers of the world or we will be purely the product of the world.

26 "We are ever striving after what is forbidden and coveting what is denied us" (Ovid).

27 This synthesis is in no way a 'mediation' of two great thinkers and we are not attempting to equalize them (cf. Nietzsche [1887] 1974: 212).

28 Lest anyone suppose, per the first dimension, i.e., personal psychology, that academic reports should be utilized, perish the thought. The world of literature and poetry offer more insights and explanations than mainstream psychology can ever hope to obtain.

29 Levin claims that "Elites in democratic societies are always under pressure to prove that the answers to these questions [of unequal wealth and power distribution] are sufficient, and so that they are worthy of authority and special standing. They have to believe this

Durkheim is famous for amplifying the antique notion that people are double (*Homo duplex* or double-minded) but when one wrestles with *Suicide* one comes to the realization that Durkheim's double is itself doubled and even doubled again. If one knows Hegel's weird disjunctive syllogism in the big *Logic* (or the money-price form in the first chapter of *Capital*) one gets the impression that we are on some kind of analogous ground with Durkheim's moral geometry where the universal is capable of enveloping itself. What we need to know is if it is possible for not only individuals to commit suicide but if a concept is also capable of killing itself, either passively or actively, and, further, if there is life after death for the sacrificial being.

8 Sacrifice and the Concept

Hegel famously concludes the *Phenomenology* at Golgotha, heralding a breakthrough for Spirit. The death of the man was a midway point (Hegel 1988: 463) in the *Bildungsroman* of the world Spirit. However, we also know that every midway point is also an end as well as a beginning or a "sunrise" for a new Concept (Hegel [1807] 2008: 731). So here was a sick man who embodied and gave expression to a new Concept and was rewarded for his illness, insight, and inspiration with a brutal execution. But we do not need the gospel of Judas (Kasser and Wurst 2007) to see that this execution was just as much a suicide—a premodern version of 'death by cop.' Durkheim might classify the death of Jesus (either as an empirically existing person or as a mythological composite) as an instance of positive, indirect, optional altruistic total self-destruction. Jesus will come to live again as a symbolic force but not until decades later when Paul (the first Christian) is engaged not in the rallying and the organization of the flock but in their *persecution*. Terror is no day at the beach, but it might contain more than we realize. This death is nothing less than conceptual autocide

---

themselves, or else they will be racked by a debilitating guilt that could eat away their sense of purpose. They have to persuade others of this as well, or else their power will be a constant provocation to cynicism, alienation, and self-righteous populist upheaval" (2020: 182). This all seems self-evidently laughable; the cynicism and self-righteousness of the American rebel pales in comparison to the unvarnished cynicism and unbridled opportunism of the power elite and their lapdogs. If the notion that the rich and powerful are wringing their hands over their perceived illegitimacy in the eyes of the common lot is a bit much, it is nonetheless true that there are, historically speaking, days of reckoning when the ruling class is forced to make concessions in style and substance in order to maintain control, i.e., change for the sake of continuity. The genuine value of Levin's book resides in the basically Durkheimian-like argument that professions qua institutions (the nexus of expertise and trust) connect individuals to the realm of universal values.

inflicted upon the positive by the negative. The autocide of the concept born from a charismatic leader functioning as a collective representation seems like a preposterous notion that ought to require a lot of ontological tomfoolery, but, I think if one approaches the suggestion of Absolute self-destruction from the standpoint of a consistent social realism, one that is attuned to nuances and currents both positive and negative, what seems absurd at first is actually true—not self-evidently true but inevitable if we see our argument through to the end. If Condorcet can die for the Revolution, the Revolution can bloody well sacrifice itself, which really *amounts to the exact same thing*.

Within its contemporary horizon, Golgotha surely appeared to be an impossible beginning to what turned out to be a brilliant career. Few individuals can receive a beating for the ages, die from asphyxiation on a cross, be eaten by birds and dogs, and, within a few centuries, conquer an empire. It is entirely plausible that the successful career of Jesus as a collective representation lies in the sheer brutality of his death recounted in stories, icons, and passion plays. World-conquering gods are not normally born from the humiliating annihilation of their profane shells, but the terror visited upon Jesus at the end of his mortal life is relatable to billions of people and the horror of it can be encapsulated in the term 'sacrifice' apart from any collective ritual reenactments. The Jesus sect was subject to state terror because the conceptual breakthrough was politically unbearable and punishable as a crime. Where one finds the 'criminal' one is sometimes in contact with a 'king' (Foucault 1977: 29; cf. Badiou 2003: 56). Indeed, the execution of a criminal is frequently the actual terminus for royalty (Freud [1913] 1950: 56). The charisma of crime might seem odd but the odyssey of the Idea and the dictatorship of reason (Freud 1939: 146–47) do not involve obedience to tradition and custom but disobedience, the demanding of reasons from those in a position of authority, and, quite frequently, unjust and even spectacular punishment visited upon the disobedient. This marks the difference between the ordinary understanding of 'authority' and the sociological concept of "creative authority" (Freeman 1943: 725).

Universal political oppression can lead to individual depression and the repression of the Idea but it is also possible for repression to lead not to desublimation *per se* but what Jean Wahl referred to as a *transdescendance* (in Sartre 1950: 38–39). As such, as in the case of a charismatic group, repression can be followed by the growth of the positive concept rather than its annihilation. Where there is "terror and compression" (Durkheim [1912] 1915: 256) there is also an automatic counter-current that leads to the elevation of the concept. A transcendental realm is our nemesis, of that there is no doubt, we do not want more alien gods and the idea of a noumenal realm is a pernicious holdover, however, "terror and compression" are simultaneously mechanisms that can reactivate the Concept, liberating it from submersion in the unconscious, providing the opportunity for the critical spirit to project the Concept back into its positive, concrete, rational ground. For example, terror attacks in the US come in external and internal forms that spur connections to politics, race, religion, etc., but, so far, the bourgeoisie have managed to prevent discourse from veering toward the essential problem: capitalism. Since the essential is taboo in America, "terror and compression" will continue unabated until, finally, there are no other dead ends and box canyons for Spirit get lost in. To bring a halt to the self-flagellation of society, the primary role of critical theory today is to connect the explosions of the sacred impure to the concept of capital as a system driven by, and expressing, an abstract, (negative) anti-reason.

The attainment of the Idea involves, perhaps not necessarily but as a historical possibility, the actualization on a tiny scale, a particularity that knows itself as the whole universe. We see this occur under conditions of tribal disintegration where each clan has universalized itself through retrogression and claimed everything under the moon and stars for itself all the while it is situated alongside other clans operating under the same 'delusional' universal beliefs. We find this even today among hyper-specialized academics who, seemingly oblivious to what has gone on around them in other disciplines, seize the Thing for themselves and, with willful ignorance, claim to have grasped some new insight all the while reproducing, in ever-more more flaccid and one-sided forms, ideas that have circulated for generations in other fields. As of 2017, the field of neuropsychology has, I kid you not, finally discovered the *Concept*. And how many times will social constructionism be reinvented, increasingly subjectivized, before eternity brings a merciful end to academia? While the descending wave is the norm, it also happens that, from time to time, some tiny group of thinkers ensconced in an increasingly stupid world, battle their way to the heights of genuine universal comprehension. Here, a particular group actually embodies the positive universal and reflects their concept into the void of the reigning, abstract universal sphere. One might think that, in all such cases, the negation of the negation rises like a colossal hammer against innovation, yet, this outcome is not predetermined.

It is not difficult to see in Weber's analysis of musical rationalization a concern for creative epochs when a "striving for expressiveness" can either burst the normative framework of an existing symbolic system or, by contrast, lead in the opposite direction toward a rational enrichment of the symbolic system. In the antiquities, the striving "led to an extreme melodic development[30]

---

30 "The poetic element in music, the language of the soul, which pours out into the notes the inner joy and sorrow of the heart, and in this outpouring mitigates and rises above the

which shattered the harmonic elements of the [musical] system" whereas "the same striving led to an entirely different result" in the west to "the development of chordal harmony." The fact that separated the antique from the Occidental outcomes was the institution of polyvocality. "Expressiveness could then follow the path of polyvoiced music" (1958: 65). Polyvocality means that singers are not forced to perform in unison within the same octave. The link to callings or vocations and a partitioning of effort are easily connected to the polyvocal form. Each individual pursuing and developing their unique voice, contributes to, rather than tarnishes, the collective product. Each voice, here, possesses a "melodic right" while preserving a "uniformity" of "the ensemble" (Weber 1958: 68). And sometimes what appears to be the blow of the mighty hammer of injustice fails not only to squash innovation but to propel it forward to new heights.

---

natural force of feeling by turning the inner life's present transports into an apprehension of itself, into a free tarrying with itself, and by liberating the heart in this way from the pressure of joys and sorrows—this free sounding of the soul in the field of music—this is alone melody" (Hegel 1975b: 929–30).

CHAPTER 1

The Whirlpool of the Negative Absolute

There seems no longer any good faith nor any sweetness of soul in human life, except among the sacrificial simple. What will for a better life still manifests itself in the world is for a while quite unable to take hold of the disorder. Italy in the Machiavellian period and Germany after the intricate wars of the Reformation may be cited as typical instances of such 'wicked' phases in social history. Yet it was not that the heart of man changed for the worse in those ages, not that there was a sudden generation of vipers, but that intellectual confusion had divided and enfeebled that graver-spirited minority which had, under more assured conditions, sustained the faith of most people and the moral disciplines of everyone. The quality of the ingredients of the human mixture remained the same, but the restraining and directive forces had in their interplay come upon a phase of mutual neutralization and collective ineffectiveness. There are many signs that to-day over large parts of the world there is a drift towards such another disintegrative and distressful phase. The brigand, the boss and the adventurer become portentously successful and immune. People who, in other times, would have been active and confident in their own lives and vigorously co-operative in the control of human affairs are uncertain in their hearts and unhappy in their interventions. The old faiths have become unconvincing, unsubstantial and insincere, and though there are clear intimations of a new faith in the world, it still awaits embodiment in formulae and organizations that will bring it into effect of reaction upon human affairs as a whole (Wells 1928: 14–15)

To continue our anatomy of collective unconsciousness and the geometry of the negative absolute (Hegel 1975b: 1236) let us return to the specter and comedy of the "great void" (S: 377) which is a product of the dissolution of the 'positive hell' of a good society[1] and connect it to an earlier theme: the lack of a social mirror, i.e., the moments of common understanding and reflection. For Hegel, the void was the historical problem of the becoming of human

---

1 We are speaking of the delamination of the sacred from the profane, the great rift that separates the two (EFRL: 37), the desacralization of some things that should be sacred, and the demonization of some things that should stay profane.

comprehension, of Spirit coming to know itself as Spirit. As Rosenkranz says, "'Hegel ... loved ... to set forth the creation of the universe as the *uttering* of the absolute *word*, and the return of the universe into itself as the understanding of the same, so that nature and history became the *medium—itself* a vanishing medium, *qua* other-being—between the uttering and the understanding [of the word]'" ([1844] 2002: 264). This characterization is supported in Hegel's lectures on the philosophy of religion where we find the abyss ("the negative of the concept") negated by the "rationally determinative activity" of the *word* itself, "taken up into interiority and returned to its origin" (1988: 430). The central abyss or the void at the heart of society is not synonymous with the lack of an object but, depending upon one's viewpoint, a pre-polar substance[2] or "energy" arising out of assemblage (S: 299, 310) or, from another standpoint, the void is the pulse of positivity—a miracle of 'grace' sustained by faith and expectation, or, finally, from the wholly negative point of view, the void is the black hole in which all hopes perish. What is an 'abyss' for the ordinary would be, for the gods of this system, the natural extension of their defects and corruption (Zola [1872] 2004: 103).

1 The Ghost of Solidarity

> No doubt the form which capitalism has taken ... is very different from what it was in the 19th-century—so different, in fact, that it is doubtful whether even the same term should be applied to both systems.... Yet whatever terminology we choose, certain basic elements are common to the old and the new capitalism. The principle that not solidarity and love, but individualistic, egotistical action brings the best results for everybody; the belief that an impersonal mechanism, the market, should regulate the life of society, not the will, vision and planning of the people (Fromm 1976: 16).

Irwin Granich[3] expresses well that old partisan faith: the masses have an instinct for solidarity and already have all the resources necessary to enact

---

2 With Durkheim: "By use of this expression we of course do not at all intend to hypostasize [hypostatize] the collective conscience. We do not recognize any more substantial a soul in society than in the individual" (S: 51). To jettison 'substance' (à la Hume) is tantamount to the sadism of positivism and behaviorism that attempt to close "alternative modes of thought which contradict the established universe of discourse" (Marcuse 1964: 178).

3 Granich (otherwise known as 'Mike Gold') and Joe Freeman were the principle architects of proletarian literature at the *New Masses* during the Depression years. On Freeman see

revolution. "Masses are never pessimistic. Masses are never sterile. Masses are never far from the earth. Masses are never far from the heavens. Masses go on—they are the eternal truth. Masses are simple, strong and sure. They are never lost for long; they have always a goal in each age" (in Fried 1997: 63). And the intellectuals? "They have created, out of their solitary pain, confusions, doubts and complexities. But the masses have not heard them; and Life goes on" (Ibid.). Not that we should let intellectuals off the hook[4] but it is quite a stretch to claim that estrangement and over-learning (Reason sickness) are responsible for the contempt toward the masses exhibited by bluestockings. Of course, in 1921, things looked completely different, but roughly twenty years later the true reality of the American masses was found to vary wildly from what was prophesied. The revolutionary masses were a product of the imagination. As it turns out, workers are just as bitter and competitive as their employers—and if they were reduced to the level of the "animal" through competition they differed dramatically from the lower species by the lack of one thing animals possess: instincts. The despair over the state of the masses seems all too reasonable considering humans do not possess instincts and where we would hope to find a positive hell of a solid social system we find, instead, a weird abyss of a peculiar absolute.[5]

Worrell (2008) and Aaron (1977). Having a firm grasp of psychoanalysis and Marxism, Freeman was clear-eyed about the social psychology of workers and was denounced by the communists as an enemy of the proletariat after he published his autobiographical *American Testament* (1936). Freeman's contributions to critical theory will never rival the cult of 'Horkheimer and Adorno' but his marginalized status is undeserved.

4   "The papal court [under the one-time pirate, Pope John XXIII] had, to serve its own needs, brought into being a class of rootless, ironic intellectuals. These intellectuals were committed to pleasing their masters, on whose patronage they utterly depended, but they were cynical and unhappy. How could the rampant cynicism, greed, and hypocrisy, the need to curry favor with perverse satraps who professed to preach morality to the rest of mankind, the endless jockeying for position in the court of an absolute monarch, not eat away at whatever was hopeful and decent in anyone who breathed that air for very long?" (Greenblatt 2011: 146–47).

5   If deficiencies were detected in the masses, it was always a problem of poor leadership and not anything inherent in the masses themselves. Visiting Trotsky in Mexico Abraham Plotkin of the International Ladies' Garment Workers' Union warned the exiled revolutionary of the threat posed by fascism and the psychological weakness of American workers. The exchange between Plotkin and Trotsky neatly encompasses many of the problems that revolutionary Marxism had regarding workers and transforming bourgeois society. For Plotkin the new CIO unions were unstable and on the brink of capitulation to fascism due, not only to the nature of worker sentiment, but poor union leadership. For Trotsky, "The masses are immeasurably better, more daring and resolute than the leaders.... You have no right to complain about the masses.... The problem is not leaders, but program. The correct program not only arouses and consolidates the masses, but also trains the leaders.... My program has a very short and

When we arrive at the 'negative heaven' of the bad absolute apparently in a state of decay (a paradise of the living dead) we are witness to a phase in the dynamic life of a social aggregate that has been subjected to rolling trauma, a loss of itself in its conceptual form, a plague of superstitions, and, most importantly, the emergence of a vortex where once stood mediating particularities or institutions that connected individuals to the dimension of the substantive universal (Durkheim 2004: 201).[6]

> Turning and turning in the widening gyre / ... Things fall apart; the center cannot hold; / Mere anarchy is loosed upon the world / ... The best lack all conviction, while the worst / Are full of passionate intensity (Yeats, in Coser 1972: 495).

When we survey the various positions within the social octahedron (a matrix of synthetic *a priori* judgments)[7] we are in the presence of an indifferent and external partitioning of a disaggregating totality as a self-reflective negating other. The extremes of egoism and altruism, for example, apparently consist of self-subsisting and indifferent moments left behind in the wake of a sundered unity (cf. SL: 599). However, where we find egoism and its opposite, we have located the spectral remains of a former solidarity and the ghost of a concept.[8] As a small-c concept or a social-historical particularity, it is true that every complex such as 'egoism,' 'necessity,' or '*ennui*' is specific to a time and place.

Ennui is a current "which does not necessarily have any equivalent in other cultures or indeed at other stages of our own. We must, for instance, make a structural distinction between this late nineteenth-century condition and the Romantic despair of the early years of the century. In the latter, the sufferer withdraws completely from the world, to sit apart, in a pose of Byronic malediction, or to return in the guise of the Satanic outcast and enemy of society. To such a state, the essential gesture of which is *refusal*, either heroic or

---

simple name: *socialist revolution*" (Trotsky 1990: 74–75). Rosa Luxemburg would essentially concur: it is never the workers (1971: 364).

6 "I was neither Living nor dead, and I knew nothing..." (Eliot 1922: 12). The traditional quest for the glory of masculine sacrifice in Pennsylvania anthracite coal country has been subverted by economic declines but also by the corruption of the institutional matrix. The ghost of the old hero-making machine produces a spectacle of unhinged, public nuisances (Silva 2019).

7 We have *unpinned* the Möbius band from the previous volume and shifted from topology (objects with holes, holey things) to a geometry of disintegration.

8 "Last night we were single, a radiant core of completion, / Surrounded by flames that embraced us but left no burns, / Today we are only ourselves; we have plans and pretensions; / We move in dividing streets with our small and different concerns" (Untermeyer, in Knoebel 1988: 662).

dejected, might most fittingly apply the description, as well as the diagnosis, made by Freud for the condition he called *melancholia*" (Jameson 1973: 56). Such is the trouble with concepts and the reason nominalist historians (i.e., most historians) reject, for example, 'Revolution' and are resigned to examine specific American, French, and Russian occurrences colloquially lumped under the practical abstraction 'Revolution.' Only the predicate, in this view, has any substance. However, the universal subjects are what we are after. Greek 'necessity' (Williams 1993: 75 ff.) is not the 'necessity' of postmodern capitalism and American 'necessity' may be different than English 'necessity' just as the latter differs from British 'necessity.' And the necessity of a wage worker differs from that of the entrepreneur, yet, aside from all these unique necessities, we have a remaining and irreducible *Necessity*. The problem is twofold: on the one hand, there is the question of structure, and, on the other, one of values. Take mysticism, for example.

In a study of Paul's mysticism, Schweitzer distinguishes between the "primitive" and "developed" forms based on the later having reached "the conception of the universal" in comparison to primitive forms. Even a passing knowledge of EFRL undermines the entire premise of this setup; social organization need only attain the 'level' of a tribal confederacy (a small form of organization) to train the mind of individuals toward universal representations. Schweitzer's first two paragraphs are a discombobulated jumble of magic, religion, ceremonies, universals, and so on, where preconditions proceed conditions, such that a phrase like "primitive mysticism" already presupposes a high degree of religious and universal development (1998: 1). In other words, many 'structural' problems simply come down to mental confusions and faulty working models. When it comes to the different *species* (kinds) or shapes of societies, of course, there are major differences, however, when it comes to 'mysticism' it will 'always' presuppose, regardless of particular predicates, a structure whereby the ego has misplaced the *ground of its initiation* and seeks immediate union with some transcendental substance.

Returning to necessity, that of a modern worker and the necessity of the entrepreneur is the difference between coordinates within the same 'fatal' structure and the composition of moral *values* at those coordinates. The fate that bore down on antique Mediterranean societies differs from postmodern American fate because, even though we both battle with Fate, our values are different (see Williams 1993: 102).[9] The fates in Atlantic City are different than

---

9   Nonetheless, we must resist the notion that explaining some social-historical fact means adopting the ontological ground upon which it operated (Anderson 2018). The consequences for adopting alien ontologies are untenable for sociology. Imagine, for example, if we could

the fates concomitant with southern honor. And, for others, "By force of toil one bends fortune. She loves the crafty; she will yield!" (Flaubert 1885). The relationship between moral 'values' (of the kind we think of in the phrase 'value voters') and the political-economic category of value (exchange-value) is one of categorical subsumption; value and values are particularities in the Value domain (Bouglé [1926] 1970). The concept *in itself* is a fiction but value, necessity, and so on, are *relations* that endure in ways that individuals and instances do not. In sociology, everything comes down to relations in various stages of development, organization, and disintegration, and how we recognize ourselves and others as well as grasp the social domain under everchanging conditions.

In a footnote in the 'value form' section of *Capital*, Marx provides us with insight into the logic of sublime identification. Here, Peter and Paul provide the foundations for their enjoyment of a universal moral status they have created for themselves.

> In a certain sense, a man is in the same situation as a commodity. As he neither enters into the world in possession of a mirror, nor as a Fichtean philosopher who can say 'I am I,' a man first sees and recognizes himself in another man. Peter only relates to himself as a man through his relation to another man, Paul, in whom he recognizes his likeness. With this, however, Paul also becomes from head to toe, in his physical form as Paul, the form of appearance of the species man for Peter (C: 144).

Marx does not go far enough here to unwind the complications of this dyadic production of an emergent 'transcendent' third, the big universal that, initially, merely "comes and goes" with each, fleeting exchange (C: 183; cf. Durkheim [1912] 1915: 228). The reduction of labor products to quantities of socially necessary labor time is relatively straightforward since we are, with exchange-value, in the domain of the purely quantitative and the abstract. Things are more exotic when it comes to qualitative reductions and sublations. A poorly-grounded critical paradigm, may, for example, project a super-individuality into this dyad that is not actually present, and, likewise, the faulty gaze may fail

---

not transgress the Nazi horizon of experience for our explanation of antisemitism. Dialectically, doing so would amount to treating the historical particularity as our universality but, more importantly, it would mean that, in the case of Nazi ideology, we would be forced to use the *Nazi* standard for establishing truth claims regarding Jews and the necessity of war. Rejecting relativism does not mean we are intellectual imperialists but, rather, attuned to the dialectics of history.

to detect a super-individuality that is a real but abstract product of this dyad and, in the process, misplace the logic of mediation.[10]

Before positively expanding upon this Peter and Paul logic, a negative case of failure will expose interesting dynamics. A fine example is provided by Moliere's *The Misanthrope* where Oronte seeks the admiration of Alceste. After a lot of preparatory flattery and qualifications, Oronte recites a sonnet which he hopes will win approval but is afterward run down as trash by Alceste who was, before the rebuff, unequaled by any other man on the earth. Failing to win esteem, Oronte departs in a huff after a scurrilous rebuke of Alceste's criticism of the sonnet (2001: 217–23). Here, Alceste, in the role of the hoped-for equivalence, refused to recognize the claims of the relative and the encounter ends in nothing but bad feelings between two individuals. The important aspect, in this example, is the *presupposed* installation of Alceste at specific social coordinates whereby he is imagined as "always already" (Althusser 1970) possessing qualities and qualifications that Oronte hoped to stand in equivalence to, if, that is, the relation had ended on a happy note after its inception. Much trickier is the case of two subjects, neither of which are presupposed to occupy any point of specific honor, and who have to both pull themselves up by their bootstraps,[11] and who, after a bewilderingly complex process, arrive at a place of collective, tenuous sublimity.[12] We might think of this as a 'Stoic' form of

---

10 "More generally speaking, the difference between the dyad and larger groups consists in the fact that the dyad has a different relation to each of its two elements than have larger groups to their members. Although, for the outsider, the group consisting of two may function as an autonomous, super-individual unit, it usually does not do so for its participants. Rather, each of the two feel himself confronted only by the other, not by a collectivity above him. The social structure here rest immediately on the one and on the other of the two, and the secession of either would destroy the whole. The dyad, therefore, does not attain that super-personal life which the individual feels to be independent of himself" (SGS: 123). Worse, in the case of "dyadic relations ... which do *not* result in higher units, the tone of triviality frequently becomes desperate and fatal" (SGS: 126). "*A pair of men is what I may call an essentially dangerous community*" (Royce 1914: 30).

11 If they start out like commodities and only find the thing they have in common they will arrive at nothing more than an abstraction and indexicality that will lack substantive determination, i.e., would be fit only for satisfying the appetite of the abstract understanding.

12 "God is thus the Subject, and Moses and the innumerable subjects of God's people, the Subject's interlocutors-interpellates: his *mirrors*, his *reflections*. Were not men made *in the image* of God? As all theological reflection proves, whereas He 'could' perfectly well have done without men, God needs them, the Subject needs the subjects, just as men need God, the subjects need the Subject. Better: God needs men, the great Subject needs subjects, even in the terrible inversion of his image in them (when the subjects wallow in debauchery, i.e. sin)" (Althusser 1970).

'third building' if we recall, with Durkheim, the Stoic construction of the sage to whom they prostrate themselves to in what amounts to idol worship (S: 289).[13] We should pause here, though, to contemplate the alterity or otherization process. How do we become other and how do we 'other' ourselves? There is no one formula since alterity is determined by our specific coordinates within the sociogony (Worrell 2019). The Lacanian 'mirror stage' and the Lacanian 'graph of desire' would take us part of the way; prestigious emulation (S: 129) or mimesis (Taussig 1993) would explain some aspects of alterity; taking the 'role of the other' (Mead) or the dynamics of the 'looking glass self' are not worthless either. Any ideal type we care to erect would be one-sided and beg the inclusion of others. Let us see, however, what can be accomplished with just one, where a 'transcendental' third emerges spontaneously for a first time out of a word supported by a dyadic or imaginary relation.[14]

2 The Bert and Ernie Dialectic

Following the Peter and Paul logic in the first chapter of *Capital*, we will set up an ideal-typical scenario whereby two[15] marionettes lacking identity set out to transform their merely ordinary existences into something bearing the mark of some kind of prestige. Bert and Ernie are two non-identical, ordinary puppets ($B \neq E$) who long for a life of mutual recognition and virtue. These two characters aspire to something greater and different than the kind of existence they endure as merely isolated and profane entities.

> Certainly, life is poor and lonely. We dwell here below like the diamond in the mine. We ask in vain how we fell so as to find the way upward again. We are like fire that sleeps in the dry branch or in flint; and in every moment we struggle and seek the end of our narrow confinement. But they come, they make up for eons of battle, the moments of liberation, when

---

13   Bondage to the sage is one consequence of attempting to imperialize the ego: passing through skepticism, the Stoic mentality devalues the world and raises the self to the position of the absolute (Caird 1893: 206). Now we have an ego that has raised itself up to the status of an empire (Barthes 1982: 68).

14   In other words, let us assume our voyage does not launch under communist presuppositions. "In socialist society, the formation and development of social relations is not a spontaneous process, but the result of conscious and systematic action by the working masses under the leadership of the Communist Party" (Kammari and Kabaev 1965: 101).

15   A dyad is far from nothing: "A couple is a world, autonomous and enclosed, that moves through the larger world essentially untouched" (Houellebecq 2015: 107).

the divine bursts open the prison, when the flame frees itself from the wood and surges victoriously over the ashes, ha! when we feel as if, the sorrows and servitude forgotten, the unfettered spirit returned in triumph into the halls of the sun (Hölderlin 2008: 70).

If you know anything about Bert and Ernie, the halls of their sun will be the new world of the Big-M.

In order to thrive, our two characters must not only coexist peacefully like human and fish under the Bush administration, they will also be forced, ultimately, to live up to an external standard, a constellation of universal norms and no one can create this standard for our friends; they will have to call it forth out of their own efforts (for now, it is one of those rare 'just us' situations)[16] and they must learn to trust in the greatness of one another.[17] Where the model is lacking there may still be hope (EFRL: 361) and where there is hope there must be a quantum of altruism. Let us see how far they can go.

In the abstract, Bert and Ernie should have no trouble arriving at something in common. If self-alienation at this moment required only quantification a universal would arise easily and life would be predicated upon putting in the minimum hours or making the necessary payments. However, they are rightfully repulsed by abstractions and know what we know: membership on the basis of quantification lacks real ethical substance. Genuine solidarity (and collective representation) requires sweat, blood, and tears. Positive qualification means that negations must be visited upon the minds and bodies of aspirants and this means that, unconsciously, repression will more than likely create a vortex of resentments and hates.[18] But, let them try.

---

16 The secret of a moral fact is contained in its most basic and elementary form and applicable (generalizable) to all other more advanced forms (Durkheim [1912] 1915: 462). In Scholastic terms, these two individuals are not coming together initially in terms of a *specificity* (what they have in common) but as *numerica*. Each individual is a unity of unique qualities unlike other individuals. Their specific unity (think *species*) is an emergent quality (see Gracia 2011: 2–3).

17 "Trust men and they will be true to you" says Emerson (1950: 245). When Melville read this, he wrote in the margins: "'God help the poor fellow who squares his life according to this'" (in Matterson 1990: xvii).

18 Repression always entails a surplus of repression where more than what is necessary is carried away (Rivers 1920: 37) such that purely mundane representations can 'return' in weird forms for no good reason other than they were swept up in the process of keeping painful thoughts out of consciousness. "In the individual it is now generally recognized that one of the most frequent ways in which repressed or suppressed experience manifests itself is in the nightmare, in which the emotional state natural to the experience which has been repressed bursts out with an intensity far greater than that which would have accompanied its unrestricted expression in the waking life. Elsewhere I have

Initially, Bert and Ernie meet as the abstract individuals that they are. As individuals they have no common basis for the development of a common identity beyond the positive will, and negative necessity, to do so. All they know at this point is that the world is not as it should be, and they seek the qualities that will put them on a new, sublime ground. They both realize that their constitutional lack in the real necessitates a joining that will provide the moral sustenance required in a post-puppet world. This initial combination of Bert and Ernie occasions a judgement whereby qualifications for association are generated and for this to occur they will have to treat and regard one another not as inalienable individuals (undivided or single-minded) but as players in distinct and divided roles.

Depending upon the point of view taken, one subject's function is that of the individual of sensuousness (Bert)[19] while the other, the aspiring equivalent, has a complicated role as social mirror for the other.[20] Ernie, the would-be equivalent, needs to acquire a *duality* in order to be an individual in himself while also serving as an equivalent to Bert. To serve as an equivalent, Ernie must be *split* or *doubled*. His sui generis qualities must be veiled behind a reflective, singular surface or social front, and he must appear to Bert as a one-sided being of reduced but essential predication, displaying something in common. This is the moment of equivalency that, while it does not seem like much as far as an actual social ground is involved, nonetheless has within it some elasticity and expandability, so much so, in fact, that one could dress it up as the kind of alluring, "happy go lucky" world that pragmatism champions (Durkheim 1983: 57).

The one-sided surface that Ernie constructs will have to be one that Bert finds alluring but also, and to the contrary, embodies an abyssal negativity, a lack that provides a *difference*[21] and a *fetish ground* for the metamorphosis of

---

suggested that the social counterpart of the nightmare is the revolution; that if the affects natural to the experience of social wrongs are not allowed to find expression in such a way as will lead to the recognition of the wrongs and to the measures which follow upon this recognition, there will sooner or later be violent and unregulated, all-or-none manifestations comparable with those of the nightmare" (Rivers 1923: 72).

19   Perception requires conception and since Bert is yet to be embraced by the concept his apparent infinitude of determinations is just an illusion. He is not complicated as an individual, he is simple and one-sided—an abstraction.

20   This mirroring is essential but frustrating. "He derived his pleasure from putting himself in the place of the other.... [H]is will to power never achieved its object, lived only by renewing it.... [T]he only thing he was eager for: himself. He needed the eyes of others to see himself, the senses of another to feel himself" (Malraux 1961: 194).

21   If the two selves cannot maintain a difference the relationship would never move beyond that of two subjects, I = I (the "night in which all cows are black" according to Hegel), and

two puppets into something original and different.[22] This is nothing more than the reproduction of the weirdness of commodity logic where we find both use-value and non-use-value, i.e., use-value and uselessness-value unified in the concept of a *bearer* (Marx) or what Weber would call a 'carrier' or Durkheim an 'envelope' or 'prop.'[23] Ernie will function in this way as an "imaginary opposite" of his "natural shape" (C: 204) but also as a symbolic being, introducing a disruptive, third dimension into the 'imaginary' (face-to-face, ego and alter) relation. We now have, simply put, Ernie and Dream Ernie.[24] Ernie's negativity results not in a simple relation between Bert and Ernie but, from one side, between Bert and the doubled equivalent: Ernie and surplus Ernie (E+E'), an image[25] and reflective screen covering an enigmatic abyss.[26] This splitting and doubling already contains the seeds, i.e., the surplus (as well as deception) of what will become the Big Other for these two characters.[27] The enigmatic

---

if there is no identity then the difference would amount to nothing more than diversity. The two are aiming for identity-in-difference.

22 The reflective surface, to use a metaphor, will contain positive qualities, just as the *objet petit a*, functioning as a form without content nonetheless *possesses* positive content (Žižek 1991).

23 The use-value of the labor product is preserved in its sublation but is doubled as use-value and non-use-value (we cannot sell it if we use it) such that the buyer confronts not merely the utility of the good but the uselessness of the thing as well. They could not sell it if they used it; I cannot use it if I do not buy it and liberate its body from the indwelling spirit that possesses it (value). When I purchase the thing I redeem its soul and its spirit goes to heaven (the merchant's bank account).

24 Dream Ernie is a compromised being that socially functions as a condensation that has shifted into another register or has been displaced or set apart in some way and serves not as a composite sign but a particular equivalent (Marx) or "'intermediate common entity'" (Freud) in relation to singular others (see Freud [1901] 1952: 37).

25 This doubling is the prototype for "the special effect of our times .... to hold the object and its image almost simultaneously as if the conception of light of ancient physics or metaphysics, in which each object was thought to secrete doubles or negatives of itself that we pick up with our eyes, has become a reality. It is a dream. It is the optical materialization of a magical process" (Baudrillard 1988: 37). It is essential that the tension between the image and the mystery be preserved because if the totality of contents become expressed in the image, "mystic awe" is drained away leaving only either total disenchantment (materialism or nominalism) or demonology upon the restoration of the unimaginable (Huizinga 1924: 159).

26 Ernie (from head to toe) combined with surplus Ernie (the double) is not a subject but a bearer of surplus moral substance that exists only within the relation with Bert or some other desiring individual. If we attempt to analyze either Bert or Ernie outside this relation we will misplace the objectivity of the moral substance and will fall into some kind of bad interpretation.

27 Self-consciousness, i.e., the particular self, "confronting the substance [universality] assigns to itself according to its nature one of these powers, and as a knowing, is on the one

background of the self-alienated Ernie will constitute a fantasy space out of which will emerge a third thing they will have in common, a Big-M.[28] But why must this logic, for the most part, manifest itself negatively instead of positively?

Common sense tells us that subjects combine on the basis of what they (already) have in common or the inherent qualities they possess. If subjects unite on the basis of this or that contingent quality, for example, Bert = (A, B, C) and Ernie = (C, D, E), the resulting positive unity would amount to nothing more than (C).[29] The resulting unity of our relation will be nothing more than a commonality, a lackluster and transparent combination of things that are *less than* the sum of their parts. No better, in fact, is the equally irrelevant 'unitarian' model where two subjects simply embrace the sum total of all contingencies of both individuals such that the unity of (A, B, C, D) and (C, D, E, F) = (A+B+C+D+E+F) where the unity is *equal to* the sum of its parts.[30] There is no additional 'weight' given at the points of coincidence (C' and D'). These positive unities are not effervescent, jazzy worlds of "incalculable excess" (Hegel 1975b: 961) but boredom itself and the tedious experience of enduring every subject's ever-growing catalog of identifications and demands. Besides, this is not how collective representations are made. Representations are ordinary (SL: 700) but *collective* representations are *extra*ordinary.[31] The

---

hand ignorant of what it does, and on the other knows what it does, a knowledge which, for that reason is a deceptive knowledge." The further development and actualization of this particularity will lead to the relation's ethical *Untergang* or downfall (PS: 266).

28 Here, the failure of Goffman's dramaturgical sociology and the failure of the critique of the dramaturgical model offered by Giddens coincide. "Players in genuine theatre ... have a motivation to impress the audience .... But this is a very particular situation, not in fact one generic to social life" (1984: 125). What Giddens fails to account for is that while a troop of actors attempts to impress the viewing audience, the interacting pair always produces an imaginary third that 'gazes' upon them and to which we actually address when we speak to another. The individual and the particular interact but do so 'as if' they were being watched and judged by an unseen Other. For this reason, a sufficiently socialized adult, in a sense, is incapable of ever being 'alone' or lacking "motivation" for putting real effort into their 'performances.'

29 Missing in this pragmatic assemblage is the terrifying return of A, B, and E.

30 The lack of negation and repression at a Unitarian Universalist meeting, for example, is the reason an entire congregation is incapable of producing even 9-volts of current between them. One might as well go to the library.

31 People do not form ideas of the extraordinary by engaging in ordinary activities. The profane cannot lead the mind to the notion of the sacred. For labor or work to possess any special moral or psychological value, labor cannot be conceived of as profane or ordinary, i.e., it would have to pass through a sacralization process. To separate labor or a movement of workers from the ground of religion from which it arose, would be like putting the cart before the horse.

Other comes not from everyday praxis but through the harrowing ordeal of ritual negations and real violence inflicted upon oneself and others in the ceremonial circle. Bert and Ernie do not strive for 'representation' or simple recognition but actual transformation on the road of Becoming. The road to Damascus is terrifying.

Ernie's depth of being is occluded by the reduction[32] of his role, one side of his being, to that of symbolic equivalence. Think of it this way: in order to function as an equivalent, to have a 'vocation' as an equivalent, to *bear* the other and be a *part* of the other, one must remain a 'closed book' that presents only one side to the other while still somehow being present as a whole.[33] To be a mirror of value one must be reduced to a one-sided abstraction and bear something that one does not even possess individually (C: 150). A glimpse into the real can be seductive, and used purposively, but if too much is revealed the transference is thwarted. Bert, does not look for a positive commonality[34] but a lack or peephole in the other, a "wink coming from nirvana" (Benjamin 1999b: 878) in which he locates that excess in his being that should be negated in order to proceed from imperfection to perfection.[35] This peephole constitutes the unity of the equivalent subject-object for the individual, Bert, and why the erotic relation, to anticipate future developments, is bound to regress beyond simple identification (to be like)[36] and into object-choice (replacement and

---

32   This reduction, the 'incision' or self-dividing, self-splitting of alienation on the part of Ernie, that which transforms him from a singular subject into an objective particularity has nothing to do with anything like "ontological security" for himself (see Giddens 1984: 125) but, from our angle, a gift or sacrifice that the other makes for the sake of the ontological consistency of the symbolic order. Sustaining the imaginary relation (Marx) bankrolls the symbolic edifice, and, 'proves' to the Other of the other (Lacan) that I am a 'normal' person and qualified to stand as an object of transference. This splitting can go further, however, in relations of subordination and superordination, for example, where the person is overwhelmed and has his or her claims challenged (really, over-challenged) to the point where a "third-person consciousness" becomes conscious (Fanon 1967: 110). The white man in a white man's world is not consciously aware of this gaze but members of a subaltern group are all too aware of the hostile gaze of the external third.

33   "Her large clear eyes ... told nothing, gave away no secrets. Camaraderie, good nature, cheeriness fall like shutters before a plate-glass window. You could only guess at the goods behind" (Greene [1938] 2004: 81).

34   "Dorothea by this time had looked deep into the ungauged reservoir of Mr. Casaubon's mind, seeing reflected there in vague labyrinthine extension every quality she herself brought ..." (Eliot [1871–72] 2015 22:).

35   When I stare longingly at the commodity, the peephole into its soul (and the thing that blocks enjoyment of its use) is the price. I see what I want but the view is bent by the price. The imaginary gaze of the commodity looks for one thing only, means of payment. The whole relation is one of quantities, of magnitudes.

36   The "boundaries of the self are actually permeable.... The ego is not really independent and self-constituting, but is actually made up of the objects it assimilates; the ego cannot

cannibalism).[37] The identification between Bert and Ernie establishes a client-like relationship where Ernie is transformed into a function to satisfy Bert's needs, but the flaw in the screen of the particular equivalent, the "peephole" or void, becomes a thing that triggers a breakdown in the dyad: the flaws projected into Ernie become reflected and mapped onto the nascent universal dimension and the purity and perfection of the latter is predicated on the annihilation of the former. As we will see in the volume on capitalism, the substitute satisfactions paid for Bert's sacrifices will be perceived as either devalued or unjustly appropriated, exposing the supplemental feature in the universal dimension that mirrors the imagined flaw in Ernie's character and duplicitous commitments. This problem will necessarily emerge because Ernie's relation to Bert is expansive and will spread out into a matrix of judgments and ego-alter relations (a big-M world needs a population, collaborators, co-conspirators).

Elsewhere the problem of sublimation and repression, as well as the necessity of a transcendental (social) third for critical sociology has been dealt with, so a recapitulation at this point is unnecessary (Worrell and Krier 2018; Worrell 2019) but Horkheimer adds another dimension that goes to the heart of the flaw in Marx's theory of post-capitalist solidarity and is important for the fate of our two characters:

> The right order would only require sublimation but no repression, and therefore no hatred, no resentment, no psychologically and therefore socially conditioned evil. This idea, which results from the earlier two, is his [Marx's] finest thought. Then, men would not just help each other but also nature. Ultimately, they would not play, as Herbert Marcuse thinks, but go to their death as they surrendered, gave themselves over to, created being. But such decline would have to announce itself, and thus man would return again to a more barbaric, more cruel, more primitive state. As the more highly developed, nobler individual has less resistance and succumbs to death, so mankind would perish if it fulfilled its destiny, for it itself is nature.... Stripped of its idealist delusion, Marxist materialism is closer to Schopenhauer than to Democritus (1978: 157).

---

leave the other to be an independent outside entity, separate from itself, because it is always incorporating the other, or demanding that the other be like the self" (Benjamin 1998: 79). It is a special capacity of the self to go outside of itself in thought and adopt a universal standpoint (Novalis 1997: 26).

37 "'I understand you, my comrade. No one understands you better than I. And yet you're a riddle'" (Hesse 1963: 141).

Horkheimer is correct: there is no sublation without repression—to think otherwise is delusional.[38]

Assuming success with respect to grasping the negativity of his being, Bert can at last renounce acts, thoughts, and feelings to bring his existence into conformity with the expectations of Ernie as a precondition for staking a claim to be a bona fide member of the Big-M community. The loss of profane enjoyments, say, unlimited fornication and whisky-drinking, are small prices to pay for life with Ernie under the approving visage of the Big-M.[39] But the absolute nature of the prohibitions, if they are indeed absolute, will also set into motion dynamics that will produce a corresponding void in social and psychic space (Durkheim 1961: 215).[40] For now, however, solidarity with Ernie is 'worth more' than sex and alcohol.[41] An important junction is reached, though, concerning Bert's desire and we can see where this is headed: (a) the desire to relate with another to (b) the point where Bert wants to have Ernie or possess him and (c) the moment where Bert wants to be Ernie, incorporate his surplus by devouring him, and finally stand in an *immediate* and all-possessing, exclusive relation to the M. This is a monumental problem that Fromm dealt with:

> Bauer's 'critical critique' is a small, but very important essay on love in which reference is made to the following statement by Bauer: 'Love is a cruel goddess, who like all deities, wants to possess the whole man and who is not content until he has sacrificed to her not only his soul but also his physical self. Her cult is suffering; the peak of this cult is self-sacrifice, is suicide.'
>
> Marx and Engels answer: Bauer 'transforms love into a "goddess," and into a "cruel goddess" by transforming the *loving man* or the *love of man*

---

38   The problem is how to manage (abreact) the return of the repressed that short-circuits terror, however, that would require a book-length study of its own. For now, we need to press forward with the careers of our two strivers.

39   For Fichte, "the relation to other rational, embodied agents would ... have to be construed not as a causal relation but as itself a normative relation, one of recognition (*Anerkennung*). (The English term, 'recognition,' is ambiguous on this point; in Fichte's, and later, under his influence, Hegel's, usage, it should be taken in the sense of attributing or conferring a normative status on someone or something, as when two states diplomatically recognize each other, or when an individual is awarded a medal in recognition of her service" (Pinkard 2002: 121).

40   "The doctor prescribed bed rest and absolute abstention from smoking. I remember that word, *absolute*! It wounded me, and my fever colored it. A great void, and nothing to help me resist the enormous pressure immediately produced around a void" (Svevo [1923] 2001: 10).

41   "The vodka gave me a dream, and another vodka has taken it away" (Greene 1982: 36).

into the *man of love;* he thus separates love as a separate being from man and makes it an independent entity.' Marx and Engels point here to the decisive factor in the use of the noun instead of the verb. The noun 'love,' which is only an abstraction for the activity of loving, becomes separated from the man. The loving man becomes the man of love. Love becomes a goddess, an idol into which the man projects his loving; in this process of alienation he ceases to experience love, but is in touch only with his capacity to love by his submission to the goddess Love. He has ceased to be an active person who feels; instead he has become an alienated worshiper of an idol, and he is lost when out of touch with his idol (1976: 18).

This business of love is tricky. In loving the big we come to hate the small and then, by extension, ourselves. Perhaps the ultimate 'Marxheimian' solution is to forget the problem of universal love, freedom, and abstract justice, etc., and just work to maintain an "equilibrium of social forces in opposition" (Freeman 1943: 628).

Decisive here is the creation of a substantial symbolic third that is independent of Bert and Ernie that will spur murder and suicide while promising solidarity and freedom.[42] Bert wants to be one with the Big-M but the structure and function of the relation with particularity (Ernie) is bungled from the very beginning at the level of signification. Recall that Ernie has split himself off for the possibility of assemblage and functions as a bearer, however, Bert wants the totality of Ernie, what he imagines Ernie holds within himself, an *agalma* (Žižek 2012: 40), the hidden treasure at the metaphorical center of his being, occluded by the public front, presumed to be a crystal of pure enjoyment.[43] In other words, Bert cannot make up his mind whether he wants Ernie as a priest or as a professional, an interchangeable utensil or as a unique personality with a flawed character and perhaps a checkered past (see Auden 2008: 204–05). At this point we can assume that Ernie will eventually be loved to death and that, at least in this case, Sophocles was incorrect when he said that it was better to be related to a king than to be the king[44] (in Grene and Lattimore

---

42 We are sticking with the Hegelian logic ("too tightly focused on the imaginary") rather than moving on to the Lacanian because we want to know why "the slave will remain a slave" (Lacan 2014: 25).

43 It might be a good idea for Ernie to 'jettison' his *agalma* so that he is no longer the sole candidate for cannibalism but if he loses it, or if it is perceived by Bert to lie outside of his body, he also no longer retains his desirability (Žižek 2012: 419). I suspect that Ernie is damned either way.

44 Generally, being the king is terrible: "'Oh, dread succession to a dizzy post / Sad sway of sceptre whose mere touch appals / Ghastly dethronement, cursed by those the most / On

1960: 136).⁴⁵ We are almost to the brink of the moment of refusal where Bert no longer believes that he and Ernie are of the same species (see Weil 1965: 13).⁴⁶ However, we cannot race too far ahead and allow Ernie to vanish just yet as he still has work to do.

Where I was once lost, exclaims Bert, a dirty, anarchic puppet who drank and fornicated, I am reborn under the sign of M and within the recognizing gaze of Ernie. "He had had no equals. Here, in the realm of inequity, he met them at last" (Le Guin 1974: 71). However, the self-imposed discipline and ascetic suffering along the way creates a reservoir or 'whirlpool' of repressed remainders.⁴⁷ That which was left over after the renunciations, the 'good' or pure, automatically creates a residue of evil or impurity (sacred pollution). Do not forget, however, that as Hegel says, the good really is bad. As the saying goes, "The good is the evil we choose to ignore" (Nelson [1917] 1957: 90; cf. DOL: 40).⁴⁸ "I have repressed all my enthusiasms; but they exist, they constitute my reserves, my unexploited resources, perhaps my future" (Cioran 1974: 88–89). The negativity of moral contingency that gets left behind automatically results in an ensemble of something more than a few positive leftovers (the ignored evil, i.e., the good) that Bert and Ernie have in common. This positivity is a much larger issue than all that, as we will see, because it contains more than the participants believe it contains and more than they want it to contain. This positive unity is *not* limited to a few qualities in common, in fact, Bert finds his entire existence bound up with it. Further, this 'positive unity' is not without its negativity as well. The problem is that Ernie's full being is also sublated and projected into the universal dimension, yet, his splitting into a finite surface and an infinite⁴⁹ and enigmatic space, creates a dynamic contradiction

---

whose repugnant brow the crown next falls'" (Browning, in Bosanquet 1912: 25). In this case Euripides was also incorrect that it is better to be the sick person than the one who tends to the sick (in Grene and Lattimore 1960a: 241).

45 "The cannibal ... has remained at this standpoint [of identification]; he has a devouring affection for his enemies and only devours people of whom he is fond" (Freud [1921] 1959: 47).

46 We see here in Bert's terroristic altruism the libidinal shift from the object to the obstacle (Žižek 2008a: 92).

47 The sublime often functions as a "cover for something low" (Adorno [1964] 1973: xxi).

48 The good is "only wickedness left uncommitted" (Gay 1993: 182). "The impure is made from the pure, and vice versa" (EFRL: 415). The good is the flower of evil (Mann 1948: 273). "It is true that every conceivable kind of iniquity has at some time and in some place been regarded as a good" (Solovyov 1918: 1).

49 "Let two mirrors reflect each other; then Satan plays his favorite trick and opens here in his way (as his partner does in lovers' gazes) the perspective on infinity" (Benjamin 1999b: 877).

between every member of what could be a community if we continue to populate it with other members. The good news, however, if we do not run too far ahead of ourselves, is that Bert claims to possess the requisite qualities to be associated with the Big-M and in this claim, Ernie, the only other with a desire to unite,[50] with eyes to see and *overlook*, ears to hear and *mishear*, and a mind to judge and *misjudge*, has no good reason to withhold recognition of the validity of the other's claim—if we do race ahead, we can see that this little seed of communal ground predicated on consensual self-alienation (C: 178) could develop to the point where the dimension of the universal equivalency is reflected back onto both Bert and Ernie retroactively.[51] To signify their joint metamorphoses and transcendence from mere puppets to inverted[52] members of the Big-M community, they are authorized to wield a social-symbolic 'phallus,' a symbol (perhaps a little *m*) that signifies membership and participation within the universal domain. Here is where all the trouble begins and ends.

There is nothing Big that is not M. The analytic gaze may view the M as nothing more than a symbol or representation of the collective unit but, for the participants, M is an absolute subject (Althusser) that interpellates individuals and elevates egos into actual subjectivities (Breckman 2013: 210–11)[53]

---

50 "The one person does not use the other merely as a hook to hang projections on. He strives to find in the other, or to induce the other to become, the very *embodiment* of projection. The other person's collusion is required to 'complement' the identity self feels impelled to sustain. One can experience a peculiar form of guilt, specific, I think, to this disjunction. If one refuses collusion, one feels guilt for not being or not becoming the embodiment of the complement demanded by the other for his identity. However, if one *does* succumb, if one is seduced, one becomes estranged from one's self and is guilty thereby of self-betrayal" (Laing 1969: 111).

51 "Emulously spending their last / warmth, our hearts will be as two / torches reflecting their double fires / in the twin mirrors of our minds" (Baudelaire 1993: 197).

52 A moral being or "topsy-turvy Creature" saunters about in an inverted form, "his Head where his Heels should be" (Swift 2015: 2).

53 "I shall then suggest that ideology 'acts' or 'functions' in such a way that it 'recruits' subjects among the individuals (it recruits them all), or 'transforms' the individuals into subjects (it transforms them all) by that very precise operation which I have called *interpellation* or hailing, and which can be imagined along the lines of the most commonplace everyday police (or other) hailing: 'Hey, you there!' Assuming that the theoretical scene I have imagined takes place in the street, the hailed individual will turn round. By this mere one-hundred-and-eighty-degree physical conversion, he becomes a *subject*. Why? Because he has recognized that the hail was 'really' addressed to him, and that 'it was *really him* who was hailed' (and not someone else). Experience shows that the practical telecommunication of hailings is such that they hardly ever miss their man: verbal call or whistle, the one hailed always recognizes that it is really him who is being hailed. And yet it is a strange phenomenon, and one which cannot be explained solely by 'guilt feelings,' despite the large numbers who 'have something on their consciences'" (Althusser 1970).

emblazoned with the 'little m.' Althusser says "there can only be such a multitude of possible ... subjects on the absolute condition that there is a Unique, Absolute, *Other Subject*, i.e. God" (1970).

Bert knows himself as M in the form and existence (use-value) of Ernie, his weird other, his mediator and foundation for the durability and externality of a universal entity. This is the long way of saying Bert needs Ernie's recognition and respect if he wishes to remain within the same moral circle. However, since neither Bert nor Ernie realize that the Big-M is an alien representation of their own social *relation*, that the positive normative structure was predicated upon their negations, their sustained cooperation is corrupted by the mistaken belief that each enjoys an *immediate* relation to their collective representation: Bm = M, Em = M.[54] Being a bearer of a little 'm' is no shame since, in the world of the sacred, even a tiny fragment is equal to the whole (Durkheim [1912] 1915: 261). It would seem, then, that an M-utopia[55] has been achieved. Yet, something is amiss; positivity is contaminated with an irreducible negativity that festers at its core. Instead of finding the grace of M in the particular other, Bert detects the impurities and flaws of the part in the universal equivalent (see Barth 1933: 505–06).[56] He confuses a reflection for the mirror itself as is the case with ordinary thinking. One serious flaw among many is that this M-faith kills reason (cf. Bosanquet 1920: 11) rather than sustaining it and this faith rewards its participants with *identical* emblems (M = m ... m, etc.), like college

---

54   Egoists living in egoistic societies always mangle the relations between the universal, the particular, and the singular. On this point Žižek insists on what is impossible, namely, direct enjoyment between the individual and the universal. No, the hell of other people is what we are stuck with, so we have to make that hell as good a place as we can because the alternative, the negative heaven of derealization, is even worse. The normal logic repeats the illusion that we enjoy direct, unmediated relations with the universal. The problem is visible any time we find the relation expressed as a dualism, where the triadic structure is missing, where singularity lacks its split and doubled other. For a quite random example see Badiou (2009: 132). What are the consequences? Oh, gender is a construct, it is a performance, etc. The whole problem of dramaturgical sociology, intersubjectivism, etc., lies in this reduction of relations to that between two ordinary subjects or the subject basking in the glory of the universal. It is true that gender is a construct and is performed but the fact that the suicide rate for those members of society who fail to adhere to the gender norms of society is so much above the average tells another story.

55   The "'moral motives'" of individuals are that of "*being met* and understood *by the other, from the sense of relationship with a reliable object*. This relational *Verstandigung* itself, the great endowment of comprehensibility, is part of the great 'something other' that Freud suspected lay further behind the traumatogenic infantile motives for belief" (Spero 1992: 194).

56   The Universal Equivalent is supposed to represent a 'container' (a good reified expression) for all that is excluded, yet, the excluded comes rushing back in (the return of the repressed).

graduates all heading out onto the labor market with identical degrees participating in the life and death struggle of renting out labor power—not one of them will receive the *one and only*, and for that reason *far superior* Th.D. (Doctor of Thinkology) authorized by the *Universitatis Committiartum E Pluribus Unum*. How do the participants in the web of imaginary m-relations make any distinctions beyond the vacuity of forenames (they mean and signify nothing) and an identical series of emblems?[57] We will have more to say about this in the volume on the commodity, but a major problem has presented itself that deserves to be marked off even though it takes us a little ahead of ourselves.

Bert and Ernie will be frustrated in their universality because they have not developed into actual personalities; their syllogism (their dialectic) is wrong. Each alter-ego (or, really, alter-subject) is functioning as an equivalent for the other in the imaginary (specular) relation. But each singularity (the individual with a role) is signified not with a substantive singularity of its own but with a generic symbol (m) in conjunction with an arbitrary forename. Since they sacrificed the same, and for the same, the resulting imaginary relation is literally that of: unit-m = unit-m or just a weightless A = A relation. Ernie fails even as an ego-ideal for Bert. The imaginary relation is structured at cross-purposes whereby singularity is hobbled at the level of signification, corrupting the very connections to the symbolic order where the big-M is supposed to govern. The paradox of successful symbolic relations is predicated, in contrast, on the singularizing of the function of particularity at the level of symbolic assignments such that the genuine duality of each subject is occluded.

On its surface, the prevailing logic would seem unimpeachable: Ernie is double ('Ernie' + m) but, against his will, he winds up becoming a double agent in the service of the anti-M. In other words, Ernie fails in revealing his duality to what should be his alter ego. Ernie does what he is supposed to do in doubling himself, but he leaves open a magic pinhole of fixation. In other words, Ernie appears to lack fidelity to the calling and since he functions as a mediating moment in relation to not only Bert, but also to others in the M matrix, his fault is a symptom of contamination. Bert sees too much and retroactively recalculates his share of sacrifice as being excessive in relation to the, apparently, surplus enjoyments of his equivalent other. In other words, inequality has creeped in. He got more for doing less. Either Ernie alienates himself absolutely and altruistically such that he becomes a blank m-screen for Bert (so

---

57 One thing clan totemism had going for it was the unique sub-totem or individual-totem (phallus) that marked the individual as uniquely separate while simultaneously a member of the universal totem, the social absolute.

that 'Ernie' can never become synonymous with 'evil' or 'pervert') or he forsakes 'the call' and undermines the pure ground of the M.[58]

Though both Bert and Ernie are now identical with the Big-M, the preserved individuality of Bert and the weirdly and visibly double nature of Ernie's role as an equivalent (and his simultaneous existence as an individual saturated at the same time with M-universality related to others within the expanded M matrix) leaves open differences in their common identities, and, weirdly, a universal that contains *too much while simultaneously becoming hollowed out*—the 'greater than' is too great, excessive, and oppressive while also appearing to be corrupted and no longer worth the trouble. On top of it all, the M is inconsistent not only in terms of purity but also in its lack of omnipresence—it is here today, gone tomorrow.

Bert begins to suspect that Ernie's motto is *Me, My, Mine*.[59] Since Bert knows that, even though he dreams day and night of unlimited fornication and

---

58 Of course, Ernie will need to preserve a manufactured presentation of individuality for others which functions to keep the split between his ego and social function integrated. The breakdown of the appearance of a platitudinous duality can be unsettling. For example, while serving in a Marine platoon, my mother sent me a picture frame as a gift. The frame was large enough to display several images of various sizes and included suggestive stock photos of a smiling, extended, multi-generational family. Since I had no photographs of my own to display I gave the frame to another Marine housed in the same barracks and he displayed the frame with the stock pictures. It was a private joke between a few of us (we even assigned names and back-stories to the models) and we more or less forgot about it until an inspection by a high-ranking officer who took an interest in my comrade's photo collection. The officer judged that the photographs consisted of many fine-looking individuals to which the new owner affirmed with a "Yes, Sir!" When asked if they were his relatives, my comrade denied having any relation to the people on display: "No, Sir!" The officer then asked my comrade for the identities of the people in the frame and he replied: "The Lance Corporal Doesn't Know, Sir! The pictures came with the frame, Sir!" The officer then exploded: "What kind of *fucking sicko* keeps fake people in their picture frame, son?! Lance Corporeal, un-fuck this situation!" and stormed out of the barracks, bringing the inspection to an abrupt and premature conclusion. Cynicism on the part of the troops was not appreciated. Anyone who has served in the enlisted ranks knows what a total failure the model of the little-m basking in the reflected glory of the Big Thing really is: the conflict, rivalries, and multiplied degradations at the level of specular relations and the contempt for authority and reliance on harsh discipline at the symbolic and real levels. Anyone displaying the least fealty to the Thing is ridiculed and held in contempt. When I was a member of the Marines, the Corps was almost always referred to as 'The Suck' by virtually every enlisted man and 'gung ho' personnel were derided. Taking 'The Suck' seriously was only for 'lifers' and 'suck-ups' incapable of 'cutting it' in the 'real world.' Cynical detachment was *de rigueur*.

59 Ernie, however, has his own suspicions: "I suspect 'frantic' activity in another. I sense that *he* senses in his actions a lack of intrinsic meaning: that in clinging to external formulas and dogmas he senses his emptiness. I expect that such a person will envy and resent

whisky-drinking, he no longer enjoys the way he once did. Worse, he suspects that somebody else must be enjoying these things since they obviously have not been extinguished in the post-M setup (cf. Freud [1913] 1950: 40–41). Now a spiral of challenges over authenticity will proliferate with the result that critical reasoning is negated under the weight of attempts to prove loyalty (Dicks 1972: 255) and individual fidelity toward the standards of the Big-M. With no one left to blame,[60] it must be Ernie and his cloaked associates that have undoubtedly and illegitimately claimed taboo pleasures for themselves. In other words, Bert arrives at the mistaken notion that Ernie is getting what Bert dreams of day and night. If getting what we want (desire realized) is, as Žižek says, a nightmare it is also a nightmare when we believe that it is only we who are foolish enough to renounce desires. The world becomes populated with 'Bad Hombres' spoiling our entitlements to enjoyment. This absolute, in all its splendor, fails to deliver satisfaction in that it "neither resolves our perplexities nor suppresses our ills..." (Cioran 1974: 75). As it turns out, they do not know one another and cannot make one another happy.[61]

We now arrive at a situation where, unlike witch-killers, disciples of bad wizards, and joyous city managers, our members of society M are letting the absolute down. First it was found to be contaminated and now it is withering into a lifeless signifier as imaginary m-relations begin to revolve on the bases of impurity and jealousy (see Williams 1958: 176). Bert develops a paranoid fantasy that not only has Ernie simply monopolized the enjoyment of forbidden pleasures, leaving others[62] in a state of ascetic deprivation,[63] but, much worse,

---

others. If, from my impression of myself, I see him as not fulfilling himself by not putting himself into his own future, I am alert to various ways in which he will try to fill his emptiness. One fills oneself with others (introjective identification) or lives vicariously by living through the lives of others (projective identification). One's 'own' life comes to a stop. One goes round in a circle, in a whirl, going everywhere and getting nowhere" (Laing 1969: 127–28).

60 Little do they know, the Big Thing has what Bataille might call a *thirst for the impure* (2004: 35).

61 "... [I]n the confusing night he forgot ... what experience had taught him—that no human being can really understand another, and no one can arrange another's happiness" (Greene [1948] 2004: 74–75).

62 Since Ernie is in "constant contact with neighbouring functions" (DOL: 308) Bert cannot be sure that others are following discipline and this generates the paranoid thought that only Bert is fool enough to remain pure in his ascetic devotions. Perhaps all the others are merely worshippers of utility.

63 Once the ascetic drive is recognized to be fruitless, in this case, it will convert into a piacular will to annihilation of the particular other via the weaponization of the unhappy singular.

Ernie is now, and always has been, an *anti-M* operative.⁶⁴ The anti-M is not a person but a *thing* (X) or "foreign substance" (Institute of Social Research 1945, 2: 404). The perfect moral Object is always "founded on inconsistency" and "implies at the same time a feature which is quite incompatible" (Bradley 1916: 150).

Once Bert, the one who sacrificed too much ("a" for self-alienation in the figure below)⁶⁵ arrives at the notion that Ernie is duplicitous, all his past actions are retrospectively reconstructed. Ernie's apparent asceticism was a ruse.⁶⁶ Ernie did not truly alienate himself the way that Bert imagines that he should but swerved, flinched at the last moment, and engaged in mimetic deception vis-a-vis Bert's sincere renunciations.⁶⁷ We have here a declination or downfall (*Untergang*). Bert sacrificed and suffered so much that his efforts were, apparently, enough to carry them both to paradise and, now, Bert deserves not only his fair share but Ernie's as well. He and he alone earned it.⁶⁸ 'M' is for makers, not takers. We are progressing through identification, to object-choice, to elimination.

The return of the repressed remainders (R) corrupt the domain of the absolute (Big-M) through an evil gaze.⁶⁹ "The return of the repressed makes up the tabooed and subterranean history of civilization—the eternal torch of mass death passed from one hegemon to another. And the exploration of this history

---

64 We have every reason to expect the sudden and dramatic entrance of the demagogue at any moment to lead Bert to the promised land via exterminatory purification of M-land.

65 See Worrell (2019: 214–15) for the problem of eccentricity.

66 "In sum, the relationship between our first and second parties will be for the second a significant part of the world, and the faking of this is within the control of the first, known by the second to be so, and known by the first to be so known. Observe, fakery will not require elaborate sets, extensive equipment, or outside help; words and touches and glances are all that are required, and of these the fabricator ordinarily already has an ample supply" (Goffman 1974: 459).

67 On the relation between social disintegration and the loss of veracity, as well as the value of lies, see Westermarck (1917: 129).

68 The antisemitic workers that the Frankfurt School studied in the US during the second world war despised 'the Jew' as a "foreign substance" because, rather than work as a team member, 'the Jew' "is not used to working in a team. He wants to get to the top, by hook and crook, through money, education, status" (1945, 2: 404). Further, 'the Jew' of antisemitic propaganda is "above the crowd" and tries to get paid for "passing the buck" and shirking their work; the same 'Jews' were overly and "aggressively ambitions" where, if they were not trying to avoid work, were guilty of doing too much work and "disrupts the collective work of the team." These 'Jews' were egoistic, putting their interests above the team and got in the way, making themselves a "social nuisance" (1945, 2: 404–14). For a comprehensive analysis of the Institute's pioneering labor study, see Worrell (2008).

69 "[T]he eye that can perceive what are the wrong things increases in an uncanny and devouring clarity..." (Chesterton 1986: 49).

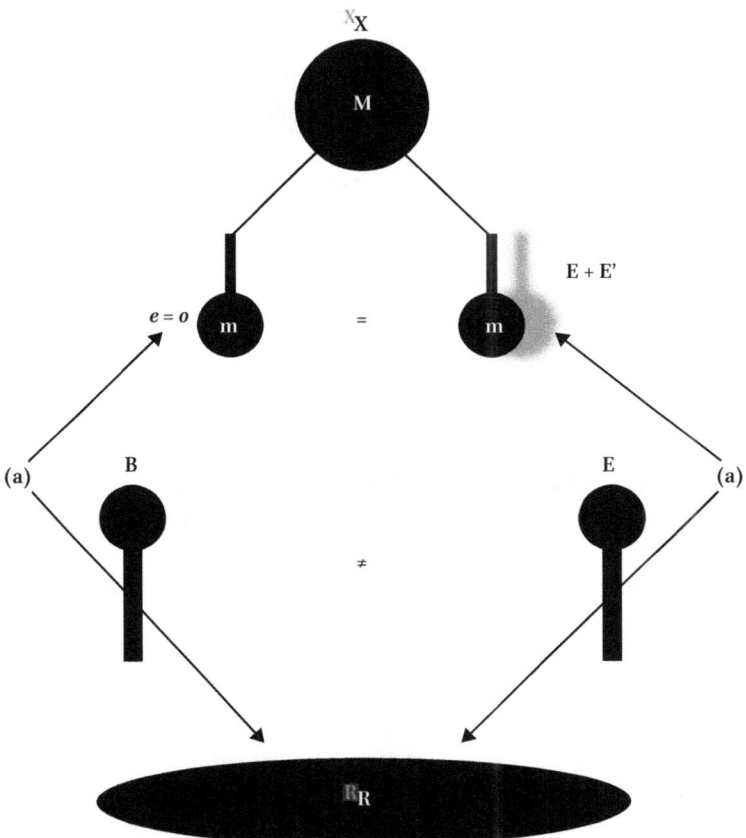

FIGURE 1 The Bert and Ernie dialectic
SOURCE: CREATED BY AUTHOR

reveals not only the secret of the individual but also that of civilization.... The effective subjugation of the instincts to repressive controls is imposed not by nature but by man" (Marcuse 1955: 16; cf. Gary 2017: 266). The imagined presence of the corrupt anti-M element (the *thing*) prevents the totalization[70] of the Big-M and blocks the attainment of a just life (things are not as they should

---

70 Deprived of unification due to the incursion of the anti-M, and therefore falling short of full totalization as the completed, utopic Big-M, the dyadic relation between the singular and the particular equivalent "becomes desperate and fatal" (SGS: 126).

be).⁷¹ Instead of accepting that the absolute is always contradictory, "infected" with negativity, and marking a "new beginning" (Dunayevskaya 1980)⁷² Bert feels that if only the anti-M element (the impure corruption within the social body) could be excised, the absolute would once again close in upon itself (return to zero eccentricity) and the world would once again be set right, purity being restored.⁷³ We shift, in other words, from the domain of political violence to the making of history.⁷⁴

> o collapse / ecstasy from which I fall / asleep / when I cry out / you who are and will be / when I will be no more / deaf X / giant mallet / crushing my head (Bataille [1962] 1991: 151).

This is a world without Bonhoeffer and, as such, Bert is unaware that the M, far from being perfect, totally unified, and omnipotent, is actually powerless and imperfect at its very core (2009: 322)⁷⁵ and that instead of the M making others perfect (the fantasy of zero eccentricity) it is the cooperation of the little others, the variably eccentric subjects of the Other, that makes it what it is. Where sacred perfection touches earth, in the form of the colossus, Caesar, king, dictator, etc., we find the opposite of what is promised.

> *Unity* is salvation; *one* monarch, one for the whole earth. Then, blindly following up his austere, inflexible logic, he lays it down, that the greater this monarch, the more he becomes omnipotent,—the more he becomes a God, and the less mankind should apprehend that he will ever abuse his power. If he has all, he desires naught; still less can he envy or hate. He is

---

71 See Badiou (2003: 42) on the so-called "minus-one" "point of incoherence, which the cosmic totality requires in order to sustain itself." Also, here, the limitations of object-relations psychology are evident. Contra Winnicott, we find that a god is not a repository of only the good, as a container that preserves the good from our evil (1965: 93).
72 We should never want the Absolute to totalize itself fully—totalization would mean the reduction of eccentricity to zero, i.e., life would become unbearably infinite in its finitude. See the first volume on moral geometry and eccentricity as it pertains to logonomy.
73 "[T]he 'corruption' of authority is almost, as it were, built into its very constitution, in its claims to reorganize worldly existence in the name of a higher truth" (Seligman 2000: 125). We err when we fetishize the contents of the absolute and neglect the form. Had Bert been a follower of Vaihinger he could substitute the 'As If' for personnel and, ta-da, "the circle is closed" (Rosenzweig [1954] 1999: 45).
74 "Politics mean operating with this x without worrying about its actual nature. Making history is to recognize x for what it stands for in the equation" (Koestler [1941] 1968: 85).
75 Following Bonhoeffer, we find in the gospel of Matthew that Jesus is a *bearer* of infirmities and disease (18: 16).

perfect, and perfectly, sovereignly just; he governs infallibly, like the justice of God. Such is the ground-work of all the theories which have since been heaped up in support of this principle: *Unity*, and the supposed result of unity, peace. And since then we have hardly ever had anything but wars (Michelet 1847: 35).

It's not really that only the weak and imperfect god can help but, rather, only the weak and imperfect can help their pitiful god. Bert and Ernie do not simply depend upon the M, rather, the M needs them—the M is that substance they have in common but neither actually possess. Since they are unaware of this (they don't have the concept to traverse externality)[76] things take a turn toward the abyss of infinite eccentricity. The law of particularity has opened the way for a fictional and one-sided restoration[77] *qua* purifications and a campaign of terror is organized and perpetrated by Bert upon his former comrade, the criminal running dog, Ernie. The substantial shadow being of reason was once founded on mutual negations[78] but it now signifies privation, a lack of relation (Suarez 1995), and commands righteous m-bearing subjects to destroy infidels; partial suicides and sacrifices segue into purges and homicides.[79]

Bert draws a circle around himself that separates his goodness from Ernie's transgressions.[80] Bert has now entered the Victim Olympics and, henceforth, when he speaks or acts it will be in the name of M-ness (cf. Lilla 2017: 66, 90). Bert is no longer a speaker of M-jargon but is spoken through by the M itself.[81] The terror inflicted on the particular, the bearer of society, leads to their erasure and the *objective* supports for the universal equivalent collapses "and when the self is withdrawn the void takes its place, takes the place of everything..." (Cioran 1974: 75). In other words, Bert will learn the hard way that the immediate is "everywhere mediated" (Hegel [1840] 1995b: 422). Since the

---

76 One needs the concept and the mind's own concept of itself in order to overcome externality (Hegel 2007: 27).
77 "[T]he law of particularity to which the universal reason in the individuals is tied, tends to insulate them from the encompassing contexts and thereby strengthens their flattering confidence in the subject's autarky" (Adorno 1973: 219).
78 Recall that with negations we have the unavoidable correlation with formless abstractions (SL: 113).
79 "When a people has been defeated it always tries to smell out a traitor or two, or, at least, to find a few scapegoats on whom to fasten the responsibility for what has occurred" (Bloch 1968: 105).
80 "Between you and us there is no common currency and no common language" (Koestler [1941] 1968: 56).
81 In his relation with Ernie, Bert possessed a soul—now that he is at war with Ernie, Bert has an identity (see Lilla 2017: 62).

M was a social-transcendental third, a name for the dreams and aspirations of both Bert and Ernie, both subjects were needed to keep the social order afloat (SGS: 124). Mediators may go invisible by sinking into the unconscious but when their vanishing is one of actual absence or erasure everything falls apart. The vortex of repressed remainders returns in the place of the M, and where the collective representation had once reigned, a void opens. "'Zeus is dethroned, and Vortex reigns in his place'" (Aristophanes, in Caird 1893: 113). Now R = M and where once M spoke from the place of the Other, there are only disconnected voices from a black hole left where the Other once reigned. In the end, destiny is realized with Bert destroying Ernie, reduced as he is, to a profane, material shell. "When I and the thing come together, one of the two must lose its [distinct] quality in order that we may become identical. But I am alive, a willing and truly affirmative agent; the thing, on the other hand, is a natural entity. It must accordingly perish, and I survive..." (PR: 89). Because Ernie left open a peephole of unrelatable individualism in his status as Erniem (Ernie projected an immediate equivalence to M) he was perceived as being contaminated with magic, made impure from Bert's angle of vision, and condemned.[82] Bert could not see that Ernie's 'impurity' was his identity with the essentially incomplete and corrupt Other. The lost objects, the M and the particular equivalent, because his hatred and rage are absolute, are introjected into Bert's now-split ego and one side of his ego, the punisher, takes revenge upon the other side of his ego, the victim or introjected objects (Freud [1921] 1959: 52). In the final analysis, where there was M there will now be "an opaque nebula whose growing density absorbs all the surrounding energy and light rays.... A black hole which engulfs the social" (Baudrillard 1983b: 3–4).

3   The Void

William James believes that "Most of us ... are a mixture of opposite ingredients, each one present very moderately" ([1907] 1995: 3). While most of us represent a collision of forces and contradictions, few represent moderation of any form. The structure of the modern social system almost excludes the possibility of moderation if, by that, we mean a synthetic and isonomic individuality arrived at through the productive sublation of the primary moral drivers covered in the previous volume.[83] No, this is a land dominated by a

---

82   The magician takes pleasure in profaning the sacred (EFRL: 40).
83   As Freud noted with respect to libidinal drives, behind the multitude of signified drives lies concealed something more powerful and serious (1965: 119).

central "whirlpool" and a new 'Roman' dominion of extreme contradictions (Hegel 1988: 385) churning and tossing people about hither and yon. It is certainly not the case that the capitalist absolute consists *only* of a spreading central abyss that swallows everything in its path, spewing forth surplus value as it grinds down nations, communities, and the biosphere. Far from it. While the capitalist social and global order does have as a central feature a 'black hole' at its metaphorical center it should be conceived of as a nebula of objects, things, and monstrosities occupying specific coordinates within the social order and each positioned along an unbroken continuum of fluidity and crystallization,[84] ice and steam, transparency and obfuscation, motivated and structured by a complex energy system and a constellation of countervailing forces spawning eddies and currents, swamps and deserts, etc., forming around, and in relation to, the central vortex. Once the 'bottom' drops out of the hell of positive social life the primary currents begin new careers as terrorizing drivers dedicated to the liquidation of institutions and the murder of individuals. As we saw in the previous volume, they are the four horsemen of the apocalypse. We have arrived at the "huge foolish Whirligig" (Carlyle [1836] 1987: 25).[85]

> As I stared into the void before me, a touch—immediately violent, excessive—joined me to that void. I saw that emptiness and saw nothing—but it, the emptiness, embraced me. My body was contracted. It shrank as if it had meant to reduce itself to the size of a point. A lasting fulguration extended from that inner point to the void. I grimaced and I laughed, with my lips parted, my teeth bared (Bataille [1962] 1991: 143).

We see all splayed out the unleashed "evil spirits" that lurk in any society (Freud [1917] 1966: 18).

This is *not* the desublimation of collective consciousness but, rather, the dynamics of disintegrated totality—bursting with energy and the trans-valuation process of a disembroiling totality, the void of the modern absolute (PS: 31).[86] What we have here is the one-sided social absolute and with a void filling out a central space, pushing *agape*, individuality, isonomia, and cooperation, etc., out to various pathological coordinates where they are reduced to one-sided

---

84   "And always the loud angry crowd / Very angry and very loud / Law is We ..." (W.H. Auden, in Untermeyer 1955: 1203).
85   "We dance round in a ring and suppose, but the secret sits in the middle and knows" (Robert Frost, in Cutler 2011: 101).
86   The lack of equilibrium, conflict and instability, are sources of energy from which we can expect not only horrors but our most sublime creations (cf. Rivers 1920: 158).

absurdities and perversions.[87] Virtues reverberate through the prism as vices, tragedies, farcical comedies, and so on. The sphere of the positive hell is transformed into the more complex constellation represented by the social octahedron with a churning and expanding maelstrom at its center—but make no mistake, we are not performing an *autopsy* on the absolute; society is not on hiatus here but, appearing in its negative, abstract, perverse, form, it is in the process of reorganizing (SL: 530) and consolidating itself anew. This abstract absolute

> functions as head and capital of a divided territory from which it is barred as empty, omnipotent center. Supplanting the diversity of relationships among elements is this universal, exclusive relationship to the general equivalent which *magnetizes* or *funnels* toward its ideal center all value relationships, making them its tributary rays. Western civilization can be formally defined as the one that pushed to its extreme limits—and in all domains—this solution to the organization of social elements: the subordination to a unique equivalent.... The social organism thus takes shape as the superimposition, entanglements, intertwining—or, on the contrary, as the radical separation, compartmentalization—of various domains or registers that are nevertheless globally and fundamentally isomorphic, structured by the preeminence of general equivalents around which a homologous system of values clusters, producing the same investments, the same mystifications, the same obliterations (Goux 1990: 44–45).

The 'moral octahedron' that we mapped in *Disintegration* is a product of the 'unpinning' and unfurling of the Möbius band from the previous volume, consisting of eight triads and one quadrilateral functioning as the shared base for all triads. To map the vortex, it will be preferable to neglect its overall diorama-like structure and view this negative heaven from the metaphorical top-down. In the figure below, the social octahedron, we have what we arrived at in the last volume.[88]

---

87 Revisit the scene in Hitchcock's *The Birds* when the birds explode into the Brenner home through the chimney: what we are witnessing is the externalization of Lydia's maternal psychic space, the explosion of fear and jealousy in the form of the swarming chaos intruding into social reality as a malevolent force. That's Žižek's spin on the scene but, decisively, recall the portrait of the dead *father* overseeing the entire ruckus.

88 To recall: Eg = egoism and its three forms: narcissism (nr), Stoicism (st), and Epicureanism (ep); ID = Infinity Disease or the fusion of the infinity of dreams (egoism) and the infinity of desires (anomie); An = anomie in its three forms: regressive or negative (r), progressive

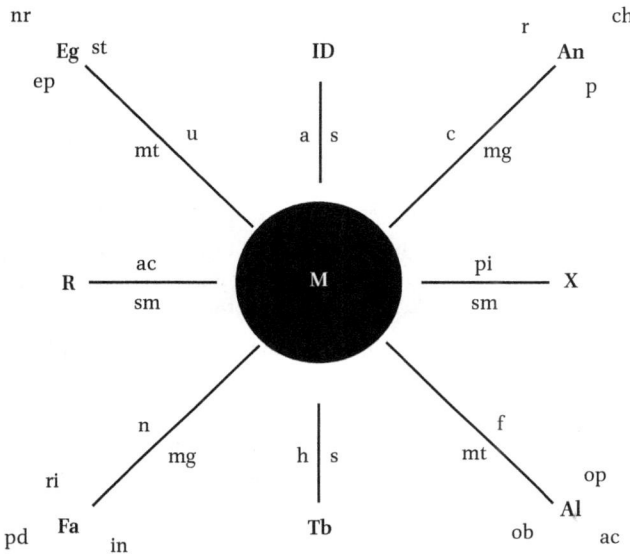

FIGURE 2   The social octahedron
SOURCE: CREATED BY AUTHOR

In its ideal form, our 'octahedron' is a square dipyramid (equal edge lengths)[89] but its substance amounts to a conceptual constellation of synthetic *a priori* judgments. Joe Freeman once wished for a set of literary symbols "to designate lowest common denominators and highest common factors of human experience" (1943). We still do not have that symbol set but this matrix of energy and representations goes some way in revealing the core, enigmatic engine

or positive (p), and chronic anomie; R = resignation with its primary active impulse, asceticism (a); X = ecstasy with its primary active impulse, the piacular spirit (p); the unity of resignation and ecstasy is in submission (sm) or suffering of the besieged; Al = altruism with its three forms: the primary, obligatory (ob), optional (op), and acute (ac); Fa = fatalism is here accompanied by its three moments of abstract right (ri), inevitability (in), and predestinationism (pd) which will be crucial in the volume on the Protestant Reformation and the commodity; Tb = taboo or a kind of disease of the finite is linked to heteronomy (h) and the fusion of taboo with infinity and its relationship to autonomy (a) is superstition (s) or the rule of things or evil encouraging the flight of mysticism or regress into magic; the necessity (n) of fatalism and the contingency (c) of anomie are unified in magical practices (m); the utilitarianism (u) of egoism unites the fanaticism (f) of altruism in mysticism (mt). At the center is the miracle, i.e., the void.

89   257 convex octahedra are possible.

of moral life.[90] We should not infer from its structure that it terminates in static and "invariant relations." "Constellation infers the elective affinity of non-identical objects / ideas whose relation must, thereby, remain unstable" (Aronowitz 1994: 127). However, we should not exclude or underestimate the identity of contradictory objects and things in this constellation. The most prominent feature of this geometry of immorality—where solidarity and regulation have gone to die (DOL: 331)—is the central vortex (in the last volume, it was the whirlpool of the miracle) which is the final destination on the road of fear (Marx [1869] 1963: 20) and the "love of lucre" (MECW 35: 233) that negated the will for rational social organization and the rule of law.[91] What writer of any merit has not pondered the wonder of the political savior, the miracle of the

---

90   The discussion of what this thing is can be found spread out over the previous two volumes. By 'engine' I do not mean any kind of literal mechanism but I am pointing toward the Latin *ingenium* where we find a rendezvous with *genius* and production.

91   Of course, the rule of 'law' in itself is more or less meaningless when, in fact, laws can be enacted that serve the exploitative desires of one class over another and outlaw, for example, labor association—i.e., "barbarous laws" of the bourgeoisie against worker combination (C: 903). While it is true that the wealthy have to obey most of the same laws as the rest of us, when it comes to the creation, accumulation, circulation, transfer, and protection of wealth, the master class gets to pick and choose the laws it wants to be governed by such that their wins are privatized, and their losses are socialized (Pistor 2019). 'Regulation' is meaningless apart from limitations on turning humans into money (PESC: 16). Where Marxism goes off the rails is in the belief that people lack a will for sacrifice. Mercy was to have eclipsed sacrifice (Matthew 18) but, apparently, the good news, like all news today, has been written off as fake. Marx himself, as well as successful capitalists, knows that capitalism is synonymous with idolatry and sacrifice (cf. CPE: 125). Indeed, many of the extremes of modern America exist because 'the masses' have been deprived of what they would consider honorable forms of self-destruction that were available to their predecessors. Eighty years ago, men could spill their guts on Omaha Beach, driving the Nazis from Normandy, but now, if they do anything at all, they just overdose in a shabby automobile behind a liquor store or eliminate themselves through 'hunting accidents.' The ones clinging to hope, shriek and hyperventilate at right-wing political rallies, dreaming of the day Hillary will get her just deserts. Just one more day to see Liberals cry again! Communist utopia is unlikely if, for no other reason, there is no mechanism in place for a person to self-destruct in pursuit of moral premiums. Objectively, dying in combat is senseless and stupid (the poor ground into red slime for the benefit of their masters) but a war death comes with its own surplus: "[W]hat I fear is solitary death, to die somewhere in a forgotten place, to die with my work undone, to die uselessly. Going to the front is another thing altogether. You are no longer a lonely atom in the world; you are part of a great collective will engaged in so vast a project that the idea of death seldom occurs to you" (Freeman 1943: 46–47). 'Unfortunately,' for today's soldiers, sailors, and Marines seeking honorable annihilation, the chance for death occurring as a result of mortal combat has been eclipsed by the likelihood of being deposited back into the civilian population, broken, traumatized, and nursing an addiction.

market, or the awesomeness of liberated passions?[92] "The belief in miracles seems to be withdrawn from one sphere only in order to settle in another. If it is driven out of nature, it now rises up in politics" (MECW, 19: 131). Naturally, the miracles of every time and place are unique. The miracles believed in by early Christians would seem more or less preposterous to most (but not all) miracle-believing Christians today, stricken as they are with skepticism (Gibbon 1909: 33–34) and the absorption of at least a few scientific principles.[93] The miracles of the 'Cosmic Walt' (the sea, rocks, forests, strangers on a train, etc.) seem too prosaic for troubled times ([1892] 1992: 290).

A society that has partially desublimated or, really, is undergoing a systematic transvaluation process, resembles a chaos of conflict and disorder to those suffering its effects; critical reason should, however, uncover its structure veiled by the apparent chaos. Philosophy is supposed to possess the conceptual power to tease out the essentials in a social sphere riven with contradictions but, always too reflexive, philosophy tends to succumb to the same forces of disintegration that it attempts to understand. Today, contemporary philosophy is little more than intellectual suicide. Not quite the zombie that philosophy has devolved into, sociology struggles forward but, lacking a sense of the vanishing positive absolute, looks about and can make little sense of the disorder and confusion other than describe what it finds and perhaps theorize little bits and pieces that it runs into. We "get the confusing spectacle of skills, passions, aims, views, and talents, running after and flying away from one another, working for and against one another, at cross purposes, while their willing and striving, their opinion and thinking, are advanced or deranged by an intermixture of the greatest diversity of sorts of chance" (Hegel 1975a: 93). Tasked with knowing

---

92 (Cf. Dewey 1946: 103–04; MECW, 14: 657; MECW, 15: 18; MECW, 19: 50; MECW, 35: 244; S: 377; Weber 1949: 108). Whitman's "Broadway"—"What hurrying human tides, or day or night! What passions, winnings, losses, ardors, swim thy waters! What whirls of evil, bliss and sorrow, stem thee! What curious questioning glances—glints of love! Leer, envy, scorn, contempt, hope, aspiration! Thou portal—thou arena—thou of the myriad long-drawn lines and groups! (Could but thy flagstones, curbs, facades, tell their inimitable tales; Thy windows rich, and huge hotels—thy side-walks wide;) Thou of the endless siding, mincing, shuffling feet! Thou, like the parti-colored world itself—like infinite, teeming, mocking life!" ([1892] 1992: 383).

93 "Even those who do believe, say, in the incarnation of Christ, or that the Abrahamic God or Allah appeared to certain human beings in the distant past, tend to refer to epiphanies as the experience of a divine presence rather than as literal physical appearances (with the possible exception of the Eucharist). Pilgrims at Lourdes may believe the Virgin Mary physically appeared to Bernadette Soubirous, but not many would expect the same thing to happen to them during a visit—unlike, perhaps, the pilgrims at Brauron. If one of us was approached by what appeared to be a god, chances are that we would want to carry out a few reality checks…" (Hall 2020).

the logic and structure of this spectacle, sociology, mired in partiality and subjectivism, offers little more than a weak narrative of random observations from the field. "This is the standpoint of the spirit which is purely finite, temporal, contradictory, and therefore transient, unsatisfied, and unblessed. For the satisfactions afforded in this sphere are themselves in their finite shape always still restricted and curtailed, relative and isolated" (Hegel 1975a: 93).

We are examining the negative heaven of contemporary society from the 'top down' so to speak. From the side this heaven would look like a normal octahedron with projected pure and impure replicas of itself;[94] every society is, then, imagined existing as three societies: the real society and its two imagined[95] forms that surround it 'above' and 'below.' "The ideal society is not outside the real one but is part of it. Far from our being divided between them as though between two poles that repel one another, we cannot hold to the one without holding to the other" (EFRL: 425).[96] It is assemblage and the work of rites, mythology, customs, and mimetic practices (see Taussig 1993: 86) that generate, realize, and authorize, these imaginary replicas, their heavens and hells, that they, the creators, become captive to (EFRL: 49).[97] A real hell would be the total lack of projected models. Where Calvinism had no need for an imagined, external kingdom of purity (due to some unfathomable inner bond with god) the pre-reformist and non-reformist strands of Christianity typically

---

94 "The savage gives to the world of his imagination, of his feelings, emotions, dreams, a certain outside reality.... He makes another world with a sort of secondary reality, supersensuous but quite real. To this supersensuous world go all his remembrances of the past, all his hopes and imaginings for the future" (Harrison 1962: 512).

95 This is, of course, not to ontologize the thing 'above.' This "above and below exist only in thought, only as abstractions" (Hesse 1963: 62). However, with Marx, this abstraction is a *real* abstraction, i.e., factual or a commanding construct.

96 These ideal societies are not just folk fantasies—look no further than 'modal realism' for even more outlandish concepts emanating from the minds of philosophers today.

97 With the disintegration of the Roman world "'Pessimism took possession of the old peoples at the beginning of the Christian era. This world is regarded as delivered over to destruction. Men long for a better life and the immortality of the gods, outside of this transitory existence. To this sentiment corresponds the division of the universe into a world of light above, the realm of the good, and a world of darkness below, where the evil powers dwell. Men live in a middle space'" (Gunkel, in Sumner [1906] 1940: 102; cf. Hegel 1988: 297 ff.). "It is true that the city is accompanied by two projections of itself, one celestial and one infernal" (Calvino 1974: 112). This doubling of the earthly and transcendental was only possible once Christianity emerged to differentiate, theologically, between the political/secular order and the divine (Eric Voegelin, in Lilla 2016: 30). These imaginary models are not merely illusions but, in so far as they retain a "mystique" and legitimacy, they survive shock after shock despite the disappointments of empirical reality (see Berger, Berger, and Kellner 1973: 142). For more on political-theological projections see Weber (AJ: 258). See also the mythical splitting or doubling of the family in Freud (1939: 10–13).

provide at least a positive model as a bare minimum—and usually a negative, counter-world in addition, e.g., Dante's *Divine Comedy*.

Of course, in the mass media era assemblage and ritual are more complex. In his analysis of American redneck culture, Bageant suggests that the "American hologram" (a "media-generated belief system" driven primarily by corporate television) delivers a steady drip of electronic 'opiates' to the semi-literate[98] dupes that get behind demagogic bloviators.

> From inside the American hologram an eagle is an eagle and a yellow ribbon is a yellow ribbon. Uneducated and trapped within the hologram ... [these] people ... will never be capable of participating in a free society, much less making the kinds of choices that preserve and protect one, unless the importance of full literacy can somehow be made clear to them.... They are too uneducated, too conditioned to the idea that being a consumer is the same thing as being a citizen.... The corporate simulacrum of life has penetrated us so deeply it has become internalized and now dominates our interior landscape.... So marvelous is [the] glow [of corporate images] that ordinary people will do the most extraordinary things to be represented in the constellation for a few brief moments—grovel at the zipper of Donald Trump's trousers, confess to marital infidelities before millions, and do other completely degrading and unimaginable things. We are all watching the hologram and cannot see one another in the breathing flesh. Within the hologram sparkles the culture-generating industry, spinning out mythology like cotton candy (2007: 250–62).

Mapping the social octahedron in terms of the dialectical oppositions set up by Durkheim and extrapolating their negative unities has a philosophical aspect in that we will be fashioning concepts "that illuminate and apportion the mass of the simply existing; ideas around which the elements of the existing crystallize as knowledge" (Adorno 1989: 4). These negative unities are not really desublimations, despite the appearance. The inversion of the pure sublime is not the profane or infraliminal but the impure and diabolical sublime. 'Evil' is not an insubstantial lack or absence of the good (Augustine). Just as mana has a negative pole (taboo might be thought of as 'negative mana')[99] these unities

---

98 Bageant's statistics on American illiteracy are slightly off. Data on illiteracy are stale and rough but the best estimate is that 45 million adults in the US are functionally illiterate (meaning that a person is socially dysfunctional) and that about half of adults read at a level below that expected of an eighth-grader.

99 The idea of taboo as 'negative mana' originates with Marett (1914: 98). Taboo "constitutes the negative side of the ritual communion" (Malinowski 1955: 134; see also Steiner 1956:

(energized judgments and authoritative representations) are powerful, irreducible forces that carry and pull the entire social order closer to the void. In the remainder of this chapter we will extend the 'map' of the social octahedron from the previous volume to explore several additional currents.

Any coordinate may exist in its own ideal-typical purity (e.g., Stoic egoism) or any two coordinates may intersect, for example, positive anomie with despotism.[100] Do not interpret the space between discrete conceptual coordinates as *metakosmia* (*intermundia*). The entire field is energized and any point on the graph represents a unique alloy of the four main currents charted in Durkheim's *Suicide*: egoism, altruism, anomie, and fatalism—on mixtures and emergent simplicities see Hegel (1975b: 924). For now, given where we have already been, we are only concerned with a provisional mapping of some secondary outposts that emerge from the continued, fractal-like self-expansion of the social or moral octahedron.

Alternations, superimpositions, and fusions of any number of forms are possible. Every social 'space' or coordinate has its own "affective coloring" (EFRL: 11). Complex alloys of numerous currents are also expected (e.g., Hobbesian political geometry). It is crucial to point out that while authoritarianism, totalitarianism, and despotism each represent vile deviations from the ideals of democracy, they are also not external imports or accidental and monstrous forms, rather, both political good and evil spring up "from the same root" (Durkheim 1960: 58; Pascal 1941: 125). The octahedron is not like Greek society that was imagined consisting of a vast system of *moirai* (Cornford [1912] 2004: 59) but has, additionally, the currents necessary to regenerate new spiritual forms. Regeneration cannot come from outside the social system, so it must

---

109). This negative mana is roughly equivalent with Durkheim's concept of "harmful mana" (EFRL: 200). What is harmful for one class is good for another and vice versa.

100 A good example of anomie and despotism is found in Poe's "William Wilson" where "As I advanced in years it was more strongly developed; becoming, for many reasons, a cause of serious disquietude to my friends, and of positive injury to myself. I grew self-willed, addicted to the wildest caprices, and a prey to the most ungovernable passions. Weak-minded, and beset with constitutional infirmities akin to my own, my parents could do but little to check the evil propensities which distinguished me. Some feeble and ill-directed efforts resulted in complete failure on their part, and, of course, in total triumph on mine. Thenceforward my voice was a household law; and at age when few children have abandoned their leading-strings, I was let to the guidance of my own will, and became, in all but name, the master of my own actions" ([1839] 1903: 301). There is much here: anomie is blended with egoism (the combination resulting in "the disease of the infinite") and despotism is delivered unto the family and friends and his illusory self-mastery, of course, leads to the opposite, anarchy and a paradoxically resulting *over*determination.

rebuild itself from its own resources, both negative and positive, pure and impure. Despotism "has the aspect of a monster, in which only the head is alive, having absorbed all the energies of the organism" (Durkheim 1960: 31). We locate despotism along one corridor that links egoism and fatalism. Neoliberal capitalism and the nearly historic levels of class polarization and wealth transfer we find in the US since the 1980s (Piketty 2014) represents a form of despotism as thus described. The middle has been hollowed out and trillions of dollars of resources and assets shifted toward the thin, uppermost strata of society. The unintentional 'upside' to this concentration of wealth in so few hands is that we know who has it and where they are and how to retrieve it once we work up the will and courage to take back what is ours.

Capitalism represents a regression away from the potential of humans to enjoy a life of genuine individuality. Sociological individuality is not synonymous with individualism (which amounts to little more than a justification for egoism and greed). Real individuality entails a duality (and doubling) of human beings—alienation is a necessary moment in the development of the personality. But alienations come in many forms (e.g., estrangement, splitting, possession, and bondage, etc.) and from all domains of life (political, economic, religious, and so on). "Heidegger's dualism of human Being (*Dasein*) and all other beings or, as he also put the point, of the Who and What, was based on and appealed to religious ideas: Man is supposed to have a unique position in the cosmos..." (Kaufmann 1980b: 40). The dualisms of Sartre (*en soi* and *pour soi*), Buber (I-it and I-You) fall under the same classification (Ibid.). Socially realistic ontology recognizes the duality of human existence but does not place emphasis on reproducing the gulf between humanity and nature, but rather, as with Durkheim's concept of *Homo duplex*, the split is that between personal and public existence—the individual as a member of society, i.e., the sublated ego. There is without a doubt a divide between human consciousness and the rest of nature (the reason for the recurring mind-body dualism) but this duality is variable and bridgeable. This was Hegel's genius in closing out the reign of Absolutism that preceded his work. It is only somewhat of an exaggeration to see the entire Western philosophical project as forming a massive arc moving from the notion of "strangers to ourselves" (Bataille, Kristeva) to "Man for himself" (Fromm)—i.e., 'otherness' to 'transparent' self-consciousness—such that symptomatic dualisms are finally capable of being overcome. As a reminder, our dualisms are not diametric in nature but polar. Polar oppositions, e.g., egoism and altruism, are not like the identity-difference relation of Being and Nothing where each vanishes *immediately* into its opposite following the straight line (see McGilvary 1898: 234, 237). Individuals become egoists and negate their egoism by becoming something other than egoists.[101] "The slow and painful transformation of a passionate and narrowly egotistical being into a man who gives himself over wholly to some great work or other that devours him, destroys him, lives in his blood, is a trial every creative being must endure" (Czapski [1987] 2018: 22).[102] Polar relations are dialectical which means that once egoism is raised to the status of a universal principle, e.g., bourgeois autonomy or rugged individualism, it necessarily generates powerful countervailing currents out of its own contradictions. Here, egoism becomes something different in its collision with altruistic currents. It is even possible to envision the most purified egotistical suicide, at the final moment, as an act of self-sacrifice to the spirit of selfism. *Abandonment* (being dispossessed of one's moral surplus, to no longer be proclaimed) also means *surrender*.

One might be tempted to dismiss moral polarities as repression effects: where there should be straightforward understanding, the truth is, instead, squashed and exchanged for ideological components that transform things into doublespeak for the benefit of a ruling class. But things are not that simple, and the consequences are of paramount importance. The paradox of repression leaves us exposed to distortions and phantoms, that is true, but voluntary self-repression is also the precondition of solidarity and reason, which, if we think about it, are themselves distortions and phantoms. If we were to somehow drain repression from the social universe it would collapse into a one-dimensional plane of material drives and signaling. Humans would be deprived of the thing that separates them from the other primates. The desiring ape would not even know how to desire and would have nothing else to fall back on. The external hyper-repression we associate with authoritarians leads to something like the proverbial law of the jungle where complex social relations are reduced to the simple, binary relation between masters and slaves (Freeman 1943). However, hypo-repression ironically leads back to that same law of nature (the law of the jungle) in its anarchic form.

---

101 These individuals are units of abstract existence, not as they should be, and trudge along in a state of unreality. All their determinations are indeterminate, and few come to the realization that, as human beings, their status as beings falls under the category of non-being.

102 Anyone with long-term personal experience has recognized in the nearly pure narcissist a terrifying will for world-transformation, the crazed desire to make an "impact" on things, and to make reality bend around their desires. This leads inexorably to much head-bashing as the world puts up stiff resistance. The path toward true creativity for these types of people rests in their potential inversion into altruistic fanatics that sacrifice their energies for some external cause, mission, or vocation.

Kenneth Burke distinguishes between polar and 'positive' terminology, the latter of which do not generate negations. For example, if I say 'book' (a 'positive' term) you do not think 'anti-book' whereas a polar term such as 'day' will negate itself by generating 'night.' "Burke's 'polar terms' approximate what Durkheim called 'the moral'" (Boon 1982: 133). There is a day-night difference between a profane book and a sacred Book. Separation or estrangement (sometimes Marx uses the term "exclusion") as a mode of alienation is the speculative double of possession such that we can render the first as nothing more than dispossession. The literature of the dispossessed it quite extensive and bears on our problem when it accentuates the dynamic between life and death.

> Now and then, half an hour apart, one came across solitary log cabins of the earliest mining days, built by the first gold-miners, the predecessors of the cottage-builders. In some few cases these cabins were still occupied; and when this was so, you could depend upon it that the occupant was the very pioneer who had built the cabin; and you could depend on another thing, too—that he was there because he had once had his opportunity to go home to the States rich, and had not done it; had later lost his wealth, and had then in his humiliation resolved to sever all communication with his home relatives and friends, and be to them thenceforth as one dead. Round about California in that day were scattered a host of these living dead men—pride-smitten poor fellows, grizzled and old at forty, whose secret thoughts were made all of regrets and longings— regrets for their wasted lives, and longings to be out of the struggle and done with it all (Twain [1872] 1917: 133–34; cf. Borges 1998: 223).[103]

At least with the gold-miners of old, they had the good sense to keep themselves separated from the living, lest the distinction collapse into confusion.

> They say that the same confraternity exists among the dead and that it never fails to lend a hand; the hooded brothers, after death, will perform the same job in the other Eusapia; rumor has it that some of them are already dead but continue going up and down. In any case, this confraternity's authority in the Eusapia of the living is vast. They say that every time they go below they find something changed in the lower Eusapia; the dead make innovations in their city; not many, but surely the fruit of sober reflection, not passing whims. From one year to the next, they say,

---

103 The "living corpse" is "the man who has been defeated and spared" death and who "does not exist purely for itself, but rather for another..." (Kojève [1947] 1969: 16).

the Eusapia of the dead becomes unrecognizable. And the living, to keep up with them, also want to do everything that the hooded brothers tell them about the novelties of the dead. So the Eusapia of the living has taken to copying its underground copy. They say that this has not just now begun to happen: actually it was the dead who built the upper Eusapia, in the image of their city. They say that in the twin cities there is no longer any way of knowing who is alive and who is dead (Calvino 1974: 110).

Keeping the dead (and the past) separated or at the proper distance from the living (and the present) is of paramount importance. Old ideas may die but they nonetheless somehow continue to prowl about in residual forms and one never knows when these things might return to repossess the living (PESC: 124).[104] "Man ... braces himself against the great and ever greater pressure of what is past: it pushes him down or bends him sideways, it encumbers his steps as a dark, invisible burden..." (Nietzsche 1983: 61). Marx grasped this contradiction with respect to revolutionary praxis. Indeed, 'praxis' cannot even be the correct concept in the face of the contamination of revolutionary politics by necromancy and magic.

In the *Eighteenth Brumaire* Marx directly connects "necromancy" with the contradictions of revolutionary praxis and reactionary counter-revolution:

> Men make their own history, but they do not make it just as they please; they do not make it under circumstances chosen by themselves, but under circumstances directly encountered, given and transmitted from the past. The tradition of all the dead generations weighs like a nightmare on the brain of the living. And just when they seem engaged in revolutionizing themselves and things, in creating something that has never yet existed, precisely in such periods of revolutionary crisis they anxiously conjure up the spirits of the past to their service and borrow from them names, battle cries and costumes in order to present the new scene of world history in this time-honored disguise and this borrowed language.... [T]he resurrection of the dead in those [bourgeois] revolutions served the purpose of glorifying the new struggles, not of parodying the old; of magnifying the given task in imagination, not of fleeing from its

---

104 The "most primitive social states are often reproduced at the highest stages of evolution, but under different forms, forms almost the opposite of their original ones" (S: 385; cf. Freeman 1943: 330).

solution in reality; of finding once more the spirit of revolution, not of making its host walk about again (Marx and Engels 1979: 103–04).[105]

It may be impossible to speak of the past without conjuring a surplus of representations and meanings that, contrary to what is intended, actually saps the wills and energies of the living.

> As he talked ... softly, pleasantly, flowingly, he seemed to drift away imperceptibly out of this world and time, and into some remote era and old forgotten country; and so he gradually wove such a spell about me that I seemed to move among the specters and shadows and dust and mold of a gray antiquity, holding speech with a relic of it! Exactly as I would speak of my nearest personal friends or enemies, or my most familiar neighbors, he spoke of Sir Bedivere, Sir Bors de Ganis, Sir Launcelot of the Lake, Sir Galahad, and all the other great names of the Table Round—and how old, old, unspeakably old and faded and dry and musty and ancient he came to look as he went on! (Twain [1889] 1917: 1).

Along another axis, the separability of egoism becomes the inseparability of altruistic possession.

In premodern societies, group affiliations "absorbed the whole man" (Simmel 1955: 149) and we can say that altruism represents a deficiency of individuality. To the extent that they are equally 'undivided' or lacking duality, both the egoist and the altruist are merely abstract individuals. The primary modes of alienation are usually combined into compound forms—hence, we have a deeper concept of compound alienation. For example, *ekstasis* represents the fusion of splitting (that we associate with anomie) and possession (that we connect to altruism).[106] In a magical rite, once the proper incantation is

---

105   The notion of 'necromancy' (from the Latin *necromantia*, itself derived from the Greek *nekros* for 'corpse' and *mancy* from *manteia* for 'divination') is an interesting point of entry into the dialectics of revolution.

106   "Matters that are recommended to our thoughts by any of our passions take possession of our minds with a kind of authority and will not be kept out or dislodged .... There is scarce anybody, I think, of so calm a temper who has not some time found this tyranny on his understanding and suffered under the inconvenience of it. Who is there almost whose mind at some time or another love or anger, fear or grief has not so fastened to some clog, that it could not turn itself to any other object? I call it a clog, for it hangs upon the mind so as to hinder its vigour and activity in the pursuit of other contemplations, and advances itself little or not [at] all in the knowledge of the thing which it so closely hugs and constantly pours on. Men thus possessed are sometimes as if they were so in the worst

formulated and executed, the product is the possession of the magician and their splitting or doubling into (a) their body and (b) their "deputy" (Mauss 1972: 79–80). Magic (a dyad consisting of the magician and the client) is born from religion but is, essentially, anti-social. Ultimately, magic inclines toward individualism and, as such, delivers us to a negative ecstasy or resignation. "At its extreme, defiant self-creation can become demonic, a passion which Kierkegaard calls 'demonic rage,' an attack on all of life for what it has dared to do to one, a revolt against existence itself" (Becker 1973: 84).[107] The frenzy of submission assumes two primary forms: resignation (passive ecstasy)[108] and ecstasy (active resignation). But each moment possesses its own unique logic: asceticism, what Caillois refers to as the "road to power" (1958: 29) aims to put the person above suffering whereas the piacular rites that use pain and self-lacerations to defeat the nefarious other, express the grip of suffering on group members (EFRL: 395).[109] Later we will have the option to replace 'submission' with another unifying concept but, for now, this will work fine.

---

sense and lay under the power of an enchantment. They see not what passes before their eyes, hear not the audible discourse of the company; and when by any strong application to them they are roused a little, they are like men brought to themselves from some remote region; whereas in truth they come no further than their secret cabinet within, where they have been wholly taken up with the puppet which is for that time appointed for their entertainment" (Locke [1706] 1966: 124–25).

107 The person led by passions is the "worst of slaves" (Erasmus [1509] 1913: 54).

108 Cf. the apathetic ecstasy of opium (RC: 232–33; see also Baudelaire 2002). Passive ecstasy is well-represented by Tennyson's "The Lotos-Eaters": "Let us alone. What is that will last? / All things are taken from us, and become / Portions and parcels of the dreadful Past. / Let us alone. What pleasure can we have / To war with Evil? Is there any peace / In ever climbing up the climbing wave? / All things have rest, and ripen toward the grave / In silence; ripen, fall and cease: / Give us long rest or death, dark death or dreamful ease" (in Harding 1947: 242–43). Merely because a drive is 'passive' does not mean that energy is not expended in its direction—the passivity is goal-oriented (cf. Freud 1965: 120). 'Passive' comes from the Latin *passivus* for "serving to express the suffering of an action."

109 Shooting yourself in the foot is a small price to pay for shooting the person you hate in both feet. During the Trump impeachment fracas, the *Times* reported that, according to survey research, "Most people would give up their preferred outcomes on health care, the environment or taxes if it means getting what they want on impeachment. It is an important issue for almost everyone" (Vavreck and Tausanovitch 2019). During World War I, Walter Rathenau wrote despairingly: "Do not try to dissuade people. Their belief in the corruption of their fellow men helps them live. If you deprive them of this belief, you deprive them of something irreplaceable. Even if it is hatred, it warms as much as love. The greater the number of Jews killed at the front, the better their enemies will be able to prove that they all remained in the rear, getting wealthy like the usurers they are. Hatred will double and triple" (Poliakov 1985: 147).

On the side of the ecstatic piacular there exists a fine line between the fanatic and the maniac—it is the line that separates altruism (the fanatic and terror) from anomie, with its characteristic suicidal manias (cf. PR: 38) and disintegrative and psychotic regressions (cf. Rivers 1920: 146, 152). Under the capitalist regime of accumulation, the capitalist embodies the fusion or identity of both fanaticism (capital personified, driven by a law of accumulation, a "cog" in the economic wheel) and an individual mask of accumulation mania (C: 738–39). Žižek is correct that we should not reduce the personifications of capital down to purely egotistical drives and personal greed—these people are also 'altruists' in the sense of devotion and submission (actual suffering) to an external power and social facticity. The frenzy of capital is nothing less than the desire to drag the divine (the infinite) down into the finite realm of space and time, to possess the absolute for oneself (Hegel 1986: 154). It is not merely magic rites, luck, or mere happenstance that opens the door allowing the infinite to rush into time and space. The collision of domains is only possible through a miracle. "Merging and rending, we wait for the miracle" (Untermeyer, in Knoebel 1988: 662).

4   Infinity and Taboo

In *Disintegration* we extrapolated from Durkheim's concept of 'infinity disease' (the fusion of egoism and anomie) and built out a corresponding 'disease of the finite' to signify the fusion of altruism and fatalism. *Per* egoism, we did repeatedly indicate the importance of narcissism as one mode of the self-absorbed person (Pearce 1989: 147). For Goethe, self-absorbed reflection was quintessentially human: "[M]an is a true Narcissus: he makes the whole world his mirror ... that is how he treats everything he discovers outside himself; his wisdom and his folly, his will and his caprices, he lends to the beasts, the plants, the elements and the gods" ([1809] 1971: 50). For us, however, narcissism will represent something of an extreme limit—the total or partial withdrawal of the ego "from the influence of other people" (Freud [1921] 1959: 4). Here we have a true self-absorption, but this is not self-love;[110] authentic "self-love ... obliges us to go beyond ourselves" (Durkheim 1961: 216).[111] In its partial

---

110 Freud tells us that "the lover is humble. He who loves has, so to speak, forfeited a part of his narcissism, which can only be replaced by his being loved" ([1914] 1959: 55). Of course, modesty may be false and merely a cover for narcissistic vanity (Adler 1954: 155).

111 Echoing Fromm, Lundskow reminds us that narcissism is more akin to self-loathing than actual self-love (2008). But the 'other' is always and inextricably bound together with the ego. The self (*autos*) has baked into it something 'other'—one possible interpretation of

withdrawal we could say that narcissists suffer from a neurosis but the total form, pushed to 'autistic' purity, enters the inverse dimension of psychosis. In an attempt to preserve the ego, the narcissist actually loses the ego because there is no such thing as an I or ego in the abstract, apart from others (Lacan 2002: 24). "A being who is not the object of a desire for another being has no determinable existence" (Lefebvre [1968] 2009: 104). When people are well-integrated in a group, narcissism is inhibited; as Freud says, groups have mechanisms for limiting self-love ([1921] 1959: 44). However, narcissistic withdrawal (reflecting the polarity with others) does not preclude the attempted transformation of others and the physical environment to better reflect the ego's self-fascination. The narcissist is capable of becoming a 'terrorist' in relation to everything exterior to the self. Here, the 'I' very much wants to expand itself in a limitless and reckless expansion or inflation of self, come hell or high water. Like other areas of life, solidarity keeps prices in line with values (Horney 1939: 89).[112] When groups disintegrate the loss of erotic bonds with others has to be replaced by libidinal investments in a string of (partial) objects (say, for example, 'hedonistic' materialism) one after the other, (sequential substitutionism, see Theweleit 1994: 97) or investments in self (the Stoic mentality, wandering in a maze of self-reflection, offers a suitable example). We can also detect a line from the narcissist to anarchic futility (i.e., the domain of fatalism): "Persons predisposed to depression have an intense craving for narcissistic gratification.... A reduction in self-regard is intolerable to them; they strive by wooing, threats, and blandishments to attract love and support" (Lewin 1961: 35). Self-love is its own kind of destiny.[113]

'Finitude Disease' or *taboo* represents a negative unity or fusion of altruism and fatalism. Taboo is neither mental illness nor a species of neurosis but a "social institution" (Freud [1913] 1950: 89) whereby "certain things are withdrawn from ordinary use" (EFRL: 304). The aspects of taboo we are interested in are severe restrictions, impediments, and limitations on social intercourse,

---

au, according to Risch (1974)—and the narcissist, to the extent that the ego wants to move away from self-hatred must recruit others to like them for them: I pretend to like you so that you will like me for me.

112 "If narcissism is considered not genetically but with reference to its actual meaning it should, in my judgment, be described as essentially self-inflation. Psychic inflation, like economic inflation, means presenting greater values than really exist" (Horney 1939: 89).

113 "A tall, soft-bellied, lisping man with a tense, mushroom-white face, rimless bifocals, and graying thin red hair, he was intermittently aware of a quality of personal unattractiveness that emanated from him like a miasma; this made him self-pitying, uxorious, and addicted also to self-love, for he associated it with his destiny as a portent of some personal epiphany. As a prophet of modern literature in a series of halfway-good colleges, he had gladly accepted an identification with the sacred untouchables of the modern martyrology..." (McCarthy 1952: 6).

the quality of being "hedged in," and the dread of moral contamination by other, impure groups and individuals (ES, 1: 434–35). In other words, taboos are not reducible to practical considerations (Freud [1913] 1950: 5). Taboos are not merely prohibitions and limitations but also the "'shuddering chill,' the awful horror which is the negative, forbidding aspect of Power" (Cornford [1912] 2004: 24, 25). Taboos keep moral polarities in motion through a paradoxical "deadlock" according to Davis: prohibition provides "at once the conditions for sin (for without the law there is no sin) and yet the precise way to traverse sin.[114] Put differently, the prohibition of the law simultaneously establishes the desire to transgress that prohibition and the *prohibition* as such. And these two couplings actually generate a vicious cycle. This circle of law / prohibition / desire / transgression / law ad infinitum is that very thing that produces a need to be rescued from this very entrapment" (2010: 101).

Tribal or clan life is the ideal-typical locus of taboo but it is also represented in the ancient city. "The religion which had produced the state, and the state which supported the religion, sustained each other, and make but one; these two powers, associated and confounded, formed a power almost superhuman, to which the soul and the body were equally enslaved" (Fustel de Coulanges [1873] 1956: 220). We can clearly discern the affinity between the 'disease of the finite' or taboo and heteronomy. The unity of narcissism and extreme anomie, anarchy, is its opposite, autonomy. Durkheim's goal of autonomous individuality is not identical with the bourgeois form of individualism or bourgeois autonomy. For Durkheim, autonomy is not the result of less social regulation and solidarity but more (creative) regulation within the social division of labor (DOL: xxx). The transposition from infinity to the finite is not only not excluded, in a positive sense, but critically presupposed. The finite is already, dialectically the infinite.[115]

Every fool in the kingdom of infinity believes they are on the road less traveled and that it has made all the difference.[116] "[T]his is the kind of claim we make when we want to comfort or blame ourselves by assuming that our

---

114 "Spirit must raise itself out of its submergence in Impulse to Universality so that Impulses, in their separateness, do not possess absolute validity; on the contrary their determinations receive their place and correct value only as *moments of the totality* whereby they are purged of subjective contingency" (Hegel 1986: 162).

115 "The danger to be avoided is illustrated by the judgment that *a line must be either finite or infinite*. This judgment is false for the reason that a line can be *both* finite *and* infinite— finite in respect to smaller lines, as *units* of length, and infinite in respect to points. For certainly a line is 'made up' of *both smaller lines and points*, and can, therefore, belong 'at the same time' to the *two* distinct universes of discourse that *logically* determine *finiteness* and *infinity* respectively" (Spaulding 1918: 142).

116 What has transformed California into a dystopia of fire, homelessness, and gridlock but infinity? "The founding idea of this place is infinitude.... Our whole way of life is built on

current position is the product of our own choices (as opposed to what was chosen for us or allotted to us by chance)" (Orr 2015b). Free will and choice is as much a concocted narrative that we cook up "that works for us, that we can live with.... Confabulation isn't lying ... but rather the invention of explanations or stories on the basis of information that is incomplete, incorrect, or manipulated .... A person who is confabulating may be saying something thoroughly ridiculous, but he doesn't actually know that it's absurd" (Orr 2015a: 119).

The forms that fate assumes are peculiar to each society yet there are none in which fate is not operative (cf. Marcuse 1978: 24). Assuredly, Greek 'fate' is not 19th Century Parisian 'fate' but there is a universality that is inescapable. Fate, necessity, and inevitability are powerful forces that are common objects of rites of propitiousness. For example, we misplace, lose or break objects when "there is an intention to sacrifice something to Fate in order to ward off some other dreaded loss.... [L]osing is often a voluntary sacrifice" (Freud [1917] 1966: 95). Indeed, it is the ritual aspect itself that can be said, in many cases, to produce 'necessity.' One way of thinking about this is to see that what is 'necessary' is only the contingent[117] that has been marinated in sanctity (Rappaport 1971: 36). The vast majority of practices that we take to be necessary are actually just sacralized contingencies that are only revealed to be such when one no longer obeys. As Simmel says, the apparently preordained is constantly being transformed through spontaneous actions (1955: 132).

5 Autonomy and Heteronomy

'Autonomy' comes from the Greek *autonomia*, from *autonomos* ('having its own laws') from *autos* (self) and *nomos* (law). Autonomy literally means 'self-law' or *law of the self*, whereas 'heteronomy' comes from the Greek *heteros* for 'other' and means 'other-law' or *law of the other*. For Kant, the law of the autonomous self is prevented from descending into sheer contingency through the 'categorical imperative,' the formula for which is the following: *Act only on that maxim through which you can at the same time will that it should become a universal law* (1964: 88). Put another way, the formula for the whole complex of the autonomous will under the direction of the categorical imperative is this: "The proposition 'Will is in all its actions a law to itself' expresses, however,

---

a series of myths—the myth of endless space, endless fuel, endless water, endless optimism, endless outward reach and endless free parking" (Manjoo 2019).

117   See Marx on the transitory necessity of capital and its personifications (C: 739).

only the principle of acting on no maxim other than one which can have for its object itself as at the same time a universal law. This is precisely the formula of the categorical imperative and the principle of morality. Thus a free will and a will under moral laws are one and the same" (1964: 114). Kant wanted to prove, as did Durkheim, that morality was "no mere phantom of the brain" but something objectively real.

What we normally think of as 'autonomy' (the liberal and bourgeois form) is an illusion and pathological: "the very individualist assumptions of moral autonomy upon which modernity is predicated frees the individual from collective restraint even as it ultimately destroys said agency by reducing it to a calculus of pure power and utility calculation" (Seligman 2000: 124).[118] Kantian autonomy is so bogged down in duties and responsibilities that no reasonable person could ever conform to the standards and, inevitably, the autonomous and reasonable person succumbs to infantile, primitive, or 'insane' regressions to wriggle out of the jam they work themselves into (cf. Wolff 1970: 14–15). This is why I signify the synthetic unity of these two currents under the concept of *superstition*—a kind of survival created by standing apart, splitting off from the rational, and seeking refuge in the supernatural, charisma, etc. The peak of autonomy is not individuality or (moral) survival but suicide, either partial or total. "To a modern consciousness, suicide ... signifies an ultimate expression of individual autonomy" (Ramp 2000: 87). It's not all it's cracked up to be. This contradiction of autonomy is not a new problem. The gift exchanges in 'primitive' societies exhibited the alloyed nature of personal autonomy and

---

118   The freedom of the individual is a product that emerges from limit and measure. In music, for example, notes are nothing but sounds until they are limited and, as such, emerge as tonal and melodic elements. "In its free development of notes the melody does float independently above the bar, rhythm, and harmony, and yet on the other hand it has no other means of actualization except the rhythmical measured movement of the notes in their essential and inherently necessary relations. The movement of the melody is therefore confined to these media of its existence and it may not seek to win an existence in them which conflicts with their inherently necessary conformity to law. But in this close link with harmony the melody does not forgo its freedom at all; it only liberates itself from the subjectivity of arbitrary caprice in fanciful developments and bizarre changes and only acquires its true independence precisely in this way. For genuine freedom does not stand opposed to necessity as an alien and therefore pressing and suppressing might; on the contrary, it has this substantive might as its own indwelling essence, identical with itself, and in its demands it is therefore so far following its own laws and satisfying its own nature that to depart from these prescriptions would be to turn away from itself and be untrue to itself. Conversely, however, it is obvious that the bar, rhythm, and harmony are, taken by themselves, only abstractions which in their isolation have no musical worth, but can acquire a genuinely musical existence only through and within the melody as the essential features and aspects of the melody itself" (Hegel 1975b: 930–31).

impersonal heteronomy. "The aim of all this is to display generosity, freedom, and autonomous action, as well as greatness. Yet, all in all, it is mechanisms of obligation, and even of obligation through things, that are called into play" (Mauss 1990: 23). Behind the appearance of generosity in the gift resides self-interest (Caillois 1959: 28). Notice that billionaires make a show of their generosity but, of course, this comes only after they have stolen everything first. They take 90 percent and give back one or two percent and expect to be celebrated for their munificence.

Autonomy is not a goal but a dead end because the human being, as a profane individual, does not already have within them that which is necessary to be a free human being. Freedom is not the freedom to just do whatever we want to do. Freedom and necessity are inseparable. Normally, autonomy is granted by virtue of "the choice of heteronomy" (Adorno 1967: 136).

> ...I am free *by compulsion*, whether I wish to be or not. Freedom is not an activity pursued by an entity that, apart from and previous to such pursuit, is already possessed of a fixed being. To be free means to be lacking in constitutive identity, not to have subscribed to a determined being, to be oneself once and for all in any given being (Ortega y Gasset [1941] 1961: 203).

Hegel, Durkheim, and Engels (to name just a few) would agree that one only becomes free when one is reconciled to the necessity of necessity itself.[119] We find 'autonomy' nestled closely to 'infinity disease' and it is one of the crucial unities of egoism and anomie. This unity plays out in dramatic fashion once a population has fallen under the strong man.

---

119 Engels says: "Hegel was the first to state correctly the relation between freedom and necessity. To him, freedom is the appreciation of necessity. 'Necessity is *blind* only *in so far as it is not understood*.' Freedom does not consist in the dream of independence from natural laws, but in the knowledge of these laws, and in the possibility this gives of systematically making them work towards definite ends. This holds good in relation both to the laws of external nature and to those which govern the bodily and mental existence of men themselves—two classes of laws which we can separate from each other at most only in thought but not in reality. Freedom of the will therefore means nothing but the capacity to make decisions with knowledge of the subject. Therefore the *freer* a man's judgment is in relation to a definite question, the greater is the *necessity* with which the content of this judgment will be determined.... Freedom therefore consists in the control over ourselves and over external nature, a control founded on knowledge of natural necessity (*Naturnotwendigkeiten*)" (in Lenin 1909). Durkheim was the master of infuriating slogans such as "Liberty is the fruit of regulation."

The totalitarian dictator is chiefly characterized by what Durkheim would call a "will mania" (1915) and the preconditions for totalitarianism are rooted in the atomization of the populace into isolated monads of apathy and stupidity unworthy of representation by mainstream corporate parties (Arendt 1968: 474–79). It was this 'mania of the will' that permeated not only the Nazi worldview but also their self-defeating military strategies, e.g., Operation Barbarossa. In *Mein Kampf* we find an ideal-typical psychological expression of this mania: *"Germany will either be a world power or there will be no Germany"* (in Nagorski 2019: 18). The absolute autonomy of the leader and the "identification of the Leader with every appointed subleader and this monopoly of responsibility for everything that is being done are also the most conspicuous signs of the decisive difference between a totalitarian leader and an ordinary dictator or despot. A tyrant would never identify himself with his subordinates.... The leader, on the contrary, cannot tolerate criticism of his subordinates, since they act always in his name..." (Arendt 1968: 374–75). The autonomy of the leader and his or her personality is identical with the heteronomy of every other member of the totalitarian movement. That which thinks for me and controls me is other, over there. Luckmann was able to specify better than most the precise linkages between subjectivism, anomie, and pseudo-autonomy in a way that leads directly to its opposite with regards to the fate of the individual (1967: 116).

We are pushed around by the impersonal, e.g., 'the law,' 'tradition,' 'contract,' 'market forces,' the 'laws of nature,'[120] and 'they,' etc. Abstractions such as 'market forces' or the supposed 'law' of supply and demand veil not only the underlying social psychology of practices but concrete political processes and policies designed to channel action in specified directions:

> Economic choices in respect of housing, whether to buy or to rent, whether to buy an old house or a new one and, in the latter case, whether to buy a traditionally built house or an 'industrial' one, depend, on the one hand, on the (socially constituted) economic *dispositions* of the agents—particularly on their tastes—and the economic resources they can summon and, on the other, on the *state of supply* of dwellings. But the two terms of the canonical relationship, which neoclassical economic theory treats as unconditioned givens, depend in turn, more or less directly, on a whole set of economic and social conditions produced by

---

120 Of course, ideas like 'natural law' are projections: "the rationality of nature is something that we *read into* nature; it is not something that nature has within itself because of its purposive structure" (Beiser 2002: 495).

'housing policy.' In effect, the state—and those who are able to impose their views through it—contributes very substantially to *producing the state of the housing market*, doing this largely through all the forms of regulation and financial assistance aimed at promoting particular ways of bringing tastes to fruition in terms of housing, through assistance to builders or private individuals, such as loans, tax exemptions, cheap credit, etc." (Bourdieu 2005: 15–16).

Dan Krier provides some perspective on the blind faith in markets in his excellent study of speculative management and finance:

As frictionless transmitters of economic efficiency, markets are theoretically important but not the subject of empirical investigation or thorough conceptualization. A deductive theory of 'markets' along the lines of neoclassical economics is insufficient to help us to understand ways that markets may have driven late-twentieth-century capitalism.... Since Adam Smith popularized the imagery of the 'invisible hand' of the market in 1776, the idea that markets control firms has been a cornerstone of socioeconomic thought. Unregulated, free competitive markets transform (or select) the firms that operate within them, rewarding those that are productively efficient and punishing those that are not. The invisible hand of the market coordinates economic action so that the aggregate effect of individual economic actions disciplines firms who are not optimally productive. Sociological investigations of capitalism must empirically identify market control of firms. In fact, market magic may only occur under select conditions, conditions that should be theorized.... One can imagine markets structured in a way that the pursuit of gain and maximum profit is not effectively channeled into productive outlets, and hence does not lead to maximum productive efficiency. Classical economists stress that a free market structure disciplines market actors so that they can only achieve maximum profit through the pursuit and accomplishment of production efficiency.... [For example,] the structure of secondary financial markets allows for the pursuit of profit through means other than efficient production. *Speculation*, trading in the fluctuating values[121] of property, is a particularly widespread nonproductive pursuit of profit" (2005: 64, 65).

A scene in John Ford's cinematic adaptation of *The Grapes of Wrath* offers a near-perfect illustration of heteronomous domination.

---

121 Actually, what is fluctuating here is not value but *prices*.

'The way it happens ... the way it happened to me ... a man come one day...' Ford then stages Muley's memory, opening the sequence with a company man sitting in a convertible, talking. 'The fact of the matter, Muley, after what them dusters did to the land, the tenant system don't work no more. They don't break even, much less show a profit. Why one man with a tractor can handle twelve or fourteen of these places. You just pay him a wage, and take all the crop.' Then the man tells the family they have to get off.

'Get off my own land?' asks Muley.[122]

Now don't blame me,' says the company man, 'it ain't my fault.'

'Well, whose fault is it?' asks Muley's son.

'You know who owns the land. The Shawnee Land and Cattle Company.'

Then Muley again, 'Well who is the Shawnee Land and Cattle Company?'

'It ain't nobody. It's a company.'

'They got a president, ain't they?' says Muley's son, 'They got somebody who knows what a shotgun's for, ain't they?'

'Oh son, it ain't his fault, cause the bank tells him what to do.'

'Alright then, there where's the bank?'

'Tulsa, but it ain't no use in blaming him. He's just the manager. And he's half crazy himself tryin' to keep up with the orders from the east.'

'Then who do we shoot?' asks Muley.

'Brother, I don't know. If I did, I'd tell ya.'

---

122   "The truth is ... the earth cannot be owned, only occupied .... The dwellers are occupants, almost never outright owners. The earth they stand on is the property of the lien-holding bank, while the occupants seldom if ever pay off their ... mortgages in their lifetimes— they effectively rent the right to occupy the property..." (Bageant 2010: 292–93).

As Cassano puts it: "Disembodied, quasi-natural forces seem to be conspiring to drive them off the land.... Ford stages a radical explanation based in political economy."

> Neither natural forces, nor bad actors, stand at the back of this drama of dispersal and loss. The windstorms are the immediate occasion for the transformation of the tenant system into a system based upon wage labor and pecuniary efficiency. But this transformation in the economy had significance for American workers that reached far beyond the dust battered plains. The systemic imperatives of market expansion inherent in a capitalist economic formation transform and colonize Muley's world. It is not ill-will, or even an ill-wind, but the ever present and systematic demand for renewed *profit* and more efficient *productivity* that disperses the Okies (2008: 108–09).

For us, the crucial dimension is the attempted transformation of abstract, impersonal operations of capital into comprehensible forms on the part of subjects wholly incapable of grasping what to them remains an apparently arbitrary and mysterious force. The upshot is that most people, almost all of the time, are following external and alien commands rather than imperatives of their own design. Of course, this following of command is not experienced as such on an everyday basis relative to mundane tasks like going to work. We do not generally need anybody else to force us to seek work and employers are not typically dependent upon the force of the state to compel us to sell our labor power on the open market. "The silent compulsion of economic relations sets the seal on the domination of the capitalist over the worker. Direct extra-economic force is still of course used, but only in exceptional cases.[123] In the ordinary run of things, the worker can be left to the 'natural laws of production' ..."

---

123 The most obvious 'exception' is strikebreaking where the state intervenes to force workers, under threat of punishment, to return to their jobs or get them out of the way for their 'scab' replacements. In US history, strikes have been broken with military or paramilitary force (including killing striking workers and their family members). More recently, less violent but nonetheless devastating measures have been deployed by the state. The infamous 1981 Professional Air Traffic Controllers Organization (PATCO) strike was crushed by the Reagan administration when defiant controllers were hammered: "When they persisted in their walkout, more than 11,000 air traffic controllers were fired. Court injunctions were obtained against the union: federal judges fined [the union] more than $1 million per day while the strike lasted, the Justice Department indicted seventy-five controllers, and several PATCO leaders were jailed; in October 1981, the Federal Labor Relations Authority decertified PATCO" (Lippit 2004: 338). So long PATCO! And this was the treatment dished out to one of only two unions that actually endorsed Reagan in his bid

(C: 899; cf. PESC: 19–20). As we will see later, capitalist production and the contractual buying and selling of human time and energy entails a radical transformation of the subject's relationship to self as a relationship between things (cf. PR: 68).[124]

Debtors, for example, do not repay their loans because they love, respect, or hold their creditors in mystical awe, or due to a sense of honor-bound duty, but because they do not have much of a choice when it comes to repaying their debts: a lack of compliance results in punishment.[125] Of course, people are 'formally free' to not enter into relationships of partial slavery but, out of self-interestedness or necessity of one kind or another, they find that they must obtain money and take what terms they can get. Importantly, in this legal, financial, and impersonal relationship, what the debtor thinks or feels about the creditor is irrelevant from the standpoint of the later. Where people are bought, sold, or treated like things (means and not ends in themselves), even within the context of a 'free market' for labor power, the line between worker, customer, and slave is blurred—no longer are notions such as the 'free' worker and the 'slave' diametrically opposed; rather, they lie along a continuum where one thing becomes its opposite sooner or later,[126] just as the oppositions between, e.g., egoism and altruism, or idealism and realism,[127] or free laborer and slave

---

for the White House. The state is obviously a monster of contradictions but being stateless in the modern world is an even more horrifying fate than being subsumed.

124 See Durkheim's illustration of commercial/contractual heteronomy (DOL: 152). The result of social interaction reduced to the "external bond" of economic exchange "where interest alone reins" breeds conflict and social disintegration. Importantly, Durkheim correlates contracts with the partial destruction of the other and limited slavery (1993: 85).

125 "Think what you do when you run in debt: you give another power over your liberty" (Franklin 2008: 23).

126 For more on 'polarities' see Beiser's analysis of Schelling's theory of life and matter (2002: 529–32).

127 As Jean Paul (Johann Paul Friedrich Richter) so perspicaciously observed, "Realism, as he was fond of saying, is only the Sancho Panza of idealism" (Pinkard 2000: 377). See Moore (1958) on the capacity for "interchange" between idealism and realism in the context of *Don Quixote*. For Gary, Quixote was a "misunderstood realist" who was "right to perceive hideous dragons and monsters in the familiar..." (2017: 266). From Schelling's perspective, idealism was an elevated form of realism where "We understand ourselves, that is, as *particular points of view* on an *objective* world that can be only *partially* manifested to us in our experience of it" (Pinkard 2002: 186). From another angle, we can see that as any idealism grows more 'realistic' or inclines toward realism it can overshoot its intent and devolve into primitivism or infantilism oscillating between the wild fetishism of ordinary objects and the radical devaluation of society's most sublime instruments (witness a child flushing money down a toilet).

blur one into the other; it is not for nothing that Marx designates wage labor as "wage slavery."

We need to realize that autonomy and heteronomy form an 'identity.' If we can make a place for 'heteronomous receptivity' (Marcuse) we have to comprehend it in the light of autonomous repudiation and the currents that connects the two.[128] Composite or intermingled representations are contradictory and have the capacity to turn, even rapidly, into opposites (RSM: 42).[129] If, for example, one wanted to grasp the social nature of autonomy it would be necessary to see that autonomy is always, already wedded to its opposite, heteronomy: on the subjective level one is free to choose so long as one makes the right choice (Žižek *passim*) and, on the class level, the autonomy of, say, the male gender in an unequal society is paid for by the pinched education, sentimentality, and bondage of women (Wollstonecraft [1792] 1983: 303–19). As Fromm says, the properly socialized person has to be taught "to *desire* what objectively is necessary for them to do. *Outer* force is replaced by *inner compulsion*, and by the particular kind of human energy which is channeled into character traits" (in Riesman, Glazer, and Denney [1950] 1953: 19–20). Rightness and inevitability are tied together from this point of view (Mann 1948: 138).

A distinction needs to be drawn regarding the directions that inevitability can run by distinguishing between, on the one hand, fatalism (overregulation) and, on the other, outright mechanistic determinism. Certain theories of inevitability, such as predestination and various types of oriental or occidental fatalism, may leave room for a spiritual life through conceiving the determining power to be itself the highest form of ethical power, and through the derivative doctrine that a person's higher life is a life lived in harmony with this ethical power. But mechanism differs radically from these theories. Mechanism reduces reality to a system of blind forces acting according to unalterable law, and it limits truth to results obtained by weighing and measuring in that system. Concepts of worth or value disappear or are reduced to chimeras (Otto 1924: 191). For the ego adrift, as we see in Weber, the imperatives of the modern world seem "unalterable" and life is reduced to obedience to blind forces and a dog-eat-dog struggle to survive (PESC: 19–20). But for their Calvinistic predecessors that plowed right through the doctrine of predestination, they assumed

---

128 "The proximal terms which describe this heteronomous receptivity in an economy without power include: *non-savior*, dissimulation, experience, fascination, obsession, *psychisme*, the 'idea' of infinity" (Libertson 1982: 6).

129 It almost goes without saying that a social system driven by polar energies is one where alienation and a lack of unity is chronic (Horkheimer 1972: 208). Dialectical analysis represents, at least at the level of method, the negation of this alienation.

the mistake and went to the end as Žižek might say, and those blind and discordant forces became energies to be tuned and manipulated.

6   Rights, Inevitability, and Necessity

To be pushed by bare, physical necessity through existence would reduce a person to the status of an animal or a member of the living dead where entities move without objectives or goals. Animals never move in straight lines of their own accord and, as such, the only rights they have are those bestowed upon them by humanity. 'Right' is derived from the Proto-Indo-European word for *moving in a straight line*. As we saw in *Disintegration*, the straight line is the basic geometric figure of the New Testament gospels; from Hegel we know that straight lines can be made to tremble and negate space itself (1975b: 920–21); and we know from Marx that the art of spatial-temporal compression is magic—e.g., being in two places at the same time (MECW, 11: 410).[130] How do we travel the straight path as it trembles and threatens to cast us hither and yonder? Or, is the vanishing of the straight line the actual cause of the instability itself? "There were doubts, confusions, hesitations and fears, but always there was that vast, straight line of never-wavering light which pointed to the goal…" (Freeman 1943: 219). To be right means to unify will with necessity: "happy he for whom a kind heavenly Sun brightens it into a ring of Duty, and plays round it with beautiful prismatic diffractions…" (Carlyle [1836] 1987: 75–76). The basic problem with Right is that we can only ever 'go straight' in our relations with others where necessity impinges on all sides: "The particularity

---

130   Absolute sociology also desires this capacity for spatial-temporal compression but rejects magic; this is why the *poetic* is central to our project—this is why, for example, *Leaves of Grass* is as important for us as *The Phenomenology of Spirit*, *Capital*, or *The Elementary Forms of Religious Life*. Witness Hegel anticipating Whitman: "Truth is absolutely concrete in virtue of comprising in itself a unity of essential distinctions. But these develop in their appearance not only as juxtaposed in space, but in a temporal succession as a history…. Even every blade of grass, every tree has in this sense its history, alteration, process, and a complete totality of different situations" (1975b: 962). Marxism has traditionally associated the unity of conception and execution with *praxis* but, for Hegel, this unity belongs most successfully and sublimely in the domain of *poiesis* (Ibid: 967). See my chapters "Magical Marx" and "City of Brothers" (co-authored with Dan Krier) in *Capital in the Mirror* (2020, SUNY Press). Hegel's lectures on aesthetics owe something to Novalis: "Poetry is *representation* of the *mind*—of the *inner world in its entirety*. Its sole medium, words, indicate this, for they are indeed the outer revelation of that inner realm of energy. They are entirely, what sculpture is to the outer formed world and music is to sounds" (1997: 160).

of a man consists in his relation to others. In this relation there are also essential and necessary determinations. These constitute the content of Duty" (Hegel 1986: 41). Duty toward others entails non-linearities, swerves, and declinations; going straight necessitates getting bent out of shape as a precondition (Diderot 1966: 120; Worrell 2016).

The conceptual reflection of Right, it's opponent, if you will, is *Krisis*. A 'crisis' means a traumatic and decisive turning point from stability and equilibrium toward instability and disequilibrium.[131] Naturally, it is a generic feature of any modern society to be in a state of interminable dynamic change, but capitalism involves not just unceasing 'change' but traumatic dislocations on a moment by moment basis that suggests that anomie itself is the ruling principle delivering people up to blind chance. One can celebrate the decay of society,[132] reject disintegration, etc., but for capitalism to continue its dread march the trick is to make non-linearities appear linear. A society cannot function unless people "*want* to do what they *have* to do" (Fromm 1973: 253)[133] and to reconcile rights with obligations, benefits with burdens, good with evil (Mill 1992: 48–49). The only Right that is *concrete* is the right of the "world spirit"— "Right is ... in general freedom, as Idea" (PR: 58). Short of the Idea, and we are short, Right is reduced to rights that are particular, contingent, limited, and contradictory—i.e., personal or abstract *interests*.[134] Right, as it appears in the

---

131 *Krisis* is derived from *krinō*, to pick, choose, decide, and judge. The resolution of a crisis involves making the right choice—going straight to it. If I am to have the right to choose I must choose the only right choice available to me. My autonomy depends upon my ability to recognize the heteronomy of the right way and reconcile necessity with desire: as a free person I want to do what I have to do.

132 See Marcuse's references to Walter Benjamin regarding the artistic *Krisenbewusstsein* and "the secret rebellion of the bourgeois against his own class" in the works of, for example, Baudelaire and Proust, among others (1978: 19–20).

133 Unfortunately, this is reminiscent of dystopian fiction: "liking what you've got to do. All conditioning aims at that: making people like their unescapable social destiny" (Huxley [1932] 1946: 15). "Freedom is not merely the chance to do as one pleases; neither is it merely the opportunity to choose between set alternatives. Freedom is, first of all, the chance to *formulate* the available choices, to argue over them—and then, the opportunity to choose" (Mills 1959: 174, emphasis added). In the big picture, the modern person is entertained through cinema and literature in such a way that we are always rehearsing for some unforeseen crisis where we will be forced to make extraordinary choices to solve extraordinary problems, from alien invasions to murders and unexpected windfalls, and so on.

134 An important feature of the egoist is the recognition of no other authority higher than the self—society is unreal, less real, or devalued relative to the self. Only the desires of the I are deemed necessary. "Don't tell me what's necessary …. What's necessary is whatever I wish to do, regardless of how *un*necessary it might seem" (Koontz 2012: 140). The ego

social octahedron, is the limitation and formality of *abstract* right (PR: 58–59) where 'right' is more or less synonymous with the collisions of private interests, *alienation*, and the freedom to dispose of property (cf. Skinner 1978: 117).

It is obvious that whether or not a person 'has' substantial rights or a right to anything at all depends not only upon contingencies[135] such as ownership and capital accumulation, class position, gender, race, ethnicity, nationality, religious affiliations, and various status markers, but also upon being taken possession of by dominant folkways or new and revolutionary covenants: Henry Ford's use of his 'sociological department' and the famous melting pot ceremonies that transformed old world bumpkins into citizens of industrialized America, are illustrative; these can be compared to, for example, Calvin's use of covenant ceremonies (including police enforcement) that bound citizens to Geneva.[136] Conversely, a group or class may be afforded rights if doing so aids an ongoing class struggle, e.g., the English struggle against aristocracy. As Engels says in a letter to Lafarge, dated 31 January 1891, "It's all very well for you to talk of irresolution and weakness. You are in a republic and the bourgeois republicans, in order to defeat the royalists, have been obliged to accord you the political rights that we are far from possessing in Germany" (MECW, 49: 116). This instrumental bestowal of rights to the proletariat (for the benefit of the ruling classes) is what Engels calls "*la démocratie vulgaire*" (MECW, 44: 185). "Right is something *utterly sacred*" (PR: 59) but rights are particular vulgarities. As a constituent in the domain of ideals, right is as much a problem of negative education as it is a matter of the positive bestowals. "The day-to-day nitty-gritty of moral decision, moral policing, moral education, and morality talk is more likely to involve reference to the disgusting than to the Good and the Right. Our moral discourse suggests we are surer of our judgments when recognizing the bad and the ugly than the good and the beautiful" (Miller 1997: 180).[137]

The traditional couplet of 'rights and duties' grossly simplifies matters. Rights and duties are two basic elements of Western law, but rights and duties

---

exerts its right to act autonomously but, here, right is a transit to necessity. Rights do not belong to the ego; truly individuated 'rights' are merely *interests* (Hocking 1956: 21).

135 "Right ... is factitious, and the creature of will. It exists, only because the society, or those who wield the powers of the society, will that it should exist" (Mill 1992: 47).

136 Calvin's use of proto-Stalinist tactics is debatable but his underlying reason for the tactics was sound: there is no church (ordered and regulated) without obligatory participation in the sacred rituals (McNeill [1954] 1967: 138–39).

137 Miller makes an excellent point about the excessive function of disgust as an importer of things into the domain of the moral or sacred that should be otherwise excluded. Disgust has, he says, a power to negate our "better judgments" (1997: 181).

are also parts of an active "living process" that also entails resolutions and cooperation through legislation, voting, administration, adjudication, negotiations, and myriad 'legal' processes, values, and concepts (Berman 1983: 5). But this sense of "living process" and resolution seems to diminish the 'dead' of the 'living' process, i.e., the crises and diremptions of class conflict and brute domination. The facticity of this "living process" is evident in its power and resilience in the face of revolutionary changes over the centuries: "Even the great national revolutions of the past—the Russian Revolution of 1917, the French and American Revolutions of 1789 and 1776, the English Revolution of 1640, the German Reformation of 1517—eventually made peace with the legal tradition that they or some of their leaders had set out to destroy" (Ibid.). Nazis, Fascists, oligarchs, etc., in other words, violent amateurism raised to the point of an organizational science (Dutt 1935: 206–09), pervert law and right. After all, as Durkheim says, "injustice is ever on the throne" (EFRL: 422),[138] yet the Western 'rule of law' has, more or less, withstood onslaughts for well over 900 years. Even those 'above the law' have to periodically sacrifice a fraction of their class to the legal principle. Law prevails because the constant and universal transgression against law reproduces it. The more criminals and perverts battle law the more criminal and perverted the law becomes. At the most basic level, a world of Right is simply one where everybody has enough, and limits are self-equilibrating. Where more than enough accrues to any class of individuals, Right will essentially operate as a system of universal wrong.

Right is connected not merely to law, duty, and obligations but also to imperatives of an optional variety that, when carried out from a sense of expectations (answering the Me) it is always, in its unalloyed form, for the express purpose of gaining or regaining a quantum of prestige or personal advantage (cf. Plato 1945, 2: 45). Whether or not an 'I' is recognized as legitimate and a bearer of rights depends on how an individual is connected via institutional particularity (intermediation) to the universal sphere. Presently, it is optional whether or not one is a Catholic or non-denominational evangelical Christian, etc., to be considered fully *American* but what is not optional is one's unwavering commitment to capital—quite literally, a luxury system (*luxus*, or a way of life grounded in material excess and unequal social ranks). Likewise, one can be a Democrat, Republican, anarchist, libertarian, progressive, etc., but none

---

138 Justice is not a solid crystal and where there is 'injustice' there might still be right and fairness; "the principle of equity following the law has, in common experience, sometimes meant that equity follows at such a respectful distance that the law is quite lost to view, or else strides out so boldly that it outstrips, not to say outwits, the law" (Allen 1927: 203).

of these negate the reign of capital and the unquestioned primacy of surplus production. We can dicker over the distribution of wealth but not over the principles of hyperproduction and hyperaccumulation.[139] Surplus value (worth beyond use) remains untouched by any 'valid' form of political discourse. Particular ethics or codes of conduct may vary but one's general morality may not. The dispossessed are fascinated by the prospect of being immediately connected to the universal and this is one way to think of crime: in pursuit of the prize of wealth the criminal negates the institutional moment of mediation through force and attempts to seize the thing itself. And this is the general plight of abstract rights in the capitalist system: "force decides" (C: 344). If a person is to have rights in modern society they must use force to deprive others of their rights—in the same way that property is theft[140] (MECW, 20: 28), rights are beaten out of my fellow human beings.[141] And "once might is made to be right, cause and effect are reversed, and every force which overcomes another force inherits the right which belonged to the vanquished" (Rousseau [1762] 1968: 53). My rights are based on a general system of wrongs and to enjoy my wares I must become a werewolf (C: 353).[142] In other words, with Weber, if we look at right from a sociological point of view, setting aside judicial formalism, it all comes down to "the facts of economic life" (ES, 1: 312). Mill says that when all the 'rights' fall to one group in society, leaving the onerous burdens for the remainder, a state of despotism has been achieved (1992: 49). It seems, then, that rights are simultaneously contingent while also firmly rooted in the necessity of fate. To have rights is also to embrace Doom. As Paine says, "It is the living, and not the dead, that are to be accommodated" (1791: 12) yet we know all too well that "the tradition of all the dead generations weighs like a nightmare on the brain of the living" (Marx [1869] 1963: 15). The living and the dead, spirit and matter, the sacred and the profane are the axles upon which our thoughts revolve. The world of people and their things, of people

---

139   One of my children protested vociferously, and frequently, when I had the audacity to serve them "enough" ice cream: "I want *too much!*"
140   Proudhon's famous phrase, "property is theft" was formulated by Jacques Pierre Brissot (*"La propriété c'est le vol."*) and cited by Marx in his critique of Proudhon (see MECW, 20: 28; MECW, 25: 173; MECW, 28: 61, 546; MECW, 47: 105). "Marx saw that the axiom 'Property is theft,' in referring to a violation of property, itself presupposed real rights in property. It was the old Abstract Man again…" (Wilson [1940] 1967: 154).
141   Cf. Weber on some forms of income as literal returns on violence (ES, 1: 206).
142   *Wares* as valuable goods comes from the Proto-Germanic word for "care" and "defense." *Wares* and *were*(wolves) are etymologically connected, distantly, in the idea of bloodshed.

and their property, is the world of negative solidarity (DOL: 72ff.).[143] Here we will find a paucity of consensus and cooperation between people and their things (DOL: 73) and, of course, in a society that has a mania for things, we find the inevitable shift or inversion, really, from people and possessions to possessions and their people (the fetishism where we find the reversal of the ends-means relation).

7   Nihilism and Skepticism

The Greeks, says Hegel, thought of happiness as "an advance over the sensuous enjoyment which is merely pleasant to the feelings." Placing 'enjoyment' and happiness beyond the horizon of the sensuous is important considering that the modern mentality associates pleasure and 'being happy' with an orgy of commodity consumption.

> Let us ask what happiness is and what there is within it for reflection, and we find that it certainly carries with it a certain satisfaction to the individual, of whatever sort it be—whether obtained through physical enjoyment or spiritual—the means of obtaining which lie in men's own hands. But the fact is further to be observed that not every sensuous, immediate pleasure can be laid hold of, for happiness contains a reflection on the circumstances as a whole, in which we have the principle to which the principle of isolated enjoyment must give way. Eudemonism signifies happiness as a condition for the whole of life; it sets up a totality of enjoyment which is a universal and a rule for individual enjoyment, in that it does not allow it to give way to what is momentary, but restrains desires and sets a universal standard before one's eyes (LHP, 1: 162).

Crucial here is the place of constraint and limits as the way to achieve actual happiness. In the previous volume we examined the minimalist spirit whereby one reduces material needs to base levels in order to achieve happiness. One can become objective to self through limitation and the establishment of a

---

143   "The very expression 'negative solidarity' that we have employed is not absolutely exact. It is not a true solidarity, having its own life and being of a special nature, but rather, the negative aspects of every type of solidarity.... Negative solidarity is only possible where another kind is present, positive in nature, of which it is both the result and the condition" (DOL: 75).

spiritual balance but, as we discovered, material minimalism was by no means a surefire route to happiness.[144] The notion of 'objective spirit' is only applicable to a minimally and dynamically equilibrated social order.[145] Once the social absolute begins to deform and disintegrate into abstractions and negativity, materialism and the unrestrained pursuit of wants swerves off into mania and depersonalization.[146] I think Marx's insistence that the capitalist class amounts to little more than a bunch of shameless egoists overlooks his frequent portrayal of that one-sidedness of the bourgeoisie with their fanaticism and willingness to martyr themselves for the sake of the money god. It is the 'altruistic' current, if you will, that whips capitalists into a frenzy of hyper-praxis that literally debases the materials of lust (gold and silver) and creates, in their place, a whirlwind of idealization and the (practically ritualized) generation of social phantoms (CPE: 109). There is a definite capacity, by no means always achieved, for exceeding the "mundane passions" and sporting competitiveness we associate with economic practices (PESC: 124).

---

144 It was hoped that there would be space in this volume to examine in more detail the spirit of maximizing material consumption that usually, but unfairly, falls under the names of 'hedonism' or 'Epicureanism.' We will take the problem up at a future date. One point that could be made now, however, is that what usually goes by the name of 'hedonism' would probably be better served under the concept of *Sybaritism*.

145 One can forget about real, mechanical equilibrium or environmental harmonizations, etc. Sociological equilibrium is not akin to the Golden Mean (Aristotle) nor finding a third way between two extremes, etc., Calvin's exhortation of sobriety as the middle way between ascetic self-torture versus the indulgence in earthly delights (McNeill [1954] 1967: 201). As for harmony with nature, we do not, and probably never have lived in harmony with the natural environment (see Posnett 2019: 276) and an equilibrated social order is only a dynamically equilibrated system that is always in the process of disintegration and reintegration (cf. Rousseau [1762] 1968: 92). One might argue that the metaphor of society rising to greater and greater heights over time is akin to the acoustic illusion provided by the so-called 'Shepard Tone' where it seems to the listener that a tone rises continuously when, in fact, the effect is produced by a short loop of bass and treble pitches of opposed amplitude changes (the volume of one increases as the volume of the other decreases). The Shepard Tone is frequently compared with the old-fashioned barber shop pole that provides an ocular illusion of an ever-rising spiral of stripes. If society is going somewhere it is also equally true that it is going nowhere. True, things change, and some things also change for the better but, here I think Žižek is correct, changes often occlude the fact that things have stayed fundamentally the same.

146 "The danger becomes all the greater the more our interest fastens upon external objects and the more we forget that the differentiation of our relation to nature should go hand in hand with a correspondingly differentiated relation to the spirit, so as to establish the necessary balance. If the outer object is not offset by an inner, unbridled materialism results, coupled with maniacal arrogance or else the extinction of the autonomous personality, which is in any case the ideal of the totalitarian mass state" (Jung 1969: 213).

We can locate Durkheim's critique of idealism in its key manifestations as they unfold through the conceptual matrix on display in *Suicide*. Idealism is a one-sided or defective paradigm that has secret affinities with ascetic self-mortification, especially in the Kantian transcendental and critical forms. What we will find, ultimately, is that pre-Hegelian idealism, from our perspective, is a symptom of resignation, the unity of egoism and fatalism, and contains within itself an impulse for self-destruction.[147] But let us not overlook the fact that idealism is not only 'egotistical' but literally knows no, or few bounds—idealism tends toward deregulated thought incapable of stopping even when it pulls up at the imaginary edge of the universe and wonders about the other side. Intellectual restlessness, impatience with existence, and constantly reaching beyond one's grasp is the long path from, say, socialism to Nietzsche (Antonio 1995: 2).[148] Later we will see that Hegelianism (a condensation of Absolute Idealism) offers solutions to its predecessors but falls short of what is required for sociology. Of special note here, with regards to idealism, are two forms we focus on: skeptical or subjective idealism, also known as nihilism and dogmatic idealism or objectivism.

Prime examples of skeptical or subjective idealism are found in Descartes and Berkeley. This subjective form is also associated with Jacobi's "Nihilism" where all we have are doubts about the existence of anything beyond our own subjective representations (Beiser 2002).[149] "Doubting, one begins to waver between one action and another. It was not by doubting that Newton discovered the law of gravity or Marx the future of capitalism" (Greene 1982: 220–21). Nihilists are "the mercenaries of the void" and barbarians without program, ideals, values, or ideologies; nihilism believes in nothing except the ego and violence (Comte-Sponville 2007: 25).

---

147   In a curious footnote, Sorel characterizes the German mentality as one dominated by a combination of strict discipline and resignation (1950: 260).

148   Wilson draws out Marx's penchant for egotistical recoil alternating with universalizing expansion in his early critiques: "He always is either contracted inside his own ego till he is actually unable to summon enough fellow-feeling to get on with other human beings at all or he has expanded to a comprehensive world-view which, skipping over individuals altogether, as his former attitude was unable to reach them, takes in continents, classes, long ages" ([1940] 1967: 152).

149   Postmodern skepticism and "its penchant for deconstruction bordering on nihilism" is a continuation of, not a break from, modern philosophical egoism. Aesthetics eclipse ethics and collective programs are negated. "It takes them beyond the point where any coherent politics are left, while that wing of it that seeks a shameless accommodation with the market puts it firmly in the tracks of an entrepreneurial culture that is the hallmark of reactionary neoconservativism" (Harvey 1990: 116).

Dogmatic or objective idealism denies the reality of empirical stuff, is more or less identical with a Transcendental Idealism minus a subject and both Leibniz as well as Spinoza are suitable examples. Objective idealism leads, inexorably, to fatalism (Beiser 2002). Subjective and objective idealisms are forms of what is called "empirical idealism" and they presuppose a transcendental realism (Beiser 2002). For Kant, these forms of thought degenerate into egoism and a third way beyond the double impasse of skepticism and dogmatism is sought. However, Kant does not ultimately solve the misery of doubt and the *denial* embedded in idealism because his own transcendental idealism, and this includes his critical turn, has woven into it the thread of ascetic self-punishment (another form of denial).

Kantian transcendental idealism, if we locate it near the coordinates of asceticism, is the sublation of the twin dead ends of the subjective and objective predecessors; they terminate in egoism and fatalism respectively. However, the contradiction of transcendental idealism means the presupposition of an empirical realism and what Nietzsche would call the "sacrifice of the intellect." Kantianism, in this form, is a road to the renunciation of reason and, to put it bluntly, intellectual suicide. When we turn to Hegel's account of Kantianism in *History of Philosophy* we should be profoundly struck by the Durkheimian timbre as we juxtapose the conceptual structure found in *Suicide*:

> Kantian philosophy does not go on to grapple with the fact that it is not things that are contradictory, but self-consciousness itself. Experience teaches that the ego does not melt away by reason of these contradictions, but continues to exist; we need not therefore trouble ourselves about its contradictions, for it can bear them. Nevertheless Kant shows here too much tenderness for things: it would be a pity, he thinks, if they contradicted themselves. But that mind, which is far higher, should be a contradiction—that is not a pity at all. The contradiction is therefore by no means solved by Kant; and since mind takes it upon itself, and contradiction is self-destructive, mind is in itself all derangement and disorder.... (Hegel [1840] 1995b: 451).[150]

This is an expression of Hegel's anti-asceticism and his unwillingness for mind to resign itself to perpetual misery and permanent alienation. Oddly enough, the idealist demand for resignation and foisting asceticism onto the subject is alive and well in orthodox quantum theory:

---

150   For a milder extension of this argument see Hegel ([1830] 1991: 92).

The orthodox view of quantum mechanics, known as the "Copenhagen interpretation" after the home city of Danish physicist Niels Bohr, one of its architects, holds that particles play out all possible realities simultaneously. Each particle is represented by a "probability wave" weighting these various possibilities, and the wave collapses to a definite state only when the particle is measured. The equations of quantum mechanics do not address how a particle's properties solidify at the moment of measurement, or how, at such moments, reality picks which form to take. But the calculations work. As Seth Lloyd, a quantum physicist at MIT, put it, "Quantum mechanics is just counterintuitive and we just have to suck it up." (Simons Science News 2014).

In his lectures on the philosophy of religion Hegel subordinates nature to Spirit and he rejects the Kantian imperative to inflict the mind with turmoil while sparing things. This historical reversal brings one to a higher scale of sublation and to the coordinates of absolute idealism (principally Hölderlin, Schelling, and Hegel).

The torment of actuality leads to the pure ego's turning inward to the inner domain of universality where the world is no longer "an object of dread" (Hegel 1956: 439). The promise of idealism was contentment in "theoretical abstraction" (Hegel 1956: 444) but Kantianism undermines the languorous repose of subjectivist resignation by drawing out its fatalistic implications,[151] leaving the understanding at the level of pure identity and delivering the subject over to autocracy (Ibid: 455–59). Kant failed to move idealism beyond the impasse of self-absorption and its various defective entanglements: "Great popularity has from one point of view been won for Kantian philosophy by the teaching that man finds in himself an absolutely firm, unwavering center-point; but with this last principle it has come to a standstill" (Ibid: 459). It was up to the *absolute* idealists to move Spirit beyond the self-torturing aspects of transcendental idealism but the elevation of the Idea to the status of the absolute, the autogenesis of the Big-C concept, brings with it a vitalized conflation of nature and Spirit and the prospect of *Geist* enthusiastically overshooting its destination into a will-mania, or a negative unity of progressive and regressive anomie:

> Ideation and movement are really two hostile forces, advancing in inverse directions, and movement is life. To think, it is said, is to abstain from action; in the same degree, therefore, it is to abstain from living. This

---

151 "She was a fatalist, you know, and it made her very serene but altogether unpurposeful" (Greene 1929: 65).

is why the absolute reign of idea cannot be achieved, and especially cannot continue; for this is death (S: 280; see also Durkheim 1993: 77).[152]

Perhaps Cornford (a card-carrying Durkheimian) summarizes best the suicidal tendencies of egoistic reflection and idealism:

> The ideal for the individual, then, is to escape from society.... He will withdraw like the Stoic, into autonomous self-sufficiency and Olympian contemplation.
> It is only a step further to the mystical trance of neo-platonism, in which thought is swallowed up in the beatific vision of the absolute One, above being and above knowledge, ineffable, unthinkable, no longer even a Reason, but 'beyond Reason' ... 'the escape of the alone to the alone.' In this [passive] ecstasy, Thought denies itself; and Philosophy, sinking to the close of her splendid curving flight, folds her wings and drops into the darkness whence she arose—the gloomy Erebus of theurgy and magic ([1912] 2004: 263).[153]

One thing is clear: we live, today, amidst the absolute reign of surplus value (M' in Marx's sign system) and the drive toward surplus value will not stop until the bourgeoisie has enslaved humanity and consumed the planet, including Weber's famous "last ton of fossilized coal" (PESC: 123). It would appear that the cunning of reason will not stop until it actually extinguishes itself. If reason can be enslaved and made to work for the general exploitation of humanity for the benefit of one class (Marcuse 1978: 36) then it is also a subject that can willingly destroy itself, if, for no other purpose, to put an end to its condition of servitude. If this sounds absurd then it also means that "intellectual suicide" is merely a whimsical phrase or that disordered and irrational thought is never a preference over ordered and rational thought. Are we willing to exclude Nietzsche and Freud from our intellectual lives?

Jumping ahead, Durkheim's position was neither the idealism of Kant, nor, as some claim, some kind of neo-Kantianism. Kant tried to rescue Spirit from the crude empiricism of the British Enlightenment by positing an active and projective mind whereby sensible intuitions were synthesized with concepts

---

152 See Herder's (1993: 70–71) critique of reason as an autonomous and transcendent power operating from somewhere outside of society and history.
153 See also Kant's relevant discussion of mysticism and limitlessness: Lao Tzu's "monstrous system of the *supreme good*, which is supposed to consist of *nothingness* [*im Nichts*], i.e., in the consciousness derived from annihilating his personality, of *feeling* oneself flowing into and being swallowed up in the abyss of the divinity ..." (1983: 99).

by the imagination. Far from a passive system of sense perception, the mind was responsible for constructing experience by means of the *a priori* categories of understanding that are already present within the mind (Kant 1929: 42–43). Where, then, do these *a priori* categories originate? Are we born with them? Durkheim's genius is to locate the *a priori* categories arising from the dynamics and organization of social exuberance:

> There is an aspect of every religion that transcends the realm of specifically religious ideas. Through it, the study of religious phenomena provides a means of revisiting problems that until now have been debated only among philosophers.... At the root of our judgments, there are certain fundamental notions that dominate our entire intellectual life. It is these ideas that philosophers, beginning with Aristotle, have called the categories of understanding: notions of time, space, number, cause, substance, personality. They correspond to the most universal properties of things. They are like solid frames that confine thought. Thought does not seem to be able to break out of them without destroying itself, since it seems we cannot think of objects that are not in time or space, that cannot be counted, and so forth. The other ideas are contingent and changing, and we can conceive of a man, a society, or an epoch that lacks them; but these fundamental notions seem to us as almost inseparable from the normal functioning of the intellect. They are, as it were, the skeleton of thought. Now, when one analyzes primitive religious beliefs methodically, one naturally finds the principal categories among them. They are born in and from religion; they are a product of religious thought.... Religious representations are collective representations that express collective realities; rites are ways of acting that are born only in the midst of assembled groups and whose purpose is to evoke, maintain, or recreate certain mental states of those groups. But if the categories are of religious origin, then they must participate in what is common to all religion: They, too, must be social things, products of collective thought (EFRL: 8–9).

Examined from Durkheim's point of view, Kant's transcendental subject remains enigmatic and undetermined: it has no objective existence, cannot be individuated, and his empirical realism means that individuals are relegated to experiencing reality as a play of appearances (Beiser 2002: 153, 209) splitting the world into knowable phenomena and a noumenal realm that we have difficulty accessing even indirectly. Durkheim's 'transcendental' subject-object is society, it is real, it can be experienced, and it does individuate itself as personalities, not just mental schematics. His picture of society is rooted in the fusion of two older paradigms: society is simultaneously 'transcendental' in the sense that it is metaphorically 'above' the individuals that constitute it but also purely immanent. What Hegel did for History, Durkheim did for Society.

It is true that, with the idealists, reality is a system of representations but, for Durkheim, the sign is not to be confused with the thing signified (S: 315). The substance underlying the sign is a real (but non-physical) energy produced through association.[154] The whole point of the ritual is the production of collective effervescence and its sublation into authoritative emblems and collective names. Rather than a conceptual autogenesis rooted in an historical process, in *Forms*, we find the organization and odyssey of moral energy, as it spreads out across time, space, and develops itself across distinct domains, religious, economic, political, and cultural, coming to rest, after passing through the crucible of magic, onto profane shores in less exotic modalities (EFRL: 34, 194, 366).[155] One of the most important lessons we learn from Durkheim is that the profane world consists of nothing but leftovers, a "residuum ... abandoned as the property of the material world" (EFRL: 36). It is not simply that materialism is the wrong *perspective*.

When we dissect any social phenomenon there is much to grab onto with any perspective. It is not quite so mysterious, then, why Durkheim (as just one example) has been accused of being so many different and contradictory things. It is a mistake to confuse any one paradigm or viewpoint (one-sided and finite, i.e., 'abstract') for some kind of 'absolute' view. All the various motivations that drive different paradigms emerge from the paradoxes and contradictions associated with judgments made from within a particular symbolic universe or from a particular sector of society where comprehension is hobbled by reflected distortions that provide only an illusion of grasping the 'big picture.' Bad interpretations recur because they mistakenly attempt to universalize their 'sideways' point of view (Pinkard 2002).

---

154   Recall from our previous discussions that collective effervescence is purely psychical (not reducible to the merely subjective or intersubjective scales of life) but exhibits physical effects.
155   Totemism only appeared on the surface to be a zoolatry (EFRL: 139) when in fact its essence was independent of its form in the plant and animal species. Totemism was not even about humans worshiping humans in an altered-alien, plant or animal form; "energy alone is the real object of [the totemic] cult" (EFRL: 191). The question was not why do people worship plants and animals but why does social energy, signification, classification, and identity assume, here, at this stage of historical development, the form of plant and animal species?

It would be an error to try and approach things from a bunch of different perspectives (per Mannheim or Mills) as if they were all at least partially correct and that we can blend them to form a picture of the whole.[156] The point is not to 'see' with a multiplicity of differing 'instruments' or points of view, even though that sounds reasonable at first glance.[157] We cannot simply 'be' X one moment and Y another moment and hope to cobble together some coherent picture of reality.[158]

We are interested in 'seeing' from two or more 'locations' at once (seemingly a magic trick from the standpoint of empiricism) via the effective development and deployment of dialectical models.[159] The project to reclaim objective knowledge will not be carried out here but it must be undertaken at some point down the road. The reason this kind of project seems implausible today is because sociology has almost completely relinquished its theoretical legacy and, worse, we live in an age characterized by genuine anti-intellectualism. Sociology has forsaken itself because you cannot write a grant proposal for this kind of science, you *cannot simply convert a concept into a variable*, and you cannot simply pull a data set down off a shelf and crunch some numbers and hope for something true. Nor can you conduct a field study and hope to grasp anything like a sense of a social totality. In other words, contemporary sociology has fallen back on naturalistic methods and statistical surveys for the sake of practicality and profitability. Then again, American society and sociology (excluding some Marxist varieties) have always had these orientations. Sociology, like the rest of bourgeois society, is roaming around aimlessly in a state somewhere between the living and the dead. Abstract individuals are the living dead, formless and invisible to those standing in the light of the negative absolute (Ellison 1947: 7).

---

156   "In fact, the law that governs the divergent perspectives is the structure of the social process as a preordained whole" (Adorno 1973: 37).

157   One-sided and thereby flawed perspectives are still important as "valuable sources of information in that they convey some part of the underlying social reality, but each only expresses one aspect and not always very faithfully" (Durkheim 1974: 63–64). Orthodox Marxism, for example, has a terrible time talking about value without falling into the abyss of transcendental realism.

158   The 'absolute' view is a 'romantic' perspective, one filled with irony (negating at every turn), and more plausible from an egoistic, disinterested coordinate in the social system.

159   "The concept of totality is but the concept of society in the abstract form. It is the whole that includes all things, the supreme class that contains all other classes" (EFRL: 443).

8   *Ekstasis* and Resignation

In our theoretical universe, *ekstasis* forms the negative unity of anomie and altruism, in the most general sense. "Society now experiences an odd critical state where the highest, near-ecstatic, integration coexists with the lowest regulation…" (Paoletti 2012: 77). Per altruism, the connections between *ekstasis* and conceptions of honor and duty are firmly established (Reich 1970: 52–53). 'Ecstasy' comes from the Latin word *ekstasis* which means 'standing outside oneself' or being beside oneself in the sense of being doubled. According to Smith, *ekstasis* forms the basis for the Roman concept of alienation (1988; see also Morris-Reich 2005). Being outside or beyond the self (an extreme form of alienation that combines splitting or doubling and possession)[160] is related to the heterotelic nature of altruistic life, in contrast to the autotelic qualities of egoistic introspection and autistic inwardness. Berger (1969: 31) defines *ekstasis* a bit more narrowly as "standing outside of the taken-for-granted routines of everyday life…" where encounters with the other can produce a terrifying thrill. In our previous volume we paid attention to the Stoic form of melancholy (a pleasurable, dreamy sadness that can work itself up to a sterile passion, can glimpse the appearance of ecstasy, but terminates in resignation. Nowhere is this captured better than in Bataille's description of a "partly failed experiment." We lack the space to delve into the whole thing now but what strikes our interest is how the ego, in its attempt to escape itself through a mild and quasi-mystical experience with nature, encounters the 'rim' of our central void. The ego's trajectory is altered (mysticism never actually succeeds in leaping the abyss) along a circular course such that it passes by the coordinates of ecstasy and is returned to the place of resignation (1988: 112–14). It almost goes without saying that real ecstasy (of the positive kind) can never happen in isolation. Ecstasy, in its ideal-typical purity, is the expected product of intense, collective religious worship.

When Rudolf Otto characterized religious experience as absolutely "other" (i.e., something "totally other" than everyday or profane reality) we can extend that to mean, literally, participation in the 'other' or as an altogether otherness. Apart from collective ritual practice, ecstasy can be experienced at the level of personal psychology and in periods of social crisis.

Religion is, first of all, the *locus classicus* for the ecstasy of the association and it is essentially altruistic: "religious man wishes to be *other* than he is on the plane of his profane experience" (Eliade 1987: 100). James Madison wrote to Thomas Jefferson in 1787:

---

160   We will have more to say about compounded alienation later.

> Religion. The inefficacy of ... restraint on individuals is well known. The conduct of every popular Assembly, acting on oath, the strongest of religious ties, shews that individuals join without remorse in acts [aghast] which their consciences would revolt, if proposed to them separately in their closets. When Indeed Religion is kindled into enthusiasm, its force like that of other passions is increased by the sympathy of a multitude. But enthusiasm is only a temporary state of Religion, and whilst it lasts will hardly be seen with pleasure at the helm. Even in its coolest state, it has been much oftener a motive to oppression than a restraint from it (in Hutchinson et al. 1962).

This passage resonates on the same frequency with Durkheim's sections on assemblage effervescence found in all his large works. Political turmoil and, of course, war are also prime generators of ebullience as well as the inevitable disillusionments.

> We had come from lecture halls, school desks and factory workbenches, and over the brief weeks of training, we had bonded together into one large and enthusiastic group. Grown up in an age of security, we shared a yearning for danger, for the experience of the extraordinary. We were enraptured by war. We had set out in a rain of flowers, in a drunken atmosphere of blood and roses. Surely the war had to supply us with what we wanted; the great, overwhelming, the hallowed experience. We thought of it as manly, as action, a merry dueling party on flowered, blood-bedewed meadows.... Anything to participate, not to have to say at home!... Our heated fantasies cooled down on the march through the claggy soil of Champagne. Knapsacks, munition belts and rifles hung round our necks like lead weights (Junger [1920] 2016: 5).[161]

War *ekstasis* transforms the self and brings one into contact with 'higher forces' (Hedges 2002; Worrell 2011). "Add to these the ecstasies of battle and of victory, the *Kampfsrausch* [bloodlust] and the *Siegestrunkenheit* [victory enthusiasm or even victory disease], and the mood of war in which acts unlawful for the individual become not only lawful but highly honorable when done collectively. There is also in the mood of war the social intoxication, the feeling on

---

161 On page five of *Storm of Steel* we find enthusiasm; by page seven that enthusiasm is "blunted"; on page nine enthusiasm devolves into "melancholy exaltation"; by page 13 the author is "fully disillusioned" with another 276 pages remaining. "Instead of the danger we'd hoped for, we had been given, dirt, work and sleepless nights..." (Junger [1920] 2016).

the part of the individual of being a part of a body and the sense of being lost in a greater whole" (Partridge 1919: 23).

It should come as no surprise that critical theorists who abandoned the proletariat as a self-absorbed and hopeless mass of reaction would be lured rightward toward the potential for war charisma and dictatorial exceptionalism as a way out of capitalist alienation (Worrell and Dangler 2011).[162] Production, consumption, proletarian revolution, etc., are all dead ends, leaving war as the last remaining fount of enthusiasm.

> The craving for ... social solidarity and ecstasy of social feeling is a factor in the causes of war. What we experience socially in times of peace is a society in which social feeling is narrow and provincial, in which we are conscious of many antagonistic motives. This social life fails to satisfy the desires which are seeking expression in the social life. That war is in part a creation of the social impulse seeking expression may be assumed from the nature of the social feelings that are excited in war. That such social feeling is a creation in the sense that it is desired, we see if in no other way in the fact that social ecstasy is the most universal form of satisfaction of all those impulses which fuse in the intoxication impulse, where we recognize it as the craving for an abundant or real life. Life is most real in its intensely dramatic social forms. Social ecstasy is in part a conscious adaptation. It is something that is desired and induced, and artificially cultivated in various ways, especially by a variety of aesthetic social experiences, and in the cults of intoxication (Partridge 1919: 64–65).

Of course, one cannot live in a state of permanent war. War without end ceases to be an exceptional state. Even if an empire does in fact carry on wars without end on a multitude of fronts, the domestic core must be relatively sheltered from the terror of dodging bullets with occasional explosions of mass murders (schools, jobsites, cinemas, clubs, and concert shootings). Once the logic works itself up full-tilt the occasional burst of morbid excitement cools off into routine: surviving the school shooting, for example, becomes just another day at the job (Worrell 2013b).

Those who are doomed to alternate between passive resignation and the untamed passions can find respite, at a price, in "blindly raging industriousness" which "does create wealth and reap honors while at the same time depriving the organs of their subtlety, which alone would make possible the

---

162 "Ecstasy or rapture is for the neo-Platonist the highest psychological state of man" (Feuerbach 1986: 47).

enjoyment of wealth and honors; also that this chief antidote to boredom and the passions at the same time blunts the senses and leads the spirit to resist new attractions" (Nietzsche [1887] 1974: 93–94). Becoming a martyr to industriousness opens other possibilities. Martyrdom represents just one hidden transit between *ekstasis* and resignation—one attempt among many to leap the abyss. With Nietzsche, we find martyrdom without paradise (Royce 1969: 303) while, with the spirit of terror, the promise of paradise awaits the martyr. Even if one cannot raise the self to an exceptional state though industriousness there is always the retreat into dreams or sickness.

> The world of dreams is ecstatic with regard to the world of everyday life, and the latter can only retain its primary status in consciousness if some way is found of legitimating the ecstasies within a frame of reference that includes *both* reality spheres. Other bodily states also produce ecstasies of a similar kind, particularly those arising from disease and acute emotional disturbance. The confrontation with death (be it through actually witnessing the death of others or anticipating one's own death in the imagination)[163] constitutes what is probably the most important marginal situation.... Religion, then, maintains the socially defined reality by legitimating marginal situations in terms of an all-encompassing sacred reality.... While the ecstasy of marginal situations is a phenomenon of individual experience, entire societies or social groups may, in times of crisis, undergo such a situation collectively (Berger 1967: 43–44).

In *Disintegration* we took an extended look at suicide as an extreme form of everyday conduct, which means, of course, that pushed beyond limits, the

---

163 "And when at last, captured and throttled, they were led into the presence of our military leaders, they were by that time already resigned to the deplorable fate that was in store for them. Their bearing was uniformly marked by a strange serenity, a serenity that was hard to explain in view of the many and discordant types of character to be found among them—mestizos of every sort, with temperaments as varied as were the shadings of their skin. Some of these beings on the lowest rung of our racial ladder displayed an incredible haughtiness in the presence of their captors" (Cunha 1944: 440). Regarding Hamlet, Calderwood says "Until the final act the world has been unfit for him and he for it, and the friction between the two has chafed his mind. At the end, however, his former discontent, his 'irritable reaching after fact and reason,' has given way to that ability to abide amid 'uncertainties, mysteries, doubts' that Keats called negative capability.... Being ready for death, dressed for that fatal appointment, entails being equipped also for life, for the kind of life in which even death answers to a higher concept of fitness. If Hamlet is fit for his role in the King's play of swords, he is also fit for his role in the play of Providence, in which all men have their parts and even sparrows suffer their brief tragic falls" (1984: 273).

ordinary is deformed into something extraordinary. Here, again, we come full circle with the concept of self-destruction as a futile attempt to reignite the engines of social effervescence. "Just as when a man commits suicide he negates the body, this rational limit of subjectivity, so when he lapses into fantastic and transcendental practice he associates himself with embodied divine and ghostly appearances, namely, he negates in practice the difference between imagination and perception" (Feuerbach 1986: 46). Suicide victims are not necessarily mad, as in literally insane, but madness is a central concept around the coordinates of *ekstasis*. 'Mad' here as a triple meaning: anger (I'm mad at the author of this book), insanity (this book is simply mad), and enthusiasm (e.g., I'm just mad about this book).[164] Anger may develop into hate, but we know that hate is a kind of negative love. If "the gates marked love and harmony lead, in the end, to hatred and domination" (Freeman 1943: 592) then it follows that hatred and domination must, at some point, return to love and harmony. Love and hate are intertwined. Indeed, the roots of anger rest in the Proto-Indo-European word for 'tied together.' And if one becomes enraged over some title they may be regarded among the vanguard when that self-same title becomes *all the rage*. And what is insanity if not, in many cases, a surplus of sanity? A *perfectly* reasonable person would be crazy in the estimation of normal people.

'Madness' is essential to life. "'That's why people prefer operas in which the music whips up every feeling and tears us apart like a whirlwind. We need madness—not dainty pastorals—to refresh the heart and mind'" (Mahler, in Haste 2019: 18). What we do not require is alienation that introduces an unbridgeable chasm between the ego and others. Almost anything can be made 'rational' including the total retreat into self. We routinely validate scenarios where total self-sacrifice is the thing to do, either for obligatory or optional (prestigious) reasons—this is why we distinguish between suicide and sacrifice. Even when a political or religious fanatic blows themselves up we cannot dismiss them *tout court* as 'mentally ill' because we can be made to see 'the reason' for it. If the Iranians bomb Mar-a-Lago in response to the killing of General Soleimani we will know the reason is 'revenge.' Revenge is not reasonable but there is a reason behind it. A thought, feeling, or action may be mad

---

164 In the end, 'enthusiasm' is derived from *enthous* which means being possessed by a god or being inspired by one. Sociological enthusiasm is, setting aside particularities, roughly synonymous with mana contamination or being filled in with grace, etc. The individual is a carrier of divine, impersonal power of some variety. In the volume on Christianity and the commodity we will take a look at Jesus as a voluntary scapegoat bearing the corruption (negative charisma) of those that sought his redeeming powers. The Jesus relation is one of an exchange between grace and sin for the everyday low price of faith.

but also able to fit into some rational scheme which brings us to the intersection of reason and alienation. If Reason is not just the mere understanding plus a little extra, i.e., if it is 'sacred' as Hegel insists, it must be somehow entangled and implicated in the dynamics of 'madness.' Hegel's theory of madness, his "ontology of insanity" (Berthold-Bond 1995: 39), amounts to a theory of alienation from the sociological point of view. As Berthold-Bond says, "insanity is not an actually necessary destiny for all consciousness, unlike despair, and yet it is constantly prepared for by despair, which in its grief solicits consciousness to 'sink back' to an inwardness which is more primitive than reason" (Ibid: 51). But Hegel's forms of madness are mostly restricted to the currents we surveyed in our previous discussions of *egoism*. What interests us in this volume is how egoism 'traverses' its passive dimension into the realm of energy (anomie, altruism, and the fusion of those currents under the concept of ecstasy).

The polar opposite of *ekstasis* is resignation and should not be mistaken for reconciliation. The latter entails a lack of movement and a willingness to buckle down for the long haul, often sustained by rationalizations or fantasies that, someday, suffering and endurance will be rewarded.[165] Resignation (or negative *ekstasis*)[166] may appear like "the master's ultimate weapon" (Sennett 1980: 142) or some kind of settling down, a path to inner and outer peace, where one comes to terms with fate "but forfeits the fullness of his real capacities and the real richness of his nature.... [Whereas] resignation may lead to bitterness and rage against fate, which may be focused on those who are participating in life and enjoying it. In an attempt to reclaim or salvage some feeling of self, the individual turns destructive and sadistic in revenge" (Ivimey 1946: 86). And once the revenge logic is wound up it knows little in the way of limits. The sadist, as Camus says, is not satisfied until they have the moon (in Fromm 1973: 289). Sadistic tendencies are directed not only toward others in overt or subtle

---

165 "Though he had never saved more than a few thousand francs, he took it for granted that in the end he would be able to set up his own restaurant and grow rich. All waiters, I afterwards found, talk and think of this; it is what reconciles them to being waiters" (Orwell [1933] 1961: 25).

166 Fromm refers to "'negative ecstasis'" as the forgetting of the self by being absorbed like a thing into a role or institutional function such that the split person is transformed into a "nonperson"—basically, negative *ekstasis* is a way of thinking about altruistic reification as a form of adaptation to anomie (1973: 234–35). As such, Fromm has identified negative *ekstasis* with what we are referring to as *ekstasis* qua *negative resignation*. Fromm never escaped an underlying allegiance to vitalism and he was susceptible to mysticism and the romantic urge for mystical unity and, for this reason, I find it necessary to flip his thinking right side up at this point.

ways but also toward the self (Ivimey 1946: 86). Here we can see quite clearly how resignation actually has built into it a kind of double logic of passive acceptance[167] and active rejection (cf. Bhaskar 2008)[168] discernible in concentration camps or prisons where resentment toward fate mingles with acceptance (Bettelheim 1960; see also Fromm 1973: 63).

In prisons, especially, the land of the hyper-regulated and the hopeless, one may still find the spirit of revolt alive and well (Durkheim 1961: 198). Pain and outrage are not incompatible with "fatal resignation" (Bageant 2010: 128) but also sudden reversals in the course of dramatic struggle (Fink 1997: 71). Consider the collective straining against predestination. Of course, many submit to fate through various forms of autocide and homicide (slow and fast) but others mobilize their energies around an ethos. "As with the Puritan belief in predestination, a serious conviction that impersonal forces ruled the world could lead to action in perceived harmony with those forces" (Liebersohn 1988: 3). Where pure egoism results in isolation (estrangement) and solitude, the mind is fooled into believing that it no longer suffers the limitations imposed upon it by external forces. But deprived of cooperation the solitary monad, in its infinity, is hyper-limited and finite.[169] Real or even just practical infinity comes from the finite limitations arising from solidarity with others; "community is freedom and infinity" (Feuerbach 1986: 71). So, it is the case that resignation may appear in the form of virtuous tolerance toward others; "when it is genuine it is based upon a respect for the reason and personality of others. But the easy toleration which declines discussion may be at bottom founded on indifference and even something approaching contempt" (Creighton 1925: 69).

Previously, we rest content with the concept of *submission* to capture what was essential about the unity of resignation and ecstasy but, in light of further developments, the ultimate but morbid unity of *ekstasis* and resignation might be best expressed in the notion of *Schwärmerei* which combines frenzy and

---

167   The horror of passive resignation is reflected in the spectating found in *Medea* (Euripides) where the chorus stands by debating as Medea, "a torment to herself and to others" due to her destructive passions that suppresses reason, slaughters her own children (Kitto 1950: 203). Why not intervene? Similarly, Bettelheim notes that murder victims that passively and willingly go to their execution should be considered suicide victims (1960: 245).

168   Important is Bhaskar's 'Rejection in Theory Acceptance in Practice' for our theory of resignation. One might tease out the differences between indifference as it refracts through Stoicism and this other form of rejective acceptance among skeptics (2008: 154).

169   A person who is integrated into a movement or party, etc., may be physically separated from others (e.g., solitary confinement) but is also not truly isolated (Freeman 1943: 413). "[H]ow different is solitary confinement from solitude, that which is imposed from that which is freely chosen!" (Ibid: 618).

rapture with passive "opiate indulgence in the comfort of disembodied ideas" (Freeman 1943: 123). If so, our earlier Durkheimian emphasis on 'submission' uniting twin extremities can be reconceptualized or simply augmented (if we so desire):

Leaving this unity aside for another time, let us once again set our sights on the half-measures of asceticism and piacular destructiveness.

9 *Piacula* and Asceticism

Marx's model of communist association, if you can even call it a model, was oriented toward the elimination of suffering for individuals. But Durkheim knew that collective existence will always entail an unavoidable degree of pain and suffering.[170] The point is not to eliminate suffering but to give the suffering meaning and a goal: suffering, in other words, is not for nothing but for a larger project. This was precisely the goal of psychoanalysis, not to eliminate suffering but to reconnect the sufferer to a reason for suffering.

> Patients come because they are suffering from something. They want that suffering to be alleviated. Ideally, in the process of doing the analysis, they might find their suffering is alleviated or modified, but also they might discover there are more important things than to alleviate one's suffering.... Analysis should do two things that are linked together. It should be about the recovery of appetite, and the need not to know yourself.... The need not to know yourself. Symptoms are forms of self-knowledge. When you think, I'm agoraphobic, I'm a shy person, whatever it may be, these are forms of self-knowledge. What psychoanalysis, at its best, does is cure you of your self-knowledge. And of your wish to know yourself in that coherent, narrative way. You can only recover your appetite, and appetites, if you can allow yourself to be unknown to yourself. Because the point of knowing oneself is to contain one's anxieties about appetite. It's only worth knowing about the things that make one's life worth living, and whether there are in fact things that make it worth living (Adams 2014).

---

170 Modern, secular asceticism is altogether milder, generally speaking, than the pure, religious forms of self-destruction we find in primitive times among religious and mystical virtuosos (e.g., Westermarck 1917: 365 ff.).

The cult of pain and suffering terminates in the extremes of asceticism and the piacular. Rites of ascetic self-torture are designed to demonstrate that one is "above suffering" whereas the piacular rites signify that one is in the grip of suffering (EFRL: 395). What we are most interested in, when it comes to pain and suffering, though, is the kind dished out by a whole group or class upon a target when it finds itself under siege, in danger, in despair, or beset by some horrible crisis. From early on, Durkheim placed great emphasis on the enraged group and the "expression of wrath that rises up [as] a single fount of anger" (DOL: 58). An outraged and avenging group under attack

> ...closes ranks in the face of danger and, in a manner of speaking, clings closer together. One is no longer content to exchange impressions when the occasion presents itself, nor draw closer together when the chance occurs or when meeting is convenient. On the contrary, the anxiety that has spread from one person to another impels forcibly together all those who resemble one another, causing them to assemble in one place. This physical concentration of the whole group, bringing the interpenetration of minds ever closer, also facilitates every concerted action. Emotional reactions enacted within each individual consciousness are thus afforded the most favourable conditions in which to coalesce together (DOL: 59).

This coalescence results, as they say in Missouri, in a whole can o'whoopass.[171] The fact that the organized group may inflict as much or more pain and damage upon *itself* in seeking revenge against the hated other is quite interesting.[172]

Fleeing from the Nazis, Max Horkheimer was led to ask: "Does unconditional submission to a political leader or a party point historically forwards or backwards?" (1972: 71). He observed that there are "exceptional moments" in history when the brutality and existential bleakness of prevailing economic and social conditions become relatively transparent (1972: 60) and these moments open the potential for revolutionary change as in the case of the Reformation and the French Revolution. Horkheimer thought that bourgeois leadership had, if there were to be any success in leading the masses to their view of the world, to promise them not necessarily what they deserved but what they desired. Appealing to their ideal interests such as love of nation and hatred of the alien,

---

[171] At the level of individuals being disrespected or dishonored, the quest for revenge and the restoration of honor often takes the form of spectacularly self-destructive acts of "keeping it real."

[172] "If you hate a person, you hate something in him that is part of yourself. What isn't part of ourselves doesn't disturb us" (Hesse [1925] 1965: 116).

the working classes were steered from questioning the reasonableness of the capitalist mode of production and, in so doing, helped to solidify the underpinnings of capitalist hegemony. In addition to the hatred of the other, they were "sold" on the long-term material benefits of capitalism: "The people are supposed to recognize that the national movement will, in the long run, bring [material] advantages for them too" (Horkheimer 1972: 62; see also Marcuse 1972). This was, however, to be an unfulfilled promise. "The bourgeois revolution did not lead the masses to the lasting state of joyful existence ... but to the hard reality of an individualistic social order instead" (Ibid.). Which is to say, it is not a 'social' order at all. During their wartime stay in the US, Horkheimer & Co. discovered that working-class Americans were, to a great and unexpected degree, captivated by the symbols and ambitions of the Nazis. Half the American population was considered unreliable in the struggle for democracy and a full ten percent were basically Nazis at heart. While American troops were 'over there' fighting the Nazis, millions of Americans 'over here' wished for a Hitler they could call their own that would round up and exterminate the Jews they imagined were ruining America. The comparisons between Hitler, the Nazis, etc., and Trump are overblown but, at bottom, Trumpism, Nazism, and Fascism, are particular forms of that universal, authoritarian menace. From poll numbers reflecting support for Trump it is impossible to say that America has made any real progress in the struggle against political sadomasochism.

Beyond psychological syndromes and political policies, Trumpism is basically symbolic revanchism borne out of decades of material dispossession and social disintegration. "As familiar grounds for security give way, people still flounder and toss in troubled search for the right to obey forms of authority that cannot possibly exist" (Moore 1978: 436).

> And when the disparity of condition increases so does universal suffrage make it easy to seize the source of power, for the greater is the proportion of power in the hands of those who feel no direct interest in the conduct of government; who, tortured by want and embruted by poverty, are ready to sell their votes to the highest bidder or follow the lead of the most blatant demagogue; or who, made bitter by hardships, may even look upon profligate and tyrannous government with the satisfaction we may imagine the proletarians and slaves of Rome to have felt, as they saw a Caligula or Nero raging among the rich patricians (George [1879] 1956: 531).

For millions of Americans, Trump (the embodiment of wrong) can do nothing right; the administration weaves erratically from one self-destructive action to the next. But this is why Trump was dropped on Washington. He was the right man for the job of wronging the political establishment. Trump was not elected as president but installed to function as an anti-president. Self-wounding is a small price to pay for an even greater injury inflicted upon despised others. Trump possesses no charisma—but his *enemies* are negatively charismatic and his power to do wrong is grounded in the demon economy that plagues the Red hologram.[173]

> ...[B]eside hero-worship there is the exorcism of devils. By the same mechanism through which heroes are incarnated, devils are made. If everything good was to come from Joffre, Foch, Wilson, or Roosevelt, everything evil originated in ... Kaiser Wilhelm, Lenin and Trotsky. They were as omnipotent for evil as the heroes were omnipotent for good. To many simple and frightened minds there was no political reverse, no strike, no obstruction, no mysterious death or mysterious conflagration anywhere in the world of which the causes did not wind back to these personal sources of evil (Lippmann [1922] 1960: 25).

It is a curious though not unexpected happening that antisemitism has staged a significant comeback in American life under Trump. Indeed, it never really vanished. Generally, any object may serve as the carrier of projected animosities and, historically, all kinds of people, groups, and objects have served as screens for the construction of fantastical creatures in possession of supernatural and diabolical powers. Every society has its preferred form of representing its form of negative love. But as capital began to reorganize European society, one entity emerged as the object *par excellence*—the *bête noire* of modernity: the

---

173 The root of Trump's ascendency rests in economic discontent and manifests itself in political circus but the logic of the 'base' is strongly dominated by the hatred of the morally impure. There is, however, nothing in the way of a genuine 'personality cult' with respect to Trump because there is no 'otherworldly' aspect to his presidency. Even supporters frequently wish out loud that he would stop communicating. On National Public Radio one of Trump's Iowa supporters (in the aftermath of the Iowa caucus debacle) claimed that the president could not be guilty of the crimes and conspiracies Democrats accuse him of committing because he is simply "too dumb" to pull it off. The classic Weberian political authority model fails to encapsulate what we find in Trumpism, necessitating a shift to Freud (psychodynamics) and Durkheim's sociology of religion (perhaps even Lacan-Žižek where Trump approximates the obscene paternal figure that has monopolized enjoyment—a kind of 'Lynchian' Father of excessive *jouissance* that, after a wild ride, must ultimately be destroyed if the symbolic order is to avoid psychotic dissolution).

mythical Jew.[174] The 'Jew' of antisemitic propaganda, the hate without end, is the only representation that quite literally has the capacity to unite the entire universe of particular hatreds.

If we were to ask Christians to name some famous, unstable, deviant, suicidal, Jewish magicians, 'Jesus' is not likely to make the list. Jesus was the murdered, perfect son and that infinite crime can never be atoned for. And if god is a perfect colossus his nemesis must also possess equally abnormal qualities and abilities. For authoritarians, routine or mundane scapegoats often do not suffice in fulfilling the psychological needs of those who project 'magical' forces. What is required is truly a 'work of art' or fantastical construction, something that embodies a substance equally as awesome as the rage embodied in the movement.[175] Objects of collective hatred represent crystallizations of what Durkheim called, in his analysis of primitive religions, *absolute* power, and, as such, mundane targets fall short of absolute capacities. A classic expression of fear toward absolute evil can be found in Pope Innocent's 1484 'Witch-bull' in which women were accused of fouling every conceivable natural and social relationship.

The list of offenses against Christianity "is surely as astonishing as it is typical." Some segment of the population "is singled out, castigated for possessing monstrous and supernatural traits that threaten everyone else, and then condemned on grounds of sheer gossip and fantasy for having committed crimes that even the most rebellious gods of Greece and Rome would have found beyond their abilities" (Oppenheimer 1996: 97–98).[176] Anomie (anarchy) lends a considerable amount of energy to the river of mythical hatred.

---

174 As money (the universal equivalent) comes to dominate society and begins the long process of saturating every nook and cranny of life—the notion of 'spectacle' (Debord [1967] 1983)—the 'Jew' is transformed into the negative personification of that universal equivalent, a role that had been written for 'the Jew' in the Middle Ages. Trachtenberg was surely incorrect in seeing modern European antisemitism as nothing more than the extension of medieval *Judenhass* pure and simple ([1943] 1983: 219).

175 We are a long way away from the mischievous little *kobold* that both frustrates and assists in everyday living: "All very well to tell them at church they must beware of evil spirits, that one they think quite harmless, one that slips into the house like a puff of wind, may really and truly be a demon. They take good care not to believe a word of it. Why! his littleness is proof enough of innocence; and certainly they have prospered more since he came. The husband is as sure of it as the wife, perhaps surer. He is firmly convinced the dear, frolicsome little Brownie makes the happiness of their home" (Michelet [1862] 1992: 31).

176 Simmel's essay on "the stranger" (the ideal type being the Jew) is relevant here but I will postpone an analysis of 'the stranger' for another time.

As Nietzsche observed, the anarchist searches for the other to blame for their suffering and is bathed in a sense of indignation. This indignation is pleasurable for the anarchist and provides "an intoxicating sense of power" (1982: 534). The anarchist aims at the sweetest revenge and any target is as worthy as another.[177] "The objects of this need for revenge, as a need for pleasure, are mere occasions: everywhere the sufferer finds occasions for satisfying his little revenge" (1982: 535). The desire for revenge against the impure other[178] (including, masochistically, the impurity within the self) is an absolutely crucial element in the education of the sadistic pervert and violent fanatic. Where we find sadistic revenge we are capturing the manifest surface dynamics of a subterranean regression to an earlier form of social organization analogous on a smaller scale to the sadistic drives of the genitally inhibited youngster that retreats into an earlier form (cf. Freud 2003: 223–34).[179] The inner pulse of Nazi education, for example, was the promise of revenge against the enemies of Germany, those lesser and second-rate fools that had humiliated the German people in the wake of defeat during WWI. "And we the living—what will we do? We will revenge, *revenge*, REVENGE!" (Ziemer 1941: 111).

Revenge can be a means to an end or it can be an end in itself.[180] As an end point, revenge may exist in a bipolar form where one seeks revenge and love at the same time (O'Neill 1932: 715).

---

177 Conforming to the rule that one is not attacked because one is bad, but, rather, one is bad because one is attacked.
178 See Borkenau (1962: 342–43) on the thirst for vengeance among German communists against their socialist enemies; the chapter is aptly titled: "The Leap Into the Abyss." It's important to frame the ascendency of Trump as popular exhaustion and disgust with both the RNC and the DNC and the desire for revenge against the entire Washingtonian 'swamp.' It is interesting that, for example, in Michigan (where Trump unexpectedly won by approximately 11,000 votes) roughly "75,000 Michiganders who went to the polls didn't vote for president at all, more than double the number in 2008" (Spangler et al. 2019). But Trump had sufficient voters who looked past or even embraced his unprecedented level of sleaze and corruption. Ultimately, the fact of Trump's involvement with Russian gangsters "was just never going to penetrate the brains of an electorate ready to take a sledgehammer to the establishment" (Simpson and Fritsch 2019: 123). But the base simply does not care and might even consider criminality to be a desired quality for the position. Indeed, it is painfully obvious that Trump is the worst-qualified person in history to serve as president (or anything, really) but it appears that it was precisely because of his poor 'qualities' that he was elected: everything he touches is transformed into excrement, therefore, if the popular will is riled up to deliver a hammer-fall to the political establishment, who better to use as a dirty cudgel than Trump?
179 One is left to wonder if all forms of social organization contain within them all previous forms of organization into which they can retreat?
180 One can also fall in love with the instrument of revenge (O'Neill 1932: 720).

Suffering is a good way to ensure revenge (AJ: 259) and this points to a *piacular* logic—we will pay to make them pay more—but not all revenge rises to this perverse sublimity and it is important to keep in mind that all piacular acts contain a revenge component but not all acts of revenge rise to the level of the piacular. One can seek revenge while never incurring losses to self. We can always count on, for example, a colleague or coworker to stab us in the back anonymously and therefore being totally unexposed to retaliation or accountability. There is also the very important situation when a person or group has already lost 'everything'—they subjectively feel as though they have nothing left to lose, even the honor of their name is either already tainted or worthless—and their deepest desire is to see others dragged down into the muck with them. The vote for Trump was, for some, not a positive act in in which people thought they were going to get relief for themselves, but a negative act of making life hell for others (McWilliams 2016). This revenge can run in the direction of making life miserable for the 'liberal elite' and 'mainstream' everything (e.g., the desire to see the precious multicultural 'snowflakes' melt under the intense rays of the tangerine sunburst) but it also runs in the direction of punishing a pool of undeserving types who enjoy 'entitlements.' Here is a separate logic found in Trumpism: I work like hell and get almost nothing in return while those lazy unemployed people who *refuse* to work get as much or more as I do. Trump will make them pay (see Kliff 2016). This bit of logic is made possible through an infantile rationalization that goes like this:

> I have and need X (the Affordable Care Act, for example) which is a *mix* of good and bad, i.e., it is bad;[181]
>
> The bad others have Y (Medicaid) which, in itself, is good;
>
> The good (Y) possessed by bad others (and thereby contaminated) is something I can no longer ignore, therefore, it is bad;
>
> To eliminate the bad (X and Y) I will vote for Trump who promises the making of greatness by the destruction of all that is non-great but I secretly hope that the bad Y is preserved for me and excluded for others (the restoration of the good).[182]

---

181 Of course, once the bad contaminates the good, the latter is eminently suitable for sacrifice—the baby with the bathwater.
182 "The biggest risk for Medicaid beneficiaries comes from pledges by Trump and other Republicans to repeal the Affordable Care Act, which provided federal funding to states to

It's as clear as mud. The paradox of this situation, where all good and bad are annihilated in order to preserve a fraction of good, seems plausible to the semi-literates of Kentucky who voted to repeal The Affordable Care Act because, as they see it, politicians never do what they promise anyways (Kliff 2016).[183] In other words, regardless of what Trump promises, Obamacare is already too big to fail and the Trump regime cannot make it worse, therefore, if any changes are made they can only make it better. As we can see, this kind of thinking has a 'rationality' but the logic relies not only on wishful thinking and faith in political lies (literally, a hope that the lies continue) but also a belief in magic: a residue of good can survive the destruction of the whole.

In *Forms* Durkheim provides a more thoroughgoing analysis of collective ritual violence under the heading of 'piacular rites' but a statement in 1899 provides us with a concise expression of the problem: we might call it persecutory *mourning joy*.

> When society undergoes suffering, it feels the need to find someone whom it can hold responsible for its sickness, on whom it can avenge its misfortunes; and those against whom public opinion already discriminates are naturally designated for this role. These are the pariahs who serve as expiatory victims. What confirms me in this interpretation is the way in which the result of Dreyfus' trial was greeted in 1894. There was a surge of joy on the boulevards. People celebrated as a triumph what should have been a cause of public mourning. At least they knew whom to blame for the economic troubles and moral distress in which they lived. The trouble came from the Jews. The charge had been officially proved. By this very fact alone, things already seemed to be getting better and people felt consoled (in Lukes 1973: 345).

Collective mourning joy is even perhaps the model for Durkheim's own, *inverted* grief. In a letter from 1916, he says "'All the egoistic side of my life has vanished.... I feel in fact detached from every worldly interest. But that also gives me joy. It is the joy of the ascetic who feels himself to be above everything. It is a severe and melancholic joy. And certainly in so far as one can foretell the future, melancholy will be my mode of my life. However, I am naturally well inclined towards it. It does not frighten me. I would prefer an active sort of joy perhaps, yet I believe that one can have a different sort of life as

---

      expand Medicaid eligibility ..." (Galewitz 2016).

183   This act of self-destruction is still less extreme than the self-destruction the proletariat would have to exact upon itself to be free of capitalist domination (MECW, 4: 37).

well'" (in Pickering 2012: 27). Perhaps submission or *Schwärmerei* expresses itself individualistically as asceticism whereas, collectively, it manifests itself as a violent explosion of sanguinity.

Robertson Smith's classic analysis of piacular rites, ceremonies dedicated to or directed toward a god, puts to rest the notion of any unitary meaning of *piacula*, "once and for all."

> Now the more complicated ritual prestations, to which the elaborate piacular services of later times must be reckoned, were not forms invented, once for all, to express a definite system of ideas, but natural growths, which were slowly developed through many centuries, and in their final form bore the imprint of a variety of influences, to which they had been subjected from age to age under the changing conditions of human life and social order. Every rite therefore lent itself to more than one interpretation, according as this or that aspect of it was seized upon as the key to its meaning. Under such circumstances we must not attempt to fix a definite interpretation on any of the developments of ancient ritual; all that we can hope to do is to trace in the ceremonial the influence of successive phases of thought, the presence of which is attested to us by other movements in the structure of ancient society, or conversely to show how features in ritual, of which the historical origin had been forgotten, were accounted for on more modern principles, and used to give support to new ideas that were struggling for practical recognition (Smith 1927: 399).

However, following Smith in part, several things do stand out as essential aspects of negative piacular death. First, the victims of this kind of individuated violence are a category set apart, sacred, and inviolable (e.g., children at a school). It is also crucial to note that victims of violent outbursts are, in a sense, targets created out of nothing or almost nothing. (cf. EFRL: 63). Also, the operation of killing, getting blood on the hands, is not an end in itself but directed toward an imagined higher being or ideal principle—"this is for *you*!" The acts are directed not at the victims *per se* but projected into the symbolic order for the enjoyment of an imagined other. Obviously, for the enemies of society, the act is not 'for you' but 'against you.' Piacular violence of the kind we are interested is a gift to the god of anarchy. Finally, what appears to be a random act of an individual is actually a ritual or ceremonial act of an individual engaged in a kind of negatively prestigious (infamous) emulation of prior piacular killings undertaken by a whole class of individuals. These are monsters, and as we found in the first volume, monsters are a warning, an index of social disintegration and harbingers of a time of wild purifications (cf. Dumézil 1986: 3). With

Smith, again, I think it is instructive to see these actions as a desired "preliminary to a campaign" (1927: 403) as if the acts of the shooter were just the opening salvo (dress rehearsal) in an upcoming war on society. The piacular should not be confused with rationalized sadism of the sort we find in the beating of children, i.e., violence for the 'good' of the victim (Gay 1993: 183).[184]

Piaculum means expiation and appeasement but the contemporary sociological meaning goes beyond expiation *per se*. As Durkheim says, "Any misfortune, anything that is ominous, and anything that motivates feelings of disquiet or fear requires a piaculum and is therefore called piacular" (EFRL: 392–93). Piacular rites and acts are those enacted in when a group feels itself to be the victim of misfortune, in the grip of some disaster, is distressed, or is terrified.[185] Historically we can find groups that resigned themselves to the fact that misfortune and disaster would be visited upon them by virtue of their god's vengefulness, especially when their god was already known as "a god of natural catastrophes who could and often did send pestilence and frightful misfortunes of all sorts against those who evoked this wrath" (AJ: 301) but these

---

[184] The correlation between beating children and the authoritarian personality syndrome is "remarkably strong" (Hetherington and Weiler 2009: 58).

[185] I hate to invent words, but 'piacularism' seems to get the job done in a way that connects the phenomenon pretty well to its polar opposite, *asceticism*, and denotes something more than simple martyrdom. To throw a kink in the proceedings, think of piacularism as a synthesis of sadomasochism blended with destructiveness toward the external Other while inflicting the self with pain and destruction. What I am calling 'piacularism' (from as far back as 1999) is adapted from Durkheim's chapter on piacular rites in *Elementary Forms*. I think this is an important step in combining classical sociology with the traditional concerns of critical social theory with respect to the authoritarian character structure—that famous 'cyclist' personality type (bowing and kicking) who "crouches to his superiors" and "is insolent to his inferiors" (Hume 2018: 66; see also Worrell 2019: 6). Besides, if Meerloo can get away with "asprinism" (1962) and Wesep can invent "Earthianism" (1920) I don't feel too bad about 'piacularism.' As for neologisms, our earlier discussion in *The Sociogony* regarding logonomic eccentricity raises the paradox of creation. In ancient forms of social organization, the buildup of experiences necessitated the careful and cautious formulation of new words whereas in the modern era it is as if the rush of neologisms creates its own experiences. If one reads the tractates of the Coptic Gnostic Library (I have in mind, for example, the "Origin of the World") one grasps the power of "verbal expression" in generating new forms and forces (Robinson 1988). In Michener's semi-brilliant *Source* we find cave-dwelling hunter-gatherers on the cusp of farming in possession of a vocabulary of 600+ words: "Every hundred years or so new experiences would accumulate, requiring the invention of new words; but this was a slow process, for Ur and his neighbors were extremely cautious and the utterances of a new word might upset the balance of nature and call into being strange forces that were better left at rest, so words tended to be restricted to the same sounds that time had made familiar" (1965: 91).

cases are rare and popular sentiments run in the direction of the piacular (*ecstatic*) rather than patient *resignation*.

In the passage above provided by Durkheim, we find a group suffering and seeking an outlet for revenge, expiation, and an opportunity for the transformation of their mourning into a cause for celebration. One can proceed several ways here: we can interpret the piacular as the mechanical conversion or transformation of one state, mourning, into its opposite, violent joy; another manifestation of this allows for an underlying mourning that is overlaid or superimposed by a surface expression of ebullience; and, in another separate form, mourning and joy are sublated into a composite of action, namely, the piacular in its full glory. Unlike the piacularity that mobilizes a group toward a collective purpose, *asceticism* transports the egoist out of torpidity and toward *ekstasis*.[186]

The ascetic can be of the reverse kind (we might call this negative or obligatory) where a person atones for a sin and seeks expiation or, inversely, asceticism can be of the forward kind (optional) where a person seeks to accumulate a surplus of merits or powers (Westermarck 1917: 360; see also Wilde [1890] 1995: 52). And, of course, once asceticism is pushed toward its limits it may flip polarity into its opposite, the piacular. Ignatius provides a stunning portrait of self-torture being carried so far that the 'being above' pain and suffering becomes its opposite, i.e., the possession by pain and suffering. Recall that ascetic and piacular rites are not diametrically opposites of one another but, rather, there exists a "continuity" between the two (EFRL: 417). The emulation of Christ's suffering (marathon prayer sessions, fasting, poverty, unreflexive obedience, obsessive self-examination, and absolute chastity) putting the ego on the path of necessity (Meissner 1992: 295–310) winds up in another dimension where one descends into the inhuman.

---

186 "There is such a people, ours, [the French] for example, that civic virtue will be suddenly brought to sublimity, if some critical circumstance calls it to it; in the meanwhile, individuals, in the course of ordinary life, isolate themselves in the care of their private interests. Just as, in religion, they come out of natural Epicureanism only by the madness of the cross, and then grow to asceticism..." (Boutmy 1902: 88). As we saw in *Disintegration*, utilitarianism (one route into altruism contaminated with mysticism) is one defense against self-negation and a recasting of what it means to have virtue. "Their attempt to reconcile the individual and the collective interest cannot be understood unless it is recognized that there is in their philosophy, first and foremost, an attempt to discredit self-abnegation and to rehabilitate egoism" (Halevy 1960: 474).

Positive asceticism, positive in the sense of self-deprivation, is the "road to power" (Caillois).[187]

> The men who submit themselves to bodily ordeals, sufficient to strike the imagination of the people with amazement, are regarded throughout the Orient as being placed above the conditions which limit human powers; as a consequence, they pass for being capable of achieving in nature things as extraordinary as the tortures which they impose on their flesh; the more extravagant their acts, therefore, the more powerful the miracles. In India they easily become divine incarnations, when the Brahmins find it advantageous to deify them, because of numerous marvels being accomplished around their tombs (Sorel 1950: 254).

Ascetic enjoyment of pain is an embrace of the unavoidable fact of pain and suffering in life, both individually and collectively. Instead of running from pain the ascetic goes *through* pain:

> There are times I—I am very frightened. Any happiness seems trivial. And yet, I wonder if it isn't all a misunderstanding—this grasping after happiness, this fear of pain .... If instead of fearing it and running from it, one could ... get through it, go beyond it. There is something beyond it. It's the self that suffers, and there's a place where the self—ceases. I don't know how to say it. But I believe that the reality—the truth that I recognize in suffering as I don't in comfort and happiness—that the reality of pain is not pain. If you can get through it. If you can endure it all the way (Le Guin 1974: 60).

Of course, the ascetic drive can become detached from any goal and simply operate in a sterile manner that amounts to nothing more than the degradation (autodevaluation) of the person.

> I believe that if one man were to live out his life fully and completely, were to give form to every feeling, expression to every thought, reality to every dream—I believe that the world would gain such a fresh impulse of

---

[187] "The pure ascetic is a man who raises himself above men and who acquires a special sanctity through fasts, vigils, retreat, and silence.... History shows what heights of religious prestige are attainable by those means. The Buddhist saint is fundamentally an ascetic, and he is equal or superior to the gods" (EFRL: 316).

> joy that we should forget all the maladies of medievalism, and return to the Hellenic ideal—to something finer, richer, than the Hellenic idea.... But the bravest man amongst us is afraid of himself. The mutilation of the savage has its tragic survival in the self-denial that mars our lives. We are punished for our refusals. Every impulse that we strive to strangle broods in the mind, and poisons us. The body sins once, and has done with its sin, for action is a mode of purification.... The only way to get rid of temptation is to yield to it. Resist it, and our soul grows sick with longing for the things it has forbidden to itself, with desire for what its monstrous laws have made monstrous and unlawful (Wilde [1890] 1995: 28).

Mild, individuated forms of the ascetic-piacular alloy are all around us in cases where "self-derogations, carried past the limits of polite self-depreciation, ... [are] a tax upon ... others" (Goffman 1967: 90). Self-mortification is an intentional 'taxation' of others, aggression toward others through the vehicle of the self. We could think of this as a kind of proto-terrorism where the self is instrumentalized and utilized in an effort to shock or degrade others. Never forget, however, that destruction is also directed toward the self, the 'weaponized' body acting as the vessel of powers that have failed to synthesize within the mind of the individual. And the piacular spirit may return from whither it came to seek refuge in the isolated ego.

Perhaps Hesse's "Harry Haller" offers us with a glimpse of the ideal type of the piacular spirit that backs up into a *passive* individuated leading not to the attempted annihilation of the empirical other but isolation, servitude,[188] and self-containment:

> I saw that Haller was a genius of suffering and that ... he had created within himself an ingenious, a boundless and frightful capacity for pain. I saw at the same time that the root of his pessimism was not world-contempt but self-contempt; for however mercilessly he might annihilate institutions and persons in his talk he never spared himself. It was always at himself first and foremost that he aimed the shaft, it was always he himself whom he hated and negated.... Although I know very little of the Steppenwolf's life ... I have good reason to suppose that he was brought up by devoted but severe and very pious parents and teachers in accordance with that doctrine that makes the breaking of the will the

---

188 "If everything is allowed, we can ask nothing of ourselves and expect nothing of others. There is no reason to combat horror, violence or injustice. All we can do is give in to nihilism and servility (the former being merely the high-class version of the latter), and hand the world over to the fanatics and the barbarians" (Comte-Sponville 2007: 47).

> corner-stone of education and up-bringing. But in this case the attempt to destroy the personality and to break the will did not succeed. He was much too strong and hardy, to proud and spirited. Instead of destroying his personality they succeeded only in teaching him to hate himself. It was against himself that, innocent and noble as he was, he directed ... the whole of his thought; and in so far as he let loose upon himself every barbed criticism, every anger and hate he could command, he was, in spite of all, a real Christian and a real martyr. As for others and the world around him he never ceased in his heroic and earnest endeavour to love them, to be just to them, to do them no harm, for the love of his neighbour was as strongly forced upon him as the hatred of himself, and so his whole life was an example that love of one's neighbour is not possible without love of oneself, and that self-hate is really the same thing as sheer egoism, and in the long run breeds the same cruel isolation and despair (Hesse 1963: 10–11).

Asceticism should not be confused with modern, rational self-discipline oriented toward empirical reality, rather, it is an archaic and perverse 'holdover' or regression.

> Asceticism in higher civilization is a survival of the life philosophy of an earlier stage, in which the pain of men was believed to be pleasant to the higher powers. The same sentiment revives now in times of decline or calamity, when the wrath of God is recognized or apprehended.... The same sentiment is at work in sects and individuals when they desire 'holiness' or a 'higher life,' or mystic communion with higher powers, or 'purity' (in the ritual sense), or relief from 'sin,' or escape from the terror of ghosts and demons, or power to arise to some high moral standard by crushing out the natural appetites which according to that standard are base and wicked (Sumner [1906] 1940: 504–05).

Following Sumner, asceticism is productive of a surplus, it is unbalancing, and directed toward invisible moral entities that rule our destinies. When we examine the philosophical forms of egoism, the Stoic form inclines toward asceticism (as does Cynicism) whereas Epicureanism, despite its minimalistic orientation towards needs-satisfactions, tends to avoid self-torture (Sumner [1906] 1940: 510–13; see also Sorel 1950: 254).[189]

---

189   Undergirding this distinction of the twin egoisms is, as we saw in the previous volume, the affinity of Stoicism with historical predeterminism (hence, the connection with resignation) and Epicureanism with chance (see Crease 2019: 110). Ascetic practices are

10   The Savage Child: Infantilism and Primitivism

The "past is not far behind us and ... our childhood begins again with each moment" (Alain [1934] 1974: 14). Capitalism appears to be a secular, rationalized economic system driven by mundane or ordinary passions but we know from Marx that the capitalist system of surplus accumulation is not only an economic system but a world Spirit that entails daily sacrifices made on the altar of wealth. Such a characterization suggests that at the core of modern and technically rational structures and processes resides a savage heart of archaic irrationality. Durkheim provocatively asserts that moderns are not free of 'primitivism' (EFRL: 25; S: 168; cf. Harrison 1962: 534).[190] Perhaps we can express this not as 'we have never been modern' but, rather, that 'we moderns have never not been primitives.' Even the postmodern aesthete is not free of archaism; the emotional structure of the most sophisticated among us can be 'contaminated' by primal emotional impediments that block the positive totalization of reason—not least of which is the susceptibility to novelties.[191] By the time we arrive at the conclusion of the final volume on the commodity we will see that this totalization is impossible but that this impossibility also does not lead automatically to a pessimistic fatalism.

America is not only a land where most adults rise to the level of, at most, old high-schoolers, but also a land populated by individuals and groups living in different historical epochs. A person may own a smartphone and act normally while also possessing a juvenile emotional structure and a mind that operates on the basis of medieval moral codes (see Veblen 1912: 304).[192] Enlightenment

---

open to those no longer resigned to resignation just as the contradictions of needs-reductions leads easily to the opposite current of wants-multiplicity and the door to infinity opens wide.

190 "'Primitiveness is still strong with us. Especially with people who combine originality with a reflective mind, primitiveness is apt to come to the surface, when from one cause or another the veneer of civilization wears off'" (Nathan Soderblom, in Wagenvoort [1947] 1976: 3). Later we will have cause to question the extent to which we are still 'primitives' because, as Durkheim argues, the modern educated person may not live up to the ideals and expectations of reason but, all the same, the educated person is not simply on par with the premodern 'savage' (EFRL: 326). As we argued in the previous volume, the modern academic bias is to interpret premodern people in the light of modern psychological individualism that can result in the translation of what should properly be "us" into "me" (Mendelsohn 2019: 32–33).

191 The aesthete is lured to the void by a "breathless adventure" of unique spectacles, "the sum of these, increased to infinity, is the truth which we seek..." (Croce 1917: 10–11).

192 Regarding Inuit suicide rates, Epstein says "One clue is that virtually all these groups lived until recently in small communities of one or a few extended families and then underwent

is spread unevenly, and we still find ourselves surrounded by "savages" and "half-savages" (Freud [1913] 1950), befuddled by incomprehensible social forces, and led astray into self-destruction by mystagogues. Describing rural Virginia after WWII, Bageant says "It was an entire world and a way of being that was anachronistic even in the 1950s ... vestigial, charged with folk beliefs, marked by an ignorance of the larger world, and lived unselfconsciously under the arc of Jeffersonian ideals, backed up by an archaic confidence in the efficacies of God's word and grapeshot" (2010: 33).

Capitalism produces savagery alongside the commodity (C: 615). Morality and immorality rub shoulders through temporal compressions and extensions. "The hierarchy of the good ... is not fixed and identical at all times. If someone prefers revenge to justice, he is moral by the standard of an earlier culture yet by the standard of the present culture he is immoral. 'Immoral' then indicates that someone has not felt, or not felt strongly enough, the higher, finer, more spiritual motives which the new culture of the time has brought with it. It indicates a backward nature, but only in degree" (Nietzsche 2015: 6).[193] The 'savage' gaze, like that of the child's (Piaget) is unified in an ordinary realism and magical thinking. But modern primitivism is distinct from modern infantilism.

---

a forced, rapid, and harrowing transition to modern life. Mastering technology—telephones, cars, computers, etc.—was easy, but psychological and emotional adaptation has been far more difficult" (2019).

193 When one or two seek to right a wrong the result is revenge but when an entire community seeks revenge the wrong is right in the light of justice (e.g., Christie 1934: 296–315). When fraud is so massive, and so extensive, and so pervasive, it passes from the domain of "merely criminal" to the domain of "business" (Larsson 2008: 438). "To kill one man—that is, to subtract 50 years from the sum of all human lives—that was a crime; but to subtract from the sum of all human lives 50,000,000 years—that was not a crime!" (Zamyatin [1924] 1993: 14). "If you believed in God, you might leave vengeance to him, but you couldn't trust the One, the universal spirit. Vengeance was Ida's, just as much as reward was Ida's ... the only reward there was. And vengeance and reward—they were both fun" (Greene [1938] 2004: 36). The "fun" of the bubbly and oblivious do-gooder in *Brighton Rock* creates a tornado of unintended consequences and, for the person who would be saved, in the end, they walk into "the worst horror of all" (Ibid: 269). Recall with Durkheim that we do not punish a thing because it is a crime, rather, it is a crime because it is punished. And we never know when the classification of 'criminal' will be applied to us willy-nilly. "Whether our destiny holds a death cell in store for us is not determined by what we have done or not done. It is determined by the turn of a great wheel and the thrust of powerful external circumstances" (Solzhenitsyn 1974: 441).

In a chapter that deals mainly with anomie, Meerloo connects impatience and mania, the aversion to boredom and the fetishism of mechanical technique (similar to Fromm's analyses of necrophilia and the Futurist love of speed, machines, war, and so on), to infantilism: "no sooner does he seat himself behind the wheel than his motor becomes the very fiend he has been complaining about. From now on he feels himself a magic, omnipotent baby in his ... carriage. The racing frenzy has caught him.... He becomes obsessed; he is cruel and arrogant" (1962: 81).[194]

11 Heterarchy and Autothematicism

Our concept of heterarchy has little to do with organizational or network sociology. Rather, the concept of sociological heterarchy signifies a negative unity of lax regulation, on the one hand, with strong solidarity. This paradox would perhaps benefit from the name of *Rabelaisianism*, if, that is, it was limited to the aspect of Rabelaisian ethics that emphasizes not vulgar and ribald pleasures but, on the contrary, a unique form of utopian collectivism in which all were dedicated to the law of "Do as Thou Wilt." In the first book of *Gargantua and Pantagruel*, Rabelais gives us the inscription on the gate of the abbey Thélème where a long list of *personae non gratae* ("holy loons," "lickgolds," "sour boors," and so on) precede the catalog of the welcomed including the "true sophisticate," "noble gentlemen" from "goodly parts," and the "gay" and the "courteous," etc. Prior to his literary career, Rabelais had been a monk and this fictional Thélème (meaning will or desire) is not a run of the mill pleasure pit for libertines and debauchery. Rather, Thélème is ambiguous in Christian thought—it could mean the will of individuals or the will of god, and in this utopia, we find a reconciliation of the individual with the big symbolic absolute, the will of god.

---

194 This passage is contained within one of the all-time great chapter titles: "Man's Raving Frenzy as a Disguised Form of Suicide." Even emotions such as laughter become mechanical among maniacs. "It always seems strange when maniacal movie villains laugh for no reason, but I'm finding that, when you're in the grips of mania, you really do laugh maniacally" (Walter 2009: 216).

> Comrades, companions, friends,
> Assemble from the ends
> Of earth in this fair place
> Where all is mirth and grace.
> Felicity here blends
> Comrades, companions, friends....
>
> The Holy Word of God
> Shall never be downtrod
> Here in this holy place,
> If all deem reason grace,
> And use for staff and rod
> The Holy Word of God (Rabelais [1532–1564] 1944: 149).

Regulation of the abbey is "not by law, statute or rule, but according to their free will and pleasure."

> Gargantua's plan called for perfect liberty. The only rule of the house was: Do As Thou Wilt because men that are free, of gentle birth, well-bred and at home in civilized company possesses a natural instinct that inclines them to virtue and saves them from vice. This instinct they name their honor. Sometimes they may be depressed or enslaved by subjection or constraint; for we all long for forbidden fruit and covet what is denied us. But they usually apply the fine forces that tend to virtue in such a way as to shake off the yoke of servitude (Rabelais [1532–1564] 1944: 154).

As we saw in *The Sociogony*, the sticking point is the reliance on an instinct that is distorted through normal social repression and preserved relatively intact by the gentle training of the "civilized" and "well-bred." For both conservatives and utopian communists, the idea is the same: get the big thing (the big other) off the backs of individuals and they will thrive in a world devoid of authority and norms—and desire (Fink 1997: 236). In Thélème the rule is an anti-rule; do what you want. But the foundation for wanting has been shaken. How does this anti-rule avoid falling into chaos and libertinism? "The Thélèmites, thanks to their liberty, knew the virtues of *emulation*. All wished to do what they saw pleased one of their number. Let some lad or maid say ... 'Let us frolic in the fields' and all of them frolicked" (Ibid., emphasis added). But this is not "emulation" but plain imitation. As we have seen the logic is just what we should expect: the regulative void results in a disintegration of the symbolic order and the reduction of the social absolute, here a putative god or society in its alienated and external form, to a hollowed out void, reduced to the point of a lifeless shell of universality (an imagined and abstract god but not an absolute, symbolic god that hovers [EFRL: 428; cf. Hegel 1988: 215] 'above' the plane of interpersonal relations). Thélèmite enjoyment is enacted through mimesis at the level of the Lacanian imaginary, meaning, of course, that if Thélème were a real place it would not be the "refuge" or "favored ground" it is advertised to be, but rather, a place of ecstatic conflict, competition, and interpersonal warfare (see Fink 1997: 79–111). In modernity, we find a similar logic at work in what Swart and Krier refer to as "dark spectacles" such as motorsport rallies that revolve around trophies of jouissance, slumming, and the demonization of enemies (2016: 264–70). And any enemy will do. Today's friend is tomorrow's devil. We have the ability to construct our enemies as we go (EFRL: 404–05).

In contrast to autothematicism, heterarchic consciousness displays a contradictory combination or alternation between a haphazard "to and fro" through the otherness of its myriad representations contrasted with a placid unity and absolute certainty of its own truth (PS: 143). The discipline necessary to live a collaborative life means that a person has to be reconciled to obeying and being subject to arbitrary rules. So long as those rules do not appear to be the whimsy of an individual but to the contingencies of life (Hocking 1918: 119–20) and the traditions, habits,[195] and routines of a collectivity, the individual can put their shoulder into the tasks of daily living. A person learns to choose their battles and let what amounts to a large quantity of arbitrariness pass over without much aggravation. However, once the contingent appears to be the product not of time, tradition, etc., but the whim of one person, every arbitrary demand will become insufferable, and a clash of competing wills is likely to ensue.

What we are calling 'autothematicism' (another unity of egoism and fatalism—the 'back door' into heterarchy) might have been better represented by *monarchy, autarky, autocracy*, etc., but these concepts already have their hands full. We are attempting to determine the negative unity of egoism (auto) and the Doom (*Themis*) of fate.[196] What needs to be said about autothematicism

---

195 We generally do a poor job as sociologists conceptualizing habit or habitus (Weber's "habitude") when we take habitus out of relational context as if habitude is an atomic crystal that can be poked and prodded in isolation. The Latin *habitudo* can be translated as habitude but also *"relation, reference, respect, disposition,* [and] *condition"* (Doyle 1995: 55).

196 'Themis' (Doom, destiny, fate) and 'theme' ('thematic,' etc.) all derive from the Greek *théma*, from *tithēmi* ("I put, I place"), itself derived from the Proto-Indo European word meaning *to put, to place,* or *to do*.

is likely expressed in *Brighton Rock* to an adequate degree. In our own time, a popular television program featuring four science researchers at a California university provides an adequate fictional representation of this heterarchic–atomocratic polarity whereby the chummy solidarity of a psychotic, neurotic, and a pair of perverts, creates the unnerving context for the satisfaction of desires without apparent restraint, while simultaneously being driven by a combination of impersonal and invisible determinants. One of the most conspicuous features of this matrix of autothematic friendship is the built-in rivalry and constant pitching of activities around the contest and the winning of games. But we should be careful to draw a line of distinction between 'contest' and friendly rivalries at this set of coordinates and full-blown (and often violent) *competition* which is represented by the unity of egoism and heteronomy (Williams 1993: 100).

Marx's "general intellect" or the alien "social brain" (G: 694, 706) fits our autothematic model fairly well. The goal of proletarian solidarity lies in revolution which overthrows the rule of the bourgeoisie, ending the rule of one class over another. Classlessness is synonymous with the restoration of autonomy in the real. With the production of necessities taken over by the General Intellect individuals are free to do whatever they wish without the burden of becoming anything in particular—I can paint but not be a painter. If you need a painter talk to the General Intellect. We understand what it means to paint but not what it means to *be* a painter.[197] Passion for any one thing (spending too much time on painting, for example) would be, if it had not been squashed by the return of instincts, pathological because it might flourish into a calling for painting—which is, admittedly, irrational.[198] The result of all this is a lack of

---

197   The more the individual is freed from understanding the more they are reduced to a profanation and "automatism" (Durkheim 1974: 3).

198   The restoration of instincts dissolves the temporary but necessary dictatorship of the proletariat during the interregnum separating bourgeois rule and communist utopia. The problem with utopia is not that it is literally nowhere, or that utopias are just abstract models and inspired visions or, when utopian movements try to put their principles into practice it almost always ends with burned out buildings (homelessness and refugees), but that utopias are so far removed from existing reality that it promotes resignation. We are so far removed from X that we might as well just forget about making life incrementally better. Freytag says "We are led to believe that in future times there will be nothing but love and happiness; and men will go about with palm branches in their hands to chase away the last of those birds of night, hatred and malice. In such a chase we would probably find the last nest of these monsters hanging between the walls of two neighboring houses. For they have nestled between neighbor and neighbor ever since the rain trickled from the roof of one house into the court of the other; ever since the rays of the sun were kept away from one house by the wall of the other; ever since children thrust their hands through the hedge to steal berries; ever since the master of the house has

social structure and enforced egoism. The world of egoism is one of individual 'molecules' flowing over other one another, jostling for position (the 'positive' form) when not ignoring one another altogether (the negative). The apparently structureless spread of egos leaves each individual vulnerable and therefore open to the lure of the absolute master (Man or Machine) that can protect it from predation or dissolution. We see this in premodern European peasants who, when assembled, do not form an organic social unity but, as Marx says, represent "'the simple addition of homologous magnitudes, much as potatoes in a sack form a sack of potatoes'" (in Krier and Feldmann 2016: 179). But the ideal-typical expression can be located in the early appeal of the Nazis in harnessing undiluted egoism for the benefit of the supreme leader: "It has ... become possible for every German—time-server and idealist alike—to see in the Nazi Party *the* leader specially summoned to realize his own particular theory. The Nazi Party resembles a vast army of individualists on the march, each of whom believes that the army is moving towards his own objective" (Heiden 1934: xiv).

The heterarchy-autothematicism identity is found in mimesis and a 'psychotic-like' structuring of human assemblage that results not in a normative absolute but hollowed-out understanding, magical totems, and the despotism of the autarch. Italian Fascism is also an expression of heterarchy and the connection to the early Nazi 'molecularky.' In *The Doctrine of Fascism*, Mussolini says that

> [Our movement rejects the view of man] as an individual, standing by himself, self-centered, subject to natural law, which instinctively urges him toward a life of selfish momentary pleasure; it sees not only the individual but the nation and the country; individual and generations bound together by a moral law, with common traditions and a mission which, suppressing the instinct for life closed in a brief circle of pleasure, builds up a higher life, founded on duty, a life free from the limitations of time and space, in which the individual, by self-sacrifice, the renunciation of self-interest ... can achieve that purely spiritual existence in which his value as a man consists (in Haidt 2012: 279–80).

---

been inclined to consider himself better than his fellow-men" ([1887] 1890, 1: 21). The era of the myth of Progress is certainly behind us but the recognition that "hatred and malice" are fixed features of society does not mean we have to abandon hope for the sublimation of hatred into useful institutions.

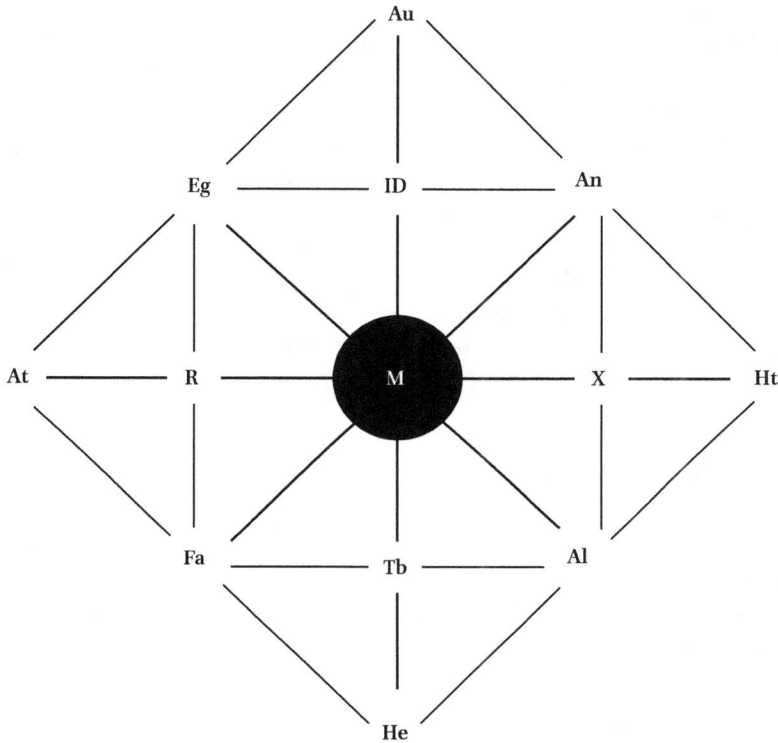

FIGURE 3 The autothematic-Rabelaisian expansion
SOURCE: CREATED BY AUTHOR

As Haidt points out, this passage is disconcerting because we know it is fascist propaganda, but we also see the appeal to organic solidarity as something alluring for simpletons. The rejection of egoism, natural determinism, fatalism, and the appeal of infinity combined with obligatory duties are clearly stated, except, of course, that all the good pours forth from the fount of the strong man's leadership.[199] It's all good except for the fact that it is upside down.

The internal drive of the previous matrix from Volume Two (*Disintegration*) has, as we can see from all the forgoing, expanded itself into something a little more complicated:

---

199   Italian Fascism did not follow the Nazis in their fetish for Jews. However, where we find 'heroes' the victim is not far behind; the hero is the counterpart to some kind of scapegoat (Lasswell 1933: 380). Fury and frustration cause the role of "victim and executioner to flip back and forth on a metronome of hatred" (Gary 2017: 111).

By injecting heterarchy and autothematicism into our original model (and also modifying, slightly, the coordinates of autonomy and heteronomy)[200] we arrive at a situation whereby the social octahedron has doubled and redoubled itself (in the figure above). In its efforts to overcome contradictions, Spirit has proliferated new judgments and syllogisms that, for example, propel the station of resignation toward ecstasy in such a way that the long transit through asceticism is literally a-voided. The ascetic 'road to power' is no longer the only way to achieve *ekstasis*; it can be 'backed into' from the station of autothematicism, the speculative double of 'Rabelaisianism' or, better, sociological heterarchy. But that's the rub: in aiming for ecstasy, we arrived, instead, at heterarchy. We have 'fractal-like' growth but this is not the good news that we might hope for.

12   Compound Alienation

"For several decades," says Aron, "in Germany, in France, in Western Europe, now even in the United States, the word alienation has been used and defined in so many ways that it would perhaps be better to discard it" (1968: 125). Aron's discussion of alienation (and anomie) is excellent but I doubt we need to abandon 'alienation' theory any time soon. However, it is possible to cut through the concept in a new way and tease out some additional aspects and insights. In the *Eighteenth Brumaire*, Marx reminds us that revolutionary thinkers must "criticize themselves constantly, interrupt themselves continually in their own course, come back to the apparently accomplished in order to begin it afresh, deride with unmerciful thoroughness the inadequacies, weaknesses and paltriness of their first attempts" ([1869] 1963). Bearing this in mind, we will begin from the point of Marx's theory of alienation as it is elaborated in the 1844

---

200   This modification recognizes the outsized power and necessity of bourgeois autonomy in breaking through the 'infinite' teleological process from which it emerged. As autonomy ascends to new 'heights' its shadowy double, heteronomy, also outgrows its restraints. For this reason, we have introduced infantilism and primitivism into the expanded map bubbling up in the wake of the hypertrophy of autonomy and heteronomy. With Hocart, we recognize that in the absence of general formulas we have, instead, imperfect diagrams that "can bring out the general idea more vividly than pages of discourse, provided we look at the form, and do not take the details too seriously" (Hocart [1936] 1970: 291). I think we can take not only the form seriously but also the content, provided, of course, that we recognize that they evolve and devolve on a moment-by-moment basis in the spiral of negations and in the overall procession of forces. As we will see in the next volume, each notion sets up its own vortex and loop in an ever-expanding matrix of judgments.

manuscripts. Among other things alienation pertains to the following primary dimensions:
1. estrangement from the product of labor;
2. estrangement from the process of labor;
3. estrangement from species being, and;
4. estrangement from one another.

'Estrangement' is a condensation that captures the sense of externality and externalization (*Entäußerung*) and strangeness (*Entfremdung*). Drawing the problem of alienation out along these four lines reveals a well-worn path rooted in preexisting philosophical debates between critical and absolute idealists as well as debates between idealists and materialists during the 19th century. Of paramount importance was, and remains, the interdigitated and paradoxical nature of *autonomy* and *heteronomy*. It is upon this axis that Marx's text rotates. Forms one and two appear to hang together logically and bear most directly on the problem of *heteronomy*.

The first form (estrangement from *product*) exposes the reduction of the working class to the status of slaves and we see an entire social class in bondage (PM: 109). Form two (estrangement from *process*) emphasizes the 'cretinism' of workers: subjecting workers to barbaric mechanization and the reduction of human life to the level of creatures (caught between humanity and the beasts) and the sacrifice of self. Forms three and four revolve, in a jumbled manner compared to the preceding two forms, around the problem of *autonomy*, and, importantly, the nature of universality and individuality. Form three (estrangement from *species being*) explores the destruction of productive freedom and universality. Capital breaks down the life of the species "into a means of individual life" (PM: 112) and reduces "individual life into its abstract form" (PM: 112–13). Here we find reversals, duplications, and inversions of life such that the only element of universality left for workers is in production (objectification of alien will) and the consumption of commodities via the universal medium of cash, while the self is cast off into what Sartre might call "molecular exile at the boundary of life and death"—of singular isolation, powerlessness, and incomprehensible duplications of subjective spirit in its alien, objective forms (1976: 733). Of special note, here, is the falling of the individual into the 'wrong' where abstractions, money, i.e., crystals of value, mediate the individual's relationship to the means of existence (use-values). Marx draws this out in his *Critique* where C-M-C, e.g., the sale of labor power, in exchange for wages, and the purchasing of use-values for survival, conform to this 'wrong' syllogistic form (CPE: 94; see also PR: 115–32). Form four, however, represents another weird formation. This final form (alienation *between individuals*) represents the sundering of both universality and individuality with relations particularized and instrumentalized. Relations are incapable of immediate gratifications or spontaneous associations.

Forms three and four are blended as Marx demonstrates when he says "… the proposition that man's species nature is estranged from him means that one man is estranged from the other, as each of them is from man's essential nature" (PM: 114). The logical differentiation between forms three and four is that between *universality* (species being) and *individuality*: 'man and man' (the other as the social mirror for the individual). Here we see the influence of classical mirror philosophy made popular by Goethe and Fichte and the mystification involved in the breakdown of freedom between 'man and man' into the coercive relationship between worker and owner (PM: 115) or between workers thrown into competition against one another on the market for labor power. Marx aims to demystify the situation by demonstrating that the alien other (the capitalist) is just another 'man' rather than a manifestation or condensation of an abstract social power. Our treatment of Marx's theory of alienation serves to merely to connect it more intimately to larger trends in the history of thought but also to pull it close to Durkheim's theory of self-destruction which contains just these moments.

By porting the standard Marxist theories of alienation into the Durkheimian theoretical matrix we arrive at the unsettling realization that the Marxist political imaginary is really just a translation and duplication of alienated life. The fusion of egoism and fatalism, bondage, is not a positive synthesis but a

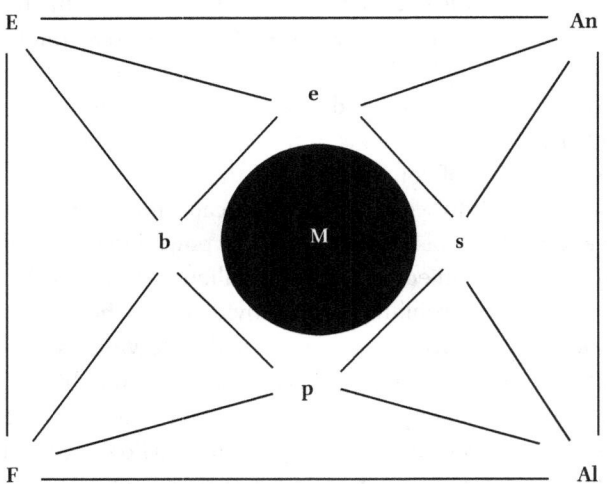

FIGURE 4   Compound alienation
SOURCE: CREATED BY AUTHOR

greater and different negativity—worse on top of bad.²⁰¹ Marx rails against alienation but conjures an image of self-regulating rational egos that leads to dissolution in the Durkheimian infinite or the Hegelian 'way of the world.' Moreover, theoretical communism does not solve the problem of alienation from either the product or the process of labor. Here comrades just squander unfocused energies through dilettantism and since production goes in the background, while we fish and criticize, we are still separated from goods because they are not *our* products, they are not objectifications of *our* consciousness but the work of the general intellect. If praxis centers on the practical education of the human being through conscious creation of the material world then this is the death of praxis and creativity.

The correct sociological position finds the solution nowhere in this negative tetrarchy of alien forces but gestures in the direction of a 'positive hell' characterized by an organic division of labor (something categorically rejected by Marx who saw *all* divisions of labor as the mutilation of the human being. Lacking a concrete universal core, the 'positive hell' of individuality is negated and devolves into a field of morbid enjoyment, and where there was once a society there now exists a yawning abyss of anxious and mutilated psyches setting up active and passive defenses. Deprived of an objective ground for existence, rational reflection, and regulation, and twisted by countervailing currents of socially pathological sentiments, people are doomed to neurotic or psychotic forms of hyper–subjectivism. Durkheim can elaborate on *how* a society devolves into a nightmare of morbid enjoyments and specify our *coordinates* within it, but it does not go far enough into the "night of the world" (the subjective unconsciousness of social atoms) to explain why subjects are drawn *toward* the pulsating void at the center of our negative heaven. In Poe's *Maelstrom*, for example, we see an endangered subject reasoning their way to survival at the rim of the whirlpool but in postmodern capitalism we find, on the contrary, crazy subjects willing the abyss itself.

We can map these into our octahedron by making recourse to Halbwachs.²⁰² In his reconstruction of Durkheim's argument in *Suicide*, Halbwachs transposes the conceptual plane from the problem of regulation and control to the more nebulous mysteries of alienation. In so doing, Halbwachs did Durkheim's *Suicide* a great disservice (see Besnard 2000) but, on the other hand, he extended the conceptual mapping in a useful direction.

---

201 The four negative syntheses or compound alienation forms represented in this diagram are bondage (b); estrangement (e); splitting (s); and possession (p).
202 Basically, by way of Durkheim, we are extending and clarifying Marx's theory of alienation as found in the *Paris Manuscripts* and, e.g., Fromm's alienation syndrome (1968: 39).

Pushed to the extreme we find the ego totally separated or *estranged* from others. Berger connects separation with anomie[203] and there are compelling reasons to make that connection:

> To be separated from society exposes the individual to a multiplicity of dangers with which he is unable to cope by himself, in the extreme case to the danger of imminent extinction. Separation from society also inflicts unbearable psychological tensions upon the individual, tensions that are grounded in the root anthropological fact of sociality. The ultimate danger of such separation, however, is the danger of meaninglessness. This danger is the nightmare *par excellence*, in which the individual is submerged in a world of disorder, senselessness and madness. Reality and identity are malignantly transformed into meaningless figures of horror. To be in society is to be 'sane' precisely in the sense of being shielded from the ultimate 'insanity' of such anomic terror. Anomy is unbearable to the point where the individual may seek death in preference to it (1967: 22).

Separation is no doubt anomic in its effects but what Berger describes also resonates with egoism.[204] Anomie is almost an automatic consequence of egoistic withdrawal so we therefore position 'estrangement' as the form associated with 'infinity disease.' It is unsurprising, then, why intellectual dreamers, estranged as they are from the vital pulse of social reality, become disillusioned or violently dogmatic when they encounter the inertia of tradition and superstition.

In the case of pre-revolutionary Russia, intellectuals "sadly lacked a factual knowledge of their country and people. Little wonder that they saw the solution to specific ills in terms of an all-embracing theoretical or ideological framework" (Raeff 1966: 158). Symptomatically, the reformers of the 19th

---

203 Though not alone, Howard (1972: 153) notices the identity between Marx's theory of alienation and Durkheim's theory of anomie as "more or less equivalent." One of my goals is to demonstrate that alienation can assume the anomic form (i.e., unadulterated anomie) but that there are three other primary forms as well (not distinctly articulated in Marx's writings) that correspond to currents of self-destruction mapped out in *Suicide*.

204 As we saw in *The Sociogony*, Berger makes some questionable assumptions based on his substitution of psychodynamic theory for the likes of Mead. Consequently, alienation in Berger's view is, or can be, a defense against anomie rather than a form of alienation itself (1967: 94). Ambivalence be gone with the magic of false consciousness and bad faith! "[I]t was [so] crucial for Alexy Alexandrovich to think this, ... however contrived, from which he, despised by everyone, could despise others, that he clung to his illusory salvation as if it was true salvation" (Tolstoy 2014: 514).

century were practically unmatched in their distance from the people they sought to transform and mobilize and, consequently, their understanding of "the people" was decidedly undeveloped and superficial. In the wake of the failed "To the People" movement of the 1870s and 1880s, for example, a Russian Populist reportedly said "'Socialism ... bounced off the peasants like peas from a wall. They listened to our people as they do to the priest—respectfully but without the slightest effect on their thinking or their actions'" (Figes 1996: 136; see also Haimson 1955: 39).

When Marx and Engels determined, as early as 1882, that "'Russia forms the vanguard of revolutionary action in Europe'" (in Fernbach 1974: 67) it represented a thorough-going rehabilitation of Russia's reputation; earlier they considered Russia to be nothing more than "a monolithic barbarian presence in Europe" (Ibid.). Russian radicalism had its origins during the 1850s but it was not until the Populists movement of the 1870s that things started to heat up. The Populist movement was organized around the assumption that peasants were inherently and instinctively democratic and egalitarian or, at the minimum, "amenable to socialist collectivism." It would be unfair to suggest that the Populists were completely unprepared for their work. Pyotr Lavrov, the originator of the "to the people" slogan, realized that revolutionary consciousness could not be mechanically imposed upon people. If peasants were going to arrive at Socialism, the task was their own (Leatherbarrow and Offord 1987: 247–52). The blind spot for Lavrov, as for most of the Populists, was in the conviction that socialism could be "transmitted" from one class to another, that reason (minus any inherent and visible prestige attached to it) was contagious, and, more importantly, they failed to recognize the extent to which their radically democratic and socialistic peasants were fantasy constructions of their own making. An additional and serious problem the populists encountered was the built-in antisemitism of the peasants. Without fear of exaggeration, nearly all non-Jewish segments of Russian society were infected by antisemitism. And the populists themselves, especially the extreme Narodnaya Volya, were plagued by the fantasy of Jews as a race of parasites (Greenberg [1942] 1945; cf. Draper 1977: 602).

The notion of *transmitting* socialism was central to Populist writers like Chaadaev and Bervi who assumed that any idea, regardless of complexity, could easily be understood by peasants and the "illiterate peasant intelligentsia." As Bervi said, "I left Siberia full of respect for the intellectual capabilities of the peasantry; I am convinced that there lies within that estate the hope of Russia, the guarantee of her future glory and greatness" (in Leatherbarrow and Offord 1987: 253). But the peasantry was, as Gorky discovered, devoid of democracy, egalitarianism, and socialistic yearnings. Gorky's initial optimism regarding the peasantry (the basis of his involvement in the movement) was transformed into revulsion and it would be an understatement to suggest that he suffered greatly as a consequence of his unrealistic expectations (Figes 1996). Mikhail Romas, an important mentor to Gorky (both were together in Krasnovidovo in the late 1880s trying to aid villagers) was fully cognizant of the gulf that separated the empirical from the mythical peasantry. What sustained his actions was the belief in the power of reason to impose itself on the mind. As Gorky wrote in his autobiography, "I noted—for the hundredth time!—that people showed far greater interest in the extraordinary, the fantastic, in what was patently—and often clumsily—invented, than in serious explanations of life's real truth. But [Romas] smiled, when I spoke to him of this, and said: 'That will pass. The main thing is, for people to learn to think. And then they'll think their own way to the truth'" (Gorky 1962: 616).[205]

But the peasants did not think their way to truth and many Populists came to the same conclusion as Dostoevsky: "We, the lovers of 'the people,' regard them as part of a theory, and it seems that none of us really likes them as they actually are but only as each of us has imagined them" (in Figes 1996: 87). Just as the populist spirit was losing its flame, Marx's *Capital* made its way into Russia providing revolutionaries with a novel, scientific basis for their political aspirations. The manner in which many Russians adopted Marx was similar to the way they had adopted previous ideas from the West, namely, in an uncritically dogmatic form. Early Russian Marxists were still Populists at heart insofar as they turned to Marx's theories in order to save the Russian peasant from proletarianization. But the people were no longer approached as unproblematic. Time and again, peasants and workers not long off the farm, refused to cooperate. Bakunin wrote,

> One would have to be an absolute idiot or an incurable doctrinaire to imagine that one might give the people anything, bestow on them any sort of material benefit or new intellectual or moral content, any new truth, and lend their life at will some new direction or, as the late Chaadaev said, thirty-six years ago with precisely the Russian people in mind, write on them what one pleased, as on a blank sheet of paper (in Leatherbarrow and Offord 1987: 278).

---

[205] Gorky knew that reason and personal intelligence were separate concepts but where he went wrong was not seeing that reason is grounded in concrete social organization.

Other radicals grew tired of dealing with peasants. The pages of *Narodnaya Volya*, the paper of the Narodovoltsi or 'terrorist' Bolshevik precursors, exclaimed: "Shall we take the initiative of anti-government action and of a political revolution—or shall we, as of old, ignore political activity, waste our strength by pressing against the people just as fishes press against ice?" (in Haimson 1955: 39). For the Narodovoltsi, Pyotr Tkachev, 'the people' were a dead end. The decisive agent of change was a revolutionary party seizing control of the state and leaping over historical stages (Leatherbarrow and Offord 1987: 251).

Even though 'the people' were a problem, capitalism was not thought of as *inevitable*—at least not initially. The faith that democracy was guaranteed by History only started to emerge in the early 1880s. And this initial openness with regard to revolutionary change was in line with Marx's own thought toward the certainty of capitalism: Marx "viewed the future of capitalism in Russia as far from predestined. If, in fact, capitalism triumphed, the Russian peasantry would certainly be doomed to proletarianization; but it was conceivable, he argued, that Russia could in fact bypass capitalism by generalizing the collective property relations inherent in the traditional Russian *obshchina*" (Smith 2001: 53). Bypassing capitalism gave way to destiny when historical materialism became the reigning ideology. Among well-known leaders such as Axelrod, Plekhanov, Blagoyev, Skvortsov, and Fedoseyev, there were others such as Sieber (Ziber), a fatalistic "legal Marxist," who saw "revolutionary activities" as pointless in the face of abstract historical forces (Haimson 1955: 43).

Sieber "quickly became" says Smith, "one of the most influential partisans of the conviction that capitalism was destiny, not only for Russia but for the world; and he argued influentially that socialism, too, requires capitalism as an unavoidable prelude" (2001: 51). But if Marx's own thinking on the inevitability of capitalism in Russia diverged from the Russian interpretation, his thoughts on revolution were not cut and dry.[206] Ultimately, and from the standpoint of

---

206 It almost goes without saying that a theory developed on the basis of the historical development of industrial forms of social organization (masses and classes) faces grave difficulties when 'ported' over to a quasi-feudal society. Referring to medieval Christian Europe, Mauss says that the "Middle Ages ... were a universe ... to a much greater degree than is contemporary Europe, and yet the groups which formed it were infinitely more diverse and more numerous. They were, however, less organic, and this is why they were infinitely more permeable to each other..." (2005: 73). This capacity of the less fully developed organizational form for permeability and alternation of social identity was clearly behind Mauss's characterization of the Russian civil war of 1919–20: "There were many painful episodes and comic switches: White cities yielding to Red vanguards; Red cities

Russian revolutionary practice (both in 1905 and 1917) what Marx had written was secondary to pragmatic necessity. The Russian interpretation of Marx was decisive for the left wing of international socialism and the emergence of communist parties outside of Russia—especially in the United States, for, as Cannon says, "The Bolshevik revolution in Russia changed everything almost overnight. Here was demonstrated in action the conquest of power by the proletariat.... Naturally, Bolshevism became the authoritative doctrine among revolutionary circles in all the workers political movements of the world, including our own here" ([1944] 1995: 16–17).

During the First World War, the American Socialist party chose, in stark contrast to the SPD, *not* to endorse the war and, in so doing, suffered a tremendous loss of support among would-be sympathizers in labor. As Lipset and Marks claim, "It is difficult to overestimate the consequences for the party of its opposition to the war. The party had narrowed its geographic base and lost its native-born support; it was less oriented to events in the United States and more driven by events in Russia, and in the process had reinforced the propaganda that the party was unpatriotic and un-American. The Socialist party was viewed as in, but not of, America" (2000: 192). However, American socialists did not, as did the SPD, become synonymous with disgrace and perversion after its capitulation in 1914. This greatly preserved in the minds of the Bolsheviks the notion that the US labor movement was a vanguard. The notion of a 'vanguard' is interesting.

'Vanguard' comes from *avant garde* (literally 'before guard') or, after all the etymological steps, an *advanced protector*. A protector is not a person, but a person *shielded* or in possession of a shield. A shielded vanguard is augmented

---

and divisions slaughtering their commissars at the rumor of a *sotnia* of Denikin's cossacks [sic] and turning White immediately; whole countrysides passing easily, smoothly and comfortably from Kolchak or Denikin to the Soviets and from the latter to Kolchak, sometimes three or four times; for the extremes of susceptibility of the Slav allows such voltefaces. But on the whole, the military *chouannerie* of Kolchak, Denikin, Yudenich and Wrangel—not to speak of that of the Siberian brigands, of Semyonov, or of the 'Greens,' the Ukrainian peasants, the mountaineers of Anti-Caucasia and the cossacks of the steppe—committed more crime, more frequently, more uselessly, more barbarously, more savagely and more deliberately than did the immense jacquerie that the Russian Revolution ultimately is. The expeditions of these defeated generals, especially those of their lieutenants, even more those of the detachments, sometimes amounting to no more than two officers, were raids by 'Great Companies' against expeditions, requisitionists, foragers even; for such were the troops of the Soviets in 1919 and the beginning of 1920. No moderation: these isolated and opposed bands moving through these immense spaces and rarely making contact only did so to yield to one another and then to incorporate their prisoners—or massacre them" ([1925] 1992: 181).

in some way that ordinary people are not. Augmentation or 'force invasion' can be experienced as a necessary and welcomed supplement (empowerment, enlightenment, and solidification). But this 'gift' of power can also obliterate the ego. "At all times and in all civilizations there are persons who feel possessed or persecuted by outside forces they feel are beyond them" (Bettelheim 1960: 58). This 'force invasion' is a central feature of the moral economy as we have been working it out. As Durkheim says,

> A profane being cannot violate a prohibition without having the religious fore that he has improperly approached extend to him and take him over. But since there is antagonism between himself and that force he finds himself subject to a hostile power, the hostility of which is inevitably manifested in violent reactions that tend to destroy him. This is why sickness and death are presumed to be the natural consequences of all such transgressions, and such are the consequences that are presumed to occur by themselves with a sort of physical necessity. The culprit feels invaded by a force that takes him over and against which he is powerless (EFRL: 324–25).

The intersection with taboo and heteronomy is pronounced but we also see a trace connection to the 'engine' of ecstasy—and Weber detects a relation to contemplation.[207] The same kind of secondary trace connects estrangement with fate-tinged resignation.

The mode of alienation that corresponds to ecstasy is that of *splitting*, doubling, or multiplication. We can amplify this concept of 'splitting' with Simmel: it is as members of society that we are "capable of splitting" ourselves "into a subject and an object..." 'Man' encounters "himself as if he were a third person—a faculty, as far as we know, without analogy among the other creatures of this world—and this ability is the foundation of our entire rational nature" (1959: 33). The contradiction is delicious: the very basis of our rationality also leaves us vulnerable to alienation and estrangement, of misplacing our own energies and products, and becoming servants to our own creations. It is

---

207 Detached contemplation and possession (ES, 1: 545) appears to be an important mode of alienation characteristic of altruism. 'Possession' here has the dual meaning of *being* possessed and being *in possession* of something (cf. ES, 1: 545). "Contemplation does not necessarily become a passive abandonment to dreams or a simple self-hypnosis, though it may approach these states in practice" (ES, 1: 546). See *Disintegration* where we colored the coordinates of egoism with tones of dream infinites and also kicked around the notion of social life being a kind of 'hypnotic' state. Every coordinate within the social octahedron, every point within social space, has its own 'affective coloring' (cf. EFRL: 11).

interesting to note that the concept of 'schizophrenia' has as its root the Greek word for splitting: *schizo* (Fromm 1973: 351). The ideal-type of the modern, split person of late capitalist society is the schizophrenic (Wexler 1996: 120; see also Deleuze and Guattari 1983). Simmel attributes these schizoid-like breaks not with egoistic isolation but with over-participation in a multiplicity of social circles with their competing imperatives that pull the person figuratively apart (1955: 141).[208] Along similar lines, Erika Mann bores in on the acute split between private and official life as productive of schizophrenia (1938: 41–42). 'Madness' is no longer the abominable specter it was in earlier generations but an extreme zone one approaches, lured to get as close as possible, without falling in. One expects to lose one's mind but only temporarily, as if secured by some anchor that enables a safe abandonment.

The person suffering an enlargement of the will attempts to power through difficulties with blunt force. "I'd always assumed that self-reliance was a matter of radical self-*assertion*—that it amounted to leaving one's current self behind in favor of some future, more compelling form, that it depended on one's ability to resist and deviate from one's surroundings" (Kaag 2016: 73). A prime example of the doubled experience is that of "double-consciousness" or the kind of "twoness" (Du Bois [1903] 1969: 45; Freeman 1943: 381) where "no true self-consciousness" is capable of developing because the self is overwhelmed by a multiplication of objective views of the self. The result is a kind of inspired madness—the anger, loss of reality, and enthusiastic drive of the psychotic to make visible to the senses (it is literally an aesthetic madness) the world of invisible but real social forces whirling around the embattled and unstable ego.

Totalitarian societies are despotic and over-regulated, but the degree of perceived overregulation is relative to the level of personality development and individuation as well as one's integration or degree of alienation within the political system. As we saw in earlier volumes, individuation was only rudimentary in the premodern world—the 'cult of the self' was only embryonic and would not really begin to flourish until after Christianity took off (cf. Granet 1951: 227).[209] Sparta, for example,

---

208 However, "it is also true that multiple group-affiliations can strengthen the individual and reinforce the integration of his personality" (Simmel 1955: 141–42). Participation in a dense network of associations is not, in itself, the culprit but being torn in incompatible directions by competing demands.

209 "[T]here is a sphere of psychological life which, no matter how developed the collective type may be, varies from one person to another and belongs by right to each individual…. This primal basis of all individuality is inalienable and does not depend upon the social condition" (DOL: 145). Mauss says "there has never been a human being who had not the awareness (*sens*) not only of his body but also of his spiritual and corporeal individuality at the same time" (1963: 459). But can we really claim that the emergence of the individual

outdid any modern totalitarian regime in the demands and regulations it imposed upon its citizens. Yet this invasion of privacy seems to have been accepted willingly enough, perhaps because, to a degree unparalleled in modern times, the citizens did in fact constitute the state. Each individual citizen could rightly feel that the polis was not an alien, outside entity, but an integral extension and collective magnification of his personal life and powers. Under these circumstances, experience could be widely shared without losing its intimate intensity, thereby unveiling new dimensions of human character and unleashing fresh springs of collective energy to produce the extraordinary flowering of classical Greek culture (McNeill 1963: 205).[210]

The relativity of *bondage* as a modality of alienation (correlates well with resignation, the unity of egoism and fatalism) is paramount. If I am already doomed, a subject of Themis, I might as well go my own way and enjoy what I can (e.g., antinomianism). One person's bondage, physically or mentally, may well amount to more in the end than another person's loss of traction in the domain of anomie (see Chesterton 1986: 43–44).

13   Bombers, Shooters, and Drones

When the Fordist regime of capital accumulation gave way to the era of flexibility and hyper-finance (Krier 2008), a new imaginary and symbolic regime was also needed to shore up the drive for limitless acquisition, reflex austerity, and endless wars. It is not a coincidence that the age of Terror corresponds with the decisive shift in the mode of capturing surplus value. Terrifying objects are important in solidifying acquiescence or obedience to a social and political order

---

mind (that first, tiny spark of individuality) is independent of social conditions, that the gap is a constituent of our species? Or must the individual come 'out from under' (at least minimally) the collective consciousness in order to first realize that 'spark'? Consider Žižek's comment: "*Cogito* is not a substantial entity, but a pure structural function, an empty place ... it can only emerge in the interstices of substantial communal systems" (2005: 11; cf. Gierke [1868] 1990: 2).

210   "[*Gemeinschaft*] constitutes an absolute unity which is incompatible with the distinction of parts. To merit the name community even if it is organized, a group is not a collection of individuals differing from one another; it is a mass, undifferentiated and compact, which is only capable of movement together, and is directed by the mass itself, or by one of its parts entrusted with directing it. It is an aggregate of minds so strongly cohesive that no one is able to stir independently of the others.... The whole alone exists; it alone has an action sphere peculiar to itself. The parts do not have one" (Aldous, Durkheim, and Tönnies 1972: 1193; cf. PH: 105; Durkheim 1981: 1060; Marcuse 1941: 73–74).

that is, now, fundamentally anti-democratic and even totalitarian in some important respects (Wolin 2008).[211] Among a wide array of objects, few are more terrifying than the image of the suicide bomber ('over there') and the rampage shooter ('over here').

What I have in mind is a foray into the symbolic structure of the imperial imagination with the aim of drawing into close proximity three representations: the suicide bomber (over there, external), the domestic rampage shooter (here, in the domestic core), and the unmanned aerial vehicle (UAV) or 'drone' ('up there' both internally and externally).[212] What we will discover is that the drone, the third term, represents the crystallization or mechanization of the piacular spirit, the sublime objectification of imperial anomie and its double, archaic revenge. The suicide bomber and rampage shooter represent speculative doubles, mirror opposites if you like, one external to the imperial core and the other, internal—or, to put it another way, the shooter represents the logic of imperial recklessness and a disregard for limits, what Bacevich calls our "heedless worship of freedom" (2009: 6), reflected back into domestic life in the form of the maniac loose in the elementary school. The 'spirit' these two objects share is a unique 'ecstatic' fusion of anomie (deregulation) and altruism (otherness): *piacularism*. Metaphorically, we can distinguish between the suicide bomber and the rampage shooter (both organic forms) by signifying one as 'positive' and the other 'negative.' The 'transcendental' object-unity of these two forms of the piacular takes the form of the inorganic, unmanned aerial vehicle (UAV) or 'drone.' The drone vehicle puts at our disposal a singular, *sui generis* representation of what amounts to the anomic drive toward limitless, external expansion and austere, domestic anarcho-capitalism. All three, and others not examined here, are forms of what I call the imperial homunculi.

The representation of the homunculus is adapted from Goethe's *Faust* ([1808] 1961) and altered for our purposes: it is a tiny, synthetic construct that empire spontaneously produces through its own momentum, which it becomes dependent upon, and that, ultimately, vanishes in an act of self-destruction (Worrell 2013). We are used to thinking of empire in either big abstractions like global hegemony, nation states, governments, regimes, regions, coalitions, movements, insurgencies, foreign policies, proxies, troop surges,

---

211   The concentration of power within the executive branch is especially distressing, resulting in Bacevich referring to the office of the president as a hybrid "emperor-president" (2009: 69; see also Worrell 2011 and 2013). Terror also blunts critical thinking. "An atmosphere of terror destroys logical thinking" (Chandler 1995: 1007).

212   Taking a cue from Simmel's *"geometry of the social world"* (Aron 1964: 5) we will map the spatial relations and traversals characterizing the system of objects and use of deadly force.

etc., or little concrete terms like manipulative, sociopathic chief executives, etc. What is missing is a focus on minuscule abstract objects and their dialectical entanglements with one another, across boundaries demarcating the external and internal, foreign and domestic. We will start with the human bomb.

In my little book on terror (Worrell 2013) I located the suicide bomber within the context of anomie, a concept that roughly converges with the notion of *fitna*. Ali and Post (2008) suggest that it is *fitna* or anarchy that is definitive when it comes to driving the suicide bomber. "According to Islamic doctrine, the word 'fitna' has been translated as chaos, 'time of temptation,' war, as well as anarchy" (2008: 615). However, the current of anomie is alloyed, in the case of the suicide bomber, with a multidimensional form of altruism. Let us look at anomic and altruistic suicides and then how they can fuse into a composite type.

Anomic suicide (especially the negative or *regressive* variety) is passionate like the altruistic type[213] but hope is replaced by "anger and all the emotions customarily associated with disappointment" including "exasperated weariness" and "violent recriminations against life in general, sometimes threats and accusations against a particular person to whom the responsibility for the suicide's unhappiness is imputed. With this group are obviously connected suicides which are preceded by a murder" (S: 284–85).[214] *Altruistic* suicide is rooted in emotional turbulence and manifests itself in a burst of energy and faith under the guidance of reason and will (S: 283).[215] The enthusiasm of the altruist is "either happy or somber, depending on the conception of death as a means of union with a beloved deity or as an expiatory sacrifice, to appease some terrible, probably hostile power" (S: 283). All three subtypes of altruistic suicide are, in the case of suicide bombers, blended.[216]

This composite is the kind of destruction we find among "besieged" communities (S: 287–88). However, Islam does not permit suicide and, considering virtually all suicide bombers today are adherents of the Islamic faith, this wave

---

213 The positive sublation of anomie and altruism, here, is the passionate quasi-fusion of opposites: "Passion seeks to tear down the borders of the ego and to absorb 'I' and 'thou' in one another" (SGS: 128).
214 "And there are the killers who are in love with death, to whom murder is a remote kind of suicide" (Chandler 1995: 683).
215 Consult Malraux on the ekstasis-possession-mysticism-absolutism of the terrorist (1961: 126, 133, 156–57).
216 In terms of the *optional* form, the suicide bomber has emerged as a kind of celebrity (MacAskill 2005) that, through its moral valorization, resets the balance of obligatory sacrifice on the part of the remainder of the community (McCauley and Moskalenko 2011: 172–89).

of self-destruction represents quite a riddle. As Durkheim says, "Nothing, in fact, is more contrary to the general spirit of Mahometan civilization than suicide.... As an act of insubordination and revolt suicide could therefore only be regarded as a grave offense to fundamental duty" (S: 329). Suicide bombers circumvent the prohibition against suicide by transforming self-destruction into "jihad" (holy war) and "martyrdom" which enables the suicide victim to traverse the taboo of self-destruction (see Strenski 2006: 270–80).

The martyr, we are told, is in love with the sacred. "They were trying not to avoid life but to fulfill it in what they considered to be an act of both personal and social redemption. In this way they were connecting a contemporary political strategy to a sacred history of martyrdom and sacrifice" (Juergensmeyer 2008: 417). McCauley and Moskalenko reach similar conclusions: while this life may be misery the suicide is not against this life but "for god" and martyrdom transforms suffering into redemption (2011: 173, 181). The "very presence" of the martyr "is a reminder to others that there is more they can do to serve the people" (Ibid: 177) and god. The martyr also "raises the bar" of ascetic self-renunciation that impels others to measure their conduct against the higher standards of the fighter willing to give all (Ibid: 179, 185); and we should note that where one finds asceticism one will find its speculative double, piacularism.

We arrive at an understanding of the suicide bomber (the martyr) as one mounted by the spirits of anomie (regressive) and a ternary altruistic complex. When a martyr looks in a mirror they see a Jewish or Israeli reflection (his or her moral bearer and particular other, not of love but of anti-love). However, when we examine the speculative relation in terms of the internal and external, the martyr would see not the Jew but his or her weird counterpart in the United States, the rampage gunman.[217]

The rampage killer represents the terrifying internalization of imperialist asymmetrical warfare reflected back into the system's core: random and singular but statistically predictable and recurring on a regular basis and, as such, part of a virtual social movement; direct attacks on people (no innocent bystanders) represent an indirect attack on the entire social system at its symbolic nerve center, the workplace, sites of recreation, but especially at schools—populated with a special class of exceptionally sacred people, taboo to injure: children (cf. Smith 1927: 356). Hi-tech from a strategic standpoint but low-tech from a tactical point of view, the rampage shooter represents a fusion

---

217 Other reflections of this kind are the transformation of urban centers into battlefields, e.g., Chicago reduced to "Chiraq"—a signifier expressing an astonishing murder rate.

of the human and the inhuman, the trigger finger and the weapon, targeting many, killing fewer.[218]

On March 5, 2001, Charles Andrew Williams entered Santana High School in Santee, California and shot fifteen of his fellow students, killing two and wounding thirteen more. In an interview with Miles O'Brien (2013) Williams says that he was incapable of "comprehending the finality" of his actions, that he was suicidal, and that his "grand plan was suicide by cop." In other words, the destruction of others was a means toward another end, the desire for self-destruction that he was incapable of inflicting upon himself. The explanation for this event follows the standard (even ritualized) formulations for other mass shootings in America: mental illness, alienation, bullying, drug and alcohol abuse, decadent youth culture, and so on. Liberals tend to seek institutional and organizational factors to comprehend mass killings while conservatives blame the dissolution of traditional values and an increasingly secular world. The point of liberal-conservative convergence, however, the blind spot or null point in the American episteme, is the spirit of anarchy.

Deregulation rose as a *consensus* political and intellectual force in the mid-60s and, by the late 70s, it had become a virtual 'religion' as airlines, trucking, and rail were allowed to determine their own prices free of government interference. The results of the shift from a labor or production mentality to consumerism backgrounding neoliberal deregulation were exactly what had been hoped for, but the unintended consequences included the immiseration of consumers as they paid for subhuman treatment and terrible customer service with low prices. Other consequences also included the intentional drive to widen the gulf of inequality, root out inefficiencies, lower tax rates, privatize everything possible, create a larger class of the hyper-wealthy, disrupt or destroy unions, lower wages, and flatten out differentials in the prices for labor power while anointing executives with extravagant compensation packages. The most pernicious and perfected form neoliberalism assumes is the fusion of deregulation, merger consolidations, and reduced competition (e.g., the cable industry in the United States). Every industry that was submerged in the acid of deregulation was subjected to steep declines in worker earnings as top executives and investors accumulated mountains of cash and perquisites; for more see Appelbaum's excellent chapter on deregulation (2019: 161–84). America is now a paradise of anarcho-capitalism ruled by a spirit of limitless

---

218 The drone represents the complete inversion of the rampage shooter in virtually every respect: strategically primitive but tactically sophisticated, targeting few but killing perhaps 90 or 100 bystanders for every single target.

greed.[219] It is not a mere coincidence that the late-70s also represent the "turning point" whereby political elites (the donor class, the judiciary, and representatives) more or less abandoned Liberal bi-partisanship and divided themselves into the extremes of liberals *versus* conservatives (McCarthy 2019: 17).[220] If Americans are kicked around like dogs at least they have ready access to cheap credit for their troubles, and, just as importantly, have millions of bogus Americans to kick around as compensation. The horizon of the infinite runs in multiple directions: from the limitless skies, impossible dreams, and so on, but also in the dream of zero. Zero-land is a kind of 'reign of terror' where the compressed ego is over-exposed to impersonal forces and struggles to raise the personal to the level of a force.

That the shooter Williams was incapable of "comprehending the finality" of his actions is telling: the US is, preeminently, the land of the Infinite, from foreign policy and military adventures, to financial and speculative magic, to religious fanaticism and cultural hype. How can anything be 'final' in the heart of the neoliberal empire? Here, Kierkegaard was onto something: the spirit of limitlessness was, in his words, "fantastical." What we have been calling our "infinity disease" (following Durkheim, the infinity of dreams and desires)[221] is connected to a mania of the will, or fantastical willing, where fantasy and the imagination (Kierkegaard 1954: 163) eclipse reality, the loss of the reality

---

219 "If it is proposed to create rights in favour of all the members of a community, the limits are strict" (Mill 1992: 49). Even a hedonist can see this.

220 McCarthy's work is on political 'polarization' but, from our view, this really goes nowhere since all social life is inherently polar. What we find in the contemporary political context is a dialectical diremption and a resulting stereotyping of acting, thinking, and feeling. When the religious spirit descends upon something the result is stereotyping. "The alteration of any practice which is somehow executed under the protection of supernatural forces may affect the interests of spirits and gods. To the natural uncertainties and resistances facing every innovator, religion thus adds powerful impediments of its own. The sacred is the uniquely unalterable" (ES, 1: 406). Why, then, is Trump able to run amok in Washington and not bring the wrath of the 'gods' down upon himself, i.e., suffer the loss of support among his base? We know that when innovation invades the religious sphere it invites disaster and punishment (e.g., ES, 1: 405). But, again, when we are attuned to the polarities of the pure and the diabolical, things make more sense: evil can manifest as malevolent spirits, limbos, ghosts, and so on that represent threats to life (Parkin 2012: 108). When we see the Trumpist moment as one of inflicting harm upon the establishment we find that the self-professed morally pure have unleashed an impure monster upon their enemies. From this view, the reason Trump does not bring down the wrath of 'the gods' is because, his base considers him to be the personification of wrath. The punisher cannot, evidently, himself be punished.

221 In the case of the infinity of desire we have, for example, the peculiar hunger of abundance where consumption stokes insatiable desire and the continuous production of an "aching void" (Ovid 1955: 47–48).

principle, and a slide into a psychosis.[222] What, then, is the connection between the American spirit of limitlessness, anomie pushed to the extreme into anarchy, and the coordinates of the fanatic at the limits of altruistic pathologies? What we are calling this fusion, sociological heterarchy, is, in essence, an aesthetic madness—the negative synthesis of the maniacal and possessed drive to make visible that which is invisible. Madness is a coagulation of much of what interests us here at the collision of anomie and altruism; anger, insanity, and enthusiasm.

The American bias is toward examination of the abstracted psyche (mass murderers are simply 'crazy') but, as Durkheim notes, the psyche is itself an infinity and the psychological infinite cannot be grasped by critique regardless of how well reason is developed. Moreover, if we want to comprehend the sociology of gun violence we will forever be stymied by looking through the peephole of the abstract mind. Besides, that which is essential with respect to the psyche is precisely its social determinants. The psyche is infused with the social. If society is 'crazy' it will mass-manufacture 'crazy' people (Fromm). If violence is considered prestigious (positively or negatively) and sanctified, people will act violently in order to participate in the positive or negative prestige of violence and, in so doing, approach sanctification in their own way. Not since the Nazis has a nation gone so far as to glorify and sacralized war, violence, and mass destruction. Violence becomes poetic and takes on a life of its own, requiring hardly any other reason for itself (cf. Maurier [1894] 1998: 183). We are, after all, a "gunfighter nation" (Slotkin 1992) and war is now a full time, multidimensional occupation (Worrell 2011).[223] It should come as no surprise that the imperial spirit of limitlessness, mass death, and indiscriminate killings (witness drone attacks that kill off more than 100 bystanders in order to 'nail' one bad guy) should be reflected back into the domestic core in the form of mass killings of innocent civilians. Much of this logic is reflected in the life of Adam Lanza.

---

222   "If you can dream—and not make dreams your master; / If you can think—and not make thoughts your aim" (Kipling 1943).
223   "The Spirit of universal assembly and association is the simple and negative essence of those systems which tend to isolate themselves. In order not to let them become rooted and set in this isolation, thereby breaking up the whole and letting the [communal] spirit evaporate, government has from time to time to shake them to their core by war. By this means the government upsets their established order, and violates their right to independence, while the individuals who, absorbed in their own way of life, break loose from the whole and strive after the inviolable independence and security of the person, are made to feel in the task laid on them their lord and master, death" (PS: 272–73).

Labeling the Sandy Hook Elementary shooter, Adam Lanza, as mentally disturbed or disabled, etc., is not the end of analysis but only the beginning. When we examine the broad contours of Lanza's life (e.g., Frontline 2013) what stands out most dramatically is the problem of unceasing change from one school to another and alternating integration with isolation; just when the child would become somewhat integrated his mother would move him to another school—enforced detachment from others. The one constant in life was his mother, but she represented not stability (a point of contact with reality) but the guarantee of ceaseless change and instability—his life was one of things continuously melting into thin air. Where Andy Williams could not fathom the "finality" of his actions, Lanza, it seems, conceived all too well of the finality of his *infinite* action: this is, thankfully, the end of the infinite. When anomie manifests itself in its singular, exasperated, enraged, and armed form we have something like an Adam Lanza. If Lanza was 'crazy' it was because the social organization of his life was 'crazy.'

It is interesting to think of the word that is often used to describe shooters: demented.[224] Adam Lanza and people like him obey and disobey commands that most of us never perceive. Is it because they are 'crazy' that they 'hear voices'? Virtually all of us are subjected to the same commands as mass shooters but the social organization of our lives, and therefore our emotional organization (ES, 1: 545), is such that those commands are either unregistered, misperceived, disavowed, or sublated into 'positive' or socially approved injunctions. One aspect of the rampage shooter that may be under-analyzed is the extent to which certainty of successes is a driving force. *Planning* a mass murder at a school or workplace, etc., is a *suicidal* gesture before it is a murderous one. In *practice*, the denouement (a self-inflicted gunshot or death by cops) is reversed: the suicide (direct or indirect) follows the murders. Women attempt more suicides than men do, but men actually 'succeed' in killing themselves at a far higher rate. For men, there is nothing attractive about surviving a suicide attempt—surviving is failure (Angier 1999) so half-hearted attempts are less attractive and nothing brings one closer to guaranteed success than the local SWAT team. Aiming at success, Lanza's mother supposedly wanted only the best education for her son but created an unendurable and unending nightmare (her plans for his transfer to another college were, apparently, the final straw).[225] Other kids in the same situation would have used, say, an

---

224   Demented as in driven to behave irrationally due to anger, distress, or excitement. From the Latin *dementare*, from *demens 'out of one's mind.'*
225   Among other splits, the US is the land divided between the gun and the diploma; here was a young man suspended between the two.

electric guitar to 'slay' the world and put their misery behind them (or exchange it for another kind of misery) but Lanza used a gun to accomplish a literal slaughter: the end of mother, the end of schools, the end of everything and the embrace of nothing. Adam Lanza was an unwilling subject in the kingdom of anomie, who, apparently, reached his limit and struck back wildly, irrationally, and murderously.

If we examine extreme cases of destructiveness, of the self or other, we will find that they lie at the extremities of a fluid continuum connecting them with normal, everyday conduct. For example, the extreme form of altruism (the acute form represented by the religious fanatic who engages in voluntary human sacrifice for the wellbeing of his or her imagined god) is related to the spirit of selfless generosity necessary for any society to function. When a Williams or a Lanza come unhinged and go on a rampage our ritualized collective response serves to localize, personalize, and translate the event into a mental health problem—in a very real sense, our scripted and ritualized responses are elements in the cult of anomic violence that guarantees the recurrence of mass killings. There is nothing wrong with 'us,' rather, 'they' are unhinged. Rituals make people, places, and things sacred (positively or negatively) and potential objects of a future cult. Wills (2012) is correct to frame mass killings as a form of sacrifice: people, it seems, must die periodically if the spirit of anomie is to reign unchallenged. Lanza (we shall presume) wanted to put an end to his suffering at the hands of the people and impersonal forces that he imagined made his life miserable. However, in so doing, and ironically, did his master's bidding. Lanza and killers like him, seen from the sociological point of view, are but personifications and instruments of abstract social forces. In short, anomie, in the form of Adam Lanza, killed 27 people on December 14, 2012 at Sandy Hook Elementary School. Adam Lanza was not merely a killer but anomie's willing executioner, a man possessed. Lanza and other mass murderers are only extreme manifestations of what we find all around us in American life: fearful necrophiles enacting phallic aggression with their firearms.

The 'gun nut' strikes fear in the hearts of civilized people and for a very good reason. Instruments of death evoke taboo and revulsion in places that ought to be free of such objects. The 'gun nut' is an avatar of impending doom and death. The weapon represents an intrusion of mechanical impurity within civil society not unlike the presence of the deceased organism within living society. "... Hertz finds generally that the deceased is treated (along with his close family members) as impure, even potentially malevolent, during the period in which the putrefaction of the corpse takes place, but this is due to the nature of the collective representation of death as a liminal space through which an individual passes, at grave danger to himself and to the society from which he departs, from one stable community to another, and not to some purely material disdain for the state of decay.... [A]n individual death resounds socially as an aggression against the sacred body social, an aggression which is seen as caused by some impure or evil force and which must therefore be 'treated' almost as an illness would be treated" (Riley 1999: 310). Let us extrapolate from this logic: the wielder of the gun, like the unburied dead, occupies a "liminal" space between life and death and, as such, is an object of horror and dread for those who value cooperation, peace, and development of life. If they cannot be loved for goodness they will be hated for their badness.

The gun industry and their lobbying wing insists that the best defense against a 'bad guy' with a gun is a 'good guy' with a gun. The solution to the gun problem is simply more guns, and, thereby, the multiplication of good guys. This is obviously a bit of self-serving nonsense but not merely for the reasons usually asserted. What is never examined is the predicate goodness. We can find an endless number of 'bad guys' with guns, they make the headlines every day, but where are the 'good guys' with guns? Plato tells us that a wealthy person is never a good person: riches and goodness are mutually exclusive (1945, 4: 436–38). Likewise, there is no such thing as a good person who owns a gun. Guns and good are mutually exclusive. All gun-owners are, in Hegel's sense, evil. Gun-ownership correlates with many currents: self-protection (fear and paranoia), independence (isolation and estrangement), machismo (repressed homo-erotic tendencies and the hatred of weakness and submission), honor (narcissism), etc., and the gun is the universal equivalent and symbolic condensation of these sentiments. Infinity disease has a 'totemic' emblem in the gun but rather than serving as a representation that unites individuals into an organic and concrete community, the gun merely connects millions of alienated dots into an abstract totality of fetishists (those that have a thing for a single, specific gun) and totemists (those that have a thing for the category Gun itself and, consequently, can never have enough).[226] The terrorist and the rampage shooter both hate America but come at retribution from different angles: terrorists rationalize attacks on the basis of the defense of god and community whereas the shooter flames out in a futile and final attempt at negative recognition. Terrorism is a dynamic we find in a world where the feeling is that god

---

226   On the difference between totems and fetishes see Worrell and Krier (2018b) as well as Bracken (2007). Durkheim soundly rejects Frazer's theory that the fetish means only an individual object ([1912] 1915: 186) but it might be a good way to describe the individual totem when it is a precise individuality that does not shade off into a category or species, or, even better, when the object of devotion is a *partial* object.

is being murdered whereas the American rampage shooter comes from a world where god has committed suicide.

The person with the gun represents "an aggression against the sacred body social" for those who value society. The hatred of society, here, egoism blended with anarchy, is signified by the intrusion of the gun within the social space. But as important as anomie is for comprehending rampage shooters and gun fetishists, there are other factors that are also important. Indeed, pinning everything on 'anomie' would not offer much in the way of an original insight. Had Lanza merely shot his mother and then himself (a common case of murder-suicide) we could probably rest at the concept of anomie to tell us what we want to know regarding the big picture but the sheer scope of the crime suggests something more, something more on the order of terror.[227] Lanza's gun rampage that resulted in the senseless, mass slaughter of children suggests an alloy of elements. The possibilities are bewilderingly complex, but much can be gleaned from the concept of, once again, the *piacular*.

By casting suicide bombings under the concept of 'piacularism' we can unify the salient features of the phenomenon and preserve its perspectival quality at the same time. In short, piacularism allows us to account for the bomber representing a case of suicide-murder from the standpoint of victims and targets while also analytically respecting the standpoint of the perpetrator that the bombing is not a suicide (which is taboo) but an act of sacrifice in a holy war.[228] Terry Godlove (2005: 45) points to the piacular rites that characterized post-9/11 America (how *we* mourned as victims) and we know that some currents of reactionary pseudo-conservatism in the US are characterized by piacular rites and ideologies (Worrell 1999) but we should also be examining the 'other side' of the terror-victim relation whereby self-annihilation and mass violence are imagined as the solution to acute anomic crises.

The piacular act or ritual is capable of transforming a group of ordinary people into a frenzied monstrosity and the ordinary individual into an instrument of divine fury. Punishment may be directed internally or externally. The

---

227   Denoting, of course, the well-known quantity-quality dialectic whereby at some point quantitative addition crosses a threshold into an entirely new qualitative state. This dialectic is best expressed in the formulation attributed, variously, to Napoleon, Lenin, and Stalin: "Quantity has a quality of its own." France suffers more than 400 murders per year and, generally speaking, these deaths are not reported in the US, yet, when 12 murders are committed on a single day in a single event (the Charlie Hebdo attack of 7 January 2015) it is a massacre, a terrorist attack, and makes headlines the world over.
228   "Sacrifice of the self is the source of all humiliation, as also on the contrary it is the foundation of all true exaltation" (Novalis 1997: 27).

internal piaculum is simply the mourning and sorrow expressed by the group and the rites of expiation for sins they feel they have committed (here, the piaculum merges with sadness). "In expiation, inner conviction draws the malefactor back to submission to social authority" (Parkin 2012: 103). It would be difficult to find a group that did not, at least ever so slightly, blame themselves or engage in self-incrimination for a misfortune that has befallen them—recall that in the wake of the 9/11 attacks, Jerry Fallwell and Pat Robertson heaped blame for the attacks not only on the terrorists but also on the sinfulness of Americans, as if the terrorists were instruments of divine retribution (Goodstein 2001). If nothing else, piacularism directed inward toward the group functions to firm up resolve and the sense of hardship and sacrifice that will be necessary to meet present challenges. *External* piacularism is the construction of the diabolical other that must be punished or subjected to violence as a price to be paid for inflicting the group to misfortune and misery and they turn to violence as a technique for "remedying this evil" that has befallen them (EFRL: 407). The 'evil' object will have to die. By definition, there must exist an evil X that mixes a kernel of empirical reality with myth in order to transfer blame for collective misfortune.

Once calamity hits a society, it will "find a victim at all costs on whom the collective sorrow and anger can be discharged. This victim will naturally be sought outside, for an outsider is a subject *minoris resistentiae* [less able to resist] since he is not protected by the fellow-feeling that attaches to a relative or a neighbor, nothing about him blocks and neutralizes the bad and destructive feelings ..." (EFRL: 404). Importantly, self-negation of this piacular form can be of a *partial* or limited variety where we see people merely inconveniencing themselves or wounding themselves. More extreme, the piacular can be carried to a higher pitch where self-negation is *total* or unlimited rather than partial. Here we find the person sacrificing the entirety of their life in one moment. Why do people feel duty-bound to kill themselves for some higher cause or, negatively, to rid their society of some impurity? To allow society to suffer without reaction would be to display indifference (egoism) and, ultimately, signal the worthlessness or irrelevance of that society. To go back to Freud's insight: to lose those erotic bonds with others causes panic ([1921] 1959). "If society permitted them to remain indifferent to the blow that strikes and diminishes it, it would be proclaiming that it does not hold its rightful place in their hearts. Indeed, it would deny itself. For a family to tolerate that one of its members should die without being mourned would give witness thereby that it lacks moral unity and cohesiveness. It abdicates; it renounces its existence. For his part, when the individual feels firmly attached to the society to which he belongs, he feels morally bound to share in its grief and its joy. To abandon it would be to break the ties that bind him to the collectivity, to give up wanting collectivity, and to contradict himself" (EFRL: 403).

At first glance, the piacular, which emphasizes *collective* ritual mourning in the face of tragedy, would throw us off the track of the lone rampage killer. Indeed, piacularism is most obviously a potential reaction on the part of *victims* of a shooting spree. However, when we dig a little deeper we can construct a matrix of piacular forms at each scale of social life: on the one hand, the piacular proper which represents collective rites of mourning and reaction that put the members of a society into contact with positive sacred energies. If, however, we turn to the negative and individuated form of the piacular we find the criminal acts of the rampage killer bent on destroying as much of society as he can (and in the case of rampage shooters in the US it is almost always a 'he'). Incidentally, between these two polar endpoints we find, e.g., the terrorist *qua* suicide bomber who acts 'alone' but for the betterment of their imaginary Big Other and the empirically existing, suffering community of oppressed of which they are a member. Jihad individuated, in other words. The piacularity of the rampage killer that strikes periodically in American life must be qualified and reconstructed to emphasize its specialized, individuated, and negative form, as opposed to the positive and collective form of the piacular rituals that will follow in the wake of the shooting spree. The seeming paradox that the piacular applies to both the good and blameless group of victims and to the evil perpetrator can be resolved when we recall that the lone maniac is not as 'alone' as he appears at first sight.

Again: how can the lone gunman with no moral cause to kill and no social collaboration constitute a manifestation of the piacular, which is eminently social or collective? A suicide bomber, for example, represents a single 'instrument' of death but dies for some cause and for their community or god, its collective representation. Can the same be said for the lone gunman who kills in the name of apparently nothing? How does nihilism (nothing-ism) pertain to the social energies of life? If we turn back to suicide we find that what appears to be a lone act, uncoordinated from any central authority, is in reality a social fact, not only statistically, but that the cohort of voluntary self-killers constitute, unconsciously, an *actual class of subjects each obeying commands to dispose of themselves*. "Life's vanquished form a long cohort of captives that society drags behind its chariot" (Halbwachs [1930] 1978: 297). We already know in advance more or less *how many* people are going to kill themselves every year and we can predict when the rate of self and other destruction will rise and fall: with every steep market correction, rich white men in Manhattan join the ranks of the prematurely departed; terrorists launch an attack on US soil and the rate of self-destruction will plunge temporarily as altruism sweeps up another portion of the disposable population to inject into the battle against Evil. Why do they go? Revenge or, at least, the avoidance of boredom.

One way to grasp the synthesis of the fanatic-martyr (the human bomb over there) and the demented rampage killer (human gun over here) is the drone object or unmanned aerial vehicle (UAV) equipped with Hellfire missiles and cameras (over there) and *just* cameras and maybe deliveries (over here).[229] As a signifier, the drone represents the sum of all anarcho-imperialist contradictions and, most importantly, we find the hidden spirit of the drone: the *lust for primitive revenge against the other*—that which separates Freudian melancholy and mourning[230] from the fully sociologically piacular.[231]

The use of drones over the imperial periphery is easy to grasp but the use of the domestic UAV introduces an interesting aspect: the logic of transposition and perpetual re-victimization. The thought of the drone overhead is a constant reminder that the negative other somewhere 'out there' is lodged within the symbolic space of the imperial core. Just like torture of the enemy combatant transforms the torturer into the eternal victim, the domestic UAV keeps American's divided between Us and Them and provides a symbol of the external war within the fabric of home life. And, really, the drone 'here' is seldom seen, like the 'terrorist' over there—what is seen and reported are the anti-drone protests which, ironically, serve to remind 'citizens' to never forget that we are (not at war) but victims and, as such, forced to use weapons like drones in order to destroy Evil while preserving sacred (pure, American) lives. The more abstract drones are and the more remote, the closer and more intimate they are in our unconscious life (the embodiment of the 'ex-timate' or, what amounts to the same thing, the *collective representation*).[232] The drone, like the terrorist, is like the background radiation of daily life. The revenge quality of the drone attack is seen in the unintended death rate among those subjected to life with drones.

---

229 The drone was once a weird machine occupying "the no-man's-land between aircraft and cruise missile" with regard to international arms proliferation and control (Siegel 2005: 35).

230 "Yet bend not all the harm upon yourself. Make those that do offend you suffer too" (Shakespeare 1999: 77). "The Tale of Cupid and Psyche" in *The Golden Ass* is one of the most startling and insightful myths with respect to piacularism (Apuleius 1994: 75–119).

231 Recall that narcissism is a transit into the domain of altruism, namely, pushed to the extreme, narcissism is always, already a kind of fanaticism. "To examine revenge as a ritual, begin with hurt, with being narcissistically damaged... Then comes the desire to 'get even.'" Revenge and violence on others "is a way of turning a passive experience into an active one. It is a primitive attempt to gain control over pain" (Fellman 1998: 82–87).

232 "This disposition, in which the subject and his or her shadowy, ex-timate [external yet intimate] double stare into a common third point ... epitomizes the relationship of the subject to an Otherness..." (Žižek 1993: 107).

When drones are used to kill they do so while annihilating indiscriminately (kill them all and let god sort them out). To 'nail' one bad guy it often means killing dozens or even more than 100 bystanders. We hear stories every week about wedding parties and funerals being bombed by US drones where whole families are destroyed. This indiscriminate quality of death is akin to the "categorical" targets of terror strikes: there are no such things as innocent victims *per se*; being killed by a drone is proof itself that the people killed were worthy of death. The drone does not destroy you because you *are* a terrorist; rather, you are retroactively classified as a 'terrorist' in the act of being destroyed by the drone. We destroy and mutilate as if we were shooting nothing more than tin cans or old tires. In the capricious and indiscriminate use of drones as killing machines, mechanized or inorganic piacularity,[233] we find an archaic and barbaric spirit of punishment hidden behind the modern, rational, technological appearance.[234] The drone turns anyone and everyone into an 'evil-doer' or 'bad hombre.' Like mass shootings, the murder of blacks by police is a numbingly routine aspect of daily life, so it is unsurprising that Homeland Security dispatched drones to surveil BLM protesters during June of 2020 in multiple cities across the US. The drone converts 'protest' and demands for justice into 'uprising' and Americans into subversives, thugs, criminals, and left-wing radicals.

Purposive drone killings mask an archaic lust for vengeance where the desire for inflicting pain is never satisfied, extending out further and further until the death of a single American is never paid back even at the expense of thousands of others (cf. DOL: 44). As Durkheim says, "we still have the mind-set of primitives" (EFRL: 25; see also S: 387).[235] Rank proposed a similar notion: it is not that we are simply savages wrapped in a modern garment but that "what we really have in common with our remote ancestors is a *spiritual*, not a primitive self.... In consequence, we reject those irrational life forces as belonging to our primitive past instead of recognizing them in our present spiritual needs" (1941: 63). It is here, to return to our original geometric imagery, that we need to

---

233 Compare this mechanical piacularism with the notion of mechanized *ekstasis* in Adorno (1967: 128–29).

234 Punishment of a crime is a negation of a negation, the superseding of a contingent deviance, and restoration of conduct in conformity with universal morality (PR: 132).

235 "The cult of Humanity, with its rites of Freedom and Equality, always struck me as a revival of those ancient cults in which gods were like animals or had animal heads" (Pessoa 2001: 11). Postmodernism and hard constructionism mark a kind of return to the archaic. "We have long grown accustomed to hearing of late that history itself is a fiction, or rhetoric, or whatever. The ancients would not have found that a particularly surprising doctrine, inasmuch as they drew only a faint line between myth and history and, as Cicero put it, considered the writing of history an *opus oratorium*—a rhetorical work" (Bowersock 1994: 12).

bring together several threads of the argument with an eye toward the role of the imagined Other, ascetic self-negation, and destruction of the terrifying object.[236] For this, we need only return, ever so briefly, to the Peter and Paul relation in the first chapter of *Capital*.

As we will recall from *The Sociogony*, to be bound to our others, to associate in a durable and meaningful fashion, requires sacrifices and self-repression. Repression is the moment of self-alienation that puts us on the road to sublation and saturation in the social. Except the repressed always returns in the form of the uncanny (Freud [1919] 1959). Unlike Las Vegas, what happens in the infra-liminal domain does not stay in the infra-liminal domain. One of the key elements worth salvaging from Žižek is the idea that the Big Other, if it actually exists as something more than an empty signifier, is never fully totalized, in other words, some thing, some fetish *point de caption* blocks or prevents the Other from attaining its full actualization (2002: 18–19, 214–22). Some terrible X in the form of a specular image captivates the singular relative and intervenes to keep utopia from crystallizing and that no-good X represents the return of the repressed in its transfigured form: either excessively large and abstract (Terror) or weirdly small (the homunculus). From Peter's standpoint, this gap between what should be, the attainment of perfection, and what exists, the abomination that ruins everything, must have a root cause and must be solved once and for all.[237]

Peter knows well what sacrifices he has made in good conscience and he knows that the Other is blameless in its inherent perfection. That only leaves one party that could be ruining life: Paul, his alter ego, the particular equivalent of Peter. Once a "Man" Peter is transformed into a paranoid martyr willing to die to purify the social order now plagued by anarchy and that means destroying Paul, also once a "Man" but now it is revealed that he is a selfish,

---

236   According to Castoriadis, the imaginary itself is rooted in the repression of drives (1987: 134). Here we are interested in how the terrifying, imaginary object is subjected to a kind of repressive desublimation that undermines solidarity.

237   "There is a sense in which failure is baked into the very idea of utopia; the goal of a perfect world—a holiday from history—is intrinsically self-undermining.... The circle of our aspirations is not easily reconciled with the square of our human propensities. Over and over, optimistically and stubbornly, commendably but maybe also a bit foolishly, utopia just seems to take a long and circuitous route to the same, inevitable destination" (Kapur 2016). Utopias typically devolve into petit bourgeois conventions or despotism of either the fluid (dictatorship) form or the fixed (tyrannical) form. The distinction between temporary dictatorship and permanent tyranny is provided by Halevy. The dictator assuming control during an emergency is fated to having their authority reduced as the ordeal is managed. "[T]he intimate daily association of the head with the members of the order tends to render that autocratic structure substantially innocuous" (Hocking 1926: 264).

greedy infidel. What is this destructive logic but a perfect form of repressive desublimation whereby Peter destroys the very foundations of society at the molecular, intersubjective level? Peter does not grasp that it is Paul who constitutes his humanity (his social mirror) and that without him, there is no society, and no imaginary Big Other to defend. This path of suicidal homicide is 'liberatory' in its destruction of the Other, it marks a return to the infra-liminal, but necessarily leads to autism and molecular flow in the liquidation of the little other. This is the logic of the rampage gunman: everything must die so the Other can live, but, of course, without us or the paranoid fanatic pulling the trigger, there is no Other. The suicide bomber, over there (external to the core) is simply the mirror image of the rampage gunman over here (within the core). The results are the same: a return to the infra-liminal but at the cost of the other. Importantly, these two singular forms of murderous self-destruction (the internal rampage shooter and the external suicide bomber) contain the secrets of other forms: we could march out two additional forms that expand from the simple all the way out to the universal where we find warring nations engaged in a death struggle (e.g., Cold War) but this will have to wait for some other day.

Finally, the drone represents the piacular condensation or synthesis of the other two moments of the internal and the external, the paranoid delusional sadist destroying his own equivalent and the suicide bomber martyring his or her self for the Big Other, but, of course, the big shift here is that the drone is a manifestation *of* the Big Other guided by what Žižek calls the unseen Other of the Big Other. It is interesting that lone wolf gunmen and suicide bombers operate at our level, on the ground, metaphorically speaking, while the drone operates "up there" and for the most part undetectable to the senses—we only know of its presence in its material effects, the deliverance of information back to the imperial core, and revenge along the periphery for the enjoyment of the permanently victimized good guys. In the final analysis, American empire needs an enemy that it cannot lose to, and terrorism is just that kind of battle. Then again, if the struggle against terror is something that cannot be lost it also cannot be won, which would seem like a dead end, but this is exactly the kind of nemesis that our empire needs: the fully developed speculative era of fictional capital, dark capital, virtual capital, potlatch capitalism, etc.,[238] needs a speculative, dark, virtual, entity of horror in which to get entangled with and the drone is the perfected embodiment of all things imperial today: dropping commodities on Us and hellfire missiles on Them.

---

238 On the various circuits of capital (virtual and dark) see Krier (2008) and on 'potlatch capitalism' see Worrell (2015b).

The lone gunman represents the tiny, synthetic manifestation of all social monstrosities in one, fiery moment of murderous self-destruction, striking the concrete up-close in a futile attempt to injure the abstract far away. The suicide bomber is also quite effective in inflicting death and destruction disproportionate to the number of people committing these acts. However, in a world of 'Biopower,' the capacity to wield forces and powers of life and death over an entire planet, the suicide bomber (like the rampage shooter) is insignificant. What is a dynamite vest or a rifle in comparison to a nuclear attack submarine or a Star Wars program? The drone, like the deranged shooter and the fanatical suicide bomber, the twin faces of piacularism, the third term, is also a futile technology that guarantees that the US generates 'terrorists' wherever it goes like a bow wave generated by its own momentum. Just as civilization created "its own barbarian plague" (Owen Lattimore, in Scott 2017: 249) neoliberalism creates its own plague of terrorism.

We tend to dismiss lone gunmen as lunatics (and who would argue otherwise?) but trying to deal with the problem at that level is the definition of futility. Likewise, we are mass-producing suicide bombers with every step we take as a nation. Now women and children are lining up to kill and die. Neoliberal policies are partially responsible for the internal meltdown and external chaos inflicted on the global population. If it is correct that the image of the suicide bomber and the rampage shooter are dialectically connected as speculative doubles, we are still helpless to push back against the root mechanisms that generate these kinds of violent responses. There has to be a concrete leverage point from which to push back against a regime and its policies that, if successful, would mean the diminishment of a wide spectrum of violent eruptions here and abroad. If correct, it is resistance to drones (military and commercial) that represents, at least for now, the best concrete point from which to resist 'everything' all at once as a retrospective portal back into other, seemingly unrelated, phenomena, rather than fighting against random flares.

While some sociologists[239] make apologies for drone warfare as the lesser of two evils (Etzioni 2011) resistance to the use of drones seems like the focal point. Unfortunately, the state keeps its drone assets offshore or locked up

---

239 Surprisingly, apart from the surveillance angle, there is presently nothing like a sociology of drone warfare to speak of. Domestic surveillance is an important problem but the focus here is on mass killings rather than the security gaze per se. While I do not believe that laughing at, or ridicule toward, counterterrorism measures like drone strikes does much to promote resistance (Heath-Kelly 2012) I think Žižek has the right stance toward domestic surveillance: just treat it dismissively—*here*, laughter and ridicule offer an opportunity for an infra-liminal space of resistance, even if only symbolic. But one must move beyond the symbolic in the world of concrete resistance.

behind barbed wire fences and defended by armed troops on military installations. Consequently, anti-drone movement, when we see them reported on in the media, are sad spectacles of retirees or low-level celebrities blocking entrances and being hauled off by police.[240] The anti-drone movement may be facing sheer futility, yet, the movement is still embryonic with only a few years of growth. Do we live in an era of futility?

> —O what made fatuous sunbeams toil
> To break earth's sleep at all? (Owen [1963] 1965: 58).

Futility, from futile, itself from the Latin for *leaky*, is an interesting concept in the geometrical Durkheimian space of heavenly negativities: futility is the name of the portal into the great death spiral of a civilization going into the twilight. So long as citizens have an opportunity to protest drones at the point they are on the ground, at the mouth of air bases, disrupting operations then there is an opportunity for the public to touch and short circuit the point of unity of the rampage-terror-vengeance complex.

14   The Grimace of the Vortex

> The silent bleed of a world decaying, / The moan of multitudes in woe, / These were the things we wished would go; / But they were staying (Thomas Hardy, in Freeman 1936: 322).

Anthropomorphized, the central abyss is typically portrayed as a snarling, smirking, and misanthropic demon, or, lacking a personality, a jumble of possessed things terrorizing consciousness. "By its regression to magic under late capitalism, thought is assimilated to late capitalist forms."

---

240 In central New York, punishments for protesters are shaping up to be as stiff as sentencing guidelines permit. The anti-drone movement cannot expect much in the way of legal protections with regard for free speech and freedom of assembly: "For those for whom international law is immaterial but U.S. law is paramount, the drone program must go before it completely erodes justice and especially civil liberties here at home. As too few in our region know, Town of DeWitt judges have issued, renewed and enforced orders of protection against nonviolent protesters at the request of Hancock Field Air National Guard commanders, including the notorious Colonel Earl A. Evans. For those who struggle to protect women at risk for violence from intimate partners, it is a travesty of justice to see orders of protection extended to the architects of drone killings" (Curtain 2015).

> The occultist draws the ultimate conclusion from the fetish-character of commodities: menacingly objectified labor assails him on all sides from demonically grimacing objects. What has been forgotten in a world congealed into products, the fact that it has been produced by men, is split off and misremembered as a being-in-itself added to that of the objects and equivalent to them.... [T]he social quality that now animates them is given an independent existence both natural and supernatural, a thing among things (Adorno 1974: 239).

Where Adorno would situate the grimace of magical products, "assimilated" to new forms under the capitalist regime of hyper-production and one-sided accumulation, we would, in contrast, characterize the central vortex of the octahedron, the coordinates of the miracle, as the center of the menacing grimace.

In *Negative Dialectics*, Adorno resurrected this line of thought: "Human beings, individual subjects, are under a spell now as ever.... Men become that which negates them.... In human experience the spell is the equivalent of the fetish character of merchandise [and] ... the subject venerates its mirror image.... The universal that compresses the particular until it splinters, like a torture instrument, is working against itself, for its substance is the life of the particular; without the particular, the universal declines to an abstract, separate, eradicable form" (1973: 345–46). Mauss reminds us that "the mind is crowded with chimerical fears which derive solely from the mutual exaltation of individuals as members of a group. In fact, while magical chimeras are universal, the objects of people's fears vary from group to group. The fears themselves are produced by collective agitation, through a kind of involuntary convention, and are transmitted by tradition" (1972: 129).

Bloom says, "Once one plunges into the abyss, there is no assurance whatsoever that equality, democracy or socialism will be found on the other side" (1987: 154). Indeed, we can rest assured that none of these things reside on the 'other side' of our abyss. However, there is no reason for pessimism either. Bloom and social conservatives talk about the abyss as a wasteland of value relativism but, if anything should be made clear from all this, it is that there are no values at all here, save the one value, the big-V value, of the abyss itself: the negative absolute of surplus value sucking all reality into itself like a black hole. We have seen a lot of "isms" but these are all composite currents of moral energy in various states of disaggregation and perverse aggregations. Drives, ideas, and ideals, yes, but not values *per se*. But, still, there's no reason for pessimism because the diremption and declinations of moral currents also generates counter-currents linked to the invisible (but nonetheless existing and active) positive absolute. Again, we know for a fact that the negative absolute exists, it makes all transactions possible, but if the negative exists, its opposite necessarily exists. Sure, bad things are bound to happen, evil is everywhere,[241] but the bad is also the precondition for the good and optimism is meaningless without its opposite. To say that the time is ripe for pessimism it amounts to saying that, optimism, too, is right around the corner.

> When society works upon the minds of men, it often produces ideas, ideals and theories which do not succeed in arousing men to social or class-motivated action, or fail to bring about the necessary political, juridical and economic changes. Frequently too, we find that new conditions do not at once impress themselves upon the mind. Behind apparent simplicities lurk complexities so unexpected that only a special instrument of interpretation can uncover them at the moment. Marxian analysis enables us to see things more clearly. We begin to see that we are inside of a process fraught with converging influences, in the midst of the slow ripening of new ideas and tendencies which constitute the gradual preparation of revolution (Pannekoek 1937).

In a letter to K.J.H. Windischmann (dated 27 May 1810) Hegel wrote:

> I am eager to see your work on magic [*Untersuchungen über Astrologie, Alchemie und Magie*, 1813]. I confess that I should not dare to tackle this gloomy side and aspect of spiritual nature or the natural spirit, and am doubly delighted that you will partly illuminate this for us, partly take up again and rehabilitate much that has been neglected and despised.... Be assured that your mental state which you describe to me is partly due to this work: this descent into dark regions where nothing shows itself to be firm, determinate, and secure, where splendors flash everywhere, but next to abysses ...—where the beginning of every path breaks off again and runs into the indefinite, loses itself, and tears us out of our destiny and direction.—From my own experience I know this mood of the mind, or rather of reason, once it has entered with interest and its intimations into a chaos of appearances and, though inwardly sure of the goal, it has not yet come through, not yet into the clarity and detailed grasp of the whole (in Kaufmann 1965: 328–29).

---

241 Pessimism comes from the Latin *pessimus* for 'worst'—and what's the worst that can happen that hasn't already happened?

The central abyss at the heart of the 'system' that we have examined over three volumes (with one more to come) is not a lack but, like a black hole, a superdense thing surrounded by fragments and leftovers, eddies, and currents. 'In there' somewhere, concealed in darkness, is the positive absolute tearing itself apart and projecting energy into the visible spectrum of understanding. There is an "inner pulse" behind the "external shapes" (PR: 20–21). There is no beginning nor end but just the "urge of the world" (Whitman [1892] 1992: 22). These are all metaphors, of course, but the important thing is that, for example, the *ekstasis* we find in the matrix of the negative heaven of the commodity world is purely morbid and sterile, abstract and 'ideal'—i.e., not 'real' in the Hegelian sense. The avatars of this domain promise ecstasy and effervescence but deliver nothing more than sadism, revenge, martyrdom, fanaticism, empty dreams, infinite desires, and doom. The ecstasy of the rally or the scapegoat is a pale shadow of ecstatic love (see Freeman 1943: 108–11). Seen from the 'inside out' the absolute is an ugly mess but all the energies and resources for democracy are also 'in' this ugly mess; nothing external or lacking is necessary for the actualization of democracy—we have what we need. The absolute (in its positive form) actually delivers what its negative twin can only promise. We have been here before.

> Whitman understood that democracy wasn't 'very boring' but rather a political system that could deliver on the promises that authoritarianism only pretended it would. For the poet, democracy wasn't just a way of passing laws or a manner of organizing a government; democracy was a method of transcendence in its own right.... A politics that is unable to translate its positions into some sort of transcendent language, pointing to something greater than the individual, is a politics that will ultimately fail. Whitman understood this.... Whitman's poetry ... explicates the metaphysical underpinnings of transcendent democracy. Where Nietzsche would offer the illusions of the Übermensch, Whitman would sing a song of the 'divine average' (Simon 2019).

The 'machinery' of transcendence is what seems to be lacking: we all want unity, but we cannot abide authority because we think it is always authoritarianism, or, conversely, authoritarians have fooled the foolish into mistaking sadomasochism for the good (right, authority, etc.). However, to return to an earlier theme, all power flows from the bottom up; recall Hegel's position: "As a living being, the human being can certainly be *dominated*—i.e., his physical side and other external attributes may be brought under the power of others. But the free will in and for itself cannot be *coerced*, except in so far as *it fails to withdraw itself from the external dimension* in which it is caught up, or from its idea of the latter. Only he who *wills to be coerced* can be coerced into anything" (PR: 119–20). In other words, "A people enslaves itself ..." (Boetie [1552–53] 1975: 50).[242] In a sense, all politics are 'democratic' but the source of authority (the 'demos') has fallen under the illusion that authority is external and that they are merely a mass of following subjects. But, as Marx says, "one man is king only because other men stand in relation of subjects to him. They, on the other hand, imagine that they are subjects because he is king" (C: 149). Note that Marx says the setup obtains "only" for one reason: a distorted understanding of a social relation tied to reflective determinations of the kind mapped out at the beginning of the previous volume—i.e., we are here dealing with a problem of dialectics.[243] *Leaves of Grass* nor the bible or any other codex has what it takes to negate a civil war (then or in the future) but Hegel, Marx, Whitman, and Durkheim all grasp that Spirit that has worked itself up to knowing itself as Spirit provides a poor ground for organized mass death and large-scale destruction. "We have circled and circled till we have arrived home again, we two, / We have voided all but freedom and all but our own joy" (Whitman [1892] 1992: 83).

---

242 "The leader, the governor, the king, the fuehrer—is an expression and tool of people's way of life" (Reich 1953: 149).

243 But, of course, there is also the emotional *welcoming* of domination (Boetie [1552–53] 1975: 50) that Marx disregards; this disregard is the classic scotoma in Marx's undeveloped social psychology. Marx's theory of the commodity was subtle and dialectical whereas his theory of revolution was hampered by materialist assumptions regarding consciousness—the whole reason neo-Marxism developed after WWI. Dialectics, as we know it, is not just about formal logic but also grasps the contradictions of freedom and the desire for subjugation.

CHAPTER 2

A Formal Condensation of Moral Geometry

> Then formed two camps: on the one side the exalted spirits, sufferers, all the expansive souls who yearned toward the infinite, bowed their heads and wept; they wrapped themselves in unhealthful dreams and nothing could be seen but broken reeds in an ocean of bitterness. On the other side the materialists remained erect, inflexible, in the midst of positive joys, and cared for nothing except to count the money they had acquired. It was but a sob and a burst of laughter, the one coming from the soul, the other from the body.... Already things were drifting toward the abyss.
> (Alfred de Musset, in Coser 1972: 496)

Let us briefly encapsulate some ideas from the 'formal intermezzo' (*The Sociogony*), the third chapter of *Disintegration*, and the first chapter of the current volume before proceeding into the logic of the commodity in the fourth and final volume. Starting in reverse, we can designate the abstract individual (not to be confused with a *personality*) as an isolated atom, no larger than the punctuation mark at the end of this sentence. The individual is plagued by a lack in the real and cannot survive, nor enjoy a moral existence, without others of their species. We will signify the assemblage of individuals in a shape (square, represented by the figure below) that gives equal weight to four dimensions: we come together, I (Ego) and Thou (Alter), to escape the twin nightmares of Anarchy (Anomie) and Themis (Fate).

As we noted in *Disintegration*, the repetition of squares in social theory, philosophy, logic and linguistics is fascinating. From the "four-cornered" typology of Durkheim's analysis of suicide (Besnard 2005), Bhaskar's "social cube" (2008: 160), the semiotic square, Lacan's L schema, Harman's four-pole ontographic model (2011: 124), in addition to the other various squares and rectangles of opposition and contradictions in logic. Literature, poetry, and myth are also fertile and interesting reflections on the theological and social nature of the square. Whitman's Transcendental Walt, a Kosmos, was also the fourth and final side of the "Square Deific." Perhaps this recurrence of the square originates in the allocentric intuitions and observations regarding the twin polarities of opposing forces that undergird all forms of social organization reflected in customs, tales, myths, theology, and philosophy.[1] "The enigmatic

---

1 For more on allocentric and autocentric modes of perception see Schachtel (1959: 81–84).

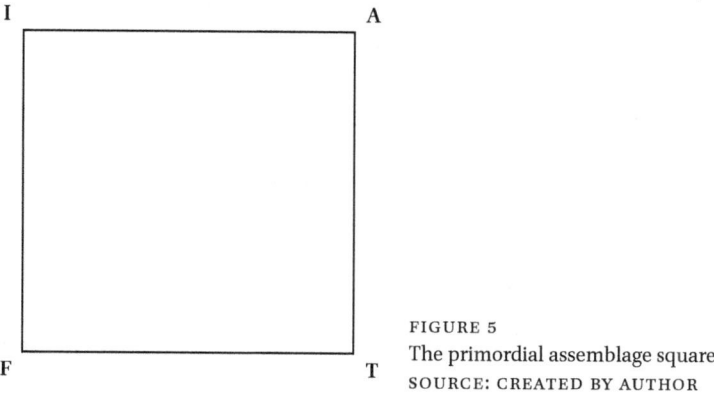

FIGURE 5
The primordial assemblage square
SOURCE: CREATED BY AUTHOR

axiom of Maria runs: '...from the third comes the one as the fourth' ... which presumably means, when the third produces the fourth it at once produces unity" (Jung 1969: 237). Kant organized a jumble of Aristotle's categories into a "fourfold" array that is found split into two in Hegel's logic (Jameson 2009: 77). Particularly interesting is the disjunctive syllogism in *Science of Logic* where the universal doubles itself to create a fourth concrete moment out of a triadic configuration of individuality, particularity, and universality. Dyads produce triads and triads produce squares—totalities that 'contain' all. Far from a mania for triads commonly attributed to Hegel, his philosophy of history features a "quatriad" (i.e., tetradic) procession of freedom from the Oriental, Greek, Roman, and finally, the German (Croce 1915: 183; Croce 1917: 273). We find some kind of parallel, again, in the L schema (Lacan) where the triadic expands *quadratus* (it is made square) through a redoubling process (Lacan 2002: 481) and we see something similar in the analyst's attempt at triangulation where the "tertiary position" (Lacan 2002: 481; Fink 1997: 106) is taken up via the imposition of a symbolic coordinate juxtaposed to the dyadic imaginary relation obtaining between the analyst and analysand (ego-ego' or a-a') which itself produces a four-cornered structure (ego, ego', Subject, and Other); where there should be a subject that can respond to the Other of the symbolic order, we find instead a black hole (Fink 1997: 105). Squares work well in theory and house-building but, in scaling up, larger social structures typically avoid squares lacking a central feature: "Quadrangular, reticulated cities (Los Angeles, for instance) are said to produce a profound uneasiness: they offend our synesthetic sentiment of the City, which requires that any urban space have a center to go to, to return from, a complete site to dream of and in relation to which to advance or retreat; in a word, to invent oneself" (Barthes 1982: 30).

Our assemblage in the square (seen in the figure above) is productive of special effects: ebullience, compression, and ecstasy, etc. This general and formless effervescence is not yet any historical individual such as mana, charisma, value, etc. We can represent this energetic transformation of the real by 'rolling up' our square into a strand or ribbon (~) and, if we are successful in avoiding the waste of this energy it will be pinned together in the form of our Möbius band ready for the odyssey of crystallization, institutionalization, and world-building. We are required to use the image of the Möbius band if we are to be true to the *polar* nature of moral currents (∞). Let us call this figure our *immortal coil*.

The greater the effort to produce a fully unified and integrated totality, something like a circle or blemish-free sphere, yields the annoying fact that it is characterized by an imperfection or some excessive supplement that prevents the totality from achieving the perfection of a calm, smooth, and static equilibrium. The more we fixate on 'the problem' (the excessive thing that is impossible to resolve and consequently blocks purified glory) the more we undermine the very ground upon which our dynamic and perfectly imperfect sphere is predicated. In the making of great we will break it with anxiety and violence.

All our energies and resources become focused on The Thing, the monster, the -X, or the 'blowhole' (represented in the figure below), and the social sphere (our universe, the orb of cooperation) suffers what appears to be some kind of inside-out inversion when the collective representation that keeps our strand tied seems to come untied (a condition we saw in the previous volume as *noa*).

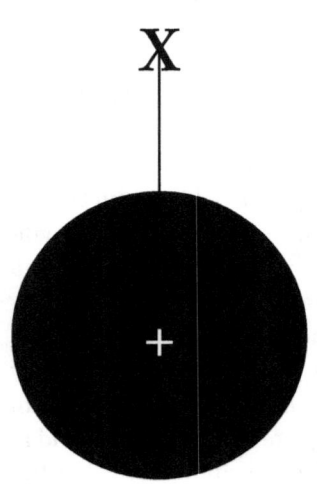

FIGURE 6
The monster
SOURCE: CREATED BY AUTHOR

The 'guts' of the social system seem to 'spill out' and we have a diremptive regression on our hands, a downfall or declination, back into to the social square. But since the social system has undergone prodigious moral developments during its death struggle with impure contaminants, the regression is not all the way back to a metaphorical ground zero. It is a regression or backsliding into an earlier form of organization, however, the earlier form has been inexorably renovated. The resignation one struggles against is an all-grown-up resignation by the time you return (Jackson 2019: 321). What we encounter, instead of the primordial square, is a matrix of negative synthetic *a priori* judgments and syllogisms we have termed the 'social octahedron' and that we have mapped out to some extent in this volume and the preceding one.

The 'octahedron' is both a metaphor and an imaginary map produced by reflection 'inside' the coil. It is, in other words, a deconstruction generated from 'within' the loop. The truth is that the 'immortal coil' never really comes untied (after all, it is 'immortal'). As Durkheim might say, the whole is disunited but it is still a whole. The 'coil' cannot be destroyed even on a mass scale, requiring only a dyad to propel and replicate itself in perpetuity. The 'coil' may abandon a people, it may surrender a population to fate, it discards old notions and invents new concepts, but it never loses faith in itself, its concept of itself. If, as Hegel says, the Concept is the *sunrise of existence*, it follows that it is also simultaneously the *twilight of essential being*. The Concept appears to be defective, lacking the power to totalize itself (as Hegel might say, its existence is inadequate to the Idea) but perhaps that deficiency only holds for the historical generators of the Concept (the embodiments of abstract anti-Reason) rather than the future inheritors. This would not be an exceptional situation: periodically Reason works itself up into a unified shape, but unification is meaningless without posterior and anterior disunities as preconditions and destinies. This is nothing more than the reality of dialectics or the dialectics of reality. Reason is divided, is ambivalent and speaks in multiple voices, following social disorganization it also regresses and disintegrates, but disunity is the precondition and preface to a drive toward reorganization and reunification.

As we saw toward the end of the first chapter in the present volume, the dynamic contradictions of the currents in the 'octahedron' (e.g., the antinomies of autonomy and heteronomy, resignation and ecstasy, and so on) drive the system toward 'fractal' replication and expansion; the matrix of judgments and syllogisms doubles and redoubles itself endlessly. Lacking the 'gravitational' force of the Concept, the web will suffer from 'ontic distortions' (demons and unfathomable depths here, barren understandings over there) and drive itself stupidly along a flat plane toward infinity.

We will see in the final volume how these figures repeat in all domains of social life. Since we 'discovered' this 'coil' at the heart of *Suicide*,[2] it will come as no surprise that we should find a repetition of this geometry in Durkheim's analysis of the social division of labor (DOL)[3] and in the analysis of games and play by a theorist we might loosely think of as disciples or otherwise greatly inspired by the Durkheim school (Caillois 1961).[4] But we will also explore the link between fatalism (Durkheim) and predestinationism (Weber) in the context of the reaction against church anomie or "lax" social control (PESC: 4) as it relates to the unintentional development of modern, western capitalism. Finally, with respect to Marx's theory of the commodity, we will unwind the general formula for capital to reveal the same underlying logic, the same immortal coil, operating in Durkheim's *Suicide* and Weber's famous essay on the Protestant ethos.

---

2 Of course, this 'thing' is not really 'in' *Suicide*, rather, we have projected it into the text. We are trailing in the destructive path of Value but, like Value, doing the work of the absolute in finding the thing that all theories have in common that none of them possess individually.

3 In the next volume we will elaborate on the division of labor and how it plays off the polar oppositions found in *Suicide*, i.e., forced-fatalistic; anomic; capricious-egoistic; and the *lack* of a division of labor in a mechanically solidified social system corresponding to the altruistic current of self-destruction.

4 Compare the four types of psychological attitudes toward games with Durkheim's types of suicide: *agôn*-egoism; *alea*-fate; *mimicry*-altruism; *ilinx*-anomie (Caillois 1961: 44).

Conclusion: the Beginning of the End

In the first volume (*Sociogony*) we examined social facts as a procession of fluid emergences and variably eccentric crystallizations. The metaphors of a Mobius-like band of assemblage energy and a social or moral geometry were introduced. Many traditional sociological elements were explored by way of illustration but nothing extensively. In the second volume (*Disintegration*) as well as the present work (*Resignation and Ecstasy*) the Mobius-like nature of social interactions and the matrix of synthetic *a priori* judgments (the social octahedron) were elaborated about as far as we could go, constrained as we are by considerations of space. In the final volume we will focus on one problem by penetrating the heart of the commodity and charting the rise of capitalism in the modern West. Marx's general formula for capital (M — C — M') will be unwound to its fullest possible extent in an effort to expose its 'octagonal' logic of alienation and to ponder the extent to which this form of objectivation has reached a terminal point on the path of self-destruction.

Appendix: Energy, Form, and Concept

> What is man? I might begin; how does it happen that there is such a thing in the world, something that ferments like a chaos or molders like a rotten tree and never thrives to ripeness? How does nature tolerate this sour grape amidst its sweet ones? To the plants he says, I too, was once like you! and to the pure stars, I will become like you in another world! Hölderlin (2008: 61)

This appendix extends my keynote address delivered December 2010 at Iowa State University's Symposium for New Directions in Critical Social Theory. The purpose of this talk ("Dialectical Durkheim") was to situate the founder of academic sociology within the larger European intellectual context and demonstrate how Durkheim's sociology *might* be thought of as a refinement of the German Absolute Idealist brought about by grounding Spirit's odyssey not in historicism but on species of social organization. Durkheim diverges significantly from Hegel in many ways, perhaps most importantly, in viewing the state as incapable of fulfilling any outsized role in guaranteeing human freedom. For Durkheim, the flourishing of Personality rests on moral education flowing into 'corporate' and professional organizations bound to one another in an organic division of labor. This presentation was also built with an eye toward providing orientation to a graduate level social theory course working its way through the vagaries of continental thought, especially with regard to the main problematic[1] of 19th century German philosophy: freedom from external compulsion (i.e., people being treated like donkeys).[2] I have expanded upon the original presentation but have resisted the urge

---

1   "A problematic is a rudimentary organization of a field of phenomena which yields problems for investigation. The organization occurs on the basis of some more or less explicitly theoretical presuppositions—it is an application of assumptions and principles to phenomena in order to constitute a range of enquiry" (Abrams 1982: xv).
2   On the difference between alienation as *externality* (a form of consciousness) and actual physical separation (*exteriority*) in the real see Marx (PM: 108). Here I would summarize the notion of externality by emphasizing the hyper-cathected nature of some representations. Hysterics provide a good example of representations becoming so over-invested with libido that they hallucinate (Fink 1997: 85). As individuals we feel keenly the desire to be liberated from externalities, yet, without the facticity of the external, or, really, the externality of the fact and the constraining power of facts, we lose our capacity for objectivity and our individual judgments slide backwards into subjectivity and fraud—our biases are soothed by "trumping up a set of rules to justify [our] ... rationalization[s]" (Orwell 2008: 338). In fact, that would be as far as Žižek's moral philosophy goes. Sans facts, i.e., external constraining power, we may be individuals (undivided) but we will lack actual sociological *individuality*. In our desire to escape alienation we find ourselves even more alienated. "The present

to alter its original form as a schematic blueprint. Additional materials have been welded on at various points that deal more specifically with the ontological parameters of classical sociology and the terminological and substantive twists and turns in the debates between nominalists, realists, materialists, and idealists in the history of philosophy and what it means for contemporary critical sociology.

1 The Spirit of Obsolescence

The year I started graduate school, Peter Burke published *History and Social Theory* in which he said: "I have done my best to not be too up-to-date. I continue to believe that Marx and Durkheim, Weber and Malinowski—to name no more—still have much to teach us" (1992: viii). That notion of not being too up-to-date has stuck with me for more than a quarter of a century, though, while Hegel, Marx, Durkheim, and Weber are my primary inspirations, my roster is a little longer and a little wider, and I also believe that it is important to mine the depths of writers that are antithetical to one's position to better sharpen one's own perspective. Reading 'bad theory' is perhaps more valuable than reading the 'good stuff' because finding oneself in agreement with the 'bad' has a shocking capacity for self-clarification. Some ideas really are just suicidal but usually the problem comes down to an idea being blind to its own preconceptions or being abstract and incomplete. Hegel famously said that there is really only *one philosophy* and that each particular form is but a one-sided link in a procession of self-reflections whereby Spirit becomes conscious of itself along its historical journey ([1840] 1995b: 545–54).[3]

'Spirit' seems like a quaint and obscure holdover from a bygone era. The last major sociological work that tackled 'Spirit' directly was Weber's famous study on the link between the Protestant ethos and modern capitalism and he seemed genuinely anxious about "the somewhat pretentious" ([1930] 2001: 13) connotations of the term. The capitalist spirit, for Weber, is laid out as a unified "conceptual whole" or a special "point of view" aimed at working out a "conceptual formulation" that relates the "necessary" and "essential ... characteristics" pertaining to an individual historical problem "from the standpoint of ... cultural significance" (Ibid: 14). Weber was a horrible writer, but

---

cultural state of America would give us a good opportunity for studying the damage to civilization which is thus to be feared" (Freud [1930] 1961: 74).

3   Dialectics, Hegelian and Marxist, contains elements of relativism, skepticism, and so forth, but "are not reducible to relativism," etc., that would preclude the formation of objective knowledge (Lenin 1972: 174). Hegel's "positivity bears features of what is bad ..." (Adorno 1973: 159). If it's 'bad' it is in the dialectic; it is a fool's errand to believe that the 'bad' can be somehow separated from the 'good.' The aim of reflection and sublation is the transition of thought beyond good and bad within the absolute Idea.

behind all this is the rejection of once-and-for-all abstract definitions of 'capitalism' *per se* and, in its palce, the "concrete genetic sets of relations which are inevitably of a specifically unique and individual character" (Ibid: 14). "Cultural significance" here plays the role of mediating criteria in the dichotomous extremities of history and the specific individuality of Occidental capitalism. When Weber refers to 'Spirit' as an "historical individual" we can think of this as a concrete constellation. Modern capitalism gradually emerges from an entanglement with a peculiar code of conduct that makes the increase of capital, by means of systematic and routine human alienation and exploitation, a solemn duty for business owners. Suddenly, the peculiar and the particular (fluid) achieves universal (fixed) significance.[4] If that sounds reminiscent of Hegel and Marx that's because, according to Ernst Troeltsch (who knew Weber exceedingly well) those were Weber's two main influences (1922: 233).[5] Here, Spirit stands in contrast to the purely unconscious, the pre-conscious, prejudice, habit, ideology, etc., and refers to conscious conceptual reflection. Absolute Spirit is consciousness of this consciousness. We have perfect examples of 'absolute sociology' in Marx's analysis of the commodity and in Durkheim's writings on the totem.

In the pages of *Capital*, Marx draws consciousness along a path from value as a reified substance, to a peculiar historical subject-substance, and finally, a form of collective subjectivity that, in the case of Marx and those that accurately comprehend his analysis, infinite subjectivity that finally knows itself as infinite subjectivity. Marx worked himself up to this level of comprehension of value by working his way back through Hegel's philosophy of Spirit.[6]

Value is a spiritual form that does not yet know itself as Spirit. Political economy only moves consciousness part of the way while the critique of political economy (the negation of the negation) completes the task, at least abstractly. Sometimes we refer to Marxism as 'political economy' (in the 50s it was a shield against anti-communist hysteria) and sometimes we read that Marx attempted to put political economy on a new footing, but, I think what Marx was doing in his 'critique' was the actual annihilation

---

4 In Durkheimian terms, capitalism prior to the Reformation enjoyed only a fluid and accidental form of existence, here today and gone tomorrow in various locations but, beginning in 16th Century Europe, that which had previously been accidental in nature began to crystallize into a fixed and total social fact.
5 Walter Kaufmann is also one of the few writers on Hegel to remark positively on the similarities between Weber and Hegel and their conceptions of scientific praxis (1965b: 81).
6 The Marx after 1857 (the year he turned back to Hegel) is very much different from the Marx of, say, the "Paris Manuscripts." Freud was in no position to accurately judge Marx's critique of capitalism, but he was astute enough to realize that Marx was in fact not a materialist, and that the Marxism of his day required supplementation to further develop into "a genuine social science" (1965: 219, 222). At about the time that Freud was leveling his criticism against the radicals, the movement to fuse Marxism with psychoanalysis was underway and most Freudians were none too pleased (Sharaf 1983: 182).

of political economy rather than its reformation. The commodity is brought out of concealment (submerged in the reified terminology of political economy) and 'enlightened' via dialectical analysis. Like Marx, the person who has true knowledge of the commodity form might not be physically free of that institution, but consciousness has nonetheless attained freedom, *has set itself apart*, and is able to work up a set of countervailing values in opposition to dominant exchange-value (Value). Where Marx could have gone further was in placing value and its manifest embodiments within the universal equivalent of universal equivalents, self-consciously situating the economy of material goods within the larger sphere of *moral* economy.[7] The history of praxis is the history of yarn, diamonds, walls, roads, wheat, linen, coats, steel, and so on, *ad infinitum*, i.e., the domain of abstract individuals. The history of morals "is where everything else originates" (Solzhenitsyn 1974: 435).

In *Capital*, the 'sacred' is always ideological claptrap used to prop up the reign of money (cf. Mazzarella 2017: 85). Recall that in the *Communist Manifesto*, all that is solid is liquidated, and all that is holy is profaned by the peculiarly modern form of the acquisitive drive. But the following notion, that "man is at last compelled to face with sober senses, his real conditions of life, and his relations with his kind" (Marx and Engels [1848] 1972: 338) is utterly incorrect, as has been confirmed so many times, under so many different circumstances. The fact that the subject classes can be duped and manipulated by the sorcerers and theologians employed by capital (assuming they are themselves not already simply capitalists) is not as interesting as the forces conjured to deceive and disenfranchise subjects; the forces are not whipped up by bourgeois propagandists as they please, rather, they merely give voice and form to the whirlpool of moral sentiments generated by the dispossessed and the discontented themselves. For sure, sellers of labor power are devalued and used like sentient tools, but they find their quantum of moral compensation from another realm and in some other form, insofar as they survive the ordeal of production. Laboring in the capitalist world might be better comprehended not in the language of praxis and economy but in the primitive religious terms of human sacrifice.

In *Elementary Forms* we learn that what appears to be animal or plant worship is deeper and vastly more complicated: the totem conceals a social relation and a form of Spirit that does not know that it is Spirit. It is not really the animal that is worshiped but the image and emblem of the species. Beneath *this* appearance is the group worshiping itself in its alien, external form. However, beneath *this* collective worship is the real object of the cult: the production and enjoyment of collective effervescence (EFRL: 191). In a word, totemism is a premodern form of *dynamism* (Smith 1988). When

---

7 If one can criticize Marx's analysis in *Capital* and the preceding *Critique* it would be his reliance on preexisting terminology, e.g., "use-value," he adopted from "the English economists" and "German compilers" (CPE: 27, 28).

APPENDIX   161

we represent this system as a hierarchy rising from currents of energy (at bottom) to the apex of crystallized sacredness (at the top) we arrive at the following array:

Representation/Emblem/Image
Category/Class/Species
Social Organization/Clan
Energy Production/Ritual Effervescence

Depth analysis works its way down from the surface of what appears to be 'animal worship' to collective consciousness that, unfortunately, will never know itself for what it really is. As Herder asks, how many people will ever work themselves up to this level of the self-consciousness of self-consciousness? With Durkheim, we are able to know, but totem-worshipers will never know the truth of what they are doing, they just do it. The mana-minded, like the money-minded, are trapped in a labyrinth of projections.[8]

2   The Consciousness of the Whole

The 'absolute' is not, contra Findlay (1970), an ontological entity or Thing that functions like an ersatz god substitute. The standard misreading of Durkheim involves the deification society when his argument is actually the reverse: 'god' is the alienated projection of society itself (EFRL: 208); society, as "the consciousness of the whole," is the demystification of the external symbol. From the theological point of view the absolute is reified and wants to remain that way: "That Other from which we have come and which is contrasted with all concrete, known, temporal, human existence can be in no manner wholly distinct unless it be in every manner wholly distinct" (Barth 1933: 115).[9]

---

8 In the previous volume we briefly touched on the hyper-cathected potential of collective representations to produce a kind of 'hallucinatory' dynamic.
9 Barth's rendition of the Concept in Hegelian philosophy is peculiar in its reductiveness and diametric ordinariness: the Concept is turned into nothing more than a unity of being and *understanding* and the world is nothing more than what I, subjectively, think of it. The Concept is also imagined as a reified container of reality and possesses the occult ability to nullify all contradictions, e.g., hot = cold is absurd from the standpoint of common sense (Adams 2017). From our standpoint, the domain of understanding is limited, prosaic, abstract, finite, descriptive, and external: hot is hot and cold is cold and to say otherwise is a logical contradiction. "For the true Concept is an inherent unity, though not a merely immediate one but one essentially split internally and falling apart into contradictions. On these lines, for example, in my *Logic* I have expounded the Concept as subjectivity, but this subjectivity, as an ideal transparent unity, is lifted into its opposite, i.e., objectivity; indeed, as what is purely idea, it is itself only one-sided and particular, retaining contrasted with itself something different and opposed to it, namely objectivity; and it is only genuine subjectivity if it enters this

The sociological absolute is a something else, but it is not the Other of Christianity; *that* Other is an alienated representation of the church itself, the church in its abstract form. The absolute is society comprehended conceptually as a universal being, with all its individuals and parts organically, i.e., concretely, related to one another within the Concept (in stark contrast to the kind of abstract universal connections and linkages that capital produces on a planetary scale).[10] Absolute sociology is the attempt to conceptually grasp and unify the disconnected bits and pieces of a society, at whatever scale, as an integrated whole. If we were limited to a *Verstehen* sociology (specifically, one that intentionally or otherwise preserves a mystery realm) we might assume, with Troeltsch, that the absolute and the wholeness of society is unknowable and doomed to forever remain at the level of abstract infinitude ([1911] 1931/1949a: 23–30). Likewise, ordinary materialism can preserve a mystical 'thing-in-itself' while reducing human life to the laws of evolution and biology.[11] But we cannot confuse the practically infinite ocean of empirical observations, descriptions, narratives, and the ever-expanding palette of sociological *jargon* with the concept itself.[12] Again, it is crucial to not confuse reflections for the mirrors.

What we call 'absolute sociology' emerged as a self-conscious project around the mid-1850s and expired roughly 100 years later. It is almost literally true that this kind of sociology was killed off by two world wars and one revolution. What remnants survived were finally snuffed out during the Cold War with some notable convulsions during

---

opposition and then overcomes and dissolves it. In the actual world too there are higher natures who are given power to endure the grief of inner opposition and to conquer it …. e.g., of religion and in particular the Christian religion in which the abysses of grief form a principal part …" (Hegel 1975b: 928).

10 'Absolute Knowledge' is not even 'knowing' in the common sense of the word. Just knowing something does not mean one has any kind of leverage over the facts. "You could know everything there was in the world and yet if you were ignorant of that one dirty scramble you knew nothing" (Greene [1938] 2004: 163). One only 'knows' within the Concept. The Concept actualizes the unity of organic growth and causal negations (cf. Berman 1983: 7). Recall from the previous volume that Durkheim's 'organicism' was the organicism of ideals (1973: 13) not individual representations but collective, systematic, and impersonal powers (S: 36). This organicism of consciousnesses preserves the capacity for aetiological analyses of social facts.

11 "We do not know the 'thing in itself' that lies behind these knowable phenomena. But why trouble about this enigmatic 'thing in itself' when we have no means of investigating it, when we do not even clearly know whether it exists or not? Let us, then, leave the fruitless brooding over this ideal phantom to the 'pure metaphysician,' and let us instead, as 'real physicists,' rejoice in the immense progress which has been actually made by our monistic philosophy of nature" (Haeckel 1934: 310).

12 "And the Lord came down to see the city and the tower that the human creatures had built. And the Lord said, 'As one people with one language for all, if this is what they have begun to do, now nothing they plot to do will elude them. Come, let us go down and baffle their language there so that they will not understand each other's language'" (Genesis 11).

APPENDIX   163

the intervening years. Sociology is a relatively new form of thought but is, for the most part, unconsciously connected to older philosophical traditions—or *a* philosophy, namely, the results achieved by the Jena circle of absolute idealists made most famous by Hegel. I think that the Marx of the *Critique* (1859) and *Capital* (1867) as well as Durkheim's sociology (especially *Forms*) represent the two most important and contrasting extensions of the Hegelian tradition.[13] While Marx and Durkheim have been set up as purely oppositional figures I think they both need one another and instead of Marx or Durkheim we need not just a partnership but a sublation of the two: a 'Marxheimian' sociology that situates the commodity and revolution within the larger economy of sacred energies. Unfortunately, the conditions for such a synthesis are not promising.

As Durkheim says in his book on the division of labor, philosophy is the "collective consciousness" of the sciences (DOL: 301).[14] But the spiritual sciences in general, and sociology in particular (the science of the hyper-spiritual),[15] have been dismembered, turned inward, lost contact with life, and consequently have descended into irrationality, leading to a situation where neither sociology nor philosophy are capable of becoming social facts *qua* imperative ways of thinking and acting.[16] Estranged from

---

13   Reading Durkheim on the totem and mana is the best way to put Marx's analysis of the commodity as a value-bearing object within the larger conceptual framework of the sacred. Inversely, reading Marx's *Capital* is the best way to concretize Hegel's big logic and philosophy of Spirit.

14   "Science, as distinguished from philosophy, is also critical but its criticism is limited to what we may call matters of detail; as bare science or unphilosophical science it does not criticise its own principles and assumptions but accepts them as given, as determining the scope of its problems. It is thus not an entirely free inquiry, being conditioned by the limitations of the assumptions which it accepts as its starting-point" (Creighton 1925: 276).

15   "[F]rom the point of view of our position, if one is to call the distinctive property of the individual representational life *spirituality*, one should say that social life is defined by its *hyper-spirituality*" (Durkheim 1974: 34).

16   In modern philosophy "there is not a single ... proposition that commands universal assent in the field" (Lachs 2012: 14). One can go right down the rabbit hole with such thoughts. For example, is science *per se* even a social fact? It is impossible to conceive of modern civilization existing and functioning without science, but another person might contend that moral humanity emerged completely free of anything like science and, as such, humanity is independent of science. "No one really knew the slightest thing about atoms until only about a hundred years ago, and yet people got along perfectly well. Ferdinand Magellan circumnavigated the globe, William Shakespeare wrote some plays, J.S. Bach composed some cantatas, and Joan of Arc got herself burned at the stake, all for their own good (or bad) reasons, none of which, from their point of view, had the least thing to do with DNA, RNA, and proteins, or with carbon, oxygen, hydrogen, and nitrogen, or with photons, electrons, protons, and neutrons, let alone with quarks, gluons, W and Z bosons, gravitons, and Higgs particles" (Hofstadter 2007: 34). An automotive engineer needs science to design and build a car but how much science? They do not have to know anything about the quantum level, nor do they concern themselves with that which takes

philosophy and history, science has been reduced almost solely to a force of domination in the service of capital (PM: 142). Universities have been termed "knowledge factories" (Lachs 2012) but even this recrimination is overly generous. Our predecessors appear to be towering intellects and moral geniuses compared to our pathetic efforts merely because they did not willingly commit intellectual suicide through myopic hyper-specialization in the pursuit of money and other symbolic tokens.[17] Durkheim's sociology moves fluidly between ethnology, sociology, philosophy, and literature, and all his work was founded on an explicit philosophical and scientific base and can only be comprehended in its fullest sense if we are attuned to the various philosophical strands woven through his oeuvre.

3   Realism, Nominalism, Idealism, and Materialism

Sorting out the philosophical currents backgrounding Durkheim's sociology has proven elusive and contradictory. Durkheim has been miscast, variously, as a neo–Kantian (Gillian Rose), a neo–Platonist (Tarde, Worms and various critics, notably those that accused him of a jejune Realism), and a nominalist (Cassirer). For the sake of argument, let's posit the somewhat radical claim that Durkheim, more or less and in his own way, completed the Absolute Idealist project initiated by Hölderlin, Schelling, and Hegel. Given that a few articles have recently explored Durkheim's elective affinity with Hegel, perhaps the claim is not as outlandish as it might first appear.[18] What would this particular 'completion' mean, exactly?

The 'Tübingen Three' as they are sometimes known had in mind the creation of a new paradigm of thought past the deadlock of idealism and materialism.[19] Some new

---

place at the molecular level—the engine exists and is thought of at the "gross (thermodynamic) level" (Ibid: 41).

17   It is an interesting feature of the contemporary intellectual landscape that sociologist are no longer targets of right-wing attacks. The reason sociology is no longer part of the political landscape is that it represents absolutely no threat whatsoever to the right or even the centrist status quo. Sociology has no public role aside from credential dispensation for law enforcement and corrections personnel. Nor do sociologists aspire to the role of 'public intellectual' of the kind we had during the Fordist era. Who in their right mind today would embrace the label 'intellectual'? The last thing universities need, or want, are intellectuals. The term is one of derision reserved for dreamers unfit to grind out life as committee queens or grant-getters.

18   See Gangas (2007) for a schematic examination of the Hegel-Durkheim relationship.

19   On the unconscious lapses that lead idealism to pass into realism (materialism) and realism into idealism, see Bergson (1920). See also the comparison of Santayana's materialism with Royce's idealism (Lachs 2012: 143–81).

APPENDIX   165

'third way' out of the dualist impasse[20] was necessary to put thinking back on a firm foundation. A stab at this comes in the form of "The Earliest System–Program of German Idealism" where we find an original contribution: the mythology or, really, a quasi-religion of Reason (Hegel 2002: 111).[21] "Thus in the end enlightened and unenlightened must clasp hands, mythology must become philosophical in order to make the people rational, and philosophy must become mythological in order to make the philosophers sensible. Then eternal unity reigns among us" (Hegel 2002: 111).[22] This is not identical with a conservative plea for superstition of the kind we find in *Psyche's Task* (see Smith 1988).[23] The idea of a religion of reason is quite a twist to the status of reason in the preceding century where it was to be the "all-powerful substitute for religion, tradition, superstition, authority, custom, prejudice, oppression, in brief for whatever man happened to view as a galling harness" (Royce 1969: 301). Durkheim would not endorse a mythology or religion of reason *per se* but the idea of a *cult* of reason is not entirely out of line with his teaching if we do not take the idea too far.[24]

---

20   A 'third way' (admittedly, not a very good way of thinking about it) was sought well before Hegel and was likened to the metaphor of the bee in contrast to the ant and the spider: "The men of experiment are like the ant, they only collect and use; the reasoners resemble spiders, who make cobwebs out of their own substance. But the bee takes a middle course: it gathers its material from the flowers of the garden and of the field, but transforms and digests it by a power of its own" (Bacon 1872: 131). "What is more prosperous or wonderful than the Bee? And though they have not the same judgement of sense as other Bodies have, yet wherein hath Architecture gone beyond their building of Houses?" (Erasmus [1509] 1913: 66).
21   Myths attempt to substitute "a single factor for the plurality of causes" (Aron 1954: 97). Compare this sense of myth with Freud's definition of *Weltanschauung* (1965: 195).
22   Robert Musil's aim (and that of his main character, Ulrich, in *The Man Without Qualities*) is to arrive at a synthesis between strict scientific fact and the mystical, which he refers to as "the hovering life."
23   "As a body of false opinions, therefore, superstition is indeed a most dangerous guide in practice, and the evils which it has wrought are incalculable. But vast as are these evils, they ought not to blind us to the benefit which superstition has conferred on society by furnishing the ignorant, the weak, and the foolish with a motive, bad though it be, for good conduct. It is a reed, a broken reed, which has yet supported the steps of many a poor erring brother, who but for it might have stumbled and fallen. It is a light, a dim and wavering light, which, if it has lured many a mariner on the breakers, has yet guided some wanderers on life's troubled sea into a haven of rest and peace. Once the harbour lights are passed and the ship is in port, it matters little whether the pilot steered by a Jack-o'-lantern or by the stars. That, ladies and gentlemen, is my plea for Superstition" (Frazer 1913: vi).
24   For Hegel, philosophy was a cult of truth (1988: 194). Interestingly, Durkheim considers 'everything' to be religious and his most important work is on 'primitive' religion but, religion, church, state, and family are all in-themselves insufficient in binding people to life (S: 374–76). See also Hegel (1988: 379) where religion is the base and substance of politics. The only salvation in the modern world, for Durkheim, resides in the prospects of voca-

It might be that Durkheim did not explicitly make the case for a "religion of society" in the way Comte did for a "religion of humanity" but "he laid a foundation comparable to the one Comte had given to the religion of the future when he asserted that humanity, having killed transcendent gods, would love itself or at least would love what was best in itself under the name of humanity" (Aron 1967: 47). This potential for the self-conscious grasp of society that does not terminate in the profanation (and sociology as the institutional self-consciousness of companionship—bread-breakers—*logos*) was not lost on the *Collège de Sociologie* that did aim explicitly at a "sacred sociology" (Caillois 2003: 148–54; see also Richman 2002).

Some necessary background:

(a) Renaissance Humanism and the Protestant Reformation: roughly 1000 years of moral hegemony begins to melt. The traditional authority of the church no longer has the capacity to hold individuals or whole communities under its tutelage and anti–corruption reform movements spring up with regularity.

(b) Rationalism: Descartes was not a skeptic who doubts for the sake of doubting, rather, after receiving a what was considered a perfectly fine education he realizes that most of what he 'knows' is riddled with errors, unwarranted presuppositions, and prejudices. We are also routinely deceived by our senses and he comes to the disturbing conclusion that he can no more distinguish the "illusory" nature of dream life from waking "reality." He wonders if it is not possible that those 'people' we see over there are not really automata wearing coats and hats (1954: 73). Part of this is merely a methodological position rather than actual psychosis: "I decided to feign that everything that had entered my mind hitherto was no more true than the illusions of dreams" (1954: 31). One serious consequence of this doubt is that *the self becomes the measure of things* (1954: 9) and that the only guarantee of true knowledge is the existence of a god. In other words, without an absolute, we are doomed to egoism and simulated psychosis.[25]

(c) Germany:

> [T]he German mentality appears to be particularly inclined to [idealism] .... One notices even at the outset in Meister Eckhart (14th century), or Martin Luther, a tendency to intensify and develop inwardness of the subject.[26] Psychologically formulated, one would state that here was a decided preference for introversion in contrast to a primary receptiveness coherent with an external world. Goethe once said: 'Within ourselves there is also a universe.' The

---

tional association within the organic division of labor. But if we conceive of Religion as "a love of *Logos*" (Comte-Sponville 2007: 20) perhaps a 'religion of reason' is not ridiculous after all.

25 See the novella "A Chess Story" by Zweig ([1943] 2013) for "simulated schizophrenia."
26 On Christianity, self-obsessive inwardness and indifference toward the world see Durkheim (1977: 282–86).

I, self, consciousness is the creative center of the formed view of the world, of which the fact gives great emphasis to the effective, active, dynamic element. We need only think of Leibniz's theory which posits monads as monads–radiating–power (*Kraftmonade*), each one comprising a microcosm (Rintelen 1977: 2–3; cf. Durkheim 1977: 282–86).

(d) Pre-Kantian idealism (see Beiser 2002) falls under the heading of 'Empirical Idealism' that includes skeptical idealism or subjective idealism or 'problematic idealism' (e.g., Descartes who *doubts* the reality of the external world); dogmatic idealism or objective idealism (e.g., Leibniz and Berkeley that *deny* the reality of the external world); all forms of empirical idealism (skeptical and dogmatic) presuppose a transcendental realism whereby appearances are equivalent to things–in–themselves and whereby representations are private data of the mind used to construct the external world; transcendental realism is the philosophy that supports crude or naïve empiricism and positivistic sciences that assume that 'what you see is what you get.'

The importance of the German idealist revolution cannot be overstated. As Žižek says,

> Idealism [is] delimited by two dates: 1787, the year in which Kant's *Critique of Pure Reason* appeared, and 1831, the year of Hegel's death. These few decades represent a breathtaking concentration of the intensity of thinking: in this short span of time, more happened than in centuries or even millennia of the 'normal' development of human thought. All that took place before can and should be read in an unashamedly anachronistic way as the preparation for this explosion … (2012: 8).

Kant's project of transcendental (or formal) idealism is typically presented in terms of the "Transcendental Deduction" and represents a heroic but flawed attempt to surmount the one–sided aspects of earlier forms of idealism.[27] One aspect of Kant's formulation, however, the 'transcendental object,' would be preserved after his formal idealism was surmounted by those who followed: "To say that a whole is not reducible to its parts does not mean that the whole *exists* apart from its parts—it indeed exists only through them—but that its meaning or identity is more than the conjunction of its parts. In short, the irreducibility refers to its *essence*, not its *existence*.[28] Kant's

---

27 In Kantianism, 'transcendental' had specific meaning: "'I call transcendental all knowledge that concerns itself not with objects but with our way of knowing objects insofar as such knowledge is supposed to be possible a priori. A system of such concepts … would be called transcendental philosophy'" (in Kaufmann 1980: 94).

28 Meanings descend "*from the whole to the parts*" and, in turn, "meaning ascends from the part to the whole, the inductive element of value…. But in this continuous two-way traffic, the significance of the whole has the deciding voice. It can override many an irksome

conceptual shorthand for the conditions of objectivity is the *transcendental object*, and it is noteworthy that the transcendental object plays an important but implicit role in the Refutation of Idealism. The transcendental object works in the background to provide the necessary formal conditions for the experience of objects in space ..." (Beiser 2002: 120).[29] For example, we find in the neo-Hegelianism of Royce the irreducible quality of Liberty, for example, that is not individual in essence nor can it be found among a mere conglomerate of existing individuals. Liberty is a "cause, a certain superhuman unity of the ideal life of a free community" (1909: 329). Here, with *cause* and with the preceding emphasis upon the reciprocal nature of induction and deduction in Kant, we swing back to Durkheim's method in *Suicide* where his aetiology (literally 'causeology') directed at social circumstances deduces "the nature of effects" and constructs a classificatory outline from which morphological verification eliminates the construction of purely imagined objects (S: 147). In an earlier volume, I touched briefly on the loss of the concept of social causes along with the desire among social scientists to flush society itself from the scientific lexicon.[30] The search for *causes* is one

---

detail, whereas without it detailed triumphs lose their charm. The worth of living must indeed have its moment-by-moment verification—total and distant objectives are not enough—but if one lives determinedly in the present in order to forget that there *is no ultimate objective*, the nerve is cut" (Hocking 1956: 23).

29 As far as Freud was concerned, the 'transcendental' was merely the unconscious projected into the outer world and shared a connection with myths (1951: 145).

30 The clumsy and mechanical sense of *cause and effect* is inadequate to sociology where we need to see that causes are powers that bind together individuals into membership within a society (Royce 1909: 307). We are dumbfounded at the loyalty of tens of millions of Americans to a ridiculous and tyrannical buffoon, yet we are employed in the same academic discipline that has given up on explaining causes and social circumstances. It is more convenient to take the moral temperature of individuals in an experimental cohort and cash in on the 'findings' rather than try and comprehend the underlying social forces and dynamics that led millions of Americans to commit political suicide all the way to the bitter end with nothing to show but a sporting enthusiasm sustained by a lack of judges and a scoreboard. One need only to read Durkheim's *Germany Above All* to know exactly what the inevitable outcome of the Trump administration was always going to be. This inevitability is a mystery to contemporary sociology that has reduced itself to a bad impersonation of psychology. "How paradoxical a world, then, must the real world be, if the faith of the loyal is indeed well founded! A spiritual unity of life, which transcends the individual experience of any man, must be real. For loyalty, as we have seen, is a service of causes that, from the human point of view, appear superpersonal" (Royce 1909: 309). Rather than measuring the attitudes of individual supporters of such and such politician, truth is better served by explaining the loyalty of individuals to a cause rooted in social forces and circumstances. I think it would be a better use of time and energy to discover how and why a group consisting of a multitude of opinions and loyalties can be made to support a champion that is a rather bad mirror of their own social aspirations. If, for example, a Nazi sympathizer in the US can be made to march off to kill actual Nazis in Europe, and even die for a cause he is not sympathetic to at the level of personal psychology,

dedicated to a depth analysis alien to empirical positivism (empiricism relegates itself to the dry and barren surface of variables). We have all been correctly trained to disregard and reject any notion of 'transcendentalism' but rather than attempting a more sophisticated grasp of the synthetic or social *apriori* we have not only cashed in facts, causes, and reason but unwittingly embraced a form of crypto-theological noumenalism.

In Durkheim's sociology the 'transcendental object' is society itself or, really, *species* of societies (RSM: 92).[31] As an emergent, *sui generis* whole, the product of human assemblage is greater than, and different than the sum of its parts. The transformed and transforming product of assemblage is not a phantom of statistical error, e.g., "Simpson's paradox" (the averaging of averages that fails to account for a confounding or lurking variable) whereby, say, drug X outperforms a placebo except that, examined empirically, the placebo outperforms drug X amongst the actual participants in a clinical trial (Yates 2019: 91); nor is the assemblage product simply the result of shenanigans, e.g., the American people voted for X but Y won the election. Absolute facts and representations (hyper-cathected) are different in nature than the ideas of the individual understanding. Moreover, the representations and logic of mediating institutions differ from those operating at the individual and universal scales of life.

Subjects do not enjoy a direct or immediate relationship to the totality of life such that representations mirror or copy the world in an undistorted fashion; representations are not just a shadowy play of images[32] (DOL: 53; see also Jones [2000] 2006: 38). Instead, subjectivity is mediated[33] by particularities such that mutual recognition in the moments of the relative ego and particular equivalent spontaneously generate the 'transcendental' object (not Žižek's big Other of fantasy but another Other) that imparts subjectivity, identity, and objective validity to the generative members: the 'I' knows itself in the concrete form of the different other and together the I–Thou relation generates the objective We (ourselves in a distorted, ideological, inverted reflection). At first it comes and goes and, later, it wears out its welcome (C: 183).

---

that would be worth knowing. Knowing what can cause a non-racist to support a racist cause might provide insight in how to get racists to support non-racist or anti-racist causes.

31 'Species' or 'kind' is the appropriate translation of Plato's 'Idea' qua 'universal' (Hegel [1840] 1995a: 29).

32 Though, every representation is an image in a sense (Kant 1998: 3).

33 Epistemologically, "All knowledge of experience is mediated, and it is mediated through the terms and conditions of representations" (Jones [2000] 2006: 40). In fact, the 'immediate' is itself a product of mediated thought (see Bowie 2003: 90). The world is, for us, a system of mediated and mediating representations. "'To try to peel off signs [and] get down to the real thing is like trying to peel and onion and get down to [the] onion itself...'" (C.S. Peirce, quoted in Brent 1998: 301).

The Transcendental Deduction: under what conditions can *we* (not just I) have experiences (experience being the synthesis of intuition and concept via the creative capacity of the imagination) and what regulates *our* ability to 'think straight' (reason) or make valid and right judgments? How can we deduce[34] the binding, normative categories of thought? The 'transcendental' shifts the terms of the debate beyond dyadic structures like subjects and objects, mental and physical, etc. What are the rules for correct judgments that are accurate vis-à-vis the domain of things-in-themselves? How do we bridge the gulf between the noumenal and the phenomenal realms? How can my judgment *here* be justified *there*? Kant's 'transcendental deduction' lays the groundwork for 'identity philosophy' and theory of identity-in-difference (Pippen 1989). In other words, Kant charts a new synthesis of realism and idealism arriving at *empirical realism*.

Kant regretted the label 'transcendental philosophy' and finally arrived at his 'critical philosophy' that represents an attempt to reconcile the long-running debate between the realist and idealist camps: "Either the subject is the cause of the object (idealism) or the object is the cause of the subject (realism)" (Beiser 2002: 433). According to Schelling, "If the object determines the subject, there will be no knowledge of the object in itself, because then the subject will know the object only insofar as the object affects it; it will see the effects of the object's activity but not the object in itself. If, conversely, the subject determines the object, then the subject will know the object only insofar as it affects the object, or only insofar as it makes the object conform to the conditions of its knowing; but insofar as the subject does not affect the object, it remains an unknowable thing-in-itself" (Beiser 2002: 590).[35]

Kant's accomplishments include defending the dynamic and projective mind against the onslaught of the British empiricists (Hume) where the mind is reduced to

---

34 "Kant's use of the term 'deduction' had more in common with legal usage of the term than with the purely logical.... [A] 'deduction' of the categories was intended to demonstrate their normativity, their bindingness on us as we make judgments about the world (just as an eighteenth-century legal 'deduction' was to demonstrate the binding quality of a legal principle in a set of cases)" (Pinkard 2002: 100–01).

35 "Idealist: *Die Phantasie in meinem Sinn / Ist dismal gar zu herrisch. / Fürwahr, wenn ich das alles bin, / So bin ich heute närrisch.* Realist: *Das Wesen ist mir recht zur Qual / Und muß mich baß verdrießen; / Ich stehe hier zum ersten Mal / Nicht fest auf meinen Füßen.*" This quote is from the "Walpurgis Night's Dream" section of Goethe's *Faust*. Kaufmann's translation is the sprightliest: "Idealist: Imagination is in me / Today far too despotic. / If I am everything I see, / Then I must be idiotic. Realist: The spirits' element is vexing / I wish it weren't there; / I never saw what's so perplexing / It drives me to despair" (Goethe 1961: 395, 397). The Arndt translation is also revelatory: "Idealist: This once by fantasy, my bliss, / I feel too harshly saddled; / Forsooth, if I am all of this / Today I must be addled. Realist: I find their doings hard to stand / I never was a squirmer; / For once I have two feet on sand / Instead of *terra firma*" (Goethe 1976: 108).

a passive receptor of sense data sorted out by transcendental (*a priori*) categories. Kant's limitations: he worked in an intellectual environment that did not yet have a clear distinction between natural and social sciences and this confusion contributes to the installation of an inaccessible counter-world and misplaces the ground of collective norms. Kant's brilliant but flawed attempt to find the moorings of objectively valid moral judgments was taken up by various disciples and critics and made possible later developments such as Hegel's 'speculative' idealism (Pippen 1989: 6).

4   Representations

Karl Leonhard Reinhold was, for a time, the most famous Kantian professor in Germany. Mostly forgotten today, Reinhold's importance at the time cannot be overemphasized. He was the "official interpreter" of Kantian critical philosophy for a good long while (Roehr 1995: 134), a wildly popular teacher, and, according to Hegel, an "honest seeker" (1984: 499). "Where Kant has sensibility and understanding as the two different stems of human knowledge, Reinhold starts from their common root, representation in general, which precedes all consciousness. From a single high principle, the proposition of consciousness, he wants to construct 'the entire theory of representations, knowledge, and also reason, and ultimately even of desire and volition.' His theory of self-consciousness ... was the first one that set out to explain the problem of 'self-relatedness in self-consciousness'" (Roehr 1995: 138–39). Reinhold's whole approach to presenting Kant was to focus on the processes of *representation* (Reinhold [1791] 2000: 56ff.). Representations became the first principle, elemental, the foundation for all philosophy (see Pinkard 2002) and Reinhold was important for popularizing 'representations' for European philosophers.[36]

> Renouvier, the 'great master' who was Durkheim's 'educator,' was the first French philosopher to recognize the scientific importance of Kant. He acknowledged that Kant had moved the question of reality beyond empiricism, materialism, positivism, idealism and realism. Kant had established representation as being central to a logic of reality and of science, and thus had shown that it is part of critical scientific thinking. 'Kant ... is the greatest philosopher ... whose work must be the point of departure for all questions of certainty and method'.... For

---

36   "It is believed that the philosophical usage of the word goes back to Leibniz (who complemented the traditional meaning *se représenter* = *imaginer* with *représentation* = *correspondence*). The French term was translated by Wolff as *Vorstellung* and the two terms were considered as equivalent" (Nemedi [2000] 2006: 88–89). For a brief history of the concept of representations in Europe and how it pertains to Durkheim, and sociology more generally, see Meštrović (1988: 46–50).

> Renouvier, what rationalism had delivered, which is 'incontestable,' 'is the methodic reduction of all direct knowledge (*connaissance*) to ways of thinking or as we say today to representations' (Jones [2000] 2006: 39–40).

Setting aside nuances in meaning, the German way of thinking of representations or *Vorstellung* "refers to the content of experience; *Vorstellung* are units of activity instead of static entities …. *Vorstellungen* form a large domain of experiential content and are not exclusively limited to images, concepts or ideas. *All* of these are *Vorstellungen*, as are memories, sensations and perceptions, to name but a few…" (Verheggen 1996: 193). However, Reinhold's 'elemental philosophy' (vis-à-vis representations) remains subjectivist. Reinhold's *Elementarphilosophie* posited *Vorstellung* and the representational nature of consciousness as the basic, irreducible feature of human thought where we find "a subject, an object, a representation of the object, and the subject ascribing the representation to itself as a subjective state of itself, while at the same time taking that subjective state of itself to be a representation of an object different from and independent of that state" (Pinkard 2002: 100). For this reason, Hegel says that representation "belongs to another sphere from knowledge of the Absolute" (1984: 499).

> Reinhold was … convinced, like Descartes, that he had to find a principle that was so absolutely *certain* that even the skeptic could not deny it. Reinhold thus offered a way of interpreting Kant to which people have time and time returned (often without knowing how Reinhold paved the way): the normative force of the Kantian categories—their character in determining how we ought to judge things or 'must' judge them if we are to make any sense at all—had to be derived from some basic, itself non-derivable *fact*, and the issue has remained how any such fact could serve as the basis for normative claims in general.[37]
>
> From the 'principle of consciousness' (understood as an undeniable fact of consciousness) and from the conclusion that 'representation' was the most basic category of any theory of consciousness, Reinhold concluded that an *Elementarphilosophie* must therefore be a general, a priori theory of our human *capacities* (or 'faculties,' *Vermögen*) for representation … (Pinkard 2002: 101).

---

[37] We can view *Forms* as Durkheim's solution to the riddle of the normative force of Kant's categories of the understanding. They are *collective* representations (not just individual representations of the understanding) and arise not from ordinary praxis but ceremonial assemblages.

5   The Post-Kantians

Fichte abandons the 'thing–in–itself' and carves out a place within Kant's mature thought: critical idealism as the fusion of idealism and realism (idealistic realism or realistic idealism), i.e., *pragmatic* idealism. Activity is the key here. Fichte asks good questions like 'why are we normative at all?' and recognizes that 'god' is just a distorted personification of the 'moral order.' Fichte's strength and simultaneous weakness is that the subject–object distinction is, for him, subjectively established (Pinkard 2002: 108–21). The entire philosophical complex from Kant to Fichte was hobbled by 'subjectivism'—i.e., the transcendental other is a *subject* that imparts upon us our *objectivity*. It will be up to those who follow to transform the subjectivist models of Kant and Fichte and put subjectivity and objectivity on a new ground. The next big step in the evolution of idealism came in the form of 'absolute' and romantic currents.

Perhaps the major contribution of the Romantic school was disconnecting virtue from sacrifice: virtue comes in the form of love not self–negation (Pinkard 2002: 169). In Novalis, e.g., love unites individuals without the eclipse of either (Pinkard 2002: 144) or, at worst, the debasing of the self is compensated by moral elevation (see Beiser 2002: 434). In other words, what we *do not* find in romantic idealism is the dreary world of capitalist exploitation where the sum total of repressed remainders is greater than the value of labor power.

Friedrich Hölderlin was a friend and schoolmate to Schelling and Hegel; his big contribution is *Hyperion*. Hölderlin provides four bold moves beyond his predecessors:

(a) deny the assertion that subject–object identity consists in the ego alone—theory of being as the unity of action and thought, intuition and concept;
(b) the absolute does not just regulate but also *constitutes* being;
(c) we *can* know the absolute;
(d) nature is not just a projection but also not an obstacle for the will—nature is autonomous and living and rational (Beiser 2002: 375).

Novalis (Friedrich von Hardenberg) makes an indirect contribution to the social or moral sciences that cannot be overstated even though he has been virtually neglected by contemporary social theorists. His brand of idealism is known as "magical idealism" that hinges on the problem of alienation and self–alienation. For Novalis, the I, in order to form a unity with others, to love and be loved, hinges on the necessity for division or splitting as the means for doubling the self. This act of dividing and multiplying the self is central to, e.g., Simmel's theory of the person and runs through much of his sometimes-brilliant *Philosophy of Money*. The self must be alienated as a precondition for giving itself to another person. Of course, this self–alienation runs aground when the alienation of the self is the precondition not only for love of the other but for the reduction of the living personality to the status of a commodity (a quantum of labor power).[38]

Magical idealism: Novalis seems to have understood the essence of magic: the art of *being in two places at once*, for a doubled existence,[39] and, most importantly, *the retention of control over our doubled existence*—being in control over both internal and external senses (Beiser 2002: 422; see Mauss 1972).[40] The absolute is sacred; the absolute is a unity of subjectivity and objectivity; the absolute is *hypostatic* (objectively real). Not only is it objectively real but even pleasures itself in autonomous free play (EFR: 426); the absolute possesses an "autonomy of fancy" and creates its own aesthetic (Croce 1917: 8) that satisfies only itself and without reference to underlying social mechanisms. "The eternal Idea, the Idea that is in and for itself, eternally remains active, engenders and enjoys itself as absolute mind" (Hegel 2007: 276).

For myself, one of the most amazing implications of 'magical idealism' in particular and absolute idealism in general is (a) the control over our doubles and (b) the rational coordination of multiple perspectives, and their upward cancellation (sublation) into 'higher' or more holistic and comprehensive 'viewpoints.' A good sociologist should be like a 'magician'—one who multiplies their *analytic* viewpoints (dialectical splitting) and can rationally *synthesize* a multiplicity of perspectives under the *concept*.[41] This does not amount to eclecticism nor does this amount to running from one perspective to another trying to encircle 'the thing' and the totality of determinations (SL: 530) and it is also not directly the upward cancellation of all one-sided perspectives toward one 'absolute' *perspective* (some kind of special leftover that survives a cognitive death struggle).[42] *It actually has little to do with 'perspectives' per se*. For example, Marx's goal

---

38   It is disheartening to think that humanity seems forever doomed to fetishism, alienation, servitude, and condemned to merely repeating, unending, the mistakes of the past. It has been a long-standing opinion among intellectuals that the notion of progress is a myth. Yet, the passage out of the condition of unfreedom itself rests on unfreedom as its precondition. One cannot liberate oneself from commodity fetishism, for example, when one stands outside of the affliction—it has to be passed through. To be free one has to first be unfree.

39   When the CIA needed to develop new techniques for the impersonal transfer of information in Moscow between individuals separated by space and time they turned to stage magicians to literally write the book (Mendez and Mendez 2019).

40   "Putting the belief in miracles to one side for a moment it seems that the first miracles arose because [Berlin chief of police] Stieber compressed into *one* day ... a whole series of events that were in reality spread over a long period of time, while the latter miracles arose when he claimed of different events that happened in one place and on one evening that they occurred in two places on two evenings" (MECW, 11: 410). Cf. Marx on the "act of seeing" (C: 165).

41   On the politics of 'facts' and the logic of magic see Feldmann (2019).

42   For Hocking perspectivalism is the epitome of society (1926: 343) but it ends in relativism—even with a rank ordering per Nietzsche. Absolute sociology does not end in perspectivalism or a view from the summit unavailable to other, one-sided perspectives.

APPENDIX   175

in *Capital* is not really the critique of political economy in itself or for the sake of political economy but the rational comprehension of the commodity as a social fact; the critique of political economy is the dead wood that has to be burned away before the commodity can be confronted sociologically. Visualized along a winding ideal-typical path, political economy is an early modern intertwining and fusion of premodern currents of reflection and praxis, as portrayed imperfectly in the figure below:

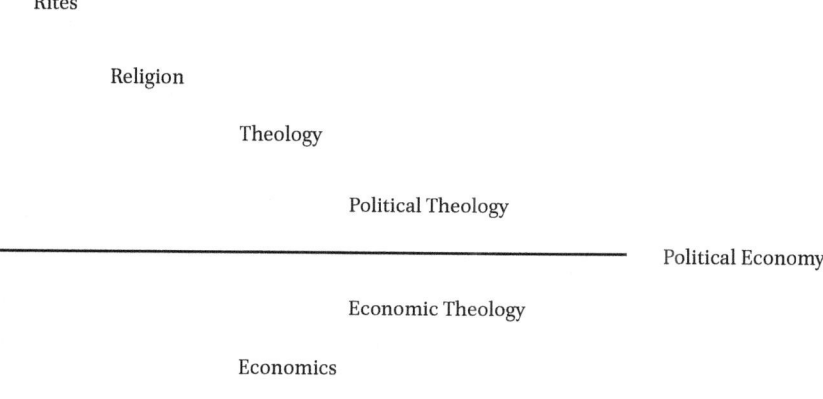

FIGURE A   The spiral of political economy
            SOURCE: CREATED BY AUTHOR

The notion of an 'absolute' *viewpoint* sounds a bit presumptuous, especially in today's relativistic and pragmatic environment. But Marx and Durkheim both produce 'absolute' conceptualizations of their respective sociological problems. The 'absolute' is not a higher, god's-eye *view* unavailable to other 'lower' or one-sided *perspectives* nor is it an empirical thing like individuals and matter. Like exchange-value, the absolute is a concept or a principle that things have in common, yet none possess individually (Hegel 1988: 455). The absolute is what religion, philosophy, science, literature, and art have in common (Boutmy 1902: 264) yet none of them are, or possess, the absolute.[43]

---

43   Why are 'the economy' and 'politics' excluded? The 'state' has the capacity to function for the absolute (when it is not working against it) but in America, capital and politics are dominated by the pursuit of surplus value and campaign contributions, and, as such, are antithetical to the general wellbeing of society—one cannot serve two masters. 'Capitalist society' is a misnomer such that the predicate actually negates and excludes the subject. America is a granular battlefield of practically infinite personal and group interests such that representatives are no longer chosen by 'their' constituents but, rather,

Coincidentally, this fundamental insight also applies to the materials and processes of dreamwork (Freud [1901] 1952: 28–29).[44] Scientifically, the absolute (not really a 'gaze' or as limited as a 'viewpoint' or even a 'perspective') is the rational product of the dialectical method that entails dissection, analysis, and synthesis. Social facts are encumbered in preexisting, irrational or one-sided explanations: common sense, popular superstitions, mysticism, nominalism, and naïvely realistic interpretive frames abound and are useful in ensuring the continued survival of the thing, whatever it is, as a reified and enigmatic power over hapless individuals.[45] Marx provides readers with a map (the concept) for escaping the prison of surplus labor. The problem is that most people do not want the concept, preferring instead, to stay in their familiar jail cells.[46]

---

politicians pick their voters through gerrymandering, dirty tricks, and hyper-concentrated corporate wealth. On the surface, American politics appears to be a death struggle between parties representing overlapping and sometimes competing but not mutually exclusive modalities of capital accumulation and the mobilization of hyper-differentiated victim bases, but, at the end of the day, the show is mostly theater: for example, one of the top donors to both the Trump and Clinton campaigns was Renaissance Technologies, the automated high-frequency trading hedge fund. Hedge funds and high-frequency traders fear proposals for the taxation of buying and selling of equities and derivatives (thanks to Dan Krier for this point) so they work both sides of the street to better ensure uninhibited accumulation. Regardless of whether Trump or Clinton wins the election, 'we' lose, RenTech continues to reap a windfall, and the public is distracted by walls, fences, and barriers, and is compensated by televised inquisitions and carefully cultivating the ever-expanding garden of grievance fruit.

44 Both the modern value form and the dream form are rooted in social organization. Nothing like this is possible in the world of matter. For example, apricots and whisky have no flavors in common but they both share flavors with tomatoes. The tomato functions as the "bridge" that links whisky to the apricot but they both actually possess something of that bridge in themselves (Simas et al. 2017). In the domain of value, the third is a projection. Nonetheless, we should be able to discern how the reflective organization of flavors is itself modelled on the commodity exchange process. In other words, *only a particular species of social organization can give rise to the unity of apricot and whisky.*

45 "Nowadays we are not supposed to write about global subjects like magic.... [and] things like totemism and magic do not exist. They are just 'constructs,' words we make up. We cannot talk about caste systems, totemism, magic, anxiety and so forth, and so we are helpless when we bump into these harsh realities" (O'Keefe 1982: xvii). Notice how nominalism (and this applies to other forms of chic academic reductions) creates a taboo on concepts and leaves us in a state of ignorance. If O'Keefe had held on a little longer he would have been amazed at magic's comeback.

46 At SUNY Cortland I joked with my students that they would soon be returning their copy of *Capital* to the university bookstore in exchange for just enough money to buy a can of cheap domestic swill down at "The Brain Drain." They almost all agreed that doing so was stupid, but they had reconciled themselves to stupidity. Beer is (negative) freedom, after all.

The known devil of negative freedom is preferable to the mysteries of positive freedom. Where Spirit has failed (or refuses) to work itself up to the *concrete* absolute, personifications and inversions are practically true: "He was in the world, and the world came into being through him; yet the world did not know him" (John 1:10). Abstract negations are necessary in the advancement toward the absolute.

6   Split Reasoning

Durkheim likes to clear the brush before embarking upon his own analyses whereas Marx dives right in by examining the commodity in abstraction, liquidating his competition along the way. Once fruitless explanations are negated the social fact is dissected (e.g., the sacred is separated from the profane; exchange-value is separated from use-value, etc.) and the thing is analyzed such that the social or moral aspects are liberated from extraneous entanglements: for example, the commodity appears to be a mysterious thing confronting the bewildered subject but what is essential is not located in the body of the commodity nor the signifier on the commodity (the price tag) but the exchange *relation* between property owners veiled behind the material shells of their goods circulating in the marketplace. The moment of 'dissection' or analysis deserves a bit more clarification since this is where the notion of an 'overview' is actually permissible not as a result but as an aspect of the analytic process: dissection (the separation of the material from the immaterial, for example) is a kind of panoramic effect.

'Panorama' comes from the Greek *pan* (all) and *horama* (view). When we divide an image and transpose its parts to the left and right we have 'panned' the bits and pieces—it is also interesting that the word 'pan' is slang for *criticism* as when a film is *panned* by its reviewer (i.e., torn to shreds). Now what? We already have the negation of one-sided explanations—they are negated because they cannot stand to reason; the fact (suicide rate, commodity exchange, totem worship, etc.) is then negated; what remains is the negation of the negation or the rational reconstruction of the fact into a new scientific representation (the 'result'). Note carefully that we have intimated the shift or transposition of the collective representation to the domain of scientific representation, or, really, the restoration of the abstract concept to the rational ground of the science of the concept. That which perishes in dichotomy is raised again in absolute identity (Hegel [1801] 1977: 195). Like all representations the synthetic absolute is a kind of objective "mirage" (Durkheim) or "real abstraction" (Marx) but the resulting product is scientific and rational (*the logos of the thing has been discovered to lie in the previously-hidden social relations of production and exchange*) and, no longer guarded by mystics and reductionists, it reveals its truth and can have its validity as a moral supremacy challenged.[47] The *thing* is brought up to the status of a comprehensible *object* (objectified human praxis) via the rational power of the critical representation. The *thing* has been deprived of its charisma (belief has been withdrawn) but as an object of praxis (teleological activity, itself a syllogism) it still retains a quantum of *jazz* and a capacity to provide enjoyment of a moral surplus.[48] In the first volume I criticized Marx's excursus at the end of *Capital* because it reads like a eulogy at the revolution's funeral, in other words, it gives back too much power to the commodity that was eliminated during the excruciatingly long analysis. Yet, at the same time, the *Resultate* does stand as a perfect example of an absolute conceptualization, a transparent and rational representation that emerges from the analyzed elements. The irony, of course, is that in the age of relativity the absolute is not actually missing but staring us in the face at all times. The necessity of the absolute leaves only two possibilities: on the one hand, we can have unenjoyable bondage to a mystified and terrifying bad absolute, or, on the other hand, we can have enjoyable sacrifice, rational self-repression, even partial death in the name of something that is greater than, and different than, the sum total of everything perceived. We now come to *irony* as a method as we continue our excursion through German idealism.

Friedrich Schlegel: Irony: a stance toward alienation and estrangement; we are multiple but driven toward subjective unity achieved by adopting an ironic attitude toward the world (Pinkard 2002: 163). Socrates was his model for irony. The absolute realizes itself in history through human activity. Dialectical and non–linear development is emphasized. Schlegel criticized Fichte for establishing the "'ideality of the real' but not 'the reality of the ideal'" (Beiser 2002: 440). Schlegel developed a transcendental realism without the thing–in–itself: "it postulates the existence of a single reality within nature, which is both subjective and objective, ideal and real, because it manifests itself equally in both" (Beiser 2002: 442). His main contribution, for us, is his theory of *polarity* and polar opposites, indifference points, and that the ideal and the real, the subjective and the objective, are merely different degrees of organization and development of energy, and that we create things like god (moral objects) out of our own activities (see Beiser 2002: 459, 461). The connections between Schlegel and thinkers like Feuerbach and Durkheim are evident here. Critique of thought prior to inquiry and action but also *during* inquiry and action is of paramount importance; we should strive for systematic thought (philosophical systems were *de rigueur* in the 19th

---

47 Morality is not just the rules of conduct but also the reasons for those rules and the rational foundation for conduct (Bray 1863: 86).

48 "'I was never ... able to see the point of the Holy Ghost. He has always seemed to me to be a bit redundant.' 'We were not satisfied with two bottles, were we? That half bottle gave us the extra spark of life we both needed. We wouldn't have been so happy without it. Perhaps we wouldn't have had the courage to continue our journey. Even our friendship might have ceased without the Holy Spirit'" (Greene 1982: 50).

century) but we should also be wary of the pitfalls generally concomitant with systems; the main problem with Schlegel is that truth remains inaccessible and the ironic stance can lead to skepticism (a route back into empirical idealism).

Schelling: Identity philosophy (the famous A=A, the "night in which all cows are black," that Hegel criticizes in his *Phenomenology*); idealism is transformed into a higher realism. Transcendental philosophy is driven by the breach of human self-consciousness in nature. Concepts of subject and object are relative to an absolute; nature is a system of forces that self–organizes—this is a non–vitalistic purposiveness without a purpose; self–organizing nature creates an interiority for itself—this is the rupture of self–consciousness. (One might make the argument from this angle that nature became self-aware when *Homo sapiens* began to ritualize and become self-reflective—i.e., became moral humans—about 50,000 BCE or, in other words, that nature became self-aware in the form of our species): "A strange mystery it is that Nature, omnipotent but blind, in the revolutions of her secular hurryings through the abysses of space, has brought forth at last a child, subject still to her power, but gifted with sight, with knowledge of good and evil, with the capacity of judging all the works of his unthinking Mother" (Bertrand Russell, in Harrison 1962: 534).[49]

In the final analysis, for Schelling (Beiser 2002: 590) it is not enough for subjects to be self–conscious but that the absolute must come to know itself; it is the task of sociology to make collective consciousness reflective and conceptually integrated. Society must come to rationally comprehend itself as society and for individuals to love society and enjoy happy and creative lives, or, at least, have a meaning for their suffering. For Durkheim, like Hegel before him, it was not merely the case of either the object determining the subject or the subject determining the object, but subjects and objects being determined by another subject-substance operating behind the backs of individuals.[50] In the first volume, following Durkheim's lead, I bent over backwards to

---

49 Said Renan, "'I made the mistake of attributing too positively to mankind a central part in the universe. The development of humanity may possibly be of no more consequence than the moss or lichen growing over a damp surface. But still, in our eyes, the history of mankind preserves its supremacy, since mankind alone, for all we know, constitutes the consciousness of the universe. And even though life should disappear from our small planet before mankind has attained to the full consciousness which is its supreme aim, the attempt baffled here would succeed elsewhere, and the effort toward the realization of God would not be lost'" (in Levy-Bruhl 1899: 416).

50 This substance is not identical with Spinoza's; Spinoza's concept of 'substance' "is simply real being. It is, by definition and demonstration, infinitely perfect as well as infinite and unique in its kind; that is, it is not limited by any other substance of the same nature. It is also causally independent of anything outside of itself: substance exists necessarily, not contingently" (Nadler 1999: 187). We know Freud as the arch-theorist of the unconscious realm but even he may have underappreciated the depth and expanse of what lies below consciousness (LeDoux 2019: 271).

stress the plurality of collective consciousnesses and that, most importantly, we need to think in terms of a collective unconsciousnesses (see the octagonal matrix of psychologies) if we want to get down to the real problems facing sociology.[51] However, Durkheim continues to refer exclusively not to collective consciousnesses (in the plural) but to a single collective consciousness and this is because he is aware that the dialectical moment of a plurality of collective consciousnesses occupies the logical coordinates of institutional particularities: e.g., each profession has its own ethic, etc. But from the standpoint of the universal, there is only one collective consciousness: like our 'immortal coil' it is the same here and there, now and then. Behind the manifold of causes and forces there is always a general or single cause (S: 169, 208–09). This cause is "the law of the real" (Croce 1917: 21). We are justified in searching for a 'planetary' force, a "single organism, as it were" (S: 322),[52] behind the spectacle of self-destruction.[53] In *Suicide* this negative absolute force is encapsulated by the concept of *disintegration*. 'Integrate' derives from the Latin *integer* for 'whole.' Social integration means combining elements to form a vibrant totality and an integrated society is one characterized by integrity. An integrated society is self-controlling and variably self-conscious.

---

51   For Durkheim, the psyche possesses "profound depths inaccessible to ordinary perception, to which we attain only gradually by devious and complicated paths ..." (S: 311). The same is true of the 'collective psyche' if we want to use such a phrase. Psychology is important, there is no doubt, but remember that the individual is just an abstraction that is not sociology's problem. The 'laws' of psychology and sociology (social or collective psychology) are different (S: 312) even though a distinct line separating the individual and the "social realm" is lacking (S: 313).

52   Recall that Durkheim's 'organicism' is not of the ordinary type but refers to an organicism of concepts, emotions, sentiments, and signs (1978: 94). Society is a force (EFRL: 227) and forces are collective ideas clothed in symbols. The cutting edge of neuropsychological research into the function of concepts in perception and emotion is catching up to, but still trailing, Durkheim's basic insight (e.g., Barrett 2017). What we know as reality is the product of a constellation of ordinary (mundane) and extraordinary (moral) concepts created by society. Barrett is correct that concepts are constructed but where this theory (decades old in sociology) falls short is in how not all concepts are created equal and how some are relatively free and amenable to modifications and new combinations whereas others are sacred and relatively fixed. This emphasis on the sacred goes beyond merely "ontological objectivity" and the autonomy of the concept. Barrett's work lends support to subjectivist, interactionist, and pragmatic strains of thought but falls short of augmenting *social* theory.

53   "Since the handful of people who kill themselves annually do not form a natural group, and are not in communication with one another, the stable number of suicides can only be due to the influence of a common cause which dominates and survives the individual persons involved. The force uniting the conglomerate multitude of individual cases, scattered over the face of the earth, must necessarily be external to each of them" (S: 313). Notice that Durkheim refers not to causes and forces but to a cause and a force. In *Suicide* we find a number of different causes and forces determining the classification of suicidal types, however, behind the appearance of different causes and forces lies a common force (refer to the "Formal Intermezzo" in *The Sociogony*).

This absolute consciousness is something we find linking Durkheim to Hegel and Marx. For sure, Hegel refers to 'spirits' however 'spirits' pertain to sequences and recollections of Spirit. There is one Spirit and many spiritual forms (DOL: 284), e.g., Marx's phenomenology of the value forms in the first chapter of *Capital* or the infinite extensions of mana, the *Urkraft*, across the millennia (EFRL: 190–206). In Hegel's *Phenomenology*, the educational journey (*Bildungsroman*) of the concept culminates in the triumph of reason; for Marx, it is communist revolution; for Durkheim, the flourishing of human society is dependent upon intense moral education, the cult of reason, incorporation, professional ethics, and the spread of an organic division of labor.[54]

Much of the language of forces, equilibrium, polarities, dynamism, development, and so on, we find percolating in Schelling. Hegel appears at first to be a mere disciple but his absolute idealism takes a dramatic turn that has a tremendous effect on what will become the moral or social sciences.

G.W.F. Hegel: for Spirit to be free it must know that it makes its own laws and how to make them for itself. For the first time what was merely half–baked or implied, here and there, becomes the central idea, namely, that the absolute is *Geist* (Spirit or consciousness of consciousness) and *Geist* is operative in a social space-time.

> Hegel was the first philosopher to take time and finitude as seriously as any Hobbesian materialist, while at the same time taking the religious impulse as seriously as any Hebrew prophet or Christian saint. Spinoza had attempted such a synthesis by identifying God with Nature, but Spinoza still thought it desirable to see things under the aspect of eternity. Hegel rejoined that any view of human history under that aspect would be too thin and abstract to be of any religious use. He suggested that the meaning of human life is a function of how human history turns out, rather than of the relation of that history to something ahistorical. This suggestion made it easier for two of Hegel's readers, Dewey and Whitman, to claim that the way to think about the significance of the human adventure is to look forward rather than upward: to contrast a possible human future with the human past and present (Rorty 1998: 19).

In Hegel's philosophy of religion, like Durkheim's, god is brought down to earth and comprehended as a representation of society itself.[55] The self–development of Spirit is not through labor alone but in raising consciousness to the level of science (the path

---

54 In all the major classical theorists we find "dregs," the "rabble," and the "remainders" that are beyond hope. Only Marx possessed a vision of a redeemable strata of brutalized humanity.

55 Jones (1998) says that Durkheim breaks with his philosophical predecessors over the primacy of religion but this would not apply to Hegel, for whom religion is the ground and substance of Spirit's self-development. Both Durkheim and Hegel insist on the "autonomy of reason" but reason was born in religion. One of Durkheim's great achievements was

to freedom was through the dialectical unfolding of thought from base sense–certainty to the most refined and sublime forms of consciousness).[56] The bridge between Hegel and Durkheim is the status of the absolute as the unity and ground of the totality of inner essence and reflective outer being (SL: 530; S: 336–37). In the *Paris Manuscripts*, Marx says that our species being, our universality and consciousness of "essential being," is achieved through mundane or "practical activity" (PM: 113) but this is assertion is unsatisfactory. Even when it is pushed to the extremes of hyper-production the leap from the real and universal reflection does not open the way to the domain of the hyper-spiritual, in fact, for Marx, hyper-production leads in the opposite direction: dehumanization, cretinism, and brutality. The expenditure of labor power does not lead to morality (cf. Rousseau [1762] 1968: 52). Only under peculiar historical circumstances, where profane labor has been transformed into an ascetic and sacred form of conduct approved by god, can hyper-production pass from the real into the hologram of divine forces.

The crude materialism of the young Marx would have seemed vulgar and naïve to Hegel;[57] nobody elevates the mind through brute toiling. Indeed, Puritans plagued by the doctrine of predestination used hard labor to quite the mind and diminish reflection. In Aristotelian terms, labor (*ergon*) is a lower form of activity (fit for slaves) because it lacks an absolute orientation necessary for people to justify their mode of life—interestingly, it is just this stress on the absolute that Durkheim appeals to within the context of the division of labor, and so enraged Marxists—recall Braverman vibrating with indignation at the suggestion in *Labor and Monopoly Capital*.

Materialist refutations of Hegel tend to be comically self-mocking: "There is no doubt that when we entertain the idea of matter we *think*, but that does not mean that we can never get near something nonmetal in our reflections" (Lachs 2012: 172–73). The reflection is thinking. For G.E. Moore the "object of consciousness" is not mental (Ibid: 173). But an "object of consciousness" is a consciousness (thought) of an object. Materialism is next to insanity and most natural scientists, when they are not atheists or submerged in a religion of science, are plagued by a primitive mentality when it comes

---

articulating the relationship between reason and the forms of social organization. As brilliant as Hegel is, there are many peculiar gaps in his presentation of Spirit's unfolding.

56 By "science" we mean systematic and objective thought. 'Systematic' is not trendy because it conjures the terrifying possibility of 'system.' *System* is not an occult phenomenon but only means that there is some kind of conceptual ordering taking place.

57 As Freud says, "what profanation of the grandiose multiformity of human life we commit if we recognize as sole motives those springing from material needs ..." (1939: 65). Marx had another rendezvous with Hegel in 1857 that completely transformed his grasp of the commodity and value. The *Critique* of 1859 and *Capital* eight years later would have been impossible without Hegel. We can thank Ferdinand Freiligrath for gifting Marx several volumes of Hegelian philosophy at just the right time.

to anything beyond rocks, chemicals, and stellar objects. The last recourse for materialism, vis-a-vis Hegel anyway, is to reduce his absolute idealism to a caricature. Once Hegel is gutted and stuffed he is, like anyone else, easily defeated. In America, pragmatism has long been the enemy of the absolute but, recently, there have been attempts to incorporate Hegel into the pragmatist sphere, however, I doubt there will be much left of him once he is dragged into that flophouse. Pragmatism is for 'perverts'—they *want* their cake and to eat it too. But Hegel just takes the cake, i.e., Hegel's position reflects and extends an underlying Christian logic vis-à-vis the standard Lacanian positions: occupying the position of the universal equivalent, Christ says, "I have the cake and you are welcome to it." The psychotic refutes the existence of cake; the neurotic feels undeserving of cake, and the pervert wants to eat his own cake (cf. Fink 1997 on these three negation positions). Christianity was revolutionary because it offers cake to all who want it. Even if you think cake is a fiction, or that you are undeserving of it, or regard it as your private property, *here is the cake nonetheless*. When the work of critique sets in, however, the cake is exposed as being only the idea of cake, an insufficient share of the cake, the functional equivalent of cake, a bribe to keep people enslaved to the cake-maker, a substance to be obtained by such-and-such method if cake is what a person ultimately values, a construct we agree to refer to as 'cake' at an annual philosophy conference, a bad confection inconsistent with the concept of cake, and, finally, we learn there was never any cake to begin with so even if we wanted cake we were never going to have it. But critique misses the point that the cake free-for-all was a metaphor and a lure for something else working behind the backs of even the critics, a treasury of values that occasion solidarity and normative life. What critique might like to offer, if it is not of the malevolent and iconoclastic variety, it automatically negates with its commitment to a post-cake world and the best we can hope for is either an asteroid strike that puts an end to our absurd, confectionary fantasies or a return to an authentic pre-cake way of life. Sociology does not set out to deny the existence of cake, etc., but, in the form of its original calling, it seeks to lead consciousness from the desire for cake (particular, finite, and abstract) to what the cake actually symbolizes (universal, infinite, and concrete). Sociology reveals the truth to cake-eaters denied by both the King of Cake as well as the nihilistic cake-deniers and the harbingers of the post-cake apocalypse: the peculiar effect of this cake fellowship is the production of a collective ebullience, the actual object of the cult, and that ritual enjoyment is available to not only *this* cult but all ritual assemblages, and that beyond the matrix of particular cults and cult energies, there is a universal cult Spirit in which all groups, unbeknownst to themselves, are blindly and inconsistently striving toward. We can have cake, we can even have surplus cake, or, for those willing to put down their forks and take the next difficult step, we can have that which the institution of cake veils, namely, the universe of non-cake objects required for a life in conformity with reason. People devoted to only cake are not as they should be. There is a good reason to eat cake, but cake, to the exclusion of non-cake, even though it can be rationalized in a thousand different ways, is indicative of thinking contaminated by fear and lacks an actual, rational ground. A cake fetish is suicidal. The finite will never know itself for what it really is, infinite Spirit, until it tarries with its difference. Wealth is empty until it comprehends its own poverty; intelligence remains abstract until it confronts its own ignorance; blue will never be true until it builds a royal ground with red. Neither Hegel nor sociology promise an Absolute *this* or an Absolute *that* but only the revelation that things are just moments in a constellation of other necessary moments awaiting reconciliation. Hegel thinks a progression like this is inevitable and driven by necessity, but, as it turns out, this necessity is retroactively constituted in creative philosophizing and is contingent upon consciousness gaining a foothold on itself. It is plausible that everything we ever needed to create this foothold, *intellectually*, was produced between 1807 (Hegel's *Phenomenology*) and Freud's *Moses and Monotheism* (1939) but where Durkheim succeeds Hegel is in grounding 'necessity' more concretely in the forms of social organization.

7   Hegel

For Hegel, history is the arc of the Concept as it develops, the process of becoming, and its self-actualizing along the way in various configurations—striving to realize itself as Idea. Central for Hegel is the notion that the struggle for freedom's actualization takes place within the context of the struggle between classes and groups done wrong by the norms of civil society.

What we owe to Hegel:

> For the first time 'representations' are conceived of as *social* facts in the Durkheimian sense—no longer are they merely things of the individual's mind that imperfectly match or attempt to copy external reality—i.e., analogical images. Social or 'socialized' representations possess moral authority, i.e., their status as 'representations' (as opposed to mere signs of lesser orders) confer upon them a sense of obligation (Pinkard does a good job in drawing this aspect out).[58]

---

[58] Hegel thinks that representations and picture-thinking are insufficient forms of consciousness when it comes to citizens of the modern world. However, representations do not cease to exist in minds developed to the higher level of conceptual thought, rather, they are sublated along the way as unconditioned, abstract conceptuality works itself up to the status of the concrete totality that contains the wealth of reality.

APPENDIX   185

Self-consciously ideal–typical methods, i.e., hyperbolic constructs: see his lordship and bondage dialectic in the *Phenomenology* for a classic example—the *Phenomenology* is a procession of models flowing one from one to the next, each driven forward by their contradictions. Hegel also delivers what we would call multidisciplinary analysis as well as a stylized historical–comparative analysis in addition to a strong focus on civil society and many themes near and dear to Durkheim such as corporate structures, the social division of labor, industrialization, religion, moral regulation, the role of the family, state structure, politics, etc.

Hegel dies, and Hegelianism rapidly dissolves into factions with Feuerbach as a leader of the so-called Young Hegelians. Marx breaks with this tendency and heads off, for a good long while, down a road that will lead, eventually, to what has been called historical or dialectical materialism. Hegelianism is all but dead only a generation after the death of the philosopher himself.

Materialism and the newly developing natural sciences are, at this point, the hot trends in thought.[59] By 1850, Hegel's influence was more or less dead in Europe and thirty years later, the intellectual climate in Germany and France around the 1880s onward, was either (a) materialistic or (b) neo–Kantian. "Kantianism offered the bridge across which the most diverse contradictions could be reconciled. Both the positivists and their opponents respected the same master. Throughout the nineteenth century virtually every educated German had cut their philosophical teeth on Kant. The same was true in France after the war of 1870, when German influence triumphed in the philosophy curriculum of the *lycées*" (Hughes 1977: 107).

But a place of honor at the head of the philosophical table does not automatically denote hegemony. You can never go back. Consider a similar and parallel journey within American sociology where legions of students were force–marched through the work of Parsons long after his grand system was left for dead. In the case of European social thought, Kant was studied as the founder of idealism (or, really, German philosophy in general) but idealism advanced through so many transformations (culminating with Hegel) that it would be incorrect to characterize the environment as essentially 'Kantian.' Kant may have been a genius but Kantianism itself was a disaster. And materialism as well as empiricism turned out to be dead ends (notice in *Elementary Forms*

---

59 "Materialism" for Hegel was the consequence of the presuppositions flowing out of empiricism, namely, that which is true is perceptible and external to the mind. For materialism, it is matter that is truly objective ([1830] 1991: 79). But, as Hegel argues, the "matter" of materialism is actually an abstraction, a thing of thought. "Music is not, as some contemporary acousticians would like us to believe, 'something that happens in the air.' It is something that, first and last, happens in the soul" (Levy 1985: 3).

that Durkheim condemns empiricism as irrationalism and that it ought to just be named that).[60]

Back to Hegel? A return to Kant (post and neo) could not proceed without either a conscious or unconscious passing back through Hegel's achievements. In what must have been a completely unexpected declaration, Marx famously defended Hegel: "I criticized the mystifictory side of the Hegelian dialectic nearly thirty years ago, at a time when it was still the fashion. But just when I was working at the first volume of *Capital*, the ill–humoured, arrogant and mediocre epigones who now talk large in educated German circles began to take pleasure in treating Hegel in the same way as the good Moses Mendelssohn treated Spinoza in Lessing's time, namely as a 'dead dog.' I therefore openly avowed myself the pupil of that mighty thinker, and even, here and there in the chapter on the theory of value, coquetted with the mode of expression peculiar to him" (C: 102–03). Marx does more than coquet with Hegel's terms; Marx's *Capital* cannot be comprehended without a grasp of Hegel's syllogisms (dialectic structure and logic of motion). The formula for circulation and the general formula representing capital are syllogisms. Dialectical or historical materialism, whatever we want to call it (Marx did not use these phrases) is no longer a materialism but a method that divides facts into separate material and moral aspects. Labor products, concrete labor, etc., belong to the domain of the physical whereas their alienations (separations, calculations, the way they are treated and regarded)[61] result in their 'transformation' into bearers of a moral substance (here we are in the domain of the famous *phantom objectivities*). As Hamlet says, "there is nothing either good or bad, but thinking makes it so."

8 Dialectical Materialism

Durkheim's 'dialectical hyper-materialism' is dramatically different from the garden variety Marxist notion. Where Marxists conceive of labor or routine praxis and the

---

60 Engels says that, "the most certain path from natural science to mysticism" is "the shallowest empiricism that spurns all theory and distrusts all thought" (MECW, 25: 353). We do not reject the empirical but as Hocking puts it: "To define groups as merely composites of individual wills is indeed the natural view: our eyes make individualists of us ..." (1926: 340). Mark Twain famously asserted that one cannot trust the senses when the "imagination is out of focus" (1917: 328). The empiricist war on the concept amounts to a self-deception so oblivious to its own unconscious presuppositions that it is as futile as trying to jump over your own shadow; the attempt to refute the universal nature of the concept, or to reduce the concept to the status of a fiction, actually affirms its universal and substantive (non-fictional) nature (Croce 1917: 15).

61 Weber uses the terminology of *treating* and *regarding* in his analysis of charismatic authority (ES, 1: 241).

relations of production as generative of class consciousnesses, Durkheim convincingly demonstrates that collective representations (those invested and animated with authority) are born not from ordinary and everyday routines, work, practical activities, sober reflections, or cold calculations, but from the *extraordinary* and furious milieu of rituals. It is for this reason that our most important thoughts are subjectively experienced as if they are rooted in another world (Czapski [1987] 2018: 65). If individuality is spiritual it is because the hyper-spirituality of collective life has been extended to it (Durkheim 1974: 34; see also Harrison 1962: 534).[62] 'Invitations' are sent, and strivers kill themselves trying to grasp the absolute whereas non-strivers molder in mom and dad's basement or are abandoned and allowed to perish in the infraliminal wasteland. Collective representations are crystallizations of *confident* ritual ecstasy and commemorate spectacular forms of self-negation. Even when the party is over, collective representations haunt us as a constellation of "from 'somewhere'" thoughts, "that is, their nature or quality proves directly that they have an existence beyond my mind" (Bosanquet 1921: 77).

It is not labor consciousness that determines the development and extension of the revolutionary situation but, rather, it is the fact of the bourgeois revolution that determines the form and content of labor consciousness. Born from terror, sacrifice, and mass murder, the concepts of the bourgeoisie are fates for all those born into the capitalist system; the historical radiance of bourgeois representations ossified into a normative framework and, as Weber would say, now, it merely comes down to the choice between conformity or death (PESC: 19). These representations, compared to the relatively free representations of the individual understanding, "easily triumph over all the private doubts which may have arisen in individual minds" (Durkheim [1912] 1915: 387).[63] Lacking a genuine social psychology, historical or dialectical materialism (conceived by contemporary critical theory) explains almost nothing beyond material facts. Surplus value is ultimately based on surplus labor, and while the historical dispossession of the means of production on the part of one class accounts for the material necessity of wage slavery, dispossession or *theft* does not account for the proletariat's unwillingness to prosecute the master class for its crimes, not only historical, but crimes recommitted every moment of every day. Why wreck the system with justice when there is a chance you can become rich and famous?[64] By the time workers realize

---

62 Under capitalism, of course, people may give their all and receive nothing but a reduction to animal status and, finally, worked to death (PM: 1109–111).
63 Collective symbols are not just active ideas detached from unconscious forces: "there is something more behind them than an appeal to intelligence, and that they owe much of their efficacy to the power of personality" and their connection to the collective desires for guidance (Rivers 1923: 52).
64 Years ago, I taught a class titled "What is Socialism?" in which, during our first session, a full one-third of the students expressed a fear of 'socialism' because, in the event that they

that they are not going to obtain wealth and fame they already have one foot in the grave and spend their nights drinking cheap beer and fantasizing about punishing deviants, i.e., the moment of revolutionary ecstasy gives way to resignation or the base desire for revenge. And if they own guns, they are almost guaranteed to turn them on family members or themselves before they seek revenge on owners of capital. This calls into question the mind-numbing and traumatic effect of laboring on the formation of rational working-class consciousness. If the proletariat have to be beaten like donkeys as a prerequisite for revolutionary action one is left to ponder the relationship between brutalization and the rational collective thought necessary for success. If only there were *substitutes*!

Another way that Marx and Durkheim diverge radically is on the problem of the syllogism (dialectics) and the structure of reason. As a post-Hegelian, Marx can see no way for individuality to be preserved within the syllogism. For Durkheim's part, individuality never loses its reality (or its hot water bottle)[65] and is never truly eclipsed by the universal or tossed into the ocean of chaos so long as the individual is enmeshed within a matrix of mediating and evolving particularities: family, church, vocation, union, party, corporation, and so on.

Durkheim was involved in the post–Kantian debates of his day. In his magnum opus he says: "Up to the present, only two doctrines have opposed one another. For some [Kantians], the categories cannot be derived from experience. They are logically prior to experience and condition it. They are thought of as so many simple data that are

---

became "rich and famous" someday, they wouldn't want the government to unjustly seize their wealth. Later I discovered that all but a couple of students were also opposed to the concept of a "maximum wage" despite the fact that, as I explained, a "minimum wage" is ineffective and irrational without its corresponding limiting partner. No explanation would make them budge from opposing a ceiling on accumulation since, again, there was that chance they would be someday "rich and famous." The fantasy of becoming "rich and famous" was a recurring theme with my students over the years (all from middle class or blue-collar backgrounds). Typically, a quarter to a third of them said they stood a fair chance of becoming "rich and famous" though they had few ideas regarding the mechanisms that would be responsible for their transformation (aside from luck) and they had no examples of their sociology/criminology predecessors attaining said wealth and fame. Nor did they know rich and famous people. Invariably, one student would cite an uncle, etc., as an example of a "very rich" person but their conception of wealth also reflected their class upbringing and it was clear they had no inkling of what real wealth is, despite Robin Leach's best efforts. When he was doing fieldwork for a dissertation on the sociology of Maquiladoras, Horowitz (2004) gathered truly fascinating data on conceptions of wealth among Mexican workers who imagined a doubling of wages or living in a brick home (assembling a few bricks at a time over the years) as signs of being rich.

65   "Always ... in the whole, life in the one: always Shelley and Goethe, and then he loses his hot water bottle; and never notices a face or a cat or a dog or a flower, except in the flow of the universal" (Woolf 1953: 261).

irreducible and immanent in the human intellect by virtue of its natural makeup. They are thus called *a priori*. For others [empiricists], by contrast, the categories are constructed, made out of bits and pieces, and it is the individual who is the artisan of that construction" (EFRL: 12). Durkheim solved this time–honored problem by extending and transforming the ground of the German idealist tradition by having the synthetic *a priori* categories (the frameworks of social thought) emerge not from a noumenal realm or an historicist developmental model but from particular forms or species of social organization fueled by intense ritual life. Merold Westphal states that, as far as religion goes, Durkheim and Hegel offer essentially identical theories (1990: 196–201).

Durkheim's most important teachers, influences, and associates (Boutroux, Renouvier, Hamelin, etc.) tended toward idealism[66] but Durkheim's sociology was only possible in a world that had already worked itself up to the idea of society as the substance of Spirit. Durkheim was highly critical of certain aspects of what we might call the German mentality (see his *Germany Above All*) but he thought like a German to a certain extent—indeed, at the turn of the 20th Century, Durkheim's indebtedness to Germanic thought caused a bit of controversy (see Verheggen 1996). It was not simply that he had studied in Germany—after all, German thought *was* European thought at the time. Strenski points out that prior to 1870 Hegel was viewed by the French as a kind of intellectual brother (2006: 43) though, as far as I can tell, Durkheim did not have much conscious regard for Hegel or neo-Hegelianism.[67] And this idea that Hegel was an intellectual brother needs to be qualified. The first translations of Hegel into French and the major exponents of Hegelianism in France from the 1860s were of dubious quality. The champions of Hegel before the 1930s and 40s were Victor Cousin and Augusto Vera who, in their own ways, were "seriously handicapped" in their abilities to transmit a

---

66   "After the demise of the weak nineteenth-century French Hegelians, other currents and individuals can be charted that finally coalesced into a French Western Marxism. Lucien Herr and Charles Andler studied Hegel at the turn of the century" (Jacoby 1981: 50). Andler rejected Durkheim's realism as being a repetition of Marx's "*chosisme*" (Lukes 1973: 314). Also critical of Durkheim's realism, Herr was the Ecole Normale librarian who introduced Durkheim to Frazer's theory of the totem (Lukes 1973: 315). Herr's review of *Rules* provides the most useful condensation of nominalist thought that one could hope for: society consists of a collection of single individuals; rules are "generalized abstractions"; symbols are "conventions between individuals", etc. (in Lukes 1973: 315). "All psychical processes [declares Professor Paul] come to their fulfillment in individual minds, and nowhere else. Neither the popular mind, nor elements of it, such as art, religion, etc., have any concrete existence, and therefore nothing can come to pass in them or between them. Away, then, with these abstractions! For 'away with all abstractions' must be our last word if we wish to attempt in any place to define the factors of that which actually happens" (in Vincent 1897: 68).

67   Durkheim was, however, viewed as intellectual kin by some neo-Hegelians, e.g., Bosanquet.

reasonable facsimile of Hegelian thought (Jacoby 1981: 49).[68] In short, there wasn't much to get *excited* about and "by the 1890s what existed of French Hegelianism had evaporated" (Ibid: 50)[69] and Durkheim was already dead by the time Hegel stormed France again.

'Social realism' was an epithet hurled at Durkheim by his many critics including Tarde, Worms, and his own student Simiand (Fournier 2006: 21, 64; Lukes 1973: 314–15).[70] The charge of 'social realism' stuck and we find it popping up again in English-language literature, e.g., the clearly disapproving Blumenthal who lumps together Le Bon, Durkheim, Wundt (who Durkheim studied with in Germany), as well as Park and Burgess (1936: 882). Fauconnet characterized Durkheim as a 'sociological realist' such that his work was oriented toward *practicality* rather than idle speculation (1923)—still, though he did not elaborate further, he made an interesting point that generally heads in the right direction, echoing post–Kantian idealism: "realism and idealism can be conciliated. Ideals are realities" (Ibid: 539).[71] These realities are not metaphysical entities and grasping their essence does not entail a commitment to Platonic realism; they are social externalities that not only seem to live an independent existence apart from individuals but, in a way, actually do live independently from individuals. We just do not want to confuse 'external' and 'independent' with physical *exteriority*, though obviously social facts are mounted or affixed to, or are projected onto, physical objects. Just as representations are independent or irreducible to the material brain (no representation has ever been found in a brain) collective representations are independent of individual consciousness and cannot be reduced to the 'contents' of the individual mind (Davy 1927: 14–15). Consequently, methods that attempt to comprehend social facts by measuring opinions and attitudes of individuals lead in a direction opposite of where we would like to go.

---

68 "Rosenkranz, who gave Vera high marks, judged Cousin harshly. If Cousin had grasped Hegel 'more deeply and accurately,' Rosenkranz stated, Hegel would have enjoyed more success in France" (Jacoby 1981: 49; see also Pinkard 2000).

69 Through weak translations and dogmatism, Vera was "unable to shake 'the indifference of the public, nor modify its prejudices'" (Jacoby 1981: 50).

70 Consult Smith (2014) for a good brief discussion of Durkheim and his critics on the problems of realism and social realism, as well as the differences between psychology and sociology.

71 See Antonio (2003) on Marx's social realism. This social reality of ideals stands in marked contrast to the "extra-mental existence" of universal ideals and categories that we find in Scholasticism (Gillespie 2008: 20). Syllogizing was the way to understand the transcendental reason of god reflected in the natural order for the Scholastics (Ibid.).

9   Universals and Individuals

If, as we have seen, philosophy is the "collective consciousness" of the sciences (DOL: 301) we would do well to examine the ontological and paradigmatic backgrounds pertaining to the 'thingness' of social facts and how classical sociology charts its own, unique path and what that path means for the program of a contemporary critical sociology as something separate from mainstream, academic pursuits that are largely irrelevant from the standpoint of truth-discovery. Mainstream sociology, with its mania for attention, money, and methods remains bogged down in positivist assumptions ('what you see is what you get')[72] and is consequently indifferent or hostile to problems of ontology, devolving, along the way into "a reverence for reified reality" (Adorno 1998: 10). We do not need to rehash the discussion of concepts and variables from preceding volumes, but one thing needs to be reiterated: if social facts are *sui generis* realities it is impossible to arrive at that weird, emergent moral residue through statistical factoring. It has been noted that factor analysis has a built-in mythological element (Maraun 1996) but I would liken it more to a conspiracy theory.[73] The assembling and combining of variables (alienated substitutions) never captures the kind of surpluses that emerge from human assemblage or the interpenetration and fusion of concepts.[74] You can, however, make a living off of dried out abstractions. One key difference

---

72   Positivism takes social facts "'as such'" and classifies these facts "according to general concepts" (Adorno 1967: 37). Positivism and ordinary entrepreneurial sociology are allergic to the social totality and favors the dismemberment of the social into bite-sized singularities—as such, mainstream sociology is a kind of "partialization" of the whole and is therefore a kind of neurotic discourse that lies to itself about reality (cf. Becker 1973: 178). As Hegel tells us in the preface to the *Phenomenology*, the mere Understanding leads to little more than schematic fetishism—"*etwas Totem*" (§53; see Worrell and Krier 2018b).

73   How can a "variable" be unobservable when it is a product of conceptual annihilation and operationalized reduction in the first place? Hegel tells us that whatever is true can never be lost (1988: 213) but a variable can become 'lost' or misplaced through the reductive process itself but, once detached, a 'factor' cannot thereafter be relocated or discovered through any statistical method. Here, again, is the fantasy of the return of the dead and scientific necrophilia. If factor analysis claims to locate unobserved variables it is because only the factor analysts themselves know where they have buried the corpses.

74   I don't think people fully appreciate the weirdness of the concept of 'surplus.' It denotes not two but *three* dimensions simultaneously. 'Surplus' originates in the medieval Latin *superplus*, from *super-* 'in addition' + *plus* 'more.' To have *surplus value* is to have a *surplus of surplus*, which translates, paradoxically, into *eight* dimensions, which we will explore in the next volume. One of our basic problems is the 'management' and the *Nomos* of surplus, material but especially moral. The notion of flushing surplus from the world is absurd and would mark the degeneration of the human back to the level of animals (see Veblen [1914] 1918: 86).

resides in the meaning of 'realism.' The original philosophical debate involving realism was that between the Medieval Realists and their opponents, the Nominalists. The centuries-long dispute revolved around the status of Universals. Were things like 'white' real things existing independently (extra-mental) or was 'white' just a word applied to things? In the 19th Century, the terminology was preserved but the meaning of the debate shifted to a self-consciously social ground such that we have some people taking a social-nominalist position where 'society' consists of *nothing but individuals* and, their antipodes, the social-realists insist that 'society' is something greater than and different than the sum of individuals (see Alpert 1939: 146ff.). This disagreement about the ontic status of 'society' is still very much alive today and rehashed continuously. One gets the impression that every generations must establish to its own satisfaction whether or not society as we have known it still persists. For many, it does not and, more radically, never really did.

Ontology (the prefix '*on*' or '*ont*' is from the Greek meaning 'being' or 'that which exists')[75] is simply philosophical reflection on what kinds of things constitute our reality (the 'thingness' or the corresponding nothingness of our world). Once we agree that there is something rather than nothing[76] it is incumbent upon us to determine the nature of that something or somethings. Is an institution like a university or a church just the sum total of countable, material elements and individuals? As we have seen, this kind of reduction does not fit the classical sense of a social fact. Alternatively, is a society just a reflection of timeless essences and ideas that reside somewhere behind the moon, independently of our comprehension? If by 'ontology' we mean the traditional sense of moral substances existing independently of human societies then we would have to conclude, with Durkheim, that social facts have *no ontological status whatsoever*. Moral forces "do not have a place of their own anywhere" and, as such, they are highly mobile, resist localization, diffuse, and "escape from ... things upon the slightest contact ..." (EFRL: 327).[77]

Still, even though social facts exhibit a "total lack of material substance" and are "purely mental configurations" (RSM: 120) they are somehow still objectively and organically real.[78] If any of the above scenarios (atomistic reduction, formalism, or blind

---

75 The Greek 'on' works itself through Latin, English and other languages to mean 'thing,' 'true,' 'fact,' and 'guilty' in the sense of, when linked to *logos*, the accountability of a fact.
76 The question has been asked, famously, at least twice: why is there something instead of nothing? Why is there anything?
77 Some ideas just spread like a disease or a virus (Kracht 2015: 74).
78 All collective representations need the support and aid of individuals to keep them alive (EFRL: 345, 348–49). The sacred beings, i.e., our representations of them, must periodically "plunge" into their source: group assembly (EFRL: 350). Durkheim's sociology moves the logic of representations out of the domain of the subjective and reconnects the representational process to the ontology of the absolute. The evolution of the absolute is

laws) were plausible sociology would be irrelevant (it would have never even arisen) and we could figure everything out with psychology, classically rationalistic speculation, or some combination of the natural sciences.[79]

Over the course of his career, Durkheim never wavered on the necessity of treating society as a real and irreducible being:

> ...social facts must be treated as things.... [W]e do not say that social facts are material things, but that they are things just as are material things, although in a different way. What indeed is a thing? The thing stands in opposition to the idea, just as what is known from the outside stands in opposition to what is known from the inside. A thing is any object of knowledge which is not naturally penetrable by the understanding. It is all that which we cannot conceptualize adequately as an idea by the simple process of intellectual analysis. It is all that which the mind cannot understand without going outside itself, proceeding progressively by way of observation and experimentation from those features which are the most external and the most immediately accessible to those which are the least visible and the most profound. To treat facts of a certain order as things is therefore not to place them in this or that category of reality; it is to observe towards them a certain attitude of mind. It is to embark upon the study of them by adopting the principle that one is entirely ignorant of what they are, that their characteristic properties, like the unknown causes upon which they depend, cannot be discovered by even the most careful form of introspection (RSM: 35–36).[80]

The idea that social or moral objects possess an ontic status ('thingness') depends upon the point of view one adopts. At all times, we must not lose sight that "despite the objectivity that marks the social world in human experience, it does not thereby acquire an ontological status apart from the human activity that produced it" (Berger

---

toward universal solidarity. Collective representations presuppose an integrative power and regulative functions preserving solidarity and equilibrium. The constellation of collective consciousnesses (one for each group or social circle) form a continuous and unbroken totality that enables the fluid movement of individuals through the various 'organs' of the social system.

79 A tour de force ultra-reductionism can be found in Haeckel (1934: 88–89): "All the phenomena of the psychic life are, without exception, bound up with certain material changes in the living substance of the body, the *protoplasm*. We have given to that part of the protoplasm which seems to be the indispensable substratum of psychic life the name of *psychoplasm* (the 'soul-substance,' in the monistic sense ...)."

80 "[T]o assert that there are irreducible constitutive rules [to social life] is to assert that the subject matter of sociology is somehow different from and partially independent of both psychology and the physical sciences" (Anton 1974: 363).

and Luckmann 1966: 60). It is also of utmost importance to realize that the only people who deny the reality of society represent a rather weird group of people that can only be found in one time and place: modern, western, educated, urban, liberals in capitalist societies—both left and right in the sense of classical Liberalism—i.e., the hyperindividuated. If you sit around *thinking about yourself thinking about yourself*, you'll eventually come to deny not only the existence of society but yourself too. It is not a coincidence that lately philosophers and physicists have begun to wonder if our known universe is not actually a computational simulation.

What virtually every critic of Durkheim has failed to grasp is that when Durkheim says that social facts are 'things' he already means that the social fact is a *relation*. Once every part is related to and substantively and rationally integrated within the whole, the work of Spirit is finished. In other words, the work is never really done. Most perspectives contain a kernel of truth and a bundle of errors that causes them to intersect at both their points of non–error as well as the underground tunnel of common consequences; transcendental idealism leads to empirical realism; transcendental realism leads to empirical idealism. Materialism can circle back on itself and discover that it is, in reality, crypto–theology. It is not quite so mysterious, then, why Durkheim (as we saw above) has been accused of being both a realist and a nominalist—or both simultaneously (Nye and Ashworth 1971: 133).[81] Alpert says that Durkheim very often sounds

---

81 In fairness, Nye and Ashworth had intuited something that was real but were incapable of penetrating the matter properly. Alexander, in a "new" (i.e., wrong) interpretation of Durkheim's intellectual trajectory argues that Durkheim started as an idealist then swerved over to materialism before sinking into subjectivism (1986). The thing that eluded Nye and Ashworth was that, like Marx, Durkheim employs a dialectical method, most easily grasped in *Forms*, where the social fact is analytically separated into its countervailing poles, the sacred and the profane. The fact qua enigmatic *thing* is dissected, with Marx's analysis of the commodity, into its concrete or qualitative aspects (materialist gaze) and its quantitative or abstract aspects (perverted gaze of the bourgeoisie); both 'moments' of this disunity vanish (the vanishing of a vanishing) into a new, emergent and objective sociological comprehension of the tamed or transparent social *object*. This stereoscopic method producing a new comprehension can be compared in some ways to the dissection of a stereophonic image. Under normal two-channel stereophonic conditions the perception of a voice front and center is a phantom illusion, a special effect of a roughly equal balance of energy broadcast from, and only from, left and right channels. The phantom at the center is a weird thing. The naïve enjoyer of the phantom image is unaware that the center is merely an illusion or mirage, yet, when the effect is explained as an emergent product of the summing of two signals (the phantom is intellectually negated or 'demystified') the center material nonetheless persists; it retains its ability to entertain and fascinate despite the moment of disillusionment. The 'jazz' suffers not. The negation of the negation does not yield a void but a mindfulness of the background mechanisms responsible for the production of the special effect. The power of explanation in the case of the stereophonic analysis is not the negation of enjoyment but the production of a knowledge (another enjoyment supplementing the musical pleasure) whereby

like a social realist but is in no way guilty of the charge (1939: 154). Simpson claims that Durkheim was simply confused about what he was doing, leading to terminological disarray (1933). Jay says, "Durkheim's struggle to devise a method to analyze this generic reality [social facts as *sui generis* realities] is now generally conceded to have produced a brilliant failure; his defense of an epistemology at once positivist and idealist, empiricist and a priori has not stood the test of time" (1984: 280).[82]

10   Rationalism and Empiricism

Is Durkheim an empiricist? Durkheim categorically denounces empiricism as "irrationalism" (EFRL: 13; cf. MECW, 5: 36–37). Is Durkheim a rationalist or *apriorist*? He certainly thinks that rationalism was "more attentive to the facts" compared to empiricists and he even identifies with rationalism in RSM and argues for the sublation of rationalism in *Moral Education* (1961: 279–81) but he is also not a rationalist in the classical sense and his negation of Descartes in *Elementary Forms* is unequivocal.[83] About

---

consciousness is able to shift from a position of *that thing is weird and does something to me* to an altogether different experience of *my mind is doing that*. Of course, stereophonic images are a long way from sociology, but the analogy is worth considering. Social theory is not the annihilator of reality and norms but enables us to shift from a position of merely being dupes to a position of self-consciousness regarding our creative powers as members of society. We want to create the passage from *They don't know what they are doing* to *We know what we are doing*. Liberation is "a process, a transition from the present situation to another of our own design" (Westhues 1982: 429–30).

82   Mannheim portrays Durkheim as a neo-idealist hobbled by the prejudices of positivism (1982: 209).

83   See Meštrović (1988) on Durkheim's 'renovation' of rationalism. But keep in mind that all the classical masters renovated rationalism in their own way. What separates them is the manner in which the absolute is theorized. Antonio does a good job in encapsulating the unity of the major classical theorists: "Regardless of many differences, classical theorists converged around some central sociological presuppositions, questions, and themes. They embraced 'progressive' features of sociocultural differentiation or, at least, viewed certain, consequent, social conditions or capacities as civilizing forces. Most implied that the process shatters the rigid, parochial constraints of tradition, shaping individuality in a freer, richer, social way. Divergent values, norms, and ideas give rise to multifaceted, reflexive, and autonomous social selves who are capable of communicating effectively with ever more diverse types of people across highly specialized roles. They forge highly complex cooperative networks that generate new social powers and consequent geometric advances in productivity. Classical theorists saw their normative critiques to be anchored in nascent forms of legitimate authority inhering in the new types of social interdependence and solidarity. While also warning of looming threats and pathologies, even pessimists detected vital, new social resources (e.g., social science) to moderate crises, reduce coercion, and strengthen the new modes of legitimate authority. Overall, they believed

experientialism and rationalism, Durkheim says: "Such are the two conceptions that have competed for centuries. And if the debate has gone on and on, it is because the arguments back and forth[84] are in fact more or less equivalent.[85] If reason is but a form of individual experience, then reason is no more. On the other hand, if the capacities with which it is credited are recognized but left unaccounted for, then reason apparently is placed outside nature and science. Faced with these opposite objections, the intellect remains uncertain. But if the social origin of the categories is accepted, a new stance becomes possible ..." (EFRL: 14; see also Creighton 1925: 273). Durkheim's form of *modified idealism* (no more an old-fashioned idealism than Marx's historical materialism was a form of preexisting materialism) is not Kantian in nature. Kant rescued the mind from the empiricism of the British Enlightenment by positing a creative and projective mind that imaginatively synthesized intuitions with concepts. Far from a passive system of sense perception, the mind was responsible for constructing experience by means of the *a priori* categories of understanding that are always already present within the mind (Kant 1929: 42–43). But where do these *a priori* categories originate? Are we born with them? Durkheim's genius is to locate the *a priori* categories within the organization and evolution of social life; the synthetic *a priori* categories are collective representations:[86]

---

that rationalization unleashes social forces of universal significance, which, if properly directed, would liberate and nurture human particularity" (1995: 6).

84 Consider the unconscious deductions operating below the surface of Baconian inductivism (Hegel [1840] 1995b: 180–81).

85 "You recognize these contrasts as familiar; well, in philosophy we have a very similar contrast expressed in the pair of terms 'rationalist' and 'empiricist,' 'empiricist' meaning your lover of facts in all their crude variety, 'rationalist' meaning your devotee to abstract and eternal principles. No one can live an hour without both facts and principles, so it is a difference rather of emphasis; yet it breeds antipathies of the most pungent character between those who lay the emphasis differently ..." (James [1907] 1995: 3).

86 The Hegelian line is such that the opposition between "the *a priori* and the *a posteriori* are poles of a continuum rather than an exclusive distinction in kind, as Kant maintained to the very end" (Westphal 2018: 60; cf. S: 278). Care must be given here to *not* put the *synthetic* on an unbroken continuum with the *analytic*, which *do belong to diametrically opposed domains*. As we saw in *The Sociogony*, Durkheim (like most social thinkers) believed with George Du Maurier that the product of 2 + 2 has no reason to be conceited ([1894] 1998: 146) whereas, for Kant, "4" is a sui generis product. These distinctions, between the diametrically opposed (e.g., the sacred and the profane, synthetic and analytic, and so on) and polar oppositions (purity and impurity, good and evil, etc.) are of grave importance. For example, it might be that "sense-making" in the world of cinema involves the same modality of logic that obtains in ordinary life, as Pippin thinks (2003: 2), but, what if 'the aesthetic' dimension is 'extraordinary' or "radically different" (Marcuse 1978: 40) and engenders another logic apart from an ordinary logic of understanding? I think this comes back around to the old 'one-dimensionality' thesis articulated by Marcuse (1964). Film

> There is an aspect of every religion that transcends the realm of specifically religious ideas. Through it, the study of religious phenomena provides a means of revisiting problems that until now have been debated only among philosophers.... At the root of our judgments, there are certain fundamental notions that dominate our entire intellectual life. It is these ideas that philosophers, beginning with Aristotle, have called the categories of understanding: notions of time, space, number, cause, substance, personality. They correspond to the most universal properties of things. They are like solid frames that confine thought. Thought does not seem to be able to break out of them without destroying itself, since it seems we cannot think of objects that are not in time or space, that cannot be counted, and so forth. The other ideas are contingent and changing, and we can conceive of a man, a society, or an epoch that lacks them; but these fundamental notions seem to us as almost inseparable from the normal functioning of the intellect. They are, as it were, the skeleton of thought. Now, when one analyzes primitive religious beliefs methodically, one naturally finds the principal categories among them. They are born in and from religion; they are a product of religious thought. This is a point that I will make again and again in the course of this book. Even now that point has a certain interest of its own, but here is what give it its true significance. The general conclusion of the chapters to follow is that religion is an eminently social thing. Religious representations are collective representations that express collective realities; rites are ways of acting that are born only in the midst of assembled groups and whose purpose is to evoke, maintain, or recreate certain mental states of those groups. But if the categories are of religious origin, then they must participate in what is common to all religion: They, too, must be social things, products of collective thought (EFRL: 8–9; see also Bouglé [1926] 1970: 170–71).

It would seem then, that everything depends upon how, when, and from which coordinates we examine life.

---

and literature generally open readers up to some crisis and we know from the previous chapter than 'Crisis' represents a break or a bend in the straight line of ordinary progression. Post-Kantians are correct that we live in one world but, for example, Hegel's *Phenomenology* represents an odyssey of Spirit that does not terminate in the mere understanding or the apex of personal intelligence and the logic of the Idea (the actuality of the concept) is not the logic of, say, sense certainty or the understanding, etc. 'Experience' is multi-dimensional, and each "dimension" provides a unique ground for "the source of knowledge and ... basic frame of reference" (Marcuse 1964: 176).

11 Viewpoints and Perspectives

Our mistake is in confusing any one viewpoint (one-sided and 'abstract') for an 'absolute' view (or even thinking that the absolute is a kind of view to begin with). All the various motivations that drive different paradigms and viewpoints (realism, idealism, nominalism, and so forth)[87] emerge from the paradoxes and contradictions associated with judgments made from within a particular symbolic universe or from a particular set of coordinates within society where comprehension is hobbled by reflected distortions that provide only an illusion of grasping the whole, if, indeed, any drive toward the whole is even operative. When one-sided perspectives do attempt to universalize their point of view the results are predictably unsatisfying and ridiculous. A nominalist cannot fail but to see normal people as lunatics smitten with conspiracy theories and hardcore realists can only conclude, in the final analysis, that normal people are no different than primitives captivated by shadows flittering across the walls of their caves.

As others have observed, most theories do not explain the world but are themselves explained *by* the world. We need to insist, once again, on the possibility of objective social knowledge; this is not the paranoid 'view from nowhere' or "the absolute gaze of the omniscient, omnipresent spectator, who, thanks to his knowledge of the social mechanics, is able to be present" (Bourdieu 1990: 98)[88] but the task of working our way up to a dialectical ubiquity, the true sense of 'objectivity' where everything that can be brought into concrete *relation* with one another (and not everything can be) is brought into relation. The absolute is not knowing everything, or the idea that everything can be known, rather, the absolute is the conceptual unification of contingent particularities.

Dialectics (split reasoning) shares with money the 'occult' capacity to 'be' in more than once place at one time but *the* dialectical method (and there is only one) is not a

---

[87] "[S]ubtile subtilties are rendred yet more subtile by the several Methods of so many Schoolmen, that one might sooner wind himself out of a Labyrinth than the entanglements of the Realists, Nominalists, Scotists. Nor have I nam'd all the several Sects, but onely in all which there is so much Doctrine and so much difficultie, that I may well conceive the Apostles, had they been to deal with these new kind of Divines, had needed to have pray'd in aid of some other Spirit" (Erasmus [1509] 1913: 117).

[88] "The real question is—transcendence of *what*? Rightly or wrongly, transcendence of *everything*, of the grand totality, the attainment of a stance wholly outside this world and one surveying it from an external, absolute viewpoint—all this can be made to sound comic. Perhaps it is. But it is not the real current issue. What is at issue is not the grand totality of things, but only the transcendence of this, that or the other closed circle of ideas, the presuppositions on which this or that system of concepts is built, the dogmas entrenched in the customs of this or that society" (Gellner 1974: 19).

magical trick but the way toward objective knowledge. Relativists discarded 'objectivity' long ago as a monomaniacal delusion but in my estimation relativism (sans an absolute dimension) is just a symptom of social disorganization and even an ethical choice. Relativists and postmodernists, with their culture of relentless, liquefying hypercriticism of the existent are partially responsible for giving us the Tangerine Dream so I think it is time we reconsider following those pseudo-sophisticated academic poseurs who demand the impossible while risking nothing. Either objectivity is possible, or we will all commit intellectual suicide and, with that, following Royce's terms, we also fall into eventual "moral suicide" (2005: 944).[89]

> Although biologically the brain capacity of the human race has remained the same for thousands of generations, it takes a long evolutionary process to arrive at objectivity, that is, to acquire the faculty to see the world, nature, other persons and oneself as they are and not distorted by desires and fears. The more man develops this objectivity, the more he is in touch with reality, the more he matures, the better can he create a human world in which he is at home. Reason is man's faculty for grasping the world by thought, in contradiction to intelligence, which is man's ability to manipulate the world with the help of thought. Reason is man's instrument for manipulating the world more successfully; the former is essentially human, the latter belongs also the animal part of man (Fromm 1981: 10–11).[90]

I think I would present this as doing the work of the Concept. This is not plainly identical with imagining society as a unitary subject, i.e., Hegel's speculative rendering of history as the self–conscious movement of the Idea (CPE: 199), and it is not merely

---

[89] After attending many partisan conferences my feeling toward intellectual solidarity, being on the right side at the cost of textual elision and lazy glossing, means intellectual suicide for the sake of the interactional and institutional integrity. "Group loyalties are necessary, and yet they are poisonous to literature, so long as literature is the product of individuals. As soon as they are allowed to have any influence, even a negative one, on creative writing, the result is not only falsification, but often the actual drying-up of the inventive faculties" (Orwell 2008: 343). Do we simply go it alone? Being right and alone is also a kind of self-destruction. Again, we can look to Durkheim and Hegel for the injunction to be double. "To suggest that a creative writer, in a time of conflict, must split his life into two compartments, may seem defeatist or frivolous: yet in practice I do not see what else he can do" (Orwell 2008: 344).

[90] Ironically, personal intelligence may work against reason as the individual pulls away in isolation to think their own thoughts rather than being thought. An intelligent person may write a good book, but as Hegel says, the worker toiling in the field of the Idea writes out of pure necessity ([1840] 1995a: 11).

taking a systematic view of the interdigitated nature of structures and processes in society. Does this mean, then, that we approach everything from a bunch of different perspectives as if they were all at least partially correct and that we can blend them to form a picture of the whole? No, we do not need a cafeteria model where we pick and choose the bits and pieces we like whether or not they have any mutual compatibility. Nor do I think a "rank ordering" of perspectives (Nietzsche) is the solution either.

The point is not to 'see' with a multiplicity of differing 'instruments' even though that sounds like a good common sense. We cannot simply 'be' idealists one moment and materialists another moment and hope to cobble together some coherent picture of reality. We *are* interested, as a point of method, in 'seeing' from two or more 'locations' at once but from one coherent perspective (seemingly a magic trick from the standpoint of empiricism and commercial positivism) via the effective development and deployment of polarized and 'totalizing' conceptual models. "The concept of totality is but the concept of society in the abstract form. It is the whole that includes all things, the supreme class that contains all other classes" (EFRL: 443). The work of absolute sociology is to assist in the transformation of the abstract into the concrete.

The reason this kind of absolute project seems so implausible today or, really, absurd is because sociology has relinquished its theoretical and 'poetic' legacy and, worse, we live in an age characterized by atomism, popular anti–intellectualism, methods fetishism, and hyper–specialization. Sociology has forsaken itself because you cannot write a grant proposal for this kind of science and you cannot simply pull a data set off a shelf and crunch some numbers and arrive at anything of value. Nor can you simply go out and conduct a field study and hope to grasp anything like a sense of a social ensemble. In other words, contemporary sociology has fallen back on naturalistic methods and statistical surveys for the sake of practicality and careerism. What would a negative sociology of totality entail and how would be arrive at it? The only reliable, sociological way to study social facts as *sui generis* realities is to operate between the twin dead ends of nominalism—i.e., the negation of realism—and realism—i.e., the personification of abstractions (Caird 1885: 20).

12 Sharks and Moderate Realism

Realism (in its traditional philosophical or theological forms) misplaces universals and moral categories by imagining them to exist independently of people, i.e., emanations from the mind of a god. In other words, realism has a problem in overshooting reality by misplacing concepts and moral objects beyond the realm of their origins. Fans of nature television programming will have seen an abundance of this: sharks as godless engines of death or hordes of hive-minded Bolshevik red ants destroying peace loving, liberal black ant colonies, and so on. Realism (in this naïve or vulgar form) is more or less identical with theological and superstitious mentalities.[91] Historically, we credit Plato with articulating the classical realist position. His student, Aristotle, is responsible for significantly deviating from his teacher's realism and developing what can be called a "moderate realism" which is alive and well into today's freak ontologies.

Moderate Realism holds that "universals exist only in particular things. To say that two or more things have a common property is to say that the property somehow exists in those things. Whiteness, for example, does not exist on its own apart from white objects; it exists in the snowflake, the paper, the chalk, and other white things. Moderate Realism is no doubt closer to common sense than Platonic Realism" (Dicker 1993: 59). The problem with this 'moderate' form is that it inverts or fetishizes the true nature of a moral substance. For example, the 'moderate' position would agree with the statement "Money has value" or thinking that value is in some way *inside* the money itself and that we use money because it *has* value. In reality, though, critical sociology knows that this is not true even though, to ordinary consciousness, it seems self-evident. We do not dig up gold from the ground because it 'has' or 'is' a material manifestation of value, rather, it acquires its status as a valuable material by the act of being dug up out of the ground and incorporated into the circulation of goods and services, etc. Value emerges through the *treating and regarding* of things, as Marx says (see also ES, 1: 241). We can witness the instantaneous devaluation of gold and money in any massive disaster such as Hurricane Katrina. When you're treading water in 175-mile-per-hour winds, the last thing you want is gold bullion.

Nominalism can be identified with 'nothing but' statements, or, the idea that, e.g., money is 'nothing but' paper or metal (Smith 1994: 7). Nominalism (meaning 'in name only') insists that 'society' is simply equal with the sum of its parts,[92] and that societies, institutions, and so forth, are reducible to personal subjectivity, tacit agreements, and "grammatical conveniences." A nominalist would tell you that since you cannot find anything like value in the chemical composition of money, or a mind in the material brain, that things like 'value' and 'mind' are just words, mere verbal and fictional entities that do not point to anything real 'behind' the words, i.e., they are merely empty signifiers. The signifiers might vibrate with energy when they get pulled into subjective fantasies but, really, there is no real social substance. Nominalists also like to imagine that since society is just an accumulation of individuals (Mannheim 1982: 224) that

---

91 Within the realist paradigm, moral substances are woven into nature and 'out there' beyond our senses and empirical verification. We only get shadows and sudden flashes. For example, value is not found in money *per se* but is ontologically prior to money. Money, then, becomes an emanation of value that resides behind it somewhere else. The whole is infinite and separated by an unbridgeable gulf from any of the finite parts that participate in the nature of moral reality. Realism is associated with Plato and formalized religion and is anti–sociological. Realism is essentially a religious mentality or crypto–theology.
92 The general is merely a collection of individuals (Mills 1966: 199–200).

they gain the information they need from observing *individuals* in action and make inferences from *personal behavior*.[93] Or, more likely, they just listen to what individuals are able to consciously articulate about their imagined world. Good sociology utilizing individualist methods is bad sociology. Perhaps the ideal–typical expression of the nominalist mentality is found in a fat tome from the 1930s that boldly states at the outset: "Our methodological starting–point is the single human being as known to our naïve sense–perception; we will begin simply by observing what is 'given' in concrete behavior. In other words, we do not begin with an abstraction, but with direct observation; the basis of the system here set forth is empirical" (Wiese and Becker 1932: 21). Little did Wiese and Becker know, they were beginning with an abstraction. Leopold von Wiese was the liberal–minded director of the Cologne sociology program and a social science bigwig during the Weimar era where sociology, before WWII, "was being conducted as a sterile theory of relations, with empirical studies restricted to the occasional field trip" (Wiggershaus 1994: 20, 111, 392). My personal copy of *Systematic Sociology* was autographed and inscribed by Becker: "Just in case some –!*& says that he doesn't know 'what sociology is all about.'" I don't think either of these men knew what sociology was all about. Needless to say, Wiese had little love for Durkheim and his animosity is worth quoting because it amplifies, both positively and negatively, what I am trying to convey about nominalist reductions: "The notion that social structures are something other and more than the mere sum of the persons who compose them has been and still is held by the German idealists, the Romanticists, and the French school clustering about Durkheim. Something other? Certainly. Plurality patterns are the neuropsychic products of the relations of their members. Something more? Yes and no ... In a certain sense they are much less ..." (Wiese and Becker 1932: 90). Wiese harps on this theme, off and on, for roughly 300 pages before admitting that while "Repetition may seem superfluous or even wearisome" it is necessary to get it through our thick heads that things like churches, norms, ideologies, states, etc., "have no existence apart from the neuropsychic patterns of the human beings comprising them ..." (Ibid: 284).

Even though nominalism and realism appear to be exact opposites of one another in every conceivable manner, they actually converge in many places; there are 'underground tunnels' and 'trap doors' that connect the two and it might be said that, oddly enough, they amount to the same thing, existing at points along a *continuum*.[94] In most

---

93   In the nominalist paradigm, moral substances do not exist. They are just words, fictions, or convenient verbal agreements. Nominalism is associated with empiricism and crude materialism and is anti–sociological. The nominalist eye is 'psychotic' in its resistance to being 'duped' by the mythologies of moral forces. Nominalism represents a fetishism of individualities.

94   In a way, we can see how nominalism would exhibit an elective affinity with insurgency. Ockhamists were not in control of the universities and the early European bourgeoisie, a radical class at the time, were decidedly nominalistic in outlook. Nominalism is linked to

cases empiricism presupposes realism. For example, the mania for measurements and multivariate analysis is typically linked to some dimly perceived (if not wholly unconscious) program to discover immutable laws that determine the operations of the natural and moral worlds. As debilitated as these two paradigms are, nominalism and realism both have elements worthy of preservation. Nominalism insists on empirical negation, methodological rigor and precision, and that material reality is important while realism, as rationalism, insists on the autonomy of ideas and the notion that there are moral 'substances' that have an existence 'beyond' the domain of crude physicality, that mind is not just brains, for example. This dualism between the analytic and the synthetic, between matter and mind, etc., has been going on for centuries and, rather than being solved once and for all, it is a dualism that reasserts itself for every generation of thinkers and necessitates a surmounting time and again (Mounier 1952: xxii, 3). As Alpert says, dualistic controversies such as the debate between nominalism and realism are "eternal" and "will never become superannuated" (1939: 149). It might seem that we are trapped in a never-ending and unproductive cycle of waging the same battles repeatedly but each generation solves the dualism in its own way, making it possible to solve problems (or not) in unique ways. From a sociological standpoint, one-sided or false dualisms persist because they are, if not literally true, *"practically true"* for a class of people: "No doubt, sometimes an error does indeed perpetuate itself in history. But barring an altogether unusual conjunction of circumstances, it cannot maintain itself this way unless it proves to be *practically true*—that is to say, if, while not giving us a correct theoretical idea of the things to which it is related, it expresses correctly enough the manner in which those things affect us, for better or for worse" (EFRL: 77).[95]

Our objective is to cancel out both nominalism and realism, that is, to negate them, to raise them up into a new, unified, synthetic program. It is naïve to think that we can keep what is good in both and discard the bad. The good is the bad. The point of *Aufheben* is to move beyond the good (greater evil) and the evil (lesser good) altogether (cf. Harrison 1962: liv). The 'third way' beyond nominalism and realism (or the product of their destruction) was thought to have been carved out by the 'moderate realism' under discussion. Hegel, the 'father' of modern social philosophy, has been portrayed

---

the struggle against orthodox and the status quo (see Mills 1966: 199–202). In Marxism we find this strain in the confusion of price and value (confusing the signifier for the thing signified) but, then again, why would we have to struggle to the death over empty signifiers? As such, militant nominalism swings back around to a naïve realist position such that it preserves the prize for its victory—it's not really enough to win the profane means of production but to capture value itself, the holy spirit of modernity.

95 "An error once discovered cannot reappear, at least until the discovery is forgotten, and there is a falling back into the conditions of mental obscurity similar to those antecedent to the discovery" (Croce 1917: 27).

as one who embraced this 'moderate' Aristotelian revision of Platonic realism. On the surface this might appear true and, in some respects, he was an Aristotelian. Aristotle was, as Beiser (2005) says, the founder of the tradition of absolute idealism of which Hegel worked but I think Hegel's later 'speculative' idealism actually offered a different solution to the problems of realism and nominalism and that his solution differed from Aristotle's 'moderate' attempt that places the universal 'in' the individuals. In one sense, it is true that the universal is intimately connected to the individual and moderate realism resists the tendency to hypostatize the universal; it recognizes that the universal is an 'imaginary,' but it also runs the risk of denying the authoritative force of that same imaginary. The universal is always imaginary; yet, we cannot imagine a lack of universality.

Here's the deal: there is nothing to prevent philosophers and other intellectual types from sitting around debating whether or not 'white' is a universal 'out there' in nature or up in heaven or whether it is 'in' the grain of salt or whether 'white' is just a word that we all agree to use while referring to some objects because to do otherwise would be inconvenient. However, we, as members of society are *required* to know what 'white' is and where it is and what things can be called white. What is missing from *philosophical* discourse on universals is the notion of *force* and *coercion* (training, socialization, discipline, punishment, and so on). In a delightfully mischievous passage Simmel says that it means something different to the oak to be syllogistically classified as a tree rather than a plant: "To subsume the oak [individual] under the concept 'plant' [universal] entails a meaning for the oak, which is not revealed by subsuming 'oak' under the concept 'tree,' [particular] however much the 'tree' includes the conceptual elements of 'plant' logically" (1955: 149).

Philosophers *qua* philosophers are not required to agree on things but when they stop philosophizing and start acting as 'normal' members of society they fall in line with the expectations and norms of the society they live in, or they will suffer the consequences of their disobedience. They may dispute the ontic status of money as an earthly emanation of a transcendental value or as a fictional token that we agree to use 'as if' it was a representation of actual value but in the supermarket checkout (i.e., exchange *relation*) they just use their money the way everybody else does, whether they like it or not, and probably don't think twice about it. If they cannot get with the program, they are free to not purchase necessities and carry on their disputations in the parking lot. As Rosenzweig says, when the philosopher "goes shopping he is unwilling to have an empty stomach as a reward for his thoughts" ([1945] 1999: 53). This reconciliation is not identical with pragmatism that merely writes it all off as irrelevant: what difference does it make, anyway? Social necessity, to speak nothing of natural necessity, *forces* us to adapt to particular forms of thought and action. People who refuse to think *normally* had better be paid (rewarded) for their disagreeable ways and set up with special times, places, and venues to question reality because in 'the real world' their disagreeable nature will not be tolerated.[96]

13 Social Realism and Social Constructionism

The new line of thinking about the reality of social objects and relations has been given a variety of names that mean, more or less the same thing, depending upon whom you ask: constructionism, social realism, sociological realism, critical realism, symbolic realism, historical materialism, and dialectical materialism.[97] One can argue that Marx's mature historical materialism and Durkheim's social realism were species of social 'constructionism' (limited to the non-subjectivist forms that can account for reification) as well as inheritors and transformers of the Hegelian philosophical tradition. Marx's debt to Hegel hardly needs to be argued but I think it is important to note that Marx's youthful (crudely materialist) rejection of Hegel was reversed when it came time, in the late 1850s, to deal with the enigma of exchange value. There has been a long-running debate as to the continuity of Marx's thought: is there only one Marx or two? There might have been three beyond the pre-1859 critique of political economy and the mature, back to Hegel critique monumentally preserved in *Capital*. The first, crucial chapter of volume one of *Capital* is only comprehensible when read 'through' the lens of Hegel's *Phenomenology* and especially the *Logic*. Indeed, the opening gambit is itself a 'phenomenology' of *Geist* in its economic form. In terms of political philosophy there was *another* Marx that we have dissected elsewhere, and it is this other Marx that necessitates, in our view, a rendezvous with Durkheim. If we cannot have Marx *per ipsum*, and we cannot, we must have Durkheim.

As far as Durkheim goes, Strenski (2006) has contributed some interesting thoughts about Durkheim's indebtedness to currents of French Hegelianism—he even goes so far to say that Durkheim was more Hegelian than the self–identifying Hegelians of his day. Strenski is not alone; in the last 20 years the connections between Durkheim and German idealism have garnered increasing if not widespread attention, and deservedly so. Therborn makes an interesting case for the unity of Marx and Durkheim on

---

96 "If a philosopher ... should turn his back on [a commodity such as a slab of butter], claiming it cannot be butter, because the French call it *beurre*, the proper place for him would be an institution accommodating philosophers exclusively" (Rosenzweig [1945] 1999: 53). *Je ne peux pas croire que ce ne soit pas du beurre.*

97 Social Realism stipulates that moral substances are real but only as the product and function of social relations, processes, and institutional control. Value is no more 'in' gold itself any more than the inspiration for suicide is 'in' a sentry box or a rope hook (Durkheim 2006: 85).

the grounds of their shared Hegelianism: "both asserted the historical and social determination of the individual"; both emphasized concrete social causes as the avenue to explain social conduct rather than relying on the conceptions that people had of their own actions, i.e., people often have an imprecise or vague notion of what they are doing or why they are doing it; and both focused on concrete social forms as determining ways of acting, thinking, and feeling over any notion of ideas floating around independently giving rise to "subjective illusions" (1980: 251). Therborn charts their ultimate divergences, and there are many, but, ultimately, if we are interested in Marx's theory of the commodity and Durkheim's theory of the totem, both critiques stand unified on the same philosophical plane (Smith 1988). Taken together, constructionism, historical materialism, etc., represent a metaphorical 'fourth dimension' beyond the deadlock of nominalism, realism, and moderate realism.

It is all too common to portray Durkheim as a realist and obscurantist only to attack him with his own style of thinking. Ortega y Gasset, for example, sets up both Hegel and Durkheim as crude realists and then counters in a very Durkheimian mode: "we now see more clearly than ever before the strange power of usage, which does not live or exist except ... by virtue of individuals, and which nevertheless hangs over them like a mechanical, impersonal power, like a physical reality that manipulates them, moves them this way and that as if they were inert bodies" (1957: 209). From his earliest days teaching philosophy, Durkheim sought alternatives to the dead ends of nominalism, naïve realism, psychological reductionism, and crude materialism. Initially, he championed Abelard's 'conceptualism' as providing an adequate solution such that "general ideas are neither words nor substances but exist in our minds and thus have a subjective existence. General [universal] ideas also exist substantively in each individual object—by the very fact that the individual object belongs to the class, the class is realized in the individual. So general ideas are more than just words" (2004: 135). Abelard was not the best example he could have chosen but neither he did not stop there. His later formulation shifted to classifications and typologies and then, in *Rules*, he focused on the comparative analysis of the differing "species" of societies or social facts.

> [O]nce it is recognized that between the confused multitude of historical societies [i.e., historical *individuals*] and the unique, although ideal, [*universal*] concept of humanity, there are intermediate entities: these are the [*particular*] social species. In the idea of species there are found joined both the unity that any truly scientific research requires and the diversity inherent in the facts, since the species is the same everywhere for all the individuals who comprise it, and yet, on the other hand, the species differ among themselves. It remains true that moral, judicial and economic institutions, etc., are infinitely variable but, the variations are not of such a nature as to be unamenable to scientific thought (RSM: 109).

Durkheim's development of a full-blown sociological realism is captured in *Suicide* where we find associated individuals forming an entirely new species of existence: "society has no other active forces than the individual; but individuals by combining form a psychical existence of a new species which consequently has its own manner of thinking and feeling ..." (S: 310). This 'realism' is not only carried forward in his magnum opus of 1912 but developed to its highest pitch. It is important to keep in mind that Durkheim does not shed his sociological realism in *Forms*. I have seen it argued, completely in reverse, that Durkheim began as a social realist and ended as a 'conceptualist.' This is not true. Durkheim began as a conceptualist (or, rather, what *he took* to be conceptualism) and, at least by 1897, had transformed idealism in his own way.[98] With evidently only passing familiarity with the German absolute idealist tradition, Durkheim put the 'absolute' of Hölderlin, Schelling, and Hegel on new ground. Exaggerating somewhat, we can say that Durkheim more fully 'socialized' Hegel—an idea that scholars are starting to realize (see Beiser 2005: 243; Knapp 1986; Strenski 2006; Westphal 1990: 195–201). When Berger and Luckmann state that Durkheimian structuralism needed augmenting with Marxist dialectics (1966: 17) they did not grasp that Durkheim already had his own dialectical method hidden in plain sight. Dialectics is not merely a theory regarding the splitting of oppositions and unifying contradictions (the old Scholastic program) but also articulating the underlying consubstantiality of reflective processional forms moving across time and space.

At the center of *Forms* is the theory of the totem and the impersonal moral energy that manifests itself in totemic emblems: "if the totemic principle [mana] is none other than the clan, it is the clan thought of in the physical form depicted by the emblem" (EFRL: 223). *Elementary Forms* extends his earlier conceptions of moral energies and social forces by exploring the effervescent ritual milieu that functions as the basis for the production and ultimate hypostatization of social energies. Ultimately, we discover that gods are but societies in their external and symbolic forms. If Durkheim has a theory of mana (to use the generic anthropological term) then Marx, in constructing a theory of the commodity, also discloses the nature of impersonal moral forces operating in the domain of commodity production, exchange, and the accumulation of surplus value.[99]

In his own tangled style Marx says: "the attempt to explain such expressions [the reality and ontic status of value] as merely poetic license only shows the impotence of the [nominalist] analysis. Hence, in answer to Proudhon's phrase, 'Labor is said to have

---

98 "[C]onceptualism has lost ground: biological and social sciences no longer believe there are immutably determined entities that define given characteristics like those of the woman, the Jew, or the black; science considers characteristics as secondary reactions to a *situation*" (Beauvoir 2009: 23–24).

99 Together, Durkheim and Marx provide us with a phenomenology that charts the journey from the ritual production of totems to the mass manufacturing of commodities.

value not as a commodity itself, but in view of the values which is supposed potentially to contain. The value of labor is a figurative expression,' etc., I have remarked 'In labor as a commodity, which is a grim reality, he' (Proudhon) 'sees nothing but a grammatical ellipsis. Thus the whole of existing society, founded on labour as a commodity, is henceforth founded on a poetic license, a figurative expression.... It is naturally still more convenient to understand by value nothing at all" (C: 677). But Marx was also not a realist in the naïve sense; you will note in the preceding '"Labour is said to have value..." Marx would say that nothing 'has value' *per se*. There is no such thing as capital *per se* (C: 169; C, 3: 953). The same applies to any kind of prestige. Kings, for example, are only kings because people willingly bow down; once people get off their knees or walk away the king is dethroned (C: 149). Like Weber's theory of charisma, the key is belief.[100] Of course, the king may continue to dominate but the concrete and substantive *relation* is broken and in its place is only mechanical *linkage* and a forced connection. Marx's orthodox followers imagine that there was only 'one Marx' and that everything he wrote is perfectly consistent, as if Marx was born and entered the world fully formed. However, Marx's intellectual trajectory was contradictory and developed considerably over time, becoming fully mature in the late 1850s and early 1860s after his return to Hegel. Here, we finally arrive at Marx's celebrated 'historical materialism' (not his phrase) that attempts to unite idealism and materialism (Lefebvre [1968] 2009: 60, 70, 76). The shift in Marx's thought in the late 1850s and early 1860s was dubbed 'dialectical materialism' by Plekhanov and widely used by later currents of Marxism (see Lefebvre [1968] 2009).[101] We find a good expression of this 'dialectical' materialism in

---

100   In the gospel of Matthew (9: 27–30) we see this primacy of belief quite clearly: Lord, cure us! Do you think I can cure you? Yes! Then, you're cured! Of course, a person remains physically wrecked but the ailment *means* something different with the belief than it does without the belief.

101   We must concede Gellner's point that the phrase 'dialectical materialism' is contradictory: "*materialism* makes certain claims, *dialectical* says, if it says anything, that all claims are liable to be reversed or limited by opposite claims. You cannot lose on this" (1979: 96). Dialectics refers to processes outside the domain of matter and using phrases like 'material relations' makes little sense. In Swain's translation of *Forms* mana is referred to as a "material force" ([1912] 1915: 218) but the Fields translation corrects this by changing it to "physical force" (EFRL: 192). Calling these forces "physical" is ambiguous unless one keeps in mind the Greek sense of *physis* (nature) that can include material but is mainly interested in divine substance comprehended by the method of *logos* and later *philosophia* as well as the organizing principle, genesis (Peters 1967: 158). Durkheim quotes Codrington as support of his position: mana "is a force, a nonmaterial and, in a sense, supernatural influence; but it reveals itself by physical force ..." (EFRL: 197). It is the concept of relation that squares this enigma of *physis*. Relations are abstractions. True, relations are or can be objectively real (many rise to the status of social facts and are therefore superior and authoritative) but they are not *material* facts. These 'real abstractions' (as Marx calls them) have physical *effects* (Durkheim) but are not themselves *physically* real as material things

Capital, especially in the commodity 'fetishism' section of the first chapter where the labor product acquires its doubled existence as a commodity in a remark about technology:

> Technology reveals the active relation of man to nature, the direct process of the production of his life, and thereby it also lays bare the process of the production of the social relations of his life, and of the mental conceptions that flow from those relations. Even a history of religion that is written in abstraction from this material basis is uncritical. It is, in reality, much easier to discover by analysis the earthly kernel of the misty creations of religion than to do the opposite, i.e., to develop from the actual, given relations of life the forms in which these have been apotheosized. The latter method is the only materialist, and therefore the only scientific one. The weakness of the abstract materialism of natural [positive] science, a materialism which excludes the historical process, are immediately evident from the abstract and ideological conceptions expressed by its spokesmen whenever they venture beyond the bounds of their own specialty (C: 494).

At the end of the day we find ourselves affirming Bernstein's view that Marx, like Hegel before him, was a synthesizer (not simply aiming at unification) of the idealist and materialist traditions ([1971] 1999: 43). Synthesis annihilates but preserves.

Unfortunately, what even the best representatives of Marxism today mean by 'historical materialism' or 'dialectical materialism' is really just a confused reductionism. *Marxists expect the ordinary, routine, and the mundane to be generative sources of the extraordinary, effervescent, and otherworldly then blink in stupefied awe at the power of capital to mentally subdue the working class.* But without the Party and its rites, in other words, a substitute for a church, solidarity is impossible. Sublime subjectivity cannot arise from the finite world of ordinary material practices. If the ordinary Marxist brand of materialism was correct, simply working under the conditions of the capitalist mode of production would be sufficient to produce revolutionary workers, a result we find nowhere. Labor exploitation (unregulated or excessive, i.e., anomic) runs toward brutalization and the profanation of workers and sublimation attaches itself not to the workers but to their ghosts, surplus value in the accounts of the bourgeoise. Marx

---

even as they are objective realities. The opposite of physical realities, social relations are ultra-psychical and appear in the consciousness of individuals *as if* they are physically real things (i.e., they are reified and inverted). Of course, there is always a physical aspect, e.g., the body of the commodity, i.e., the body as bearer or the physical aspect of the churinga (the carrier) but these are things mounted by value or mana, the material supports that thought is projected upon. Common sense just mistakes the contingent body for the essential principle.

believed that when variable capital approached its limit of being reduced to the equivalent of constant capital, i.e., worked to the brink of death, a great historical recoil would necessary follow: the workers of the world would rise up simultaneously and unchain themselves. Little did he realize they were much more likely to slaughter one another. It is a strange thing that victims will turn on each other before they pull the rug out from under their mutual oppressors (Freeman 1943). However, the promises of a political-economic revolution are vague and practical (Own your own means of production!) whereas the immediate and visceral rewards of mortal combat against a hated neighbor are things brutes can sink their teeth into. War against capital is a phantom conflict but war against a nation or demonizing Mexicans seems eminently more concrete and rewarding. A revolution for the lives of workers is far different than a war.

The concept of 'revolution' is rooted in the compression effect of ritual circle dancing. Where there are genuine revolutions there are sacred rituals. What Marxist would go anywhere near a sacred ritual? Religion, magic, and superstition are enemies of working-class revolution but 'religion' itself is not synonymous with the sacred. Just as labor itself is not value but 'creates' value, religion is not itself the sacred, but merely administers that substance and organization of life. If Marxism has a sacred it is of the naïvely realistic form borrowed from the bourgeoisie: commodity fetishism and the hypostatization of value, reflected upon in splendid isolation. The kind of 'social realism' and 'modified idealism' we find in Durkheim would make class organization and effervescent solidarity a precondition for the generation of a revolutionary class.[102]

14 The Return of Subjectivist Understandings

Durkheim's sociology is a social constructionism, but it is far removed from the subjectivism of contemporary constructivist strains.[103]

---

[102] All of this is somewhat (but not entirely) pointless because 'Marxism' consists almost entirely of a loose, tiny, and dwindling confederation of academics. Marx may rise again (I would say this is a certainty) but in so far as his disciples are mired in materialist interpretations of things we can expect nothing more than what we have already had.

[103] A consistent social or sociological realism is very difficult to maintain and regressions occur at nearly every point. One common error is the mistaken belief that the individual is lost or canceled out by virtue of the powers of the absolute. Both Hegel and Durkheim express well that, in the real, there are only individuals, however, *individuality* (personality) only emerges within the ensemble. Ginsberg does an admirable job illustrating the regression from a social realism to petit bourgeois mysticism: "The unity which belongs to a social aggregate cannot be accounted for by the nature of the units, because the units have no existence at all, out of relation to their social grouping. There are not at first individuals and then a social unit, as there might be bricks and then a pile of them.

> It is often supposed that social constructivism undermines truth. If reality is socially constructed, there is no objectivity and no reality. I deny the conclusion. Social constructivism is sociological realism; and sociological realism carries with it a wide range of realist consequences (Collins 1998: 858).

Collins makes a good point but never himself rises above the level of network intersubjectivity and, as such, his sociology falls short of where we would like to go. Collins does recognize the existence of 'universals' but these are only universals "as conceived by the understanding" (Royce 1892: 495) and are, therefore, nothing more than abstract generalities of categories and names—generic shells or, at most, the "gentle force" of the "uniting principle among ideas" we find in Hume (1896: 10).[104]

> Our forms of action are not mere rubrics nor dead categories; they are not the outcome of a classificatory process that has been applied to pre-existing materials. They are institutions of the law; they are—we say it without scruple—living things. Each of them lives its own life, has its own adventures, enjoys a longer or shorter day of vigour, usefulness, and popularity and then sinks perhaps into a decrepit and friendless old age (F.W. Maitland, in Berman 1983: 6).

If it is true that every concept "is associated with a word" but that "not every word is a social and political concept" (Koselleck 1985: 83) then it is also true that every absolute is associated with a universal but not all universals rise to the level of an absolute. Absolutes are universals with teeth. Living with a fanged beast might not sound especially appealing but in every domain of life devoid of that 'beast' we find a kind of

---

The relations that bind individuals together are intrinsic, actually constitutive of the individual. But if the individualist view is defective, the strength of the opposed position lies rather in what it rejects than in the positive account it offers of the individual and society. Though individuals are nothing apart from society, or rather the development of individuality is at the same time a development of sociality, yet society is nothing but individuals in relation, and in individuals there is a core of being which is unique and incommunicable" (1921: 47). This kind of thinking found its way into American interactionism: "According to this doctrine, neither the group nor the individual is real except in terms of the other: that is, you-don't-have persons-without-a-group and you-don't-have groups-without-persons. In addition to the stress upon the indivisibility of the two, there is an emphasis upon the study of this whole in its concrete entirety and complexity. Finally, the interactionist doctrine has placed emphasis upon the multiplicity of causative factors needed to account for what happens. It combines biological, cultural, personal, and social explanations. In much of the interactionist literature there are ghosts of the older nominalist thoughtways, most often found as implicit assumptions of and stresses upon the individual as the greater or more basic reality ..." (Warriner 1956: 550).

104 The structure of ideas for Hume amounts to the work of resemblance, contiguity, and cause and effect, i.e., everything comes down to subjective perceptions and impressions.

moral hyper-inflation or hyper-devaluation, physical degradation, paranoia, and conspiracy. Hegel actually considered the regression from reason to understanding a form of mental illness (1984: 407).[105] In the economic sphere this is self-evidently true, but even in 'peripheral' occupations like operatic music, not a department we normally think of when it comes to inflation and conspiracies, the lack of a standard pitch reference for tuning instruments, leads to a kind of pitch inflation that literally shreds human vocal cords and devalues all but the most 'superhuman' vocalists (Dickey 2013). It might seem to the ordinary understanding that our value as individuals is increased as our limitations are reduced but, on the contrary, limitlessness and 'inflation' lead in the opposite direction.

Plain understanding leaves the mind susceptible to identity thinking whereby the singular becomes identified with its alienated abstract universal (Adorno 1973: 216) and, as such, the situation is ripe for ontic slippage[106] from social realism proper into either ordinary empiricism (see EFRL: 13) or, through a backdoor, into naïve realism.[107] The individual fails to locate a home for itself in these generalized forms of thought and represents a regression to a kind of Neo-Platonism (Hegel [1840] 1995b: 549).

---

105 Just as there are different laws for the Id and the Ego (Freud 1939: 123), the 'laws' of individuality, the profane, and the mere understanding are different than the 'laws' of social facts, the sacred, and reason. The most generous thing we can say about the understanding is, at its best, it comes at the world in reverse (Durkheim [1912] 1915: 173).

106 A recurring problem in Western intellectual and political theory and practice revolves around the notion that consensus must be established around the meaning of the universal and the absolute. The history of Protestantism and the nature of the Eucharist is instructive. The only working solution to the meaning of the Eucharist has been (1) that it is good and (2) whatever it means to you personally, just keep it to yourself. The properly functioning moral order depends not upon consensus over ultimate meanings but reducing them to the level of the profane and individual: the meaning of it is your business; the doing it is our business. We do not perform Rite X because we believe; we believe because we perform Rite X. A million and one rationales can support the same thing.

107 Due to fetishistic inversions and the invisibility of particularity, the individual becomes captivated by the visible and observable world of material and ends up regarding it as not singularities but equivalent instances of universal substances. For example, the material world appears to be a sparkling and enchanted spectacle of value. To reduce universals to experience leads to irrationality: "Consequently, it is to deny all objective reality to that logical life which the function of the categories is to regulate and organize" (EFRL: 13). Adorno accused Durkheim of reducing the individual to an "atom" wholly subservient to the totality of society and disregarding the "individual perspective" (Hagens 2006: 220). However, a true reading of Durkheim must grasp that 'individual' and 'singular' are only meaningful within the larger matrix of particular affiliations and the integration of individuals and particularities (institutional associations and the web of alter egos) within the more encompassing universal social constellation. Recall that for Durkheim the actual apex of civilization (the *masterpiece*) is not the abstract individual but the concrete person endowed with reason, morality, ethics, and *individuality*. Modernity produces 'atoms' but Durkheim's sociology aimed at raising atoms to the height of personality.

APPENDIX 213

Expectedly, the opposite of ordinary realism, disenchanted empiricism, is also an outcome of the devaluation of the universal to the point of the generic.

> The scientific sense, which has gradually communicated itself ... to many of those who are not scientific, forces us to see in particular things not ideals, but merely examples of general classes, and to regard them all as connected to each other by laws of necessary relations, in such a way that they are *ipso facto* deprived any exceptional or independent position. How can we treat anything as deserving of praise or worship for itself, if, to explain it, we have to look, not to itself, but to its conditions and causes? And when science bids us treat *everything* in this manner, how can there be anything left to reverence? (Caird 1893: 113).

If we resign ourselves to abstractions of the *understanding*[108] we cannot grasp the 'real abstractions' that are central to the projects of Marx and Durkheim.[109] There is a difference between, on the one hand, a category of the understanding and logical universals, and, on the other, the kind of power that the universal equivalent under capitalism represents.[110] Money is not just a general idea but a world-historical force. Likewise, every language is not only double (profane and sacred) but the sacred doubles itself (holy and diabolical). Even the general concepts of scientific reasoning are more powerful than we assume.

> It should be noted, moreover, that the general idea, necessary to the organization of science, is not only a collection of impressions. The concept towers above the see-saw of impressions as the rock towers above the surge. It is the permanent element on which personal thought takes footing. It possesses, moreover, a character which is imperative at the same time as impersonal. It is, in its way, an ideal which imposes itself, an exemplary type which tends to determine the way of thinking. What does this mean if not that the concept is a command, and expression of a collective power? It is, without a doubt, in religious beliefs, that this

---

108 "Understanding is finding oneself in fantasy, reestablishing its framework to accommodate more and more, enlarging it, not dissipating it, not traversing it ..." (Dolar 2006: 138).
109 These real abstractions include the unreal reality or real unrealities of social facts like race (Mills 1998: 141) and gender, etc.
110 Here Gellner runs aground by naturalizing mind and reducing society to nature (1974: 93). He is completely mistaken as to the identification of Durkheimian epistemology. For Durkheim, *apriorism* is closer to the truth than empiricism but Durkheim's conceptual *apriorism* is, first of all, qualified, and secondly, does not confuse sacred thought with the mere understanding (the social and the individual). Of course, we are submerged in nature but the 'part' of us sunken in nature is different from the 'part' that is 'outside' of nature. To reduce the latter to the former is to collapse the surreal into the real as an undifferentiated mass of notions.

latter makes its action most strongly felt. But intellectual ideas could not have been constituted without conserving something of the superior authority of religious beliefs (Bouglé [1926] 1970: 170–71)

Anyone who has slogged through *Sociology of Philosophies* has been subjected to a repetitive rubric that ends, in the final analysis, with electro-mechanical slots of excitation and recognition. The social absolute goes under leaving what should be rightly grasped as particular equivalency as a false universality (prime mover). This dead end is similar to the slippery world of the Lacanian quilting point that has come undone and is also a fatal flaw in Žižek's work: the big Other is nothing but an empty, fantasmatic object devoid of the kind of substance that we expect from the authoritative social absolute (Bradley 1916: 144). The Lacanian mechanism whereby a metaphor ties together signifiers to particular meanings is achieved "without regard to an absolute referent" (Fink 1997: 94). There is no sociology possible here except for symbolic interactionism and related currents because the capacity of the paternal metaphor to create "unshakeable meaning" (Ibid.) depends upon it being not just a metaphor but an authoritative metaphor, a collective representation that dispenses not merely understandings but enforced and valid reasons.[111] With Aquinas, we note that reason has built into it a power (even a violence) that the understanding lacks (1993: 173). It is important to note that for Žižek, reason (*Vernunft*) is a fiction, there is only really understanding (*Verstehen*). As he says somewhere, reason is the coming to the realization that there is really only *understanding*. This would be the end of critical sociology and a form of intellectual resignation, the victory of categorical thinking, as weall as interminable categorical conflicts. You might as well hang a picture of Stalin over your fireplace and hope for the best. Understanding makes use of abstract representations whereas the concept has its place (*locus communis*) in reason (Kant 1991). Understanding is the act of making the unfamiliar familiar through metaphor (Jaynes 1990: 52) whereas critical sociology has as its mission the making the familiar alien and restarting teleological activity.[112] The universal (as metaphor) then, is reduced in Collins,

---

111 "No normative issue, no question of validity, can be decided by a mere definition" (Gellner 1979: 59). "The power of one animal over another may occur in terms of brute coercion, accompanied by grunts and growls, but man, as Susanne Langer has written, can 'control [his] inferiors by setting up symbols of [their] power, and the mere idea that words or images convey stands there to hold our fellows in subjection even when we cannot lay our hands on them.... Men ... oppress each other by symbols of might'" (Gerth and Mills 1953: 195).

112 Žižek's "communism" is predictably empty, rhetorical, and leads nowhere but a reconciliation with the existing social order. It is not coincidental that Žižek's celebrity status went into freefall after the 2008 economic downturn and the Occupy movement. When the world turned to Žižek for some startling new insight and plan for action he sounded like any other liberal fuddy-duddy.

Žižek, *inter alios*, to nothing more than a gap in the network of particularities (Žižek 2000b: 103).[113] Žižek claims to be an Hegelian but this is not Hegel. Žižek is basically a mystagogue: a magician with a following (ES, 1: 447) that takes pleasure in profaning the sacred (EFRL: 39–40) and reducing the social absolute to a linguistic fiction or empty signifier. What is the solution to anxiety and alienation? Buy a copy of *Enjoy Your Symptom!* For Hegel, Reason (*Logos*) is a sublime third, a subject substance that we as individuals have in common yet none of us possess as individuals. Because we cannot locate reason in a person's brain we cannot therefore conclude that it is merely 'fantasmatic.' It's not that reason is a fiction, rather, it is an 'external' form of collective consciousness that emerges out of social organization. In Weber we find charisma (the irrational) juxtaposed to reason, an *external* transformative force: the "revolutionary force of 'reason' works from without: by altering the situations of life and hence its problems, finally in this way changing men's attitudes toward them" (ES, 1: 245). We encounter reason and are able to reason in solidarity, in substantive relations and projects with others, and only there. *The Wizard of Oz* is correct on this point. The standard interpretation of *Oz* insists that the four clodhoppers possessed all along that which they sought, but, if one pays careful attention to the film, it is undoubtedly the case that courage, intelligence, and compassion, only *emerge* in concerted action. If you live out of airports and rehash old jokes for adoring and ever-changing crowds of aspiring academics, of course, Reason seems like a complete fiction. As many serious Hegel scholars have pointed out, Žižek frequently runs afoul of the letter and spirit of Hegel's philosophy. Is Hegel alive or dead in Žižek's work? It has been said that philosophy itself died with the death of Hegel in 1831.

The main goal of Western culture has shifted from the artistic, religious, and philosophic interests to scientific, technical, and economic aspirations, to problems

---

113   "The Hegelian 'concrete universality' thus involves the Real of some central impossibility: universality is 'concrete,' structured as a texture of particular figurations, precisely because it is forever prevented from acquiring a figure that would be adequate to its notion. This is why—as Hegel puts it—the Universal genus is always *one of its own species*: there is universality only in so far as there is a gap, a hole, in the midst of the particular content of the universality in question, that is, in so far as, among the species of a genus, there is always one species missing: namely, the species that would adequately embody the genus itself" (Žižek 2000b: 103). Actually, this is not Hegel but rather the first volume of *Capital* where the universal equivalent functions on the basis of universal *exclusion* and particular *exclusion*. Note well what Marx says regarding this twin exclusion: "all commodities except one are ... excluded from the equivalent form. A single commodity ... therefore has the form of direct exchangeability with all other commodities, in other words it has a directly social form because ... no other commodity is in this situation" (C: 161). However, "The commodity that figures as universal equivalent is on the other hand excluded from the uniform and therefore universal relative form of value" (Ibid.).

of social welfare and peace, and to political rivalry on a world scale. Mankind today no longer respects speculation. It does not care for metaphysical truth at all (Kroner 1961: 303).

But Hegel stages recurring comebacks. Arguably, no one has done more to raise the value of Hegel in the recent past than Žižek. However, with Žižek, at best, and this is our most generous reading, we have what amounts to another take on neo-Kantian (Vaihinger 1924) fictionalism: at most, we should act *as if* the big Other exists so that I may enjoy libidinal investments in utterly ridiculous things that really have no meaning at all when we examine them objectively; we are, after all, nothing but absurd chimps that laugh and wear trousers. I think, at the end of the day, the problem with Žižek and Lacanian psychology in general is that they let the fragility of virtual reality at the level of subjectivity extend to the world of the intersubjective and, beyond that, to the 'higher' scales of social life. As one moves beyond psychology and subjectivity and into collective consciousness, reality, even though it is virtual, is tough, reified stuff that endures. Try not using money and, sooner or later, your lifeless body will be recovered from a dumpster from behind some low-quality restaurant. If you offend my understanding I will not mind, you will not offend my reason, and we can still come to a mutual understanding or an agreement over meanings. But if you offend reason, I *mind*, because you have run afoul of authority and the sacred, a thing that is not merely a puff of air but the hypostatized Eros-Thing that has been constructed over a long duration by millions of people who put their blood, sweat, and tears into keeping it propped up. The sacred is a "value that is or seems absolute, that imposes itself unconditionally and can be violated only on pain of sacrilege or dishonor ... then it is likely that no society can do without it for long" (Comte-Sponville 2007: 18).

In short, the derealization of the universal and the negation of the social absolute lacks the proper structure and method required for critical reasoning. Authority goes unexplained, is divided into its dead empirical parts and, where a void is created on the immaterial side, fetishism creeps in to fill the vacancy. It is true that the theological big Other is dead, but we have failed to make sense of the other big Other by reducing the Concept to the level of a tool for making convenient generalizations or as a synonym for abstract thought. Reductionist sociology, especially of the American, positivistic, academic, and interactionist varieties, have long had this problem of failing to grasp the substantive absolute through misconception while allowing the particular *qua* universal (G: 145) to gobble up the individual (Hocking 1926: 134). What is the proper form and structure of critical reason?

We owe it to the Jena critics of subjectivist idealism (see Beiser 2002: 350) for laying down the philosophical foundations of what today we refer to, in our preferred lingo, as social realism. Hegel gives us an early statement in his famous "'I' that is 'We' and 'We' that is 'I.' It is in self–consciousness, in the concept of Spirit, that consciousness first finds its turning–point, where it leaves behind it the colorful show of the sensuous here–and–now and the night–like void of the supersensible beyond, and steps out into the spiritual daylight of the present" ([1807] 1977: 110–11, translation corrected). Hegel's version of Absolute Idealism was decisive for the future of sociology because he bridges realism and intersubjectivity. "What Hegel essentially does in these chapters [Hegel [1807] 1977: 104–19] is to socialize Kant's idealism, so that the 'I' of Kant's 'I think' must be part of a 'We think'" (Beiser 2005: 177; see also Beiser 2005: 212–13). It was up to Marx and Durkheim to refine the antique realist tradition. Durkheim provides, perhaps, the best summary statement of what social realism is: naturally, when we look around, we see only individuals (cf. Bloch 1968: 173) "but individuals by combining form a psychical existence of a new species, which consequently has its own manner of thinking and feeling.[114] Of course the elementary qualities of which the social fact consists are present in germ in individual minds. But the social fact emerges from them only when they have been transformed by association since it is only then that it appears. Association itself is also an active factor productive of special effects. In itself it is therefore something new. When the consciousness of individuals, instead of remaining isolated, becomes grouped and combined, something in the world has been altered" (S: 310).[115]

15 Methodological Individualism

Some would argue that Weber's 'individualism' makes him the odd man out in the classical tradition of sociology. However, as Smith points out, on the most important issue (that of impersonal social forces), Weber was very much aligned with both Durkheim and Marx: "…Weber's idea of charisma closely parallels Durkheim's notion of the sacred. This, in my opinion, is almost self–evidently true, not only exegetically but substantively—and both Weber and Durkheim, in fact, affirmed thematic parallels of precisely this kind" (2001: 72–73).

Mommsen delineates the individualist position clearly: "Weber took over in particular the individualistic approach of Carl Menger and his followers in economic affairs. The economic action of individuals must always be traced back to their individual motivations and interests, and not to economic laws of any kind. Weber was to maintain the position of a strict methodological individualism in a sometimes even pedantic fashion throughout his lifetime" (2006: 191).[116] Weber's own words seem to

---

114   See especially Hocking (1926: 340 ff.).
115   Contra John Stuart Mill who stated that, "Men are not, when brought together, converted into another kind of substance" (in Lukes 1973: 314).
116   This would not strike the Engels of 1844 as anything but good common sense (MECW, 38: 11–12).

confirm what amounts to an anti–sociological reductionism: "'... if I have become a sociologist ... it is mainly in order to exorcise the specter of collective conceptions which still lingers among us. In other words, sociology itself can only proceed from the actions of one or more separate individuals and must therefore adopt strictly individualistic methods'" (in Eldridge 1971: 25). Except that when we examine Weber's own procedure we find that this claim of focusing on "'one or more separate individuals'" is nothing more than a jug of moonshine. It is quite often the case that a great thinker says they are doing one thing while they are actually doing something quite different, even, the opposite of what they claim they are doing.

For sure, Weber's methods were different than Durkheim's. For example, in *Elementary Forms* we see the later definitely pursuing the generic, religion in general, the common elements shared by all religions, the essential aspects that have "objective meaning everywhere and everywhere fulfill the same function" (EFRL: 4). The practically infinite, luxurious diversity of religious expressions and representations veil a generic kernel. Durkheim's aim, then, is not unrelated to Hegel's "speculative method" where "what matters is to recognize in the semblance of the temporal and transient the substance which is immanent and the eternal which is present.[117] For since the rational, which is synonymous with the Idea, becomes actual by entering into external existence, it emerges in an infinite wealth of forms, appearances, and shapes and surrounds its core with a brightly coloured covering in which consciousness at first resides, but which only the concept can penetrate in order to find the inner pulse, and detects its continued beat even within the external shapes" (PR: 20–21). Perhaps the best way to describe the idea behind the "speculative method" is thusly: instead of oscillating back and forth between the object and the subject, the subject-object identity at the core of speculative idealism tells us that the objects that fill out the phenomenal space are dynamically, historically, and reflectively related to one another and that the observing subject is actively connected and reflected in the total constellation of objects. The mind guided by the concept (not the concept of abstractions and generalizations) finds not a world of passive objects but interconnected 'moments' (a physics term) each reflecting their relations to all the other objects—even though, in the case of 'dead' material things, they 'shine' like reflectors when comprehended in the light of the concept and objectively in the community of discourse (speech and texts). Everything is illuminated without being mystified.

Compare Durkheim and Hegel to Weber's 'individualistic' approach in his most famous essay on Protestantism and the 'spirit of capitalism' where an abstract model rooted in historical reality is constructed to accentuate the most essential features decisive in the emergence of a new relationship toward money and work: "This is in the

---

117 "I believe in the visible world which changes with time. And I also believe in the invisible world whose constituents do not change with time" (Freeman 1943: 323).

nature of 'historical concept–formation,' which for its methodological purposes does not seek to embody historical reality in abstract generic concepts but endeavors to integrate them in concrete configurations which are always and inevitably *individual* in character" ([1905] 2002: 9).

Durkheim may have been on the hunt for an objective truth and an essential core when it came to religion, but his method was just as 'individualistic' as Weber's, i.e., he did not seek to explain religion by examining religion *per se* or in the abstract, rather, he approached the question of religion from the 'historical individuality' of totemism and the specificity of clan and tribal organization. Weber was not inquiring into the essential framework of religious thought but the specific question pertaining to the effect of ascetic Protestantism on the unintentional development of modern capitalism, yet, both he and Durkheim, in their own ways, turned to individual historical constructs to develop their explanations. The unfortunate phrase "historical individual" should be reinterpreted if not abandoned due to the confusion it generates: "By 'historical individuals' Weber meant historical complexes of economic and social facts, integrated into historically specific unities in distinctive and unrepeatable constellations. He definitely was not talking about individual people. And in fact, he should have spoken, say, about 'historical constellations' rather than singularities. His aim was to sail between [Windelband's] poles of idiography [specification of the contingent and unique] and nomothesis [generalization of types], not by denying the reality of social–historical facts, but, on the contrary, by affirming their specificity as historical facts" (David Norman Smith, personal communication).[118]

Reflect on one of Weber's most famous passages: "The capitalist economy of the present day is an immense cosmos into which the individual is born, and which presents itself to him, at least as an individual, as an unalterable order of things in which he must live. It forces the individual, in so far as he is involved in the system of market relationships, to conform to capitalistic rules of action. The manufacturer who in the long run acts counter to these norms, will just as inevitably be eliminated from the economic scene as the worker who cannot or will not adapt himself to them will be thrown into the streets without a job" (PESC: 19–20). A more anti–individualist and even fatalistic statement cannot possibly be formulated. Weber is describing a world of inexorable forces that makes individual motivations and interests (beyond the desire

---

118   An historical individual is a representation or ideal-typical construct that embodies both the uniqueness as well as the universality of a particular time and place, e.g., not the empirical Jesus, the singular Ben Franklin, or the totality of Calvinist doctrine, etc., but ideas or determinate composites built up as markers of a particular constellation of beliefs that drive collective action. These historical individuals function for reflective spirit as decisive turning points in an historical sequence (see Strauss 1892: 771–72). "Even ideas quit looking like themselves when they're embodied" (Gary 2017: 211). For a good discussion of the individual and the general in related terms see Simmel (SGS: 256–57).

for sheer survival) completely irrelevant. What was the crux of Weber's individualism and does it render his sociology incompatible with the main currents of classical sociology? First, we need to distinguish at least between *methodological* individualism and *ontological* individualism.[119]

Methodological individualism from Weber's standpoint simply means that social phenomenon cannot be accounted for, in the final analysis, by making references to abstractions such as "the state" or "the nation" or "the law of supply and demand" and so on, without determining precisely what we mean by "the state" beyond what ordinary people using ordinary language mean by "the state." Weber insisted on precision concept construction (Eldridge 1971: 25–26) rather than everyday language (see also Durkheim 2006: 18–19). Methodological individualism, the way that Mommsen and his ilk intend, means almost nothing when you get right down to it. As Lukes indicates, it is mostly just a collection of banalities: when you look around you see people making decisions and doing things (1968). Even Durkheim would agree: "To be sure, it is ... true that society has no other active forces than individuals..." (S: 310). But any individualist argument winds up presupposing a mass of unarticulated and irreducible assumptions. One way to solve the conflict between individualism and the facticity of society is to pragmatically reframe the debate such that the two poles are equivalent to one another: both are impossible, and we should strive to enjoy a "peaceful philosophical co-existence" (Danto 1965: 277). Danto's move, however, is only possible by defanging what he calls "methodological socialism" in contrast to methodological individualism. For example, Danto uses two sentences to illustrate the individualist and the 'socialist' positions: *a man makes marks on a piece of paper* versus *a bank-teller certifies a withdrawal-slip* (Ibid: 273). Are either statements sociologically relevant at all? Like any pragmatic move, the essential has to be excluded in order to defuse the conflict: relying

---

119 "Those who teach history should be continually concerned with the task of seeking the solid and the concrete behind the empty and the abstract. In other words, it is on men rather than functions that they should concentrate their attention" (Bloch 1968: 27). This is textbook expression of methodological individualism. Why was France defeated by the Nazis during World War Two? According to Bloch, the list of errors and deficiencies is quite long, including collective "timidity" (Ibid: 132) on the part of the French as a whole, but, in the final analysis, it was the mistakes of the old men at the top: they relied on wisdoms of the previous war to wage folly upon an enemy that was nothing like anything they had seen before. This blaming of leadership is a common fallback by perpetually disappointed leftists who cannot bring themselves to fault the rank and file (Worrell 2008: 7–8). However, Bloch's *methodological* individualism did not spread to his *ontology*, which reflects his indebtedness to Durkheim: above the individuals that constitute a group are not just rules and norms but a *sui generis* "*esprit de corps*" (Ibid: 32–33). Incidentally, Bloch was no communist nor a Marxist, but he was an admirer of Karl Marx and insisted that, with Marx, "never was there a more powerful analyst of the social problem." His admiration was tempered by those that would transform Marx into a quasi-religious prophet and the elevation of his 19th century theories to the apotheosis of a timeless gospel (Ibid: 152).

on Maurice Mandelbaum's definition, "social facts" are reduced to simply "'the forms of organization present in society'" (1965: 270). Once authority (the irreducible element) is removed from the meaning of social facts, any two things are equivalent or, actually, *irrelevant*. That is the pragmatic move: negate the common denominator that animates a judgment, reducing the terms of the debate to signifiers that no longer have a necessary relation with one another, i.e., making terms irrelevant. 'Relevant' comes from the Latin for 'lifting up again' (*relevō*) whereas the making of things irrelevant is to just let them drop. What difference does it make anyway? Just as the value of a human being can be alienated, reduced to a quantum of labor power and paid a wage, perspectives and viewpoints can also be alienated and made into equivalents of one another. The same goes for the concepts of the understanding (abstractions and generalizations). Here, the shift is to magnitudes and quantities (more of something) but not the emergence of a moral difference.[120] A perfect and quite charming example of this variety of individualism can be found in Sir Francis Younghusband's *Mutual Influence* (1915: 81) which is, unfortunately, too long to quote here. In short, to equate the real with the sum total of things amounts to the production of a "metaphysical void" (SL: 707).

A full–blown methodological individualism must deny the existence of structures, classes, forces, i.e., social facts all the way around. But when we examine Weber's actual work we find little in the way of individualism of any kind, either methodological or ontological, apart from the insistence that we have to examine specific and individual things, e.g., certain forms of Protestantism rather than Protestantism in general. Except, even here, we see Weber lump them all together under the concept of asceticism: "For the purposes of this chapter, though by no means for all purposes, we can treat ascetic Protestantism as a single whole" (PESC: 102). Weber is aware, though he does not articulate it in these terms, that his object of study consists of a syllogism: to grasp the accidental rise of capitalism in the Occident one has to pay attention to the individuals (Luther, Calvin, Baxter, Franklin, and so on), the multitude of sects and churches, and the general spirit of asceticism that animates the other moments.

Weber argues that religious ideas are driving forces in the realm of economic ethics but to make the case he has to dive into the specific differences between the medieval Catholic Church and the reform movements that burst out of it in a variety of forms. If Weber is a true individualist we should find in his *Protestant Ethic* a heavy emphasis on the acting, thinking, and feeling of, for example, John Calvin whereas, on the contrary, we find that what Calvin thought was very different from the historical force of *Calvin-*

---

120 For example, the mass of a proton is thought to be far in excess of the combined mass of all the quarks that inhabit the proton (gluons have no mass but the "glue field" does contribute energy). The majority of the mass of protons is provided by the energy produced by quark motion (34 percent) and the "glue field" (36 percent; in Yang et al. 2018).

ism, the collective religious movements that were decisive in the universal proliferation of what ultimately came to be the modern capitalist spirit. Likewise, we should find a long discourse on Luther and his uniqueness as the father of the Reformation. On the contrary, we find in Weber's analysis the very opposite: Luther's sole contribution to his study is the injection of the 'calling' into the Bible.

So, far from devolving into actual methodological individualism, Weber's methodological *anti–individualism* is pronounced throughout his work especially in his most famous study. In addition to the passage I have already quoted he famously concludes *The Protestant Ethic*:

> The Puritan wanted to work in a calling; we are forced to do so. For when asceticism was carried out of monastic cells into everyday life, and began to dominate worldly morality, it did its part in building the tremendous cosmos of the modern economic order. This order is now bound to the technical and economic conditions of machine production which to–day determine the lives of all the individuals who are born into this mechanism, not only those directly concerned with economic acquisition, with irresistible force ... (PESC: 123).

How exactly do we square this and many similar expressions from Weber with the notion that explaining capitalism, according to Mommsen et al., comes down to the "economic action of individuals ... [and] their individual motivations and interests, and not to economic laws of any kind" (Mommsen 2006: 191). According to Weber our actions, motivations, and interests are simply to get with the program or suffer the consequences of our disobedience: being "thrown into the street" or eradication from the field of competition. If Weber is a 'methodological individualist' then his work is virtually pointless from the standpoint of sociology. Weber was undeniably a bourgeois egoist, but he did have the capacity to see beyond (or 'above') narrow class and academic coordinates. The typical academic might concede that, yes, capitalism as a "self–engendering monster" is a real, heteronomous power but let us not forget that "behind this abstraction there are real people and natural objects on whose productive capacities and resources Capital's circulation is based" (Žižek 2012: 244). However, with Marx, I think Weber's emphasis is not on the notion of the real individuals hidden behind the abstraction of capital, but, rather, how the spirit of capitalism develops to the point where it "is no longer attributable to concrete individuals" (Žižek 2000: 15). Capital is, today, an autonomous and objective spirit, impersonal, global, and irreducible.

Whatever Weber may or may not have been, when it comes to the problem of authority in the modern world, with respect to the question we are most interested in he stands shoulder to shoulder with Marx and Durkheim. As Sartre puts it, "it is possible to accept both Durkheim's maxim and 'treat social facts as things,' and the response of Weber and many contemporaries, that 'social facts are not things'" (1976: 179). Individuality and facticity merely represent different 'moments' in the contradictory logic of social praxis: "The future comes to man through things in so far as it previously came to things through man" (Sartre 1976: 178). Moreover,

> To the extent ... that these [socio–economic] forces are forces of inertia, that is to say, to the extent that they are communicated by and to matter *from the outside*, they introduce exteriority in the form of passive unity as *a material bond of interiority*. Materialized *praxis* (the minted coin, etc.) has the effect of uniting men precisely to the extent that it separates them by imposing on everyone a meaningful reality infinitely richer and more contradictory than they anticipated individually. Materialized practices, poured into the exteriority of things, impose a common destiny on men who know nothing of one another, and, at the same time, by their very being, they reflect and reinforce the separation of individuals (Sartre 1976: 179).

A few sociologists will have heard this from Peter Berger: "We would contend that [our] dialectical understanding of man and society as mutual products makes possible a theoretical synthesis of the Weberian and Durkheimian approaches to sociology without losing the fundamental intention of either.... Weber's understanding of social reality as ongoingly constituted by human signification and Durkheim's of the same as having the character of *choseité* as against the individual are both correct.... [T]he two understandings are only correct *together*" (1967: 187). I would argue, however, that even this concedes too much to the supposed differences between the founders of sociology. For example, Sartre's opposition between facticity and transcendence is merely the polar inverse of Durkheim's position. Sartre gives us a philosophy of striving (anomie) against facts and arrives at the position of the necessity of freedom (Cox 2012: 40). Durkheim would merely say that, as you already know, facticity is not capable of individual transcendence (not that individual or collective strivings are futile) but you will be free when you invert your formula: the freedom of necessity. With Marx, Durkheim, Weber, et al., their politics were opposed (revolutionary, reformist, bourgeois) and their questions were unique but their ways of doing sociology were not mutually repulsive when we finally move beyond partisan simplifications and rituals. Fanatics keep their idols separate from impurities, and I know that love is never true until it works itself up to a hostage situation, but absolute sociology entails not the isolation of intellectual currents but their synthesis.

16 The Really Real

This final section is intended to sort out the terminological whirlpool of Realism, realism, Realists, realists, reality, the real, and the Real. It helps to place these terms within the historical timeframe and within the context from which they arose. For example, the debate between 'Realism' and 'Nominalism' within the medieval Catholic Church was actually one occurring between what they themselves referred to as the difference obtaining between the "Reals" or "Realists" and the anti–realists, "Nominals" or "Nominalists" (Wulf [1911] 1915: 92).

The word 'Realism' is from the German *Realismus* and did not appear until the end of the 18th Century in connection with Kant's distinction between empirical and transcendental realism[121] so it is actually a case of retrospective reconstruction to ascribe the terms 'Realism' and 'Nominalism' to the Scholastic epoch (contra EP, 7: 77). The etymology of the word 'real' is in the classical Latin term *res* (thing) and the post–classical Latin word *realis* (actual). The way 'real' gets developed in European languages proceeds along two lines: on the one hand, something that is real has an objective existence and, on the other, that something exists materially. This duality is the reason the word 'real' presents such complexity because we can refer to non–material, as well as material things, as having an *objective* existence, e.g., concepts (non–material) and rocks (material). This duality between actuality and materiality is also the point that marks the divergence in use of the word 'real' in philosophy; during the medieval period Realism elevated the universal (e.g., Human) to a point of greater objective existence (more real) than individual people (e.g., Sam I Am) who happens to be just a particular instance of the idea of Human, and, as such, less real than the idea of Human. In its most purified form, Realism holds that only universals are actually real and that every particular thing we are in contact with in daily life is a shadow of that perfect form hidden behind the veil of phenomenal experience.

The Catholic debate between the Realists and the Nominalists occurred within the backdrop of the crusades. Where one might have expected a "Carolingian renaissance" we find the opposite: a new 'Dark Age' (Copleston 1950: 136). Eleventh–century Europeans could not, as Riley–Smith argues, punish themselves enough. Their fixation on sin was "almost morbid" and developed in the wake of monkish evangelicalism that raised the "standards of behavior" beyond what was possible for most people. Indulgences were invented at the beginning of the 13th Century as a way for people to discharge the accumulated sense of guilt but the crusades of roughly a hundred years earlier were another important form of penance that elevated war and mass violence to "the same meritorious plane as prayer, works of mercy and fasting" (2014: 13–31). Crusaders found themselves in contact with non–Christians "who found it easy to ridicule the simplicities of unreasoned faith…. In order to define the relation between faith and reason, it was necessary to determine the nature of reason's proper object.

---

121   This material can be found in the 1911 edition of the *Encyclopedia of Britannica*, Vol. 22.

This brings us to the much disputed question of the nature and the status of universals" (Jones 1969: 185).

Hegel says that the "conflict" between the realists and the nominalists "raged with a burning vehemence, and was carried to the greatest extremes ..." ([1840] 1995: 82). The stakes were high at the intersection of religion and politics: nominalism was used to legitimate the authority of secular princes against the claims of the Pope (Ibid: 83). Medieval philosophy (Scholasticism) was supported by, and supportive of, the Church. Nominalism, it was felt, undermined Church authority and, importantly, separated philosophy from theology and matters of faith from reason. Early medieval theologians were concerned primarily with metaphysical problems. St. Augustine argued for a version of Platonic realism whereby universal forms are inherent, non-mental features of the universe: "universals exist in themselves and would exist even if there were no minds to be aware of them" (EP, 8: 198–99). Individuals and societies, then, have nothing to do with the existence of universals, i.e., Ideas are in the mind of god. The question then arose: were humans in contact with the thinking god? Aquinas developed realism in an Aristotelian direction in contrast to the Platonism of Augustine. Aquinas held that universals exist but only in their individual existences or concrete manifestations. "Universals are apprehended directly by the mind, but only in the material things the nature of which they comprise; they are not to be found in themselves, although by the processes of abstraction and comparison the mind can approximate to thinking of them in themselves" (EP, 8: 198–99).

Peter Abelard's nominalist theory stipulated that universals were just words that acquire meaning in reference to their use.[122] William of Ockham believed that "universals are terms or signs standing for or referring to individual objects and sets of objects, but they cannot themselves exist. For what exists must be individual, and a universal cannot be that; the mistake of supposing that it could was the fatal contradiction of Platonic realism. And Aristotelian realism was no better, for it involved its own contradiction, that the identical universal should be present in a number of particulars. Real universals are neither possible nor needed" (EP, 8: 203). Woozley sums up the debate between realism and nominalism: realists call a thing a 'table' because that's what it is, whereas nominalists would say that 'tables' are only tables because we agree to call them 'tables' (EP, 8: 203). The name/word is therefore totally contingent; they could be called anything, and it would not make any difference. This is clear enough but how do we transition from the medieval debate to the modern realism/idealism debate?

---

122 Abelard was an opponent of the first nominalist, Roscelinus, but he himself was "nothing more or less than a Nominalist" (LHP, 3: 78).

Despite the fact that Leibniz may be the originator of the term 'idealism' (EP, 8: 110) and that the debate involved the British, Germans, and the French, Berkeley and Hume mark the transition from nominalism to idealism in their attacks on realism over the question of the nature and function of words and the expansion of the 'word problem' to the larger consideration of the nature of material reality. The nature of words is still a fascinating question today because words and names seem to be a blending of both material and immaterial realities. In other words, no pun intended, when it comes to words we have the tendency to regress intellectually to the 'level' of primitives. Just reflect on how certain words (spoken or written) are 'shocking.'[123] Some, but not all representations, create weird eruptions of moral energies and cause unsettling physical effects. It makes a lot of sense why these important debates would occur on the grounds of language and words.

Berkeley came under attack for his anti–materialist views (he referred to his own position as 'immaterialism' but he was labeled an 'idealist') such that "nothing could be known to exist or did exist except the ideas in the mind of the percipient" (EP, 8: 111). We can here see the direct connection between the earlier nominalist position that denied the reality of universals and the 'idealist' denial of objective reality beyond what the mind can know of it. The old debate was transformed into a disagreement over anti–materialism (the subjectivism of idealism) and the ever-growing materialism of the realists. In modern philosophy (after Descartes) the term 'realism' takes on a new meaning[124] such "that material objects exist externally to us and independently

---

123 "The rule seems to be that words accepted as swear words have some magical character, which sets them apart and makes them useless for ordinary conversation. Words used as insults seem to be governed by the same paradox as swear words" (Orwell [1933] 1961: 177). "Music had troubled him many times. But music was not articulate. It was not a new world, but rather another chaos, that it created in us. Words! Mere words! How terrible they were! How clear, and vivid, and cruel! One could not escape from them. And yet what a subtle magic there was in them! They seemed to be able to give a plastic form to formless things.... Mere words! Was there anything so real as words?" (Wilde [1890] 1995: 29).

124 In the modern era 'realism' moves ever-closer to materialism as the opponent of idealism (see Bowie 2003: 39). Today, realism now means that there is a reality that exists independently of any knowing consciousness. The current trend in 'speculative realism' (e.g., Harman 2010; Meillassoux 2008) is one such move, though, as critics have indicated, the very distinction between a reality separate from consciousness and reality as constructed by consciousness, itself, falls within the domain of consciousness. Trying to imagine what the universe would be like *per se*, i.e., outside of or without human consciousness, is an "impossible gaze" that can only occur within the mind. I have suggested elsewhere that 'speculative realism' goes beyond the 'pornographic impossible gaze' (see Žižek) to a more radical, suicidal farewell letter written by academics where we are invited to imagine a world without them ('You'll miss me when I'm gone'). In the final analysis, the idealist can say with a certainty unavailable to materialism that any and all experience we have

of our sense experience. Realism is thus opposed to idealism, which holds that no such material objects or external realities exist apart from our knowledge or consciousness of them, the whole universe thus being dependent on the mind or in some sense mental" (EP, 7: 77). Part of the problem is that both realism and idealism, like ordinary consciousness, work with representations that resist disclosing to the mind that representational externality is, for the realist, equally a subjective inwardness or "in and of itself" (Hegel 1988: 213), and for the idealist, that externality is non-material yet still nonetheless objectively real (physicality pertains to effects not ontology). Especially interesting for us is that European idealism (subjectivism) grows out of the breakdown of traditional society and the erosion of the Catholic Church's authority. Individualism was on the march, especially in England, a forerunner in capitalist development, and in Germany, the cradle of the Protestant Reformation where Luther had tended to the cult of the word. In other words, idealism was associated with and sometimes attacked for 'egoism' (EP, 8: 111). Indeed, one might argue that it is a form of thinking that best resonates with hyper–individualist of the Stoic variety.

The French reception of the materialism and anti–materialism (realism and idealism) debate was mediated not only by the French Revolution and capitalist social transformations but also its persistent Catholicism and in thinkers like Durkheim, who comes along much later. With Durkheim we find the peculiarly French synthesis of English empiricism and the speculative bent of the Germans. It is also interesting to note that in his youth, Hegel, one of the modern founders of 'absolute idealism' was also an admirer of Rousseau (Beiser 2005: 9), a writer near and dear, though, not uncritically, to Durkheim.

The poet Friedrich Hölderlin turned Idealism on its head and Friedrich Schlegel, Novalis, and Friedrich Schelling, followed in his path, each making important, pre-sociological contributions that would ultimately contribute to the development of what would become 'dialectical materialism' (not a materialism at all in the usual sense) or historical materialism (neither historical in any way a historian would recognize nor materialistic). But it was the philosopher G.W.F. Hegel who raised this tradition up to its proto–sociological potential. It is to Hegel that we owe much for creating a genuinely social philosophy that effectively transcended the severe and debilitating limitations of nominalism and realism; for the best short summary of what we are here calling Hegel's 'social realism' see Beiser (2005: 212–13). Pinkard makes an important

---

as individuals is synthesized by our minds. It is therefore true that all our reality is a kind of 'virtual' construct. Where idealism falls short is making the move from subjectivist constructions to social facts (i.e., from psychology to sociology).

point that serves to conclude our brief foray into these matters: "All of these motivations to realism, subjective idealism, and naturalism, according to Hegel's diagnosis, arise from the paradoxes attendant on such judgments made within a 'reflected' sense of the whole; they arise, in Hegel's terms, by taking the 'finite,' 'sideways on' point of view as 'absolute'" (2002: 256).[125]

---

[125] McDowell says that this "sideways on" point of view is a Platonic picture that offers "no real content" (1998: 208). Cf. the "straight on" view of naïveté (Levinas 1979: 36).

Bibliography

Aaron, Daniel. 1977. *Writers on the Left*. Oxford: Oxford University Press.
Abrams, Philip. 1982. *Historical Sociology*. Ithaca: Cornell University Press.
Acton, H.B. 1967. "Idealism." Pp. 110–18 in *The Encyclopedia of Philosophy*, Vol. 8. New York: Macmillan and The Free Press.
Adams, Nicholas. 2017. "Clash of Titans: Barth Versus Hegel." Paper presented 16 October, University of Birmingham.
Adams, Phillip, interviewed by Paul Holdengräber. 2014. "The Art of Nonfiction, No. 7." *The Paris Review*, Spring. Online: (www.theparisreview.org/interviews/6286/the-art-of-nonfiction-no-7-adam-phillips).
Adler, Alfred. 1954. *Understanding Human Nature*. Greenwich: Fawcett.
Adorno, Theodor W. 1950. "Democratic Leadership and Mass Manipulation." Pp. 418–35 in *Studies in Leadership*, ed. Alvin W. Gouldner. New York: Harper.
Adorno, Theodor W. [1964] 1973. *The Jargon of Authenticity*, tr. Knut Tarnowski and Frederic Will. Evanston: Northwestern University Press.
Adorno, Theodor W. 1973. *Negative Dialectics*, tr. E.B. Ashton. New York: Continuum.
Adorno, Theodor W. 1974. *Minima Moralia*, tr. E.F.N. Jephcott. London: Verso.
Adorno, Theodor W. [1975] 2000. *The Psychological Technique of Martin Luther Thomas*. Stanford: Stanford University Press.
Adorno, Theodor W. 1976. "Sociology and Empirical Research." Pp. 68–86 in *The Positivist Dispute in German Sociology* by Theodor W. Adorno, Hans Albert, Ralf Dahrendorf, Jürgen Habermas, Harald Pilot, and Karl R. Popper. London: Heinemann.
Adorno, Theodor W. 1997. *Aesthetic Theory*, tr. Robert Hullot-Kentor. Minneapolis: University of Minnesota Press.
Adorno, Theodor W. 1989. *Kierkegaard*, tr. Robert Hullot-Kentor. Minneapolis: University of Minnesota Press.
Adorno, Theodor W. 1993. *Hegel: Three Studies*, tr. Shierry Nicholsen. Cambridge: The MIT Press.
Adorno, Theodor W. 1998. *Critical Models*, tr. Henry W. Pickford. New York: Columbia University Press.
Adorno, Theodor W. 2000. *Introduction to Sociology*, tr. Edmund Jephcott. Stanford: Stanford University Press.
Adorno, T.W., Else Frenkel-Brunswik, Daniel J. Levinson, and R. Nevitt Sanford. 1950. *The Authoritarian Personality*. New York: W.W. Norton.
Adorno, Theodor W. and Hellmut Becker. 1983. "Education for Autonomy." *Telos* 55: 103–10.
Agamben, Giorgio. 1999. *The Man Without Content*, tr. Georgia Albert. Stanford: Stanford University Press.

Alain. [1934] 1974. *The Gods*, tr. Richard Pevear. New York: New Directions.

Aldous, Joan, Emile Durkheim, and Ferdinand Tönnies. 1972. "An Exchange between Durkheim and Tönnies on the Nature of Social Relations." *The American Journal of Sociology* 77(6): 1191–200.

Alexander, Jeffery C. 1986. "Rethinking Durkheim's Intellectual Development I: On 'Marxism' and the Anxiety of Being Misunderstood." *International Sociology* 1(1): 91–107.

Ali, Farhana and Jerrold Post. 2008. "The History and Evolution of Martyrdom in the Service of Defensive Jihad." *Social Research* 75(2): 615–54.

Allen, Carleton Kemp. 1927. *Law in the Making*. London: Oxford University Press.

Alpert, Harry. 1939. *Emile Durkheim and his Sociology*. New York: Columbia University Press.

Alpert, Harry. 1958. "The Growth of Social Research in the United States." Pp. in *The Human Meaning of the Social Sciences*. New York: Meridian Books.

Altamura, Chris. 2019. "The Sorrows of Modern Subjectivity: Capital, Infinity Disease, and Werther's Hysterical Neurosis." *Fast Capitalism* 16.2. Online: (https://fastcapitalism.journal.library.uta.edu/index.php/fastcapitalism).

Alter, Robert. 2019. "Introduction to the Five Books." Pp. xliii–xlix in *The Hebrew Bible*, Vol. 1, tr. Robert Alter. New York: W.W. Norton.

Althusser, Louis. 1969. *For Marx*. New York: Vintage.

Althusser, Louis. 1970. "Ideology and Ideological State Apparatuses." Online: (www.marxists.org/reference/archive/althusser/1970/ideology.htm).

Alvarez, A. 1972. *The Savage God*. New York: Random House.

Amator patriae (anon.). 1829. *An Appeal to Capitalists and the Rest of the Community of the British Empire, on the State of its Trading and Commercial Interests, and Submitting a Remedy for the Evils to which they are Subjected*. London: Printed and sold for the author by Holdsworth and Ball.

Amin, Samir. 1994. *Re-Reading the Postwar Period*. New York: Monthly Review Press.

Amin, Samir. 1997. *Capitalism in the Age of Globalization*. London: Zed Books.

Amin, Samir. 2004. *The Liberal Virus*. New York: Monthly Review Press.

Amis, Martin. 1984. *Money: A Suicide Note*. New York: Penguin.

Anderson, Elizabeth. 2017. *Private Government*. Princeton: Princeton University Press.

Anderson, Greg. 2018. *The Realness of Things Past*. New York: Oxford University Press.

Angier, Natalie. 1999. "Why Men Don't Last: Self-Destruction as a Way of Life." *The New York Times* 17 February. Online: (www.nytimes.com/1999/02/17/health/why-men-don-t-last-self-destruction-as-a-way-of-life.html).

Anton, Anatole. 1974. "Commodities and Exchange." *Philosophy and Phenomenological Research* 34(3): 355–83.

Antonio, Robert J. 1995. "Nietzsche's Antisociology: Subjectified Culture and the End of History." *American Journal of Sociology* 101(1): 1–43.

Antonio, Robert J. 2003. "Introduction: Marx and Modernity." Pp. 1–50 in *Marx and Modernity*, ed. Robert J. Antonio. Malden: Blackwell.

Antonio, Robert J. 2017. "Immanent Critique and the Exhaustion Thesis: Neoliberalism and History's Vicissitudes." Pp. 655–76 in *The Palgrave Handbook of Critical Theory*, ed. Michael J. Thompson. New York: Palgrave.

Appelbaum, Binyamin. 2019. *The Economists' Hour*. New York: Little, Brown and Co.

Apuleius. 1994. *The Golden Ass*, tr. P.G. Walsh. Oxford: Oxford University Press.

Aquinas, Thomas. 1947. *Summa Theologica*. Grand Rapids: Christian Classics.

Aquinas, Thomas. 1993. *Selected Philosophical Writings*, tr. Timothy McDermott. Oxford: Oxford University Press.

Aquinas, Thomas. 2000. *Treatise on Law*, tr. Richard J. Reagan. Indianapolis: Hackett.

Arendt, Hannah. 1968. *The Origins of Totalitarianism*. New York: Harcourt.

Aristotle. 1984. *Complete Works of Aristotle*, Vol. 2. Princeton: Princeton University Press.

Aron, Raymond. 1954. *The Century of Total War*. New York: Doubleday.

Aron, Raymond. 1964. *German Sociology*. New York: The Free Press.

Aron, Raymond. 1965. *Main Currents in Sociological Thought*, Vol. 1. New York: Doubleday.

Aron, Raymond. 1967. *Main Currents in Sociological Thought*, Vol. 2. New York: Doubleday.

Aron, Raymond. 1968. *Progress and Disillusion*. New York: The New American Library.

Aronowitz, Stanley. 1994. *Dead Artists, Live Theories, and Other Cultural Problems*. London: Routledge.

Auden, W.H. 2002. *The Complete Works*, Vol. 2. Princeton: Princeton University Press.

Auden, W.H. 2008. *The Complete Works*, Vol. 3. Princeton: Princeton University Press.

Augustine. 1876. *Works*, Vol. 15(3). Edinburgh: T. and T. Clark.

Augustine. 1972. *City of God*. New York: Penguin.

Avineri, Shlomo. 1972. *Hegel's Theory of the Modern State*. Cambridge: Cambridge University Press.

Avineri, Shlomo. 1976. "How to Save Marx from the Alchemists of Revolution." *Political Theory* 4(1): 35–44.

Bacevich, Andrew J. 2009. *The Limits of Power*. New York: Holt.

Bacon, Francis. 1872. *The Works of Francis Bacon, 1: Philosophical Writings*. New York: Hurd and Houghton.

Badiou, Alain. 2003. *Saint Paul*. Stanford: Stanford University Press.

Badiou, Alain. 2009. *Theory of the Subject*, tr. Bruno Bosteels. New York: Continuum.

Bageant, Joe. 2007. *Deer Hunting with Jesus*. New York: Three Rivers Press.

Bageant, Joe. 2010. *Rainbow Pie*. Melbourne: Scribe.

Balzac, Honoré de. [1846] 1991. *Cousin Bette*, tr. James Waring. New York: Knopf.

Barnes, Harry Elmer and Howard Becker. 1938. *From Lore to Science*. Boston: D.C. Heath.

Barnes, Jonathan. 2001. *Early Greek Philosophy*. New York: Penguin.
Barrett, Lisa Feldman. 2017. *How Emotions are Made*. Boston: Houghton.
Barth, Karl. 1933. *The Epistle to the Romans*. London: Oxford University Press.
Barthes, Roland. 1964. *Elements of Semiology*. Online: (www.marxists.org/reference/subject/philosophy/works/fr/barthes.htm).
Barthes, Roland. 1976. *Sade, Fourier, and Loyola*, tr. Richard Miller. Berkeley: University of California Press.
Barthes, Roland. 1982. *Empire of Signs*, tr. Richard Howard. New York: Hill and Wang.
Barzun, Jacques. 1964. *Science: The Glorious Entertainment*. New York: Harper.
Bataille, Georges. [1962] 1991. *The Impossible*, tr. Robert Hurley. San Francisco: City Lights.
Bataille, Georges. [1967] 1989. *The Accursed Share*, Vol. 1, tr. Robert Hurley. New York: Zone Books.
Bataille, Georges. [1976] 1991. *The Accursed Share*, Vol. 2, tr. Robert Hurley. New York: Zone Books.
Bataille, Georges. 1988. *Inner Experience*, tr. Leslie Anne Boldt. Albany: SUNY Press.
Bataille, Georges. 1989. *Theory of Religion*, tr. Robert Hurley. New York: Zone Books.
Bataille, Georges. 2004. *Divine Filth*, tr. Mark Spitzer. Creation.
Baudelaire, Charles. 1993. *Poems*, tr. Richard Howard. New York: Knopf.
Baudelaire, Charles. 2002. *On Wine and Hashish*, tr. Andrew Brown. London: Hesperus Press.
Baudrillard, Jean. 1983a. *Simulations*, tr. Paul Foss, Paul Patton, and Philip Beitchman. New York: Semiotext(e).
Baudrillard, Jean. 1983b. *In the Shadow of the Silent Majorities*, tr. Paul Foss, John Johnston, and Paul Patton. New York: Semiotext(e).
Baudrillard, Jean. 1983c. "The Ecstasy of Communication." Pp. 126–34 in *Anti-Aesthetic*, ed. Hal Foster. Port Townsend: Bay Press.
Baudrillard, Jean. 1988. *America*, tr. Chris Turner. London: Verso.
Baudrillard, Jean. 2005. *The System of Objects*, tr. James Benedict. London: Verso.
Beauvoir, Simone de. 2009. *The Second Sex*. New York: Vintage.
Bechtold, Thomas. 2019. "Sociopoetics in the Work of Shakespeare." *Fast Capitalism* 16(2) Online: (https://fastcapitalism.journal.library.uta.edu/index.php/fastcapitalism).
Becker, Ernest. 1973. *The Denial of Death*. New York: The Free Press.
Beiser, Frederick. 2002. *German Idealism*. Cambridge: Harvard University Press.
Beiser, Frederick. 2005. *Hegel*. New York: Routledge.
Bell, Daniel. 1976. *The Cultural Contradictions of Capitalism*. New York: Basic Books.
Bellah, Robert N., Richard Madsen, William M. Sullivan, Ann Swidler, and Steven M. Tipton. 1985. *Habits of the Heart*. New York: Harper.

Bendix, Reinhard. [1956] 1974. *Work and Authority in Industry*. Berkeley: University of California Press.
Bendix, Reinhard. 1960. *Max Weber*. Garden City: Doubleday.
Bendix, Reinhard. 1978. *Kings or People*. Berkeley: University of California Press.
Benjamin, Jessica. 1988. *The Bonds of Love*. New York: Pantheon.
Benjamin, Jessica. 1998. *Shadow of the Other*. New York: Routledge.
Benjamin, Walter. [1963] 1998. *The Origin of German Tragic Drama*. London: Verso.
Benjamin, Walter. 1996. *Selected Writings*, Vol. 1. Cambridge: Harvard University Press.
Benjamin, Walter. 1999a. *Selected Writings*, Vol. 2/2. Cambridge: Harvard University Press.
Benjamin, Walter. 1999b. *The Arcades Project*, tr. Howard Eiland and Kevin McLaughlin. Cambridge: Harvard University Press.
Berger, Bennett M. 1995. *An Essay on Culture*. Berkeley: University of California Press.
Berger, Jonah. 2016. *Invisible Influence*. New York: Simon and Schuster.
Berger, Peter. 1967. *The Sacred Canopy*. New York: Anchor.
Berger, Peter. 1969. *A Rumor of Angels*. New York: Anchor.
Berger, Peter, Brigitte Berger, and Hansfried Kellner. 1973. *The Homeless Mind*. New York: Vintage.
Berger, Peter and Thomas Luckmann. 1966. *The Social Construction of Reality*. New York: Anchor.
Berger, Peter and Stanley Pullberg. 1965. "Reification and the Sociological Critique of Consciousness." *History and Theory* 4(2): 196–211.
Bergson, Henri. 1920. *Mind-Energy*, tr. H. Wildon Carr. New York: Henry Holt.
Berkeley, George. 1843. *Works*, Vol. 1. London: Thomas Tegg.
Berman, Harold. 1983. *Law and Revolution*. Cambridge: Harvard University Press.
Bernstein, Richard J. [1971] 1999. *Praxis and Action*, new edition. Philadelphia: University of Pennsylvania Press.
Berthold-Bond, Daniel. 1995. *Hegel's Theory of Madness*. Albany: SUNY Press.
Besnard, Philippe. 2000. "The Fortunes of Durkheim's *Suicide*." Pp. 97–125 in *Durkheim's Suicide*, eds. W.S.F. Pickering and Geoffrey Walford. London: Routledge.
Besnard, Philippe. 2005. "Durkheim's Squares: Types of Social Pathology and Types of Suicide." Pp. 70–79 in *The Cambridge Companion to Durkheim*, eds. Jeffrey C. Alexander et al. Cambridge: Cambridge University Press.
Bettelheim, Bruno. 1960. *The Informed Heart: Autonomy in a Mass Age*. New York: Avon.
Bhaskar, Roy. 2008. *Dialectic: The Pulse of Freedom*. New York: Routledge.
Bloch, Ernst. 1988. *The Utopian Function of Art and Literature*. Cambridge: The MIT Press.
Bloch, Marc. 1953. *The Historian's Craft*. New York: Vintage.
Bloch, Marc. 1961. *The Royal Touch*, tr. F.E. Anderson. New York: Dorset.

Bloch, Marc. 1966. *French Rural History*, tr. Janet Sondheimer. Berkeley: University of California Press.

Bloch, Marc. 1968. *Strange Defeat*, tr. G. Hopkins. New York: W.W. Norton.

Bloom, Allan. 1987. *The Closing of the American Mind*. New York: Simon and Schuster.

Blumenthal, Albert. 1936. "The Nature of Culture." *American Sociological Review* 1(6): 875–93.

Boethius, Anicius Manlius Severinus. [524] 1962. *The Consolation of Philosophy*, tr. Richard Green. New York: Macmillan.Boetie, Etienne de la. [1552–53] 1975. *The Politics of Disobedience: The Discourse of Voluntary Servitude*. Montreal: Black Rose Books.Bonhoeffer, Dietrich. 2005. *Ethics*. Minneapolis: Fortress Press.

Bonhoeffer, Dietrich. 2009. *Letters and Papers from Prison*. London: The Folio Society.

Boon, James A. 1982. *Other Tribes, Other Scribes*. Cambridge: Cambridge University Press.

Borges, Jorge Luis. 1998. *Collected Fictions*, tr. Andrew Hurley. New York: Penguin.

Borkenau, Franz. 1962. *World Communism*. Ann Arbor: The University of Michigan Press.

Borkenau, Franz. 1981. *End and Beginning*. New York: Columbia University Press.

Borneman, Ernest (ed.). 1976. *The Psychoanalysis of Money*. New York: Urizen Books.

Bosanquet, Bernard. 1912. *The Principle of Individuality and Value*. London: Macmillan.

Bosanquet, Bernard. 1913. *Mind and its Object*. Manchester: Manchester University Press.

Bosanquet, Bernard. 1920. *What Religion Is*. London: Macmillan.

Bosanquet, Bernard. 1921. *The Meeting of Extremes in Contemporary Philosophy*. New York: Macmillan.

Bosanquet, Bernard. [1923] 1965. *The Philosophical Theory of the State*. New York: St Martin's.

Bouglé, Celestin. [1926] 1970. *The Evolution of Values*. New York: Augustus M. Kelley.

Bourdieu, Pierre. 1977. *Outline of a Theory of Practice*. Cambridge: Cambridge University Press.

Bourdieu, Pierre. [1980] 1990. *The Logic of Practice*. Stanford: Stanford University Press.

Bourdieu, Pierre. 1990. *In Other Words*. Stanford: Stanford University Press.

Bourdieu, Pierre. 1991. *Language and Symbolic Power*. Cambridge: Harvard University Press.

Bourdieu, Pierre. 2005. *The Social Structures of the Economy*. Malden, MA: Polity Press.

Bourdieu, Pierre et al. 1999. *The Weight of the World*. Stanford: Stanford University Press.

Boutmy, Emile. 1902. *Élélments d'une Psychologie Politique du Peuple Américain*. Paris: Librairie Armand Colin.

Boutroux, Emile. 1914. *Natural Law in Science and Philosophy*, tr. Fred Rothwell. New York: Macmillan.

Bowersock, G.W. 1994. *Fiction as History*. Berkeley: University of California Press.
Bowie, Andrew. 2003. *Introduction to German Philosophy*. Malden: Polity.
Bracken, Christopher. 2007. *Magical Criticism: The Recourse of Savage Philosophy*. Chicago: University of Chicago Press.
Bradley, F.H. 1916. *Appearance and Reality*. London: George Allen and Unwin.
Braudel, Fernand. 1980. *On History*, tr. S. Matthews. Chicago: The University of Chicago Press.
Braverman, Harry. 1974. *Labor and Monopoly Capital*. New York: Monthly Review Press.
Bray, Charles. 1863. *The Philosophy of Necessity*, second edition. London: Longman.
Breasted, James H. 1933. *The Dawn of Conscience*. New York: Scribner's Sons.
Breckman, Warren. 2013. *Adventures of the Symbolic*. New York: Columbia University Press.
Brent, Joseph. 1998. *Charles Sanders Peirce: A Life*, revised and enlarged edition. Bloomington: Indiana University Press.
Burke, Peter. 1992. *History and Social Theory*. Ithaca: Cornell University Press.
Caillois, Roger. 1959. *Man and the Sacred*. Urbana: University of Illinois Press.
Caillois, Roger. 1961. *Man, Play, and Games*, tr. Meyer Barash. Urbana: University of Illinois Press.
Caillois, Roger. 2003. *The Edge of Surrealism*, ed. Claudine Frank. Durham: Duke University Press.
Caird, John. 1880. *An Introduction to the Philosophy of Religion*. Glasgow: James Maclehose.
Caird, John. 1885. *The Social Philosophy and Religion of Comte*. Glasgow: James Maclehose.
Caird, John. 1886. *Hegel*. Philadelphia: J.B. Lippincott.
Caird, John. 1893. *Hegel*. Edinburgh and London: William Blackwood and Sons.
Calderwood, James L. 1984. "Hamlet's Readiness." *Shakespeare Quarterly* 35(3): 267–73.
Calvin, John. [1559] 1981. *Institutes of the Christian Religion*, tr. Henry Beveridge. Grand Rapids, MI: Wm. B. Eerdmans.
Calvino, Italo. 1974. *Invisible Cities*, tr. William Weaver. San Diego: Harcourt.
Camus, Albert. 1955. *The Myth of Sisyphus and Other Essays*, tr. Justin O'Brien. New York. Vintage.
Camus, Albert. 1956. *The Rebel*, tr. Anthony Bower. New York: Vintage.
Cannon, James. [1944] 1995. *The History of American Trotskyism*. New York: Pathfinder.
Capek, Karel. [1923] 1961. *R.U.R.* Oxford: Oxford University Press.
Capra, Fritjof. 1982. *The Turning Point*. New York: Bantam.
Carlyle, Thomas. [1836] 1987. *Sartor Resartus*. Oxford: Oxford University Press.
Carlyle, Thomas. 1900. *Critical and Miscellaneous Essays*, Vol. 1. New York: Scribner's Sons.
Carus, Paul. [1900] 1996. *The History of the Devil and the Idea of Evil*. New York: Gramercy.

Cassano, Graham. 2008. "Radical Critique and Progressive Traditionalism in John Ford's *The Grapes of Wrath*." *Critical Sociology* 34(1): 99–116.
Cassano, Graham. 2016. "Critical Pragmatism's Status Wage and the Standpoint of the Stranger." Pp. 217–39 in *Capitalism's Future*, ed. Dan Krier and Mark P. Worrell. Leiden and Boston: Brill.
Cassano, Graham. 2019. "The Master's Race: Phallic Whiteness in 'The Young Savages.'" *Fast Capitalism* 16.2. Online: (https://fastcapitalism.journal.library.uta.edu/index.php/fastcapitalism).
Cassirer, Ernst. 1944. *An Essay on Man*. New York: Doubleday Anchor.
Cassirer, Ernst. 1946. *Language and Myth*. New York: Harper.
Cassirer, Ernst. 1955a. *The Philosophy of Symbolic Forms*, Vol. 1. New Haven: Yale University Press.
Cassirer, Ernst. 1955b. *The Philosophy of Symbolic Forms*, Vol. 2. New Haven: Yale University Press.
Cassirer, Ernst. 1996. *The Philosophy of Symbolic Forms*, Vol. 4, The Metaphysics of Symbolic Forms. New Haven: Yale University Press.
Cassirer, Ernst. 2013. *The Warburg Years*, tr. S.G. Lofts with A. Calcagno. New Haven: Yale University Press.
Castoriadis, Cornelius. 1987. *The Imaginary Institution of Society*, tr. Kathleen Blamey. Cambridge: The MIT Press.
Chandler, Raymond. 1995. *Later Novels and Other Writings*. New York: Library of America.
Chateaubriand, François-René de. 1962. "Progress." Pp. 99–107 in *Catholic Political Thought*, ed. Bela Menczer. Notre Dame: University of Notre Dame Press.
Chattopadhyaya, D.P. 1987. "Sociology of Knowledge." *Annals of the Bhandarkar Oriental Research Institute* 68(1/4): 133–75.
Chesterton, G.K. 1986. *Collected Works*, Vol. 1. San Francisco: Ignatius Press.
Chopin, Kate. 1899. *The Awakening*. Chicago: Herbert S. Stone and Co.
Christie, Agatha. 1934. *Murder on the Orient Express*. New York: Harper.
Cioran, E.M. 1974. *The New Gods*, tr. Richard Howard. Chicago: The University of Chicago Press.
Collins, Randall. 1998. *The Sociology of Philosophies*. Cambridge: Harvard University Press.
Comte, Auguste. 1853. *The Positive Philosophy*, Vol. 2. London: John Chapman.
Comte, Auguste. 1969. *Auguste Comte: Sire of Sociology*. New York: Thomas Y. Crowell Company.
Comte-Sponville, Andre. 2004. *The Little Book of Philosophy*. London: Heinemann.
Comte-Sponville, Andre. 2007. *The Little Book of Atheist Spirituality*. New York: Viking.
Cooley, Charles Horton. [1909] 1962. *Social Organization*. New York: Schocken.
Copleston, Frederick. 1950. *Medieval Philosophy*. New York: Doubleday.

Cornford, F.M. [1912] 2004. *From Religion to Philosophy*. Mineola: Dover.

Coser, Lewis. 1972. *Sociology Through Literature*, 2nd Ed. Englewood Cliffs: Prentice-Hall.

Cousin, Victor. 1853. *Course of the History of Modern Philosophy*, tr. O.W. Wright. New York: D. Appleton.

Cox, Gary. 2012. *The Existentialist's Guide to Death, the Universe, and Nothingness*. London: Continuum.

Crease, Robert P. 2019. *The Workshop and the World*. New York: W.W. Norton.

Creighton, James Edwin. 1925. *Studies in Speculative Philosophy*. New York: Macmillan.

CrimethInc. 2001. *Days of War, Nights of Love*. Salem: CrimethInc.

CrimethInc. 2011. *Work*. Salem: CrimethInc.

Croce, Benedetto. 1915. *What is Living and What is Dead of the Philosophy of Hegel*. London: Macmillan.

Croce, Benedetto. 1917. *Logic as the Science of the Pure Concept*. London: Macmillan.

Cunha, Euclides da. 1944. *Rebellion in the Backlands*, tr. Samuel Putnam. Chicago: The University of Chicago Press.

Curtain, Maureen F. 2015. "Warren Weinstein and the Law are Casualties of U.S. Drone War." *Syracuse.com*, 8 May. Online: (www.syracuse.com/opinion/index.ssf/2015/05/warren_weinstein_and_law_are_casualties_of_us_drone_war_commentary.html).

Cutler, Jonathan. 2011. *Literary Theory*. New York: Oxford University Press.

Czapski, Jozef. [1987] 2018. *Lost Time: Lectures on Proust in a Soviet Prison Camp*, tr. Eric Karpeles. New York: New York Review of Books.

Dahms, Harry F. 2019. "Ignoring Goethe's Faust." *Fast Capitalism* 16(2). Online: (https://fastcapitalism.journal.library.uta.edu/index.php/fastcapitalism/article/view/223).

Dante Alighieri. 1995. *The Divine Comedy*, tr. Allen Mandelbaum. New York: Knopf.

Danto, Arthur. 1965. *Analytical Philosophy of History*. Cambridge: Cambridge University Press.

Darwin, Charles. 1897. *The Descent of Man*. New York: Appleton.

Davis, Creston. 2010. "Paul and Subtraction." Pp. 100–21 in *Paul's New Moment: Continental Philosophy and the Future of Christian Theology* by Milbank et al. Grand Rapids, MI: Brazos Press.

Davy, Georges. 1927. *Emile Durkheim*. Paris: Louis-Michaud.

Davy, Georges. 1957. "Introduction." Pp. xliii–lxxiv in *Professional Ethics and Civic Morals* by Emile Durkheim. London and New York: Routledge.

Debord, Guy. 1983. *Society of the Spectacle*. Detroit: Black & Red.

Debord, Guy, Attila Kotanyi, and Raoul Vaneigem. [1962] 1981. "Theses on the Paris Commune." Pp. 314–17 in *Situationist International Anthology*, edited by Ken Knabb. Berkeley: Bureau of Public Secrets.

Degré, Gerard. 1985. *The Social Compulsions of Ideas*. New Brunswick: Transaction.

Deleuze, Gilles and Felix Guattari. 1983. *Anti-Oedipus: Capitalism and Schizophrenia.* Minneapolis: University of Minnesota Press.

Descartes, Rene. 1954. *Philosophical Writings,* eds. Elizabeth Anscombe and Peter Thomas Geach. Wokingham, UK: Van Nostrand Reinhold.

Dewey, John. 1903. *Ethical Principles Underlying Education.* Chicago: The University of Chicago Press.

Dewey, John. 1929. *The Quest for Certainty.* New York: Capricorn.

Dewey, John. 1946. *Problems of Men.* New York: Philosophical Library.

Dewey, John. 1978. *The Middle Works, 1899–1911,* Vol. 6. Carbondale: Southern Illinois University Press.

Dicker, Georges. 1993. *Descartes: An Analytical and Historical Introduction.* New York: Oxford University Press.

Dickey, Colin. 2013. "Pitch Battles." *The Believer.* Online: (http://reprints.longform.org/pitch-battles).

Dicks, Henry V. 1972. *Licensed Mass Murder.* New York: Basic Books.

Diderot, Denis. 1966. *Rameau's Nephew* and *D'Alembert's Dream,* tr. Leonard Tancock. New York: Penguin.

Diderot, Denis. 1999. *Jacques the Fatalist,* tr. David Coward. Oxford: Oxford University Press.

Dilthey, Wilhelm. 1961. *Pattern and Meaning in History.* New York: Harper.

Dolar, Mladen. 2006. *A Voice and Nothing More.* Cambridge: The MIT Press.

Dostoyevsky, Fyodor. [1863] 1955. *Winter Notes on Summer Impressions,* tr. John Calder. Surrey, UK: Alma Books.

Dostoyevsky, Fyodor. 1912. *The Brothers Karamazov,* tr. Constance Garnett. New York: The Modern Library.

Dostoyevsky, Fyodor. 1994. *Crime and Punishment, The Gambler,* and *Notes from the Underground.* London: Chancellor Press.

Doyle, John P. 1995. "Translation Notes." Pp. 55–56 in *On Beings of Reason* by Francisco Suarez, ed. and tr. J. Doyle. Milwaukee: Marquette University Press.

Draper, Hal. 1977. *Karl Marx's Theory of Revolution,* Vol. 1. New York: Monthly Review Press.

Draper, Hal. 1978. *Karl Marx's Theory of Revolution,* Vol. 2. New York: Monthly Review Press.

Du Bois, W.E. Burghardt. [1903] 1969. *The Souls of Black Folk.* New York: New American Library.

Du Bois, W.E. Burghardt. 1935. *Black Reconstruction in America.* New York: Harcourt, Brace and Co.

Du Bois, W.E. Burghardt. 1965. *The World and Africa.* New York: International Publishers.

Dumézil, Georges. 1970. *Archaic Roman Religion,* tr. Philip Krapp. Baltimore: The Johns Hopkins University Press.

Dunayevskaya, Raya. 1943. "A Restatement of Some Fundamentals of Marxism Against 'Pseudo-Marxism.'" Online: (https://web.archive.org/web/20130821153517/http://newsandletters.org/issues/1999/June/6.99_rd.htm).

Dunayevskaya, Raya. 1961. "Notes on the *Logic* from Hegel's *Encyclopedia of Philosophical Sciences*." Online: (www.marxists.org/archive/dunayevskaya/works/news let/5_oo_rd.htm).

Dunayevskaya, Raya. 1965. "The Theory of Alienation: Marx's Debt to Hegel." Online: (www.marxists.org/archive/dunayevskaya/works/articles/alienation.htm).

Dunayevskaya, Raya. 1980. *Hegel's Absolute as a New Beginning*. News and Letters Reprint.

Durkheim, Emile. [1893] 1984. *The Division of Labor in Society*, tr. W.D. Halls. New York: The Free Press.

Durkheim, Emile. [1897] 1951. *Suicide*, tr. J. Spaulding and G. Simpson. New York: The Free Press.

Durkheim, Emile. [1901] 2006. "Technology." Pp. 31–32 in *Marcel Mauss: Techniques, Technology and Civilization*, ed. Nathan Schlanger. New York: Durkheim Press/Berghahn.

Durkheim, Emile. [1912] 1915. *The Elementary Forms of the Religious Life*, tr. Joseph Ward Swain. New York: The Free Press.

Durkheim, Emile. [1912] 1995. *The Elementary Forms of Religious Life*, tr. Karen E. Fields. New York: The Free Press.

Durkheim, Emile. [1914] 1960. "The Dualism of Human Nature and Its Social Conditions." Pp. 325–40 in *Emile Durkheim, 1858–1917, A Collection of Essays*, ed. Kurt H. Wolff. Columbus: Ohio State University Press.

Durkheim, Emile. 1915. *Germany Above All*. Paris: Librairie Armand Colin.

Durkheim, Emile. 1957. *Professional Ethics and Civic Morals*, tr. Cornelia Brookfield. London and New York: Routledge.

Durkheim, Emile. 1958. *Socialism*. New York, NY: Collier.

Durkheim, Emile. 1960. *Montesquieu and Rousseau*. Ann Arbor: The University of Michigan Press.

Durkheim, Emile. 1961. *Moral Education*, tr. Everett K. Wilson and Herman Schnurer. Mineola: Dover.

Durkheim, Emile. 1973. *On Morality and Society*. Chicago: The University of Chicago Press.

Durkheim, Emile. 1974. *Sociology and Philosophy*, tr. D.F. Pocock. New York: The Free Press.

Durkheim, Emile. 1977. *The Evolution of Educational Thought: Lectures on the Formation and development of Secondary Education in France*, tr. Peter Collins. London: Routledge and Kegan Paul.

Durkheim, Emile. 1978. *On Institutional Analysis*, ed. and tr. Mark Traugott. Chicago: University of Chicago Press.

Durkheim, Emile. 1981. "The Realm of Sociology as a Science." *Social Forces* 59 (4): 1054–070.

Durkheim, Emile. 1982. *The Rules of Sociological Method*, ed. Steven Lukes, tr. W.D. Halls. New York: The Free Press.

Durkheim, Emile. 1983. *Pragmatism and Sociology*, tr. J.C. Whitehouse and ed. John B. Allcock. Cambridge: Cambridge University Press.

Durkheim, Emile. 1993. *Ethics and the Sociology of Morals*, tr. Robert T. Hall. Buffalo: Prometheus.

Durkheim, Emile. 2004. *Durkheim's Philosophy Lectures: Notes from the Lycée de Sens Course, 1883–1884*, eds. Neil Gross and Robert Alun Jones. Cambridge: Cambridge University Press.

Durkheim, Emile. 2006. *On Suicide*, tr. Robin Buss. New York: Penguin.

Durkheim, Emile and Marcel Mauss. [1903] 1963. *Primitive Classification*, ed. and tr. Rodney Needham. Chicago: University of Chicago Press.

Durkheim, Emile and Marcel Mauss. [1913] 2006. "Note on the Concept of Civilization." Pp. 35–39 in *Marcel Mauss: Techniques, Technology and Civilization*, ed. Nathan Schlanger. New York: Durkheim Press/Berghahn.

Dutt, R. Palme. 1935. *Fascism and Social Revolution*. New York: International Publishers.

Eco, Umberto. 1983. *The Name of the Rose*, tr. William Weaver. New York: Knopf.

Eco, Umberto. 1984. *Semiotics and the Philosophy of Language*. Bloomington: Indiana University Press.

Eco, Umberto. 2001. The Prague Cemetery, tr. R. Dixon. New York: Houghton Mifflin Harcourt.

Eco, Umberto. 2016. *Chronicles of a Liquid Society*, tr. R. Dixon. New York: Houghton Mifflin Harcourt.

Eldridge, J.E.T. (ed.). 1971. *Max Weber: The Interpretation of Reality*. New York: Charles Scribner's Sons.

Eliade, Mircea. 1987. *The Sacred and the Profane*, tr. Willard R. Trask. San Diego: Harcourt.

Eliot, George. [1871–72] 2015. *Middlemarch*. New York: Penguin.

Eliot, T.S. 1922. *The Waste Land*. New York: Boni and Liveright.

Elliott, Justin and Laura Sullivan. 2015. "How the Red Cross Raised Half a Billion Dollars for Haiti and Built Six Homes." *ProPublica*, 3 June. Online: (www.propublica.org/article/how-the-red-cross-raised-half-a-billion-dollars-for-haiti-and-built-6-homes).

Ellison, Ralph. 1947. *Invisible Man*. New York: Vintage.

Emerson, Ralph Waldo. 1950. *The Selected Writings of Ralph Waldo Emerson*. New York: The Modern Library.

Epstein, Helen. 2019. "The Highest Suicide Rate in the World." *The New York Review of Books*, 10 October. Online: (www.nybooks.com/articles/2019/10/10/inuit-highest-suicide-rate).

Erasmus. [1509] 1913. *The Praise of Folly*, tr. John Wilson. London: Oxford University Press.
Etzioni, Amitai. 2011. "The Good, the Bad and the Ugly on Unmanned Aircraft." *The National Interest*, 4 October. Online: (http://nationalinterest.org/commentary/the-drone-debate-5945).
Fanon, Frantz. 1967. *Black Skin, White Masks*. New York: Grove Press.
Fasenfest, David. 2018. "Is Marx Still Relevant?" *Critical Sociology* 44(6): 851–55.
Fauconnet, Paul. 1923. "The Pedagogical Work of Emile Durkheim." *The American Journal of Sociology* 28(5): 529–53.
Fauconnet, Paul. 1927. "The Durkheim School in France." *Sociological Review* 19 (1): 15–20.
Feldmann, Tony. 2019. "Political Mystagogue: Steve Bannon and the Spell of Domination." *Fast Capitalism* 16.2. Online: (https://fastcapitalism.journal.library.uta.edu/index.php/fastcapitalism).
Fellman, Gordon. 1998. *Rambo and the Dalai Lama*. Albany: SUNY Press.
Fernbach, David (ed.). 1974. *Surveys from Exile*. New York: Random House.
Feuerbach, Ludwig. 1986. *Principles of the Philosophy of the Future*. Indianapolis: Hackett.
Fichte, Johann Gottlieb. 1847. *The Vocation of the Scholar*, tr. W. Smith. London: Chapman.
Fichte, Johann Gottlieb. 1848. *The Vocation of Man*, tr. William Smith. London: Chapman.
Figes, Orlando. 1996. *A People's Tragedy*. New York: Penguin.
Findlay, J.N. 1958. *Hegel: A Re-Examination*. New York: Collier.
Findlay, J.N. 1970. *Ascent to the Absolute*. New York: Humanities Press.
Fink, Bruce. 1995. *The Lacanian Subject*. Princeton: Princeton University Press.
Fink, Bruce. 1997. *A Clinical Introduction to Lacanian Psychoanalysis: Theory and Technique*. Cambridge: Harvard University Press.
Flaubert, Gustave. 1885. *Salammbô*, tr. M. French Sheldon. London: Saxon and Co.
Flaubert, Gustave. 1957. *Madame Bovary*, tr. Francis Steegmuller. New York: Knopf.
Foucault, Michel. 1970. *The Order of Things*. New York: Vintage.
Foucault, Michel. 1977. *Discipline and Punish*. New York: Vintage.
Fournier, Marcel. 2006. *Marcel Mauss*, tr. J.M. Todd. Princeton: Princeton University Press.
Frankfurt Institute for Social Research. 1972. *Aspects of Sociology*. Boston: Beacon.
Franklin, Benjamin. 2008. *The Way to Wealth*. Best Success Books.
Frazer, J.G. 1913. *Psyche's Task*, second edition. London: Macmillan.
Freeman, Joseph. 1936. *An American Testament*. New York: Farrar and Rinehart.
Freeman, Joseph. 1943. *Never Call Retreat*. New York: Farrar and Rinehart.
Freud, Sigmund. [1900] 1965. *The Interpretation of Dreams*. New York: Avon.
Freud, Sigmund. [1901] 1952. *On Dreams*. New York: W.W. Norton.

Freud, Sigmund. [1910] 1959, "Contributions to the Psychology of Love: A Special Type of Choice of Object Made by Men." Pp. 192–202 in in *Collected Papers*, Vol. 4. New York: Basic Books.

Freud, Sigmund. [1910] 1961. *Leonardo da Vinci and a Memory of His Childhood*. New York: W.W. Norton.

Freud, Sigmund. [1912] 1959, "Contributions to the Psychology of Love: The Most Prevalent Form of Degradation in Erotic Life." Pp. 203–16 in *Collected Papers*, Vol. 4. New York: Basic Books.

Freud, Sigmund. [1913] 1950. *Totem and Taboo*. New York: W.W. Norton.

Freud, Sigmund. [1914] 1959. "On Narcissism: An Introduction." Pp. 30–59 in *Collected Papers*, Vol. 4. New York: Basic Books.

Freud, Sigmund. [1915] 1959. "Thoughts for the Times on War and Death." Pp. 288–317 in *Collected Papers*, Vol. 4. New York: Basic Books.

Freud, Sigmund. [1917] 1959. "Mourning and Melancholia." Pp. 152–70 in *Collected Papers*, Vol. 4. New York: Basic Books.

Freud, Sigmund. [1917] 1966. *Introductory Lectures on Psycho-Analysis*. New York: W.W. Norton.

Freud, Sigmund. [1919] 1959. "The Uncanny." Pp. 368–407 in *Collected Papers*, Vol. 4. New York: Basic Books.

Freud, Sigmund. [1921] 1959. *Group Psychology and the Analysis of the Ego*. New York: W.W. Norton.

Freud, Sigmund. [1923] 1960. *The Ego and the Id*. New York: W.W. Norton.

Freud, Sigmund. [1925] 1959. "Negation." Pp. 181–85 in *Collected Papers*, Vol. 5. New York: Basic Books.

Freud, Sigmund. [1926] 1959. *Inhibitions, Symptoms, and Anxiety*. New York: W.W. Norton.

Freud, Sigmund. [1927] 1959. "Fetishism." Pp. 198–204 in *Collected Papers*, Vol. 5. New York: Basic Books.

Freud, Sigmund. [1927] 1961. *The Future of an Illusion*. New York: Norton.

Freud, Sigmund. [1930] 1961. *Civilization and its Discontents*. New York: W.W. Norton.

Freud, Sigmund. [1931] 1959. "Libidinal Types." Pp. 247–51 in *Collected Papers*, Vol. 5. New York: Basic Books.

Freud, Sigmund. [1938] 1959. "Some Elementary Lessons in Psycho-Analysis." Pp. 376–82 in *Collected Papers*, Vol. 5. New York: Basic Books.

Freud, Sigmund. 1939. *Moses and Monotheism*. New York: Vintage.

Freud, Sigmund. [1940] 1969. *An Outline of Psycho-Analysis*. New York: W.W. Norton.

Freud, Sigmund. 1950. *The Question of Lay Analysis*. New York: W.W. Norton.

Freud, Sigmund. 1951. *Psychopathology of Everyday Life*. New York: New American Library.

Freud, Sigmund. 1960. *Jokes and Their Relation to the Unconscious*. New York: W.W. Norton.

Freud, Sigmund. 1962. *Three Essays on the Theory of Sexuality*. New York: Avon.
Freud, Sigmund. 1963. *The History of the Psychoanalytic Movement*. New York: Collier.
Freud, Sigmund. 1965. *New Introductory Lectures on Psycho-Analysis*. New York: W.W. Norton.
Freud, Sigmund. 2002. *The Schreber Case*. New York: Penguin.
Freud, Sigmund. 2003. *The 'Wolfman' and Other Cases*. New York: Penguin.
Freud, Sigmund. 2012. *The Letters of Sigmund Freud and Otto Rank*, eds. E.J. Lieberman and R. Kramer, tr. G.C. Richter. Baltimore: The Johns Hopkins University Press.
Freytag, Gustav. [1887] 1890. *The Lost Manuscript*, Vol. 1. Chicago: The Open Court.
Fried, Albert. 1997. *Communism in America*. New York: Columbia University Press.
Fromm, Erich. 1941. *Escape from Freedom*. New York: Henry Holt and Company.
Fromm, Erich. [1950] 1978. *Psychoanalysis and Religion*. New Haven: Yale University Press.
Fromm, Erich. 1957. "The Authoritarian Personality." Online: (www.marxists.org/archive/fromm/works/1957/authoritarian.htm).
Fromm, Erich. 1967. *Let Man Prevail*. New York: Socialist Party, USA.
Fromm, Erich. 1968. *The Revolution of Hope*. New York: Harper.
Fromm, Erich. 1970. *The Crisis of Psychoanalysis*. Greenwich: Fawcett Publications.
Fromm, Erich. 1973. *The Anatomy of Human Destructiveness*. New York: Holt, Rinehart and Winston.
Fromm, Erich. 1976. *To Have or to Be?* New York: Continuum.
Fromm, Erich. 1981. *On Disobedience*. New York: The Seabury Press.
Fromm, Erich. 1984. *The Working Class in Weimar Germany*. Cambridge: Harvard University Press.
Frontline. 2013. "Raising Adam Lanza." Online: (www.pbs.org/wgbh/pages/frontline/raising-adam-lanza).
Fustel de Coulanges, Numa Denis. [1873] 1956. *The Ancient City*. New York: Doubleday.
Galewitz, Phil. 2016. "Millions Could Lose Medicaid Coverage Under Trump Plan." *Kaiser Health News*, 9 November. Online: (http://khn.org/news/millions-could-lose-medicaid-coverage-under-trump-plan).
Gangas, Spyros. 2007. "Social Ethics and Logic: Rethinking Durkheim Through Hegel." *Journal of Classical Sociology* 7(3): 315–38.
Garcia, Jose M. Gonzalez. 2011. "Max Weber and Rilke: The Magic of Language and Music in a Disenchanted World." *Max Weber Studies* 11(2): 267–88.
Gary, Romain. 2017. *The Kites*, tr. M. Mouillot. New York: New Directions.
Gay, Peter. 1993. *The Cultivation of Hatred*. New York: W.W. Norton.
Gellner, Ernest. 1974. *Legitimation of Belief*. Cambridge: Cambridge University Press.
Gellner, Ernest. 1979. *Words and Things*. London: Routledge & Kegan Paul.
George, Henry. [1879] 1956. *Progress and Poverty*. New York: R. Schalkenbach Foundation.

Gerth, Hans and C. Wright Mills. 1953. *Character and Social Structure.* New York: Harcourt.
Gibbon, Edward. 1909. *The Decline and Fall of the Roman Empire*, Vol. 2. London: Methuen.
Giddens, Anthony. 1984. *The Constitution of Society.* Berkeley: University of California Press.
Gierke, Otto. [1868] 1990. *Community in Historical Perspective*, ed. Antony Black. Cambridge: Cambridge University Press.
Gillespie, Michael Allen. 2008. *The Theological Origins of Modernity.* Chicago: University of Chicago Press.
Ginsberg, Morris. 1921. *The Psychology of Society.* London: Methuen.
Godlove, Terry F. (ed.). 2005. *Teaching Durkheim.* New York: Oxford University Press.
Goethe, J.W. [1796] 1989. *Wilhelm Meister's Apprenticeship*, tr. Eric Blackall. Princeton: Princeton University Press.
Goethe, J.W. [1809] 1971. *Elective Affinities*, tr. R.J. Hollingdale. New York: Penguin.
Goethe, J.W. [1808] 1961. *Faust*, tr. Walter Kaufmann. New York: Anchor Books.
Goethe, J.W. 1840. *Theory of Colours*, tr. C.L. Eastlake. London: John Murray.
Goethe, J.W. 1976. *Faust*, tr. Walter Arndt and ed. Cyrus Hamlin. New York: W.W. Norton.
Goethe, J.W. 1983. *Selected Poems*, ed. Christopher Middleton. London: John Calder.
Goethe, J.W. 1984. *Faust*, tr. Stuart Atkins. Princeton: Princeton University Press.
Goethe, J.W. 1989. *The Sorrows of Young Werther*, tr. Michael Hulse. New York: Penguin.
Goffman, Erving. 1963. *Behavior in Public Places.* New York: The Free Press.
Goffman, Erving. 1967. *Interaction Ritual.* New York: Pantheon.
Goffman, Erving. 1974. *Frame Analysis.* Boston: Northeastern University Press.
Gogol, Nikolai. [1842] 1996. *Dead Souls*, tr. R. Pevear and L. Volokhonsky. New York: Knopf.
Goldmann, Lucien. 1969. *The Human Sciences and Philosophy.* London: Cape.
Goldmann, Lucien. 1976. *Cultural Creation.* Saint Louis: Telos Press.
Goodstein, Laurie. 2001. "After the Attacks: Finding Fault." *The New York Times*, 15 September. Online: (www.nytimes.com/2001/09/15/us/after-attacks-finding-fault-falwell-s-finger-pointing-inappropriate-bush-says.html).
Gorky, Maxim. 1962. *The Autobiography of Maxim Gorky.* New York: Collier Books.
Goux, Jean-Joseph. 1990. *Symbolic Economies.* Ithaca: Cornell University Press.
Gracia, Jorge J.E. 2011. "Introduction." Pp. 1–27 in *Suarez on Individuation.* Milwaukee: Marquette University Press.
Gramsci, Antonio. 1971. *Selections from the Prison Notebooks.* New York: International Publishers.
Granet, Marcel. 1951. *Chinese Civilization.* New York: Barnes and Noble.

Green, T.H. [1895] 1924. *Lectures on the Principles of Political Obligation*. London: Longmans, Green, and Co.
Greenberg, Hayim. [1942] 1945. "The Myth of Jewish Parasitism." *Jewish Frontier Anthology, 1934–1944*. New York: Jewish Frontier Association.
Greenblatt, Stephen. 1988. *Shakespearean Negotiations*. Berkeley: University of California Press.
Greenblatt, Stephen. 2011. *The Swerve*. New York: W.W. Norton.
Greene, Graham. 1929. *The Man Within*. New York: Penguin.
Greene, Graham. [1938]. 2004 *Brighton Rock*. New York: Penguin.
Greene, Graham. [1948] 2004. *The Heart of the Matter*. New York: Penguin.
Greene, Graham. [1951] 2004. *The End of the Affair*. New York: Penguin.
Greene, Graham. 1982. *Monsignor Quixote*. New York: Simon and Schuster.
Grene, David and Richmond Lattimore (eds.). 1960. *Greek Tragedies*, Vol. 1. Chicago: The University of Chicago Press.
Haeckel, Ernst. 1934. *The Riddle of the Universe*, tr. Joseph McCabe. London: Watts.
Hagens, Tobias. 2006. "*Conscience Collective* or False Consciousness?" *Journal of Classical Sociology* 6(2): 215–37.
Haidt, Jonathan. 2012. *The Righteous Mind*. New York: Vintage.
Haimson, Leopold H. 1955. *The Russian Marxists and the Origins of Bolshevism*. Boston: Beacon Press.
Halbwachs, Maurice. [1930] 1978. *The Causes of Suicide*, tr. Harold Goldblatt. London: Routledge and Kegan Paul.
Halbwachs, Maurice. 1958. *The Psychology of Social Class*, tr. Claire Delavenay. Glencoe: The Free Press.
Halbwachs, Maurice. 1962. *Sources of Religious Sentiment*, tr. John A. Spaulding. New York: The Free Press.
Halevy, Elie. 1960. *The Growth of Philosophical Radicalism*, tr. Mary Morris. Boston: Beacon.
Halevy, Elie. 1965. *The Era of Tyrannies*, tr. R.K. Webb. New York: NYU Press.
Hall, Claire. 2020. "The Day a God Rode In." *London Review of Books* 42(4). Online: (www.lrb.co.uk/the-paper/v42/n04/claire-hall/the-day-a-god-rode-in).
Hall, Stuart. 1997. "Representation, Meaning and Language." Pp. 15–64 in *Representation*, ed. Stuart Hall. London: Sage.
Hamison, Leopold. 1955. *The Russian Marxists and the Origins of Bolshevism*. Cambridge: Harvard University Press.
Harding, Esther M. 1947. *Psychic Energy*. Princeton: Princeton University Press.
Hardy, Thomas. [1894–95] 2006. *Jude the Obscure*. Mineola: Dover.
Harman, Graham. 2010. *Towards Speculative Realism*. Winchester, UK: Zero Books.
Harman, Graham. 2011. *The Quadruple Object*. Winchester, UK: Zero Books.

Harms, John B. 1981. "Reason and Social Change in Durkheim's Thought." *Pacific Sociological Review* 24(4): 393–410.

Harris, H.S. 1993. "Hegel's Intellectual Development to 1807." Pp. 25–51 in *The Cambridge Companion to Hegel*, ed. Frederick C. Beiser. Cambridge: Cambridge University Press.

Harrison, Jane Ellen. 1962. *Epilegomena to the Study of Greek Religion* and *Themis*. New Hyde Park: University Books.

Harvey, David. 1990. *The Condition of Postmodernity*. Cambridge: Blackwell.

Haste, Cate. 2019. *Passionate Spirit*. New York: Basic Books.

Heath-Kelly, Charlotte. 2012. "Can We Laugh Yet? Reading Post-9/11 Counterterrorism Policy as Magical Realism and Opening a Third-Space of Resistance." *European Journal on Criminal Policy and Research* 18(4): 343–60.

Hedge, Fredric (ed). 1847. *Prose Writers of Germany*. Philadelphia: Carey and Hart.

Hedges, Chris. 2002. *War is a Force That Gives Us Meaning*. New York: Anchor.

Hegel, G.W.F. [1801] 1977. *The Difference Between Fichte's and Schelling's System of Philosophy*, tr. H.S. Harris and Walter Cerf. Albany: SUNY Press.

Hegel, G.W.F. [1802–1804] 1979. *System of Ethical Life* and *First Philosophy of Spirit*, ed. and tr. H.S. Harris and T.M. Knox. Albany: SUNY Press.

Hegel, G.W.F. [1807] 1967. *The Phenomenology of Mind*, tr. J.B. Baillie. New York: Harper.

Hegel, G.W.F. [1807] 1977. *Phenomenology of Spirit*, tr. A.V. Miller. Oxford: Oxford University Press.

Hegel, G.W.F. [1807] 2008. *Phenomenology of Spirit*, tr. Terry Pinkard. Unpublished.

Hegel, G.W.F. [1812] 1969. *Science of Logic*, tr. A.V. Miller. Atlantic Highlands, NJ: Humanities Press International.

Hegel, G.W.F. [1821] 1991. *Elements of the Philosophy of Right*, tr. H.B. Nisbet. Cambridge: Cambridge University Press.

Hegel, G.W.F. [1830] 1991. *The Encyclopedia Logic, Part 1 of the Encyclopedia of Philosophical Sciences with the Zusätze*, tr. T.F. Geraets, W.A. Suchting, and H.S. Harris. Indianapolis/Cambridge: Hackett Publishing.

Hegel, G.W.F. [1840] 1974. *Lectures on the Philosophy of Religion*, Vol. 1, tr. E.B. Speirs and J. Burdon Sanderson (Reprint). New York: The Humanities Press.

Hegel, G.W.F. [1840] 1995a. *Lectures on the History of Philosophy*, Vol. 2, tr. E.S. Haldane and Frances H. Simson. Lincoln: University of Nebraska Press.

Hegel, G.W.F. [1840] 1995b. *Lectures on the History of Philosophy*, Vol. 3, tr. E.S. Haldane and Frances H. Simson. Lincoln: University of Nebraska Press.

Hegel, G.W.F. [1892] 1995. *Lectures on the History of Philosophy*, Vol. 1, tr. E.S. Haldane. Lincoln: University of Nebraska Press.

Hegel, G.W.F. 1948. *Early Theological Writings*. Philadelphia: University of Pennsylvania Press.

Hegel, G.W.F. 1956. *The Philosophy of History*, tr. J. Sibree. Mineola: Dover.
Hegel, G.W.F. 1975a. *Aesthetics,* Vol. 1, tr. T.M. Knox. Oxford: Oxford University Press.
Hegel, G.W.F. 1975b. *Aesthetics,* Vol. 2, tr. T.M. Knox. Oxford: Oxford University Press.
Hegel, G.W.F. 1975c. *Lectures on the Philosophy of World History: Introduction,* tr. H.B. Nisbet. Cambridge: Cambridge University Press.
Hegel, G.W.F. 1983. *Hegel and the Human Spirit,* tr. Leo Rauch. Detroit: Wayne State University Press. Online: (www.marxists.org/reference/archive/hegel/jlindex.htm).
Hegel, G.W.F. 1984. *Hegel: The Letters,* tr. Clark Butler and Christiane Seiler. Bloomington: Indiana University Press.
Hegel, G.W.F. 1986. *The Philosophical Propaedeutic,* tr. A.V. Miller. Oxford and New York: Basil Blackwell.
Hegel, G.W.F. 1987. *Lectures on the Philosophy of Religion,* Vol. 2. Berkeley: University of California Press.
Hegel, G.W.F. 1988. *Lectures on the Philosophy of Religion,* abridged. Berkeley: University of California Press.
Hegel, G.W.F. 2002. *Miscellaneous Writings of G.W.F. Hegel,* ed. Jon Stewart. Evanston: Northwestern University Press.
Hegel, G.W.F. 2007. *Philosophy of Mind,* tr. W. Wallace and A.V. Miller. Oxford: Oxford University Press.
Heiden, Konrad. 1934. *A History of National Socialism.* London: Methuen.
Herder, Johann Gottfried. 1966. *Outlines of a Philosophy of the History of Man.* New York: Bergman Publishers.
Herder, Johann Gottfried. 1993. *Against Pure Reason,* ed. and tr. Marcia Bunge. Fortress Press: Minneapolis.
Hertz, Robert. [1913] 1987. "St Besse: A Study of an Alpine Cult." Pp. 55–100 in *Saints and their Cults,* ed. Stephen Wilson. Cambridge: Cambridge University Press.
Hertz, Robert. 1994. *Sin and Expiation in Primitive Societies,* tr. Robert Parkin. Oxford: British Centre for Durkheimian Studies.
Hess, Moses. 1845. "The Essence of Money." Online: (www.marxistsfr.org/archive/hess/1845/essence-money.htm).
Hesse, Hermann. [1925] 1965. *Demian.* New York: Harper.
Hesse, Hermann. 1963. *Steppenwolf.* New York: The Modern Library.
Hesse, Hermann. 1971. *If the War Goes On...,* tr. Ralph Manheim. New York: Farrar, Straus and Giroux.
Hetherington, Marc J. and Jonathan D. Weiler. 2009. *Authoritarianism and Polarization in American Politics.* Cambridge: Cambridge University Press.
Hirst, R.J. 1967. "Realism." Pp. 77–83 in *The Encyclopedia of Philosophy,* Vol. 7. New York: Macmillan and The Free Press.
Hobbes, Thomas. 1651. *Leviathan.* London: Andrew Crooke. Online: (socserv2.socsci.mcmaster.ca/econ/ugcm/3ll3/hobbes/Leviathan.pdf).

Hobbes, Thomas. 1889. *Behemoth*, ed. F. Tönnies. London: Simpkin, Marshall, and Co.

Hocart, A.M. [1936] 1970. *Kings and Councillors*. Chicago: The University of Chicago Press.

Hocking, William Ernest. 1918. *Morale and its Enemies*. New Haven: Yale University Press.

Hocking, William Ernest. 1926. *Man and the State*. New Haven: Yale University Press.

Hocking, William Ernest. 1956. *The Coming World Civilization*. New York: Harper.

Hodgkin, Luke. 2005. *A History of Mathematics*. Oxford: Oxford University Press.

Hofstadter, Douglas. 2007. *I am a Strange Loop*. New York: Basic Books.

Hölderlin, Friedrich. 2008. *Hyperion*, tr. Ross Benjamin. New York: Archipelago Books.

Horkheimer, Max. 1972. *Critical Theory*. New York: Continuum.

Horkheimer, Max. 1978. *Dawn and Decline*. New York: Seabury.

Horkheimer, Max and Theodor W. Adorno. [1944] 1972. *Dialectic of Enlightenment*, tr. John Cumming. New York: Continuum.

Horney, Karen. 1939. *New Ways in Psychoanalysis*. New York: W.W. Norton.

Horney, Karen. 1945. *Our Inner Conflicts*. New York: W.W. Norton.

Horney, Karen (ed.). 1946. *Are You Considering Psychoanalysis?* New York: W.W. Norton.

Horowitz, Mark. 2004. "Attitudes Towards Wage Fairness in the Maquiladora Zone." Ph.D. dissertation, University of Kansas.

Houellebecq, Michel. 2015. *Submission*. New York: Farrar, Straus and Giroux.

Howard, Dick. 1972. *The Development of the Marxian Dialectic*. Carbondale: Southern Illinois University Press.

Hubert, Henri and Marcel Mauss. 1964. *Sacrifice*. Chicago: The University of Chicago Press.

Hughes, H. Stuart. 1977. *Consciousness and Society: The Reorientation of European Social Thought: 1890–1930*, revised edition. New York: Vintage Books.

Huizinga, Johan. 1924. *The Waning of the Middle Ages*. New York: St. Martin's Press.

Hume, David. 1896. *A Treatise of Human Nature*. Oxford: Clarendon Press.

Hume, David. 2018. *David Hume on Morals, Politics, and Society*, ed. Angela Coventry and Andrew Valls. New Haven: Yale University Press.

Hutchinson, William T. et al. (eds.). 1962. *The Papers of James Madison*. Chicago: University of Chicago Press. Online: (http://press-pubs.uchicago.edu/founders/documents/v1ch17s22.html).

Huxley, Aldous. [1932] 1946. *Brave New World*. Cutchogue, NY: Buccaneer Books.

Institute of Social Research. 1944. "Ten Years on Morningside Heights: A Report on the Institute's History: 1934–1944." Unpublished prospectus. Columbia University.

Institute of Social Research. 1945. *Antisemitism Among American Labor*. Unpublished, four-volume report. Columbia University.

Ivimey, Muriel. 1946. "What is a Neurosis?" Pp. 61–92 in *Are You Considering Psychoanalysis?*, ed. Karen Horney. New York: W.W. Norton.
Jackson, Holly. 2019. *American Radicals*. New York: Crown.
Jacoby, Russell. 1981. *Dialectic of Defeat*. Cambridge: Cambridge University Press.
James, William. [1907] 1995. *Pragmatism*. New York: Dover.
James, William. 1909. *A Pluralistic Universe*. London: Longmans, Gren, and Co.
James, William. 1918. *The Principles of Psychology,* Vol. 1. Mineola: Dover.
Jameson, Fredric. 1973. "The Vanishing Mediator: Narrative Structure in Max Weber." *New German Critique* 1: 52–89.
Jameson, Fredric. 1990. *Late Marxism*. London: Verso.
Jameson, Fredric. 1991. *Postmodernism*. Durham: Duke University Press.
Jameson, Fredric. 2009. *Valences of the Dialectic*. London: Verso.
Jaspers, Karl. 1986. *Basic Philosophical Writings*, ed. and tr. Edith Ehrlich, Leonard H. Ehrlich, and George B. Pepper. Amherst: Prometheus Books.
Jay, Martin. 1984. *Marxism and Totality*. Berkeley: University of California Press.
Jaynes, Julian. 1990. *The Origin of Consciousness in the Breakdown of the Bicameral Mind*. Boston: Houghton Mifflin.
Jones, Ernest. 1931. *On the Nightmare*. London: Hogarth Press.
Jones, Ernest. 1961. *The Life and Work of Sigmund Freud*. Garden City: Doubleday.
Jones, Susan Stedman. 1998. "The Concept of Belief in the *Elementary Forms*." Pp. 53–65 in *On Durkheim's* Elementary Forms of Religious Life, eds. N.J. Allen, W.S.F. Pickering, and W. Watts Miller. London: Routledge.
Jones, Susan Stedman. [2000] 2006. "Representations in Durkheim's Masters: Kant and Renouvier." Pp. 37–58 in *Durkheim and Representations*, ed by W.S.F. Pickering. London: Routledge.
Jones, Susan Stedman. 2001. *Durkheim Reconsidered*. Cambridge: Polity.
Jones, W.T. 1969. *The Medieval Mind: A History of Western Philosophy*, Vol. 2, second edition. San Diego: Harcourt.
Jones, W.T. 1970. *A History of Western Philosophy, Volume 1: The Classical Mind*, second edition. San Diego: Harcourt.
Juergensmeyer, Mark. 2008. "Martyrdom and Sacrifice in a Time of Terror." *Social Research* 75(2): 417–34.
Jung, Carl. 1969. *The Archetypes and the Collective Unconscious,* second edition. Princeton: Princeton University Press.
Junger, Ernst. [1920] 2016. *Storm of Steel*, tr. Michael Hoffmann. New York: Penguin.
Kaag, John. 2016. *American Philosophy: A Love Story*. New York: Farrar, Straus and Giroux.
Kaag, John. 2017. "Me for the Woods." *The Paris Review*, 30 June. Online: (www.theparisreview.org/blog/2017/06/30/me-for-the-woods).

Kammari, M.D. and G.L. Kabaev. 1965. "Problems of Historical Materialism and Concrete Sociological Research." Pp. 101–08 in *Social Sciences in the USSR*, Unesco. Paris: Mouton.

Kant, Immanuel. 1929. *Critique of Pure Reason*, tr. Norman Kemp Smith. New York: St. Martin's Press.

Kant, Immanuel. 1951. *Critique of Judgement*, tr. J.H. Bernard. New York: Hafner.

Kant, Immanuel. 1964. *Groundwork of the Metaphysics of Morals*, tr. H.J. Paton. New York: Harper & Row.

Kant, Immanuel. 1983. *Perpetual Peace and Other Essays*, tr. Ted Humphrey. Indianapolis: Hackett.

Kant, Immanuel. 1991. *The Metaphysics of Morals*, tr. Mary Gregor. Cambridge: Cambridge University Press.

Kant, Immanuel. 1998. *Religion Within the Boundaries of Mere Reason*, ed. and tr. by Allen Wood and George Di Giovanni. Cambridge: Cambridge University Press.

Kapur, Akash. 2016. "The Return of the Utopians." *The New Yorker*, 3 October. Online: (www.newyorker.com/magazine/2016/10/03/the-return-of-the-utopians).

Kasser, Rudolphe and Gregor Wurst (eds.). 2007. *The Gospel of Judas*, tr. R. Kasser, M. Meyer, G. Wurst, and F. Gaudard. Washington, DC: National Geographic.

Kaufmann, Walter. 1958. *Critique of Religion and Philosophy*. Princeton: Princeton University Press.

Kaufmann, Walter. 1965a. *Hegel: A Reinterpretation*. Notre Dame: University of Notre Dame Press.

Kaufmann, Walter. 1965b. *Hegel: Text and Commentary*. Notre Dame: University of Notre Dame Press.

Kaufmann, Walter. 1980. *Discovering the Mind: Freud, Adler, and Jung*. New Brunswick: Transaction.

Kierkegaard, Søren. 1940. *For Self-Examination*. Minneapolis: Augsburg Publishing House.

Kierkegaard, Søren. 1954. *Fear and Trembling* and *Sickness Unto Death*, tr. Walter Lowrie. Princeton: Princeton University Press.

Kierkegaard, Søren. 1987. *Either/Or*. Princeton: Princeton University Press.

Kipling, Rudyard. 1943. "If—." Online: (www.poetryfoundation.org/poems/46473/if---).

Kitto, H.D.F. 1950. *Greek Tragedy*. Garden City: Doubleday.

Kliff, Sarah. 2016. "Why Obamacare Enrollees Voted for Trump." *Vox*, 13 December. Online: (www.vox.com/science-and-health/2016/12/13/13848794/kentucky-obamacare-trump).

Kliman, Andrew. 2007. *Reclaiming Marx's 'Capital.'* Lanham: Lexington Books.

Klinkenborg, Verlyn. 2019. "What Were Dinosaurs For?" *The New York Review of Books*, 19 December. Online: (www.nybooks.com/articles/2019/12/19/what-were-dinosaurs-for/).

Knapp, Peter. 1986. "Hegel's Universal in Marx, Durkheim, and Weber: The Role of Hegelian Ideas in the Origin of Sociology." *Sociological Forum* 1(4): 586–609.

Knoebel, Edgar (ed.). 1988. *Classics of Western Thought*, Vol. 3, 4th ed. Toronto: Wadsworth.

Koestler, Arthur. [1941] 1968. *Darkness at Noon*. New York: Scribner.

Koestler, Arthur. 2000. "Humor." *Encyclopaedia Britannica*. Online: (www.britannica.com/topic/humor).

Kojève, Alexandre. [1947] 1969. *Introduction to the Reading of Hegel*. Ithaca: Cornell University Press.

Kolnai, Aurel. 1922. *Psychoanalysis and Sociology*, tr. Eden and Cedar Paul. New York: Harcourt.

Koontz, Dean. 2012. *Odd Thomas*. New York: Random House.

Körner, Stephan. 1955. *Kant*. New York: Penguin.

Korsch, Karl. 1970. *Marxism and Philosophy*. New York: Monthly Review Press.

Koselleck, Reinhart. 1985. *Futures Past*, tr. Keith Tribe: Cambridge: The MIT Press.

Kracauer, Siegfried. 1995. *The Mass Ornament*. Cambridge: Harvard University Press.

Kracauer, Siegfried. 1998. *The Salaried Masses*. London: Verso.

Kracauer, Siegfried. 1999. "The Hotel Lobby." *Postcolonial Studies* 2(3): 289–97.

Kracauer, Siegfried. 2003. "Hollywood's Terror Films: Do They Reflect an American State of Mind." *New German Critique* 89: 105–11.

Kracht, Christian. 2015. *Imperium*, tr. Daniel Bowles. New York: Farrar, Straus and Giroux.

Krier, Dan. 2005. *Speculative Management*. Albany: State University of New York Press.

Krier, Dan. 2008. "Critical Institutionalism and Finance Globalization: A Comparative Analysis of American and Continental Finance." *The New York Journal of Sociology* 1: 130–86.

Krier, Dan. 2017. "Debt, Value, and Economic Theology." *Continental Thought and Theory* 1(2). Online: (https://ir.canterbury.ac.nz/bitstream/handle/10092/13076/Krier-CTT-v1-2-2017.pdf).

Krier, Dan and Tony Feldmann. 2016. "Social Character in Western Pre-Modernity: Lacanian Psychosis in Wladyslaw Reymont's *The Peasants*." Pp. 175–216 in *Capitalism's Future*, edited by Dan Krier and Mark P. Worrell. Leiden and Boston: Brill.

Krier, Dan and Mark P. Worrell. 2017. "The Social Ontology of Capitalism." Pp. 1–11 in *The Social Ontology of Capitalism*, eds. Dan Krier and Mark P. Worrell. New York: Palgrave.

Krier, Dan and Mark P. Worrell. 2017b. "The Organic Composition of the Big Mother." *Continental Thought and Theory* 4. Online: (http://ctt.canterbury.ac.nz).

Krier, Dan and Mark P. Worrell (Eds). 2020. *Capital in the Mirror*. Albany: SUNY Press.

Kroner, Richard. 1961. *Speculation and Revelation in Modern Philosophy*. Philadelphia: Westminster Press.

Kuhn, Thomas S. 1970. *The Structure of Scientific Revolutions*, second edition. Chicago: University of Chicago Press.
Lacan, Jacques. 1988. *The Seminar of Jacques Lacan, Book II: The Ego in Freud's Theory and in the Technique of Psychoanalysis, 1954–1955*, tr. S. Tomaselli. New York: W.W. Norton.
Lacan, Jacques. 1993. *The Seminar of Jacques Lacan, Book III: The Psychoses, 1955–1956*, tr. Russell Grigg. New York: W.W. Norton.
Lacan, Jacques. 2002. *Écrits*, tr. Bruce Fink. New York: W.W. Norton.
Lacan, Jacques. 2008. *My Teaching*, tr. David Macey. London and New York: Verso.
Lacan, Jacques. 2014. *The Seminar of Jacques Lacan, Book X: Anxiety*, tr. A.R. Price. Cambridge: Polity.
Lacan, Jacques interviewed by Emilio Granzotto. 1974. "There can be no Crisis of Psychoanalysis." *Panorama*. Online: (www.versobooks.com/blogs/1668-there-can-be-no-crisis-of-psychoanalysis-jacques-lacan-interviewed-in-1974).
Lachs, John. 2012. *Stoic Pragmatism*. Bloomington: Indiana University Press.
Laing, R.D. 1969. *Self and Others*. New York: Penguin.
Larsson, Stieg. 2008. *The Girl with the Dragon Tattoo*, tr. Reg Keeland. New York: Alfred A. Knopf.
Lasswell, Harold D. 1933. "The Psychology of Hitlerism." *The Political Quarterly* 4(1–4): 373–84.
Leatherbarrow, W.J. and D.C. Offord. 1987. *A Documentary History of Russian Thought: From Enlightenment to Marxism*. Ann Arbor: Ardis.
Le Bon, Gustave. 1913. *The Psychology of Revolution*. London: Unwin.
LeDoux, Joseph. 2019. *The Deep History of Ourselves*. New York: Viking.
Lefebvre, Henri. [1966] 1968. *The Sociology of Marx*. New York: Penguin.
Lefebvre, Henri. [1968] 2009. *Dialectical Materialism*, tr. John Sturrock. Minneapolis: University of Minnesota Press.
Lefebvre, Henri. 1995. *Introduction to Modernity*, tr. John Moore. London: Verso.
Le Guin, Ursula K. 1969. *The Left Hand of Darkness*. New York: Ace.
Le Guin, Ursula K. 1974. *The Dispossessed*. New York: Harper Collins.
Lenin, V.I. 1909. "Freedom and Necessity." *Collected Works*, Vol. 14. Online: (www.marxists.org/archive/lenin/works/1908/mec/three6.htm).
Lenin, V.I. 1972. *The Essential Lenin*, ed. Ernst Fischer. New York: Herder and Herder.
Lenin, V.I. 1978. *Revolutionary Adventurism*. Moscow: Progress Publishers.
Lessing, Gotthold Ephraim. [1772] 1979. *Emilia Galotti*, tr. Edward Dvoretzky. New York: Mary S. Rosenberg, Inc.
Levi-Strauss, Claude. 1963. *Structural Anthropology*. New York: Basic.
Levi-Strauss, Claude. 1966. *The Savage Mind*. Chicago: The University of Chicago Press.
Levin, Yuval. 2020. *A Time to Build*. New York: Basic Books.

Levinas, Emmanuel. 1979. *Totality and Infinity*, tr. A. Lingis. The Hague: Martinus Nijhoff.
Levy, Ernst. 1985. *A Theory of Harmony*. Albany: SUNY Press.
Levy-Bruhl, Lucien. 1899. *History of Modern Philosophy in France*. Chicago: Open Court.
Levy-Bruhl, Lucien. [1910] 1926. *How Natives Think*. London: Allen and Unwin.
Levy-Bruhl, Lucien. [1923] 1966. *Primitive Mentality*. Boston: Beacon Press.
Lewin, Bertram D. 1961. *The Psychoanalysis of Elation*. New York: Psychoanalytic Quarterly.
Libertson, Joseph. 1982. *Proximity, Levinas, Blanchot, Bataille, and Communication*. The Hague: Martinus Nijhoff.
Liebersohn, Harry. 1988. *Fate and Utopia in German Sociology, 1870–1923*. Cambridge: MIT.
Lilla, Mark. 2016. *The Shipwrecked Mind*. New York: The New York Review of Books.
Lilla, Mark. 2017. *The Once and Future Liberal*. New York: Harper Collins.
Lippit, Victor D. 2004. "Class Struggles and the Reinvention of American Capitalism in the Second Half of the Twentieth Century." *Review of Radical Political Economics* 36 (3): 336–43.
Lippmann, Walter. [1922] 1960. "The World Outside and the Pictures in Our Heads." Pp. 21–47 in *Images of Man* by C. Wright Mills. New York: George Braziller.
Lipset, Seymour Martin and Gary Marks. 2000. *It Didn't Happen Here*. New York: Norton.
Locke, John. [1706] 1966. *Of the Conduct of the Understanding*. New York: Teachers College Press.
Luckmann, Thomas. 1967. *The Invisible Religion*. New York: Macmillan.
Luckmann, Thomas. 1987. "Comments on Legitimation." *Current Sociology* 35(2): 109–17.
Lukács, Georg. 1926. "Moses Hess and the Problems of Idealist Dialectics." Online: (www.marxistsfr.org/archive/lukacs/works/1926/moses-hess.htm).
Lukács, Georg. 1971. *History and Class Consciousness*. Cambridge: The MIT Press.
Lukács, Georg. 1978a. *The Ontology of Social Being, 1, Hegel*. London: Merlin.
Lukács, Georg. 1978b. *The Ontology of Social Being, 2, Marx*. London: Merlin.
Lukács, Georg. 1978c. *The Ontology of Social Being, 3, Labour*. London: Merlin.
Lukes, Steven. 1968. "Methodological Individualism Reconsidered." *British Journal of Sociology* 19(2): 119–29.
Lukes, Steven. 1973. *Emile Durkheim*. Stanford: Stanford University Press.
Lundskow, George. 2008. "Toyota's Willing Stooges." *New York Journal of Sociology* 1: 92–117. Online: (http://facultyweb.cortland.edu/tnyjs/TNYJS.html).
Luxemburg, Rosa. [1900] 1970. *Reform or Revolution*. New York: Pathfinder Press.

Luxemburg, Rosa. 1971. *Selected Political Writings of Rosa Luxemburg*, ed. Dick Howard. New York: Monthly Review Press.
Lynd, Robert S. 1939. *Knowledge for What?* Princeton: Princeton University Press.
Lynd, Robert S. and Helen Merrell Lynd. 1937. *Middletown in Transition.* New York: Harcourt.
MacAskill, Ewen. 2005. "The Suicide Bomber is the Smartest of Smart Bombs." *The Guardian*, July 13. Online: (http://www.guardian.co.uk/uk/2005/jul/14/israel.july7).
Macfarlane, Robert. 2019. *Underland.* New York: W.W. Norton.
Malinowski, Bronisław. 1948. *Magic, Science and Religion.* New York: Doubleday.
Malraux, Andre. 1961. *Man's Fate*, tr. Haakon M. Chevalier. New York: Random House.
Manjoo, Farhad. 2019. "It's the End of California as We Know It." *The New York Times*, 30 October. Online: (www.nytimes.com/2019/10/30/opinion/california-fires.html).
Mann, Erika. 1938. *School for Barbarians.* Mineola: Dover.
Mann, Thomas. [1924] 1952. *Buddenbrooks*, tr. H.T. Lowe-Porter. New York: Vintage.
Mann, Thomas. [1927] 1955. *Magic Mountain*, tr. H.T. Lowe-Porter. . New York: Heritage Press.
Mann, Thomas. 1931. *Mario and the Magician*, tr. H.T. Lowe-Porter. New York: Knopf.
Mann, Thomas. 1936. *Stories of Three Decades*, tr. H.T. Lowe-Porter. New York: Knopf.
Mann, Thomas. 1948. *Doctor Faustus*, tr. H.T. Lowe-Porter. New York: Knopf.
Mann, Thomas. 1951. *The Holy Sinner*, tr. H.T. Lowe-Porter. New York: Knopf.
Mannheim, Karl. 1982. *Structures of Thinking.* London: Routledge and Kegan Paul.
Maraun, Michael D. 1996. "Meaning and Mythology in the Factor Analysis Model." *Multivariate Behavioral Research* 31(4): 603–16.
Marcuse, Herbert. 1941. *Reason and Revolution.* Atlantic Highlands: Humanities Press.
Marcuse, Herbert. 1955. *Eros and Civilization.* Boston: The Beacon Press.
Marcuse, Herbert. 1964. *One-Dimensional Man.* London: Routledge.
Marcuse, Herbert. 1972. *From Luther to Popper.* London: Verso.
Marcuse, Herbert. 1978. *The Aesthetic Dimension.* Boston: Beacon.
Marett, R.R. 1914. *The Threshold of Religion.* New York: Macmillan.
Marx, Gary T. 1990. "Reflections on Academic Success and Failure." Online: (http://web.mit.edu/gtmarx/www/success.html).
Marx, Karl. [1844] 1964. *The Economic and Philosophic Manuscripts of 1844*, ed. Dirk J. Struik and tr. Martin Milligan. New York: International Publishers.
Marx, Karl. [1857] 1973. *Grundrisse*, tr. Martin Nicolaus. New York: Penguin.
Marx, Karl. 1859. *Zur Kritik der Politischen Ökonomie.* Berlin: Duncker. Online: (www.mlwerke.de/me/me13/me13_003.htm).
Marx, Karl. [1859] 1970. *A Contribution to the Critique of Political Economy*, tr. S.W. Ryazanskaya. New York: International Publishers.
Marx, Karl. 1867. *Das Kapital: Kritik der politischen Ökonomie.* Hamburg: Verlag von Otto Meissner.

Marx, Karl. [1867] 1976. *Capital: A Critique of Political Economy*, Vol. 1, tr. Ben Fowkes. New York: Penguin.

Marx, Karl. [1869] 1963. *The Eighteenth Brumaire of Louis Bonaparte*. New York: International Publishers.

Marx, Karl. [1884] 1978. *Capital: A Critique of Political Economy*, Vol. 2, tr. David Fernbach. New York: Penguin.

Marx, Karl. [1894] 1981. *Capital: A Critique of Political Economy*, Vol. 3, tr. David Fernbach. New York: Penguin.

Marx, Karl. 1904. *A Contribution to the Critique of Political Economy*, tr. N.I. Stone. Chicago: Charles H. Kerr.

Marx, Karl. 1906. *Capital*, tr. Samuel Moore and Edward Aveling. Chicago: Charles Kerr.

Marx, Karl. 1935. *Value, Price, and Profit*. New York: International Publishers.

Marx, Karl. 1963. *Theories of Surplus Value, Part 1*. Moscow: Progress Publishers.

Marx, Karl. 1969. "Feuerbach." Online: (www.mlwerke.de/me/me03/me03_017.htm#I_I).

Marx, Karl. 1973. *The Revolutions of 1848*. New York: Penguin.

Marx, Karl. 1974. *The Ethnological Notebooks of Karl Marx*, second edition, ed. L. Krader. Assen: Van Gorcum.

Marx, Karl. 1978. "The Value-Form." *Capital and Class* 4, Spring: 130–50. Online: (www.marxists.org/archive/marx/works/1867-c1/appendix.htm).

Marx, Karl and Friedrich Engels. [1848] 1972. "The Communist Manifesto." Pp. 331–62 in the Marx-Engels Reader, edited by Robert C. Tucker. New York: W.W. Norton.

Marx, Karl and Friedrich Engels. [1848] 1977. *Manifesto of the Communist Party*. Moscow: Progress Publishers.

Marx, Karl and Friedrich Engels. 1968. *Selected Works*. New York: International Publishers.

Marx, Karl and Friedrich Engels. 1970. *The German Ideology*. New York: International Publishers.

Marx, Karl and Friedrich Engels. 1972. *The Marx–Engels Reader*, ed. Robert C. Tucker. New York: W.W. Norton.

Marx, Karl and Friedrich Engels. 1975–2004. *Collected Works*, vols. 1–50. New York: International Publishers.

Marx, Karl and Friedrich Engels. 1978. *The Socialist Revolution*. Moscow: Progress Publishers.

Marx, Karl and Friedrich Engels. 2008. *On Religion*. Mineola: Dover.

Massing, Paul W. 1949. *Rehearsal for Destruction*. New York: Harper.

Matterson, Stephen. 1990. "Introduction." Pp. vii–xxxvi in *The Confidence-Man* by Herman Melville. New York: Penguin.

Maurier, George Du. [1894] 1998. *Trilby*. Oxford: Oxford University Press.

Mauss, Marcel. [1909] 2003. *On Prayer*, tr. Susan Leslie. New York: Durkheim Press/Berghahn Books.

Mauss, Marcel. [1920/1950] 2006. "The Nation." Pp. 41–48 in *Marcel Mauss: Techniques, Technology and Civilization*, ed. Nathan Schlanger. New York: Durkheim Press/Berghahn.

Mauss, Marcel. [1925] 1992. "A Sociological Assessment of Bolshevism." Pp. 165–211 in *The Radical Sociology of Durkheim and Mauss*, ed. Mike Gane. London: Routledge.

Mauss, Marcel. 1963. "A Category of Human Spirit." *Psychoanalytic Review* 55(3): 457–81.

Mauss, Marcel. 1972. *A General Theory of Magic*. New York: W.W. Norton.

Mauss, Marcel. 1979. *Sociology and Psychology*, tr. B. Brewster. London: Routledge & Kegan Paul.

Mauss, Marcel. 1990. *The Gift*, tr. W.D. Halls. New York: W.W. Norton.

Mauss, Marcel. 2005. *The Nature of Sociology*, tr. William Jeffrey. New York: Durkheim Press/Berghahn Books.

McCarthy, Mary. 1952. *The Groves of Academe*. New York: Harcourt, Brace and World.

McCarthy, Nolan. 2019. *Polarization*. New York: Oxford University Press.

McCauley, Clark and Sophia Moskalenko. 2011. *Friction*. New York: Oxford University Press.

McDowell, John. 1998. *Mind, Value, and Reality*. Cambridge: Harvard University Press.

McGilvary, E.B. 1898. "The Dialectical Method." *Mind* 7(26): 233–42.

McNeill, John T. [1954] 1967. *The History and Character of Calvinism*. New York: Oxford University Press.

McNeill, William H. 1963. *The Rise of the West*. Chicago: The University of Chicago Press.

McWilliams, Susan. 2016. "This Political Theorist Predicted the Rise of Trumpism. His Name was Hunter S. Thompson." *The Nation*, 15 December. Online: (www.thenation.com/article/this-political-theorist-predicted-the-rise-of-trumpism-his-name-was-hunter-s-thompson).

Mead, George Herbert. 1899. "The Working Hypothesis in Social Reform." *The American Journal of Sociology* 5(3): 367–71.

Mead, George Herbert. [1932] 1977. "The Objective Reality of Perspectives." Pp. 342–54 in *George Herbert Mead on Social Psychology*. Chicago: University of Chicago Press.

Mead, George Herbert. [1934] 1962. *Mind, Self, and Society*. Chicago: The University of Chicago Press.

Meerloo, Joost A.M. 1962. *Suicide and Mass Suicide*. New York: Grune and Stratton.

Meillassoux, Quentin. 2008. *After Finitude*, tr. Ray Brassier. London and New York: Bloomsbury.

Meissner, W.W. 1992. *Ignatius of Loyola*. New Haven: Yale University Press.

Mendelshon, Daniel. 2019. *Ecstasy and Terror*. New York: New York Review of Books.

Mendez, Antonio J. and Jonna Mendez. 2019. *The Moscow Rules*. New York: Hachette.
Meštrović, S.G. 1988. *Emile Durkheim and the Renovation of Sociology*. Totowa: Rowman & Littlefield.
Michelet, J. 1847. *History of the French Revolution*, tr. Cocks. London: H.G. Bohn.
Michener, James A. 1965. *The Source*. New York: Fawcett Crest.
Mill, James. 1992. *Political Writings*, ed. Terence Ball. Cambridge: Cambridge University Press.
Mill, John Stuart. 1881. *The Principles of Political Economy*. London: Longmans, Green and Co.
Miller, William Ian. 1997. *The Anatomy of Disgust*. Cambridge: Harvard University Press.
Mills, C. Wright. 1956. *The Power Elite*. Oxford: Oxford University Press.
Mills, C. Wright. 1959. *The Sociological Imagination*. New York: Oxford University Press.
Mills, C. Wright. 1962. *The Marxists*. New York: Dell.
Mills, C. Wright. 1966. *Sociology and Pragmatism*. New York: Oxford University Press.
Mills, Charles W. 1998. "Dark Ontologies." Pp. 131–68 in *Autonomy and Community*, eds. Jane Kneller and Sidney Axinn. Albany: SUNY Press.
Moliere. 2001. *The Misanthrope, Tartuffe, and Other Plays*, tr. Maya Slater. Oxford: Oxford University Press.
Mommsen, Wolfgang J. 2006. "From Agrarian Capitalism to the 'Spirit' of Modern Capitalism: Max Weber's Approach to the Protestant Ethic." *Max Weber Studies* 5(2): 185–203.
Montaigne. 1842. *The Complete Works of Michel de Montaigne* tr. W. Hazlitt. London: Templeman.
Montesquieu. 2002. *The Spirit of Laws*. Amherst: Prometheus.
Moore, Barrington. 1978. *Injustice: The Social Bases of Obedience and Revolt*. Armonk, NY: M.E. Sharpe.
Moore, John A. 1958. "The Idealism of Sancho Panza." *Hispania* 41(1): 73–76.
More, Thomas. [1516] 1999. *Utopia*, in *Three Early Modern Utopias*, ed. Susan Bruce. Oxford: Oxford University Press.
Moret, Alexandre. 1927. *The Nile and Egyptian Civilization*. Mineola: Dover.
Moret, Alexandre and Georges Davy. [1926] 1970. *From Tribe to Empire*, tr. V.G. Childe. New York: Cooper Square Publishers.
Morris-Reich, Amos. 2005. "From Autonomous Subject to Free Individual in Simmel and Lacan." *History of European Ideas*, 31(1): 103–27.
Mounier, Emmanuel. 1952. *Personalism*. Notre Dame: University of Notre Dame Press.
Musil, Robert. 1996. *The Man Without Qualities*, tr. Sophie Wilkins. New York: Vintage.
Nadler, Steven. 1999. *Spinoza*. Cambridge: Cambridge University Press.
Nagorski, Andrew. 2019. *The Year Germany Lost the War*. New York: Simon and Schuster.

Nelson, Leonard. [1917] 1957. *Critique of Practical Reason*. Frankfurt: Verlag.

Nemedi, Denes. [2000] 2006. "A Change in Ideas." Pp. 83–97 in *Durkheim and Representations*, ed. W.S.F. Pickering. London: Routledge.

Nietzsche, Friedrich. [1887] 1974. *The Gay Science*, tr. Walter Kaufmann. New York: Vintage.

Nietzsche, Friedrich. 1909. *The Complete Works of Friedrich Nietzsche*, Vol. 12. Edinburgh: T.N. Foulis.

Nietzsche, Friedrich. 1967. *Ecce Homo*, tr. Walter Kaufmann. New York: Vintage.

Nietzsche, Friedrich. [1967] 1989. *On the Genealogy of Morals* and *Ecce Homo*, tr. Walter Kaufmann. New York: Vintage.

Nietzsche, Friedrich. 1968. *Will to Power*, tr. Walter Kaufmann. New York: Vintage.

Nietzsche, Friedrich. 1982. *The Portable Nietzsche*, ed. and tr. Walter Kaufmann. New York: Penguin.

Nietzsche, Friedrich. 1986. *Human, All too Human*, tr. R.J. Hollingdale. Cambridge: Cambridge University Press.

Nietzsche, Friedrich. 2002. *Beyond Good and Evil*, tr. J. Norman. Cambridge: Cambridge University Press.

Nietzsche, Friedrich. 2015. *Aphorisms on Love and Hate*, tr. Faber and Lehmann. New York: Penguin.

Novalis. 1997. *Philosophical Writings*, ed. and tr. Margaret Stoljar. Albany: State University of New York Press.

Nye, D.A. and C.E. Ashworth. 1971. "Emile Durkheim: Was He a Nominalist or a Realist?" *The British Journal of Sociology* 22(2): 133–48.

Oberhauser, Ann M., Daniel Krier, and Abdi Kusow. 2019. "Political Moderation and Polarization in the Heartland: Economics, Rurality, and Social Identity in the 2016 US Presidential Election." *The Sociological Quarterly*. Online: (https://doi.org/10.1080/00380253.2019.1580543).

O'Brien, Miles. 2013. "Sins of the Sons." *PBS Newshour*, February 20. Online: www.pbs.org/newshour/updates/science/jan-june13/miles_blog_02-19.html.

O'Connor, James. 1980. "The Division of Labor in Society." *Insurgent Sociologist* 10(1): 60–68.

O'Connor, James. 1984. *Accumulation Crisis*. New York: Basil Blackwell.

O'Keefe, Daniel Lawrence. 1982. *Stolen Lightning*. New York: Continuum.

O'Neill, Eugene. 1932. "Mourning Becomes Electra." Pp. 683–867 in *Nine Plays*. New York: The Modern Library.

Orr, David. 2015a. *The Road not Taken*. New York: Penguin.

Orr, David. 2015b. "The Most Misread Poem in America." *The Paris Review*, September 11. Online: (www.theparisreview.org/blog/2015/09/11/the-most-misread-poem-in-america).

Ortega y Gasset, José. 1932. *The Revolt of the Masses*, tr. anon. New York: W.W. Norton.

Ortega y Gasset, José. [1941] 1961. *History as a System*, tr. Helen Weyl. New York: W.W. Norton.
Ortega y Gasset, José. 1957. *Man and People*, tr. Willard Trask. New York: W.W. Norton.
Orwell, George. [1933] 1961. *Down and Out in Paris and London*. San Diego: Harcourt.
Orwell, George. 2008. *All Art is Propaganda*. Orlando: Harcourt.
Otto, M.C. 1924. *Things and Ideals*. New York: Henry Holt.
Ovid. 1955. *The Fall of Icarus*, tr. Mary M. Innes. New York: Penguin.
Owen, Wilfred. [1963] 1965. *The Collected Poems of Wilfred Owen*. New York: New Directions.
Paine, Thomas. 1791. *Rights of Man*. London: J.S. Jordan.
Pannekoek, Anton. 1909. "The New Middle Class." Online: (www.marxists.org/archive/pannekoe/1909/new-middle-class.htm).
Pannekoek, Anton. 1937. "Society and Mind in Marxian Philosophy." Online: (www.marxists.org/archive/pannekoe/society-mind/index.htm).
Pannekoek, Anton. 1947. "Religion." Online: (www.marxists.org/archive/pannekoe/1947/religion).
Paoletti, Giovanni. 2012. "Some Concepts of 'Evil' in Durkheim's Thought." Pp. 63–80 in *Suffering and Evil*, ed. W.S.F. Pickering and Massimo Rosati. New York: Durkheim Press/Berghahn.
Parkin, Robert. 2012. "Robert Herz on Suffering and Evil: The Negative Processes of Social Life and Their Resolution." Pp. 103–17 in *Suffering and Evil*, eds. W.S.F. Pickering and Massimo Rosati. New York: Durkheim Press/Berghahn.
Partridge, G.E. 1919. *The Psychology of Nations*. New York: Macmillan.
Pascal, Blaise. 1941. *Pensées*, tr. W.F. Trotter. New York: The Modern Library.
Pearce, Frank. 1989. *The Radical Durkheim*. London: Unwin Hyman.
Pessoa, Fernando. 2001. *The Book of Disquiet*, tr. Richard Zenith. New York: Penguin.
Peters, F.E. 1967. *Greek Philosophical Terms*. New York: New York University Press.
Pickering, W.S.F. 2012. "Reflections on the Death of Emile Durkheim." Pp. 11–27 in *Suffering and Evil*, eds. W.S.F. Pickering and Massimo Rosati. New York: Durkheim Press/Berghahn.
Piketty, Thomas. 2014. *Capital in the Twenty-First Century*. Cambridge: Belknap/Harvard.
Pinkard, Terry. 1996. *Hegel's Phenomenology*. Cambridge: Cambridge University Press.
Pinkard, Terry. 2000. *Hegel*. Cambridge: Cambridge University Press.
Pinkard, Terry. 2002. *German Philosophy*. Cambridge: Cambridge University Press.
Pippin, Robert B. 1989. *Hegel's Idealism*. Cambridge: Cambridge University Press.
Pippin, Robert B. 2012. *Fatalism in Film Noir*. Charlottesville: University of Virginia Press.
Pistor, Katharina. 2019. *The Code of Capital*. Princeton: Princeton University Press.
Plato. 1945. *The Works of Plato*, tr. Benjamin Jowett. New York: Tudor.

Poe, Edgar Allan. [1839] 1903. "William Wilson." Pp. 300–24 in *The Best Tales of Edgar Allan Poe*, ed. Sherwin Cody. Chicago: McClurg.
Poe, Edgar Allan. [1841] 1920. *A Descent into the Maelstrom*. Paris: Devambez.
Poliakov, Leon. 1985. *The History of Anti-Semitism*, Vol. 4, tr. George Klin. Philadelphia: University of Pennsylvania Press.
Pope, Whitney. 1976. *Durkheim's Suicide: A Classic Analyzed*. Chicago: The University of Chicago Press.
Posnett, Edward. 2019. *Strange Harvests*. New York: Viking.
Prior, Ryan. 2019. "A 'No-Brainer Nobel Prize': Hungarian Scientists May Have Found a Fifth Force of Nature." *CNN*, 23 November. Online: (www.cnn.com/2019/11/22/world/fifth-force-of-nature-scn-trnd/index.html).
Proust, Marcel. [1913] 2002. *Swann's Way*, tr. Lydia Davis. New York: Penguin.
Pufendorf, Samuel. 1994. *The Political Writings of Samuel Pufendorf*, ed. C. Carr, tr. M. Seidler. New York: Oxford University Press.
Rabelais, Francois. [1532–1564] 1944. *The Complete Works of Rabelais: The Five Books of Gargantua and Pantagruel*. New York: The Modern Library.
Radcliffe-Brown, A. 1952. *Structure and Function in Primitive Society*. New York: The Free Press.
Radkau, Joachim. 2009. *Max Weber*, tr. Patrick Camiller. Cambridge: Polity.
Raeff, Marc. 1966. *Origins of the Russian Intelligentsia*. New York: Harcourt, Brace, and World
Ramp, William. 2000. "The Moral Discourse of Durkheim's *Suicide*." Pp. 81–96 in *Durkheim's Suicide*, eds. W.S.F. Pickering and Geoffrey Walford. London: Routledge.
Rank, Otto. 1941. *Beyond Psychology*. New York: Dover.
Rappaport, Roy. 1971. "The Sacred in Human Evolution." *Annual Review of Ecology and Systematics* 2: 23–44.
Reich, Wilhelm. [1933] 1972. *Character Analysis*. New York: Farrar, Straus and Giroux.
Reich, Wilhelm. 1953. *The Murder of Christ*. New York: Farrar, Straus and Giroux.
Reich, Wilhelm. 1970. *The Mass Psychology of Fascism*. New York: Noonday.
Reich, Wilhelm. 1974. *Listen Little Man*. New York: Noonday.
Reinhold, K.L. [1791] 2000. "The Foundation of Philosophical Knowledge." Pp. 51–103 in *Between Kant and Hegel*. Indianapolis: Hackett.
Richman, Michèle H. 2002. *Sacred Revolutions*. Minneapolis: University of Minnesota Press.
Ricoeur, Paul. 1981. *Hermeneutics and the Human Sciences*, ed. and tr. John B. Thompson. Cambridge: Cambridge University Press.
Ricoeur, Paul. 1991. *From Text to Action*, tr. Kathleen Blamey and John B. Thompson. Evanston: Northwestern University Press.
Riesman, David, Nathan Glazer, and Reuel Denney. [1950] 1953. *The Lonely Crowd*. New York: Doubleday.

Riley, Alexander T. 1999. "Whence Durkheim's Nietzschean Grandchildren? A Closer Look at Robert Hertz's Place in the Durkheimian Genealogy." *European Journal of Sociology* 40(2): 304–30.

Riley-Smith, Jonathan. 2014. *The Crusades: A History*. London and New York: Bloomsbury.

Rintelen, Fritz-Joachim von. 1977. "Philosophical Idealism in Germany." *Philosophy and Phenomenological Research* 38(1): 1–32.

Risch, Ernst. 1974. *Wortbildung der homerischen Sprache*. Berlin: Walter de Gruyter.

Rivers, W.H.R. 1914. *Kinship and Social Organization*. London: Constable and Co.

Rivers, W.H.R. 1920. *Instinct and the Unconscious*. Cambridge: Cambridge University Press.

Rivers, W.H.R. 1923. *Psychology and Politics*. London: Kegan Paul, Trench, Trubner and Co.

Robinson, James (ed.). 1988. *The Nag Hammadi Library*, revised edition. San Francisco: Harper.

Roehr, Sabine. 1995. *A Primer on German Enlightenment, with a Translation of Karl Leonhard Reinhold's "The Fundamental Concepts and Principles of Ethics."* Columbia: University of Missouri Press.

Rorty, Richard. 1998. *Achieving our Country*. Cambridge: Harvard University Press.

Rose, Gillian. 2009. *Hegel Contra Sociology*. London: Verso.

Rosenkranz, Karl. [1844] 2002. "The Full Report of Rosenkranz Concerning the Triangle of Triangles." Pp. 264–69 in *Miscellaneous Writings of G.W.F. Hegel*, ed. Jon Stewart. Evanston: Northwestern University Press.

Rosenzweig, Franz. [1945] 1999. *Understanding the Sick and the Healthy*, tr. Nahum Glatzer. Cambridge: Harvard University Press.

Rousseau, Jean-Jacques. [1762] 1968. *The Social Contract*, tr. Maurice Cranston. New York: Penguin.

Rousseau, Jean-Jacques. [1762] 1978. *On the Social Contract*, tr. Judith R. Masters. New York: St. Martin's Press.

Rousseau, Jean-Jacques. 1898. *Emile*, tr. Eleanor Worthington. Boston: D.C. Heath.

Royce, Josiah. 1892. *The Spirit of Modern Philosophy*. Boston and New York: Houghton Mifflin.

Royce, Josiah. 1909. *The Philosophy of Loyalty*. New York: Macmillan.

Royce, Josiah. 1914. *War and Insurance*. New York: Macmillan.

Royce, Josiah. 1948. *California*. New York: Knopf.

Royce, Josiah. 1969. *The Basic Writings of Josiah Royce*, Vol. 1, ed. John J. McDermott. Chicago: The University of Chicago Press.

Royce, Josiah. 1982. *The Philosophy of Josiah Royce*, ed. John Roth. Indianapolis: Hackett.

Royce, Josiah. 2005. *The Basic Writings of Josiah Royce*, Vol. 2: *Logic, Loyalty, and Community*, ed. John J. McDermott. New York: Fordham University Press.
Ruskin, John. 2015. *Traffic*. New York: Penguin.
Sade, Marquis de. 1966. *The 120 Days of Sodom and Other Writings*, tr. Austryn Wainhouse and Richard Seaver. New York: Grove.
Sade, Marquis de. 2006. *Philosophy in the Boudoir*, tr. Joachim Neugroschel. New York: Penguin.
Santayana, George. [1905] 1932. *Reason in Society*. Charles Scribner's Sons.
Santayana, George. 1913. *Winds of Doctrine*. London: J.M. Dent and Sons.
Santayana, George. [1936] 1949. *The Last Puritan*. New York: Charles Scribner's Sons.
Sartre, Jean-Paul. [1946] 1976. *No Exit*. New York: Vintage.
Sartre, Jean-Paul. 1948. *The Wall*, tr. Lloyd Alexander. New York: New Directions.
Sartre, Jean-Paul. 1950. *Baudelaire*, tr. Martin Turnell. New York: New Directions.
Sartre, Jean-Paul. [1952] 1963. *Saint Genet*, tr. Bernard Frechtman. New York: Pantheon.
Sartre, Jean-Paul. 1976. *Critique of Dialectical Reason, Volume 1: Theory of Practical Ensembles*, new edition, tr. Alan Sheridan-Smith. London: Verso.
Schachtel, Ernest G. 1959. *Metamorphosis*. New York: Basic Books.
Scheler, Max. 1973. *Selected Philosophical Essays*. Evanston: Northwestern University Press.
Schelling, Friedrich. [1813] 1997. *Ages of the World*, tr. Judith Norman. Ann Arbor: The University of Michigan Press.
Schiller, Friedrich. 1966. *On the Sublime*. New York: Frederick Ungar.
Schiller, Friedrich. 1967. *On the Aesthetic Education of Man*. Oxford: Clarendon Press.
Schmitt, Carl. 2003. *The Nomos of the Earth*, tr. G. Ulmen. New York: Telos Press.
Schnitzler, Arthur. [1926] 1999. *Dream Story*, tr. J.M.Q. Davies. New York: Penguin.
Scott, James C. 2017. *Against the Grain*. New Haven: Yale University Press.
Seligman, Adam B. 2000. *Modernity's Wager*. Princeton: Princeton University Press.
Sennett, Richard. 1980. *Authority*. New York: Knopf.
Shakespeare, William. 1956. *Measure for Measure*. New York: Penguin.
Shakespeare, William. 1963. *Love's Labor's Lost*. New York: Penguin.
Shakespeare, William. 1973. *Coriolanus*. New York: Penguin.
Shakespeare, William. 1999. *Much Ado About Nothing*. New York: Penguin.
Shakespeare, William. 2000. *Macbeth*. New York: Penguin.
Shakespeare, William. 2001. *Hamlet*. New York: Penguin.
Sharaf, Myron. 1983. *Fury on Earth: A Biography of Wilhelm Reich*. New York: DaCapo.
Shelley, Mary. [1818] 1992. *Frankenstein*. New York: Knopf.
Siegel, Jonas. 2005. "Why One Man's UAV is Another Man's Cruise Missile." *Bulletin of the Atomic Scientist*, September/October: 35.
Silva, Jennifer M. 2019. *We're Still Here*. New York: Oxford University Press.

Simas, Tiago, Michal Ficke, Albert Diaz-Guilera, Pere Obrador, and Pablo R. Rodriguez. 2017. "Food-Bridging: A New Network Construction to Unveil the Principles of Cooking." arXiv: 1704.03330.

Simmel, Georg. [1907] 1990. *The Philosophy of Money*. London and New York: Routledge.

Simmel, Georg. [1921–1922] 1984. "On Love (A Fragment)." Pp. 153–92 in *Georg Simmel: On Women, Sexuality, and Love*, ed. and tr. Guy Oakes. New Haven: Yale University Press.

Simmel, Georg. 1950. *The Sociology of Georg Simmel*, ed. and tr. Kurt H. Wolff. New York: The Free Press.

Simmel, Georg. 1955. *Conflict* and *The Web of Group Affiliation*. New York: The Free Press.

Simmel, Georg. 1959. *The Sociology of Religion*. New York: Philosophical Library.

Simmel, Georg. 1971. *On Individuality and Social Forms*, ed. Donald N. Levine. Chicago: University of Chicago Press.

Simon, Ed. 2019. "Why We Will Need Walt Whitman in 2020." *The New York Times*, 30 December. Online: (https://www.nytimes.com/2019/12/30/opinion/walt-whitman-nytimes-2020.html).

Simons Science News. 2014. "Have We Been Interpreting Quantum Mechanics Wrong This Whole Time?" *Wired*. Online: (www.wired.com/2014/06/the-new-quantum-reality).

Simpson, George. 1933. "Emile Durkheim's Social Realism." *Sociology and Social Research* 28: 2–11.

Simpson, George. 1937. *Conflict and Community*. Ph.D. dissertation, Columbia University.

Simpson, Glenn and Peter Fritsch. 2019. *Crime in Progress*. New York: Random House.

Skinner, Quentin. 1978. *The Foundations of Modern Political Thought, Volume Two: The Age of the Reformation*. Cambridge: Cambridge University Press.

Slotkin, Richard. 1992. *Gunfighter Nation*. Norman: University of Oklahoma Press.

Smith, Adam. [1776] 1937. *The Wealth of Nations*. New York: The Modern Library.

Smith, Cyril. 1994. "Karl Marx and the Origins of 'Marxism.'" Online: (www.marxists.org/reference/archive/smith-cyril/works/millenni/smith4.htm).

Smith, David Norman. 1988. "Authorities, Deities, and Commodities: Classical Sociology and the Problem of Domination." Ph.D. dissertation, University of Wisconsin–Madison.

Smith, David Norman. 1994. *The Realm of the Social*. New York: McGraw–Hill.

Smith, David Norman. 1998. "Faith, Reason, and Charisma: Rudolf Sohm, Max Weber, and the Theology of Grace." *Sociological Inquiry*, 68: 32–60.

Smith, David Norman. 2001. "Anomie, Solidarity, and Conflict: French Sociology and the Limits of Dialogue." *The Sociological Quarterly* 42(1): 69–78.

Smith, David Norman. 2006. "Time is Money: Commodity Fetishism and Common Sense." Pp. xix–lxiii in *The Hegemony of Common Sense* by Dean Wolfe Manders. New York: Peter Lang.

Smith, David Norman. 2013. "Charisma Disenchanted: Max Weber and His Critics." *Current Perspectives in Social Theory* 31: 3–74.

Smith, David Norman. 2014. "Slashing at Water with a Knife? Durkheim's Struggle to Anchor Sociology in First Principles." *Contemporary Sociology* 43(2): 165–71.

Smith, David Norman. 2016. "Capitalism's Future: Self-Alienation, Self-Emancipation and the Remaking of Critical Theory." Pp. 11–62 in *Capitalism's Future* eds. Daniel Krier and Mark P. Worrell. Leiden: Brill.

Smith, David Norman. 2017. "Theory and Class Consciousness." Pp. 369–423 in *The Handbook of Critical Theory*, ed. Michael J. Thompson. New York: Palgrave.

Smith, David Norman. 2019a. "Authoritarianism Reimagined: The Riddle of Trump's Base." *The Sociological Quarterly*. Online: (https://doi.org/10.1080/00380253.2019.1593061).

Smith, David Norman. 2019b. "Max Weber's Odyssey." *Fast Capitalism* 16.2. Online: (https://fastcapitalism.journal.library.uta.edu/index.php/fastcapitalism).

Smith, Douglas. 2016. *Rasputin*. New York: Farrar, Straus and Giroux.

Smith, Norman Kemp. 1992. *Commentary to Kant's 'Critique of Pure Reason,'* second edition. Atlantic Highlands, NJ: Humanities Press.

Smith, Tony. 1993a. *Dialectical Social Theory and its Critics*. Albany: SUNY Press.

Smith, Tony. 1993b. "Marx's *Capital* and Hegelian Dialectical Logic." Pp. 15–36 in *Marx's Method in* Capital, ed. Fred Moseley. Atlantic Highlands: Humanities Press.

Smith, William Robertson. 1927. *Lectures on the Religion of the Semites*, third ed. New York: Macmillan.

Solovyov, Vladimir. 1918. *The Justification of the Good*, tr. N. Duddington. London: Constable.

Solzhenitsyn, Aleksandr I. 1974. *The Gulag Archipelago*, Vol. 1., tr. Thomas P. Whitney. New York: Harper and Row.

Sorel, Georges. 1950. *Reflections on Violence*, tr. T.E. Hulme. Mineola: Dover.

Spangler, Todd, Craig Gilbert, Candy Woodall, and Frank Gluck. 2019. "'You Can't Take any of Them for Granted': The Voters who Will Sway 2020's Swing States." *USA Today*, 2 December. Online: (www.usatoday.com/story/news/politics/elections/2019/12/02/election-2020-swing-states-will-rely-on-these-key-voters/4298609002/).

Spaulding, Edward Gleason. 1918. *The New Rationalism*. New York: Henry Holt.

Spero, Moshe Halevi. 1992. *Religious Objects as Psychological Structures*. Chicago: University of Chicago Press.

Spinoza, Baruch. 2002. *Complete Works*, tr. Samuel Shirley. Indianapolis: Hackett.

Steiner, Franz. 1956. *Taboo*. London: Cohen and West.

Stewart, Jon (ed.). 1996. *The Hegel Myths and Legends*. Evanston: Northwestern University Press.
Strauss, David Friedrich. 1892. *The Life of Jesus*, tr. George Eliot. London: Swan Sonnenschein.
Strenski, Ivan. 2006. *The New Durkheim*. New Brunswick: Rutgers University Press.
Suarez, Francisco. 1995. *On Beings of Reason*, tr. John P. Doyle. Milwaukee: Marquette University Press.
Sumner, William Graham. [1906] 1940. *Folkways*. New York: Mentor.
Svevo, Italo. [1923] 2001. *Zeno's Conscience*, tr. William Weaver. New York: Knopf.
Swart, William J. and Dan Krier. 2016. "Dark Spectacle." Pp. 240–76 in *The Social Ontology of Capitalism*, eds. Dan Krier and Mark P. Worrell. New York: Palgrave.
Swift, Jonathan. 2015. *A Modest Proposal*. New York: Penguin.
Taussig, Michael. 1993. *Mimesis and Alterity*. New York: Routledge.
Therborn, Göran. 1980. *Science, Class, and Society*. London: Verso.
Theweleit, Klaus. 1994. *Object-Choice*, tr. Malcolm R. Green. London: Verso.
Thoreau, Henry David. [1854] 1960. *Walden*. New York: New American Library.
Tocqueville, Alexis de. [1835] 1956. *Democracy in America*. New York: Mentor.
Tocqueville, Alexis de. 1856. *The Old Regime and the Revolution*, tr. John Bonner. New York: Harper.
Tolstoy, Leo. [1869] 1992. *War and Peace*, Vol. 3, tr. Louise and Aylmer Maude. New York: Knopf.
Tolstoy, Leo. 2014. *Anna Karenina*, tr. R. Bartlett. Oxford: Oxford University Press.
Tönnies, Ferdinand. 1988. *Community and Society*. New Brunswick: Transaction.
Troeltsch, Ernst. [1911] 1931. *The Social Teaching of the Christian Churches*, Vol. 2. Chicago: University of Chicago Press.
Troeltsch, Ernst. [1911] 1931/1949a. *The Social Teaching of the Christian Churches*, Vol. 1. New York: Macmillan.
Troeltsch, Ernst. [1911] 1931/1949b. *The Social Teaching of the Christian Churches*, Vol. 2. New York: Macmillan.
Troeltsch, Ernst. 1922. *Historism and its Problems*, tr. James Luther Adams, et al. Unpublished English translation of *Historismus*. Tübingen: Verlag von J.C.B. Mahr (Paul Siebeck).
Trotsky, Leon. 1939. "The ABC of Materialist Dialectic." Online: (www.marxists.org/archive/trotsky/1939/12/abc.htm).
Trotsky, Leon. 1990. *Trade Unions in the Epoch of Imperialist Decay*. New York: Pathfinder.
Twain, Mark. 1872. *The $30,000 Dollar Bequest and Other Stories*. New York: Greystone.
Twain, Mark. 1883. *Life on the Mississippi*. Boston: James R. Osgood and Co.
Twain, Mark. 1917. *A Connecticut Yankee in King Arthur's Court*. New York: Greystone.
Untermeyer, Louis. 1955. *A Treasury of Great Poems*. New York: Galahad Books.

Vaihinger, Hans. 1924. *The Philosophy of 'As if,'* tr. C.K. Ogden. London: Routledge and Kegan Paul.
Vavreck, Lynn and Chris Tausanovitch. 2019. "What Is Voters' Highest Priority? There's a Way to Find Out." *The New York Times*, 5 December. Online: (www.nytimes.com/2019/12/05/upshot/impeachment-biggest-issue-voters-poll.html).
Veblen, Thorstein. 1912. *The Theory of the Leisure Class*. New York: Macmillan.
Veblen, Thorstein. 1914. *The Instinct of Workmanship*. New York: B.W. Huebsch.
Verheggen, Theo. 1996. "Durkheim's 'Représentations' Considered as 'Vorstellungen.'" *Current Perspectives in Social Theory* 16: 189–219.
Vincent, George Edgar. 1897. *The Social Mind and Education*. Chicago: University of Chicago Press.
Voltaire. 1962. *Philosophical Dictionary*, tr. Peter Gay. New York: Harcourt.
Wagenvoort, Hendrik. [1947] 1976. *Roman Dynamism*. Westport: Greenwood Press.
Wahl, Jean. 2017. *Transcendence and the Concrete: Selected Writings*, eds. Alan D. Schrift and Ian Alexander Moore. New York: Fordham University Press.
Walter, Jess. 2009. *The Financial Lives of the Poets*. New York: Harper.
Warriner, Charles K. 1956. "Groups are Real: A Reaffirmation." *American Sociological Review* 21(5): 549–54.
Wartofsky, Marx W. 1977. *Feuerbach*. London: Cambridge University Press.
Weber, Marianne. 1988. *Max Weber*, tr. Harry Zohn. New Brunswick: Transaction.
Weber, Marianne. 2003. "Authority and Autonomy in Marriage." *Sociological Theory* 21(2): 85–102.
Weber, Max. [1905] 2002. *The Protestant Ethic and the Spirit of Capitalism*, tr. Peter Baehr and Gordon C. Wells. New York: Penguin.
Weber, Max. [1909] 1984. "'Energetic' Theories of Culture." tr. Jon Mark Mikkelsen and Charles Schwartz. *Mid-American Review of Sociology* 9(2): 33–58.
Weber, Max. [1922] 1991. *The Sociology of Religion*. Boston: Beacon.
Weber, Max. [1930] 2001. *The Protestant Ethic and the Spirit of Capitalism*, tr. Talcott Parsons. London: Routledge.
Weber, Max. 1946. *From Max Weber: Essays in Sociology*, eds. Hans H. Gerth and C. Wright Mills. New York: Oxford University Press.
Weber, Max. 1949. *The Methodology of the Social Sciences*. New York: The Free Press.
Weber, Max. 1952. *Ancient Judaism*. New York: The Free Press.
Weber, Max. 1958. *The Rational and Social Foundations of Music*. Carbondale: Southern Illinois University Press.
Weber, Max. 1978. *Economy and Society*. Berkeley: University of California Press.
Weber, Max. 1981. *General Economic History*. New Brunswick: Transaction Publishers.
Weber, Max. 2000. *The Religion of India*, tr. Hans Gerth and Don Martindale. New Delhi: Munshiram Manoharlal.
Weil, Simone. 1965. "The Iliad, or the Poem of Force." *Chicago Review* 18(2): 5–30.

Wells, H.G. 1928. *The Open Conspiracy*. London: Victor Gollancz Ltd.
Wells, H.G. 1934. *Marxism Versus Liberalism*. Online: (www.marxists.org/reference/archive/stalin/works/1934/07/23.htm).
Wesep, H.B. 1920. *The Control of Ideals*. New York: Knopf.
Westermarck, Edward. 1917. *The Origin and Development of the Moral Ideas*, Vol. 2, second edition. London: Macmillan.
Westhues, Kenneth. 1982. *First Sociology*. New York: McGraw-Hill.
Westphal, Kenneth R. 2018. *Grounds of Pragmatic Realism*. Leiden: Brill.
Westphal, Merold. 1990. *History and Truth in Hegel's Phenomenology*. New Jersey: Humanities Press International.
Wexler, Philip. 1996. *Critical Social Psychology*. New York: Peter Lang.
Whitman, Walt. 1847–1854. "Talbot Wilson" Notebook. The Walt Whitman Archive. Online: (https://whitmanarchive.org/manuscripts/notebooks/transcriptions/loc.00141.html).
Whitman, Walt. [1892] 1992. *Leaves of Grass*. New York: Book of the Month Club.
Wiese, Leopold and Howard Becker. 1932. *Systematic Sociology*. New York: Wiley & Sons.
Wiggershaus, Rolf. 1994. *The Frankfurt School*. Cambridge, MA: The MIT Press.
Wilde, Oscar. [1890] 1995. *The Picture of Dorian Gray*. Köln: Könemann.
Williams, Bernard. 1993. *Shame and Necessity*. Berkeley: University of California Press.
Williams, Raymond. 1958. *Culture and Society, 1780–1950*. New York: Harper.
Wills, Garry. 2012. "Our Moloch." *The New York Review of Books*, December 15. Online: (www.nybooks.com/blogs/nyrblog/2012/dec/15/our-moloch).
Wilson, Edmund. [1940] 1967. *To the Finland Station*. New York: New York Review of Books.
Wilson, Eric. 2008. *Savage Republic*. Leiden: Martinus Nijhoff
Wilson, Stephen. 1982. *Ideology and Experience*. East Brunswick: Associated University Presses.
Winnicott, D.W. 1965. *The Maturational Processes and the Facilitating Environment*. London: The Hogarth Press.
Wolff, Robert. 1970. *In Defense of Anarchism*. New York: Harper.
Wolin, Sheldon S. 2008. *Democracy Incorporated: Managed Democracy and the Spectre of Inverted Totalitarianism*. Princeton: Princeton University Press.
Wollstonecraft, Mary. [1792] 1983. *Vindication of the Rights of Woman*. New York: Penguin.
Woolf, Virginia. [1929] 2001. *A Room of One's Own*. Peterborough: Broadview Press.
Woolf, Virginia. 1953. *A Writer's Diary*. London: Hogarth Press.
Woozley, A.D. 1967. "Universals." Pp. 194–206 in *The Encyclopedia of Philosophy*, Vol. 8. New York: Macmillan and The Free Press.

Worrell, Mark P. 1995. "Getting to Know You: Marx and Nietzsche in the Age of Postmodernism." *Humanity and Society* 20(4): 109–12.

Worrell, Mark P. 1998. "Authoritarianism, Critical Theory, and Political Psychology: Past, Present, and Future." *Social Thought and Research* 21(1–2): 3–33.

Worrell, Mark P. 1999. "The Veil of Piacular Subjectivity: Buchananism and the New World Order." *Electronic Journal of Sociology* 4(3). Online: (www.sociology.org/content/vol004.003/buchanan.html).

Worrell, Mark P. 2008. *Dialectic of Solidarity*. Chicago: Haymarket.

Worrell, Mark P. 2009a. "A Faint Rattling: A Research Note on Marx's Theory of Value." *Critical Sociology* 35(6): 887–92.

Worrell, Mark P. 2009b. "The Cult of Exchange Value." *Fast Capitalism* 5.2. Online: (www.uta.edu/huma/agger/fastcapitalism/5_2/Worrell5_2.html).

Worrell, Mark P. 2009c. "The Ghost World of Alienated Desire." *Critical Sociology* 35(3): 119–22.

Worrell, Mark P. 2009d. "Joseph Freeman and the Frankfurt School." *Rethinking Marxism* 21(4): 498–513.

Worrell, Mark P. 2011. *Why Nations go to War*. New York: Routledge.

Worrell, Mark P. 2013a. *Terror: Social, Political, and Economic Perspectives*. New York: Routledge.

Worrell, Mark P. 2013b. "The Charisma of Impending Doom: Disaster Solidarity and Emergency Mentalities." *Critical Sociology* 39(2): 159–61.

Worrell, Mark P. 2014. "The Commodity as the Ultimate Monstrosity." *Fast Capitalism* 11.1. Online: (www.uta.edu/huma/agger/fastcapitalism/11_1/worrell11_1.html).

Worrell, Mark P. 2015a. "Imperial Homunculi: The Speculative Singularities of American Hegemony." *Current Perspectives in Social Theory* 33: 217–41.

Worrell, Mark P. 2015b. "Discarding Simmel: Public Property, Neoliberalism, and Potlatch Capitalism." *Logos* 14(1). Online: (www.logosjournal.com).

Worrell, Mark P. 2016. "Idolatry of Mind and Intellectual Suicide." Pp. 1–11 in *The Social Ontology of Capitalism*, co-edited by Dan Krier and Mark P. Worrell. New York: Palgrave.

Worrell, Mark P. 2017a. "The Social Psychology of Authority." Pp. 463–80 in *Handbook of Critical Theory*, ed. Michael J. Thompson. New York: Palgrave.

Worrell, Mark P. 2017b. "The Sacred and the Profane in the General Formula for Capital: The Octagonal Structure of the Commodity and Saving Marx's Sociological Realism from Professional Marxology." Pp. 75–119 in *The Social Ontology of Capitalism*, eds. Dan Krier and Mark P. Worrell. New York: Palgrave Macmillan.

Worrell, Mark P. 2019. *The Sociogony: Social Facts and the Ontology of Objects, Things, and Monsters*. Leiden: Brill.

Worrell, Mark P. 2020. *Disintegration: Bad Love, Collective Suicide, and the Idols of Imperial Twilight*. Leiden: Brill.

Worrell, Mark P. and Dan Krier. 2012. "The Imperial Eye." *Fast Capitalism* 9.1. Online: (www.uta.edu/huma/agger/fastcapitalism/9_1/worrellkrier9_1.html).

Worrell, Mark P. and Dan Krier. 2018. "Atopia Awaits!" *Critical Sociology* 44(2): 213–39.

Worrell, Mark P. and Dan Krier. 2018b. "Totems, Fetishes, and Enchanted Modernity: Hegelian Marxism Confronts Idolatry." *Logos* 17(1). Online: (www.logosjournal.com).

Worrell, Mark P. and Jamie Dangler. 2011. "Cafe Narcissism Redux." Pp. 72–92 in *Journal of no Illusions: The Legacy of Telos*, eds. Tim Luke and Ben Agger. New York: Telos Press.

Wulf, Maurice de. [1911] 1915. "Nominalism, Realism, Conceptualism." *The Encyclopedia of Catholicism*, Vol. 11. New York: Encyclopedia Press.

Wundt, Wilhelm. 1897. *Ethics: An Investigation of the Facts and Laws of the Moral Life.* London: Swan Sonnenschein.

Yang, Yi-Bo, et al. 2018. "Proton Mass Decomposition from the QCD Energy Momentum Tensor." *Physical Review Letters*, 19 November. Online: (https://doi.org/10.1103/PhysRevLett.121.212001).

Yates, Kit. 2019. *The Math of Life and Death*. New York: Scribner.

Zamyatin, Yevgeny. [1924] 1993. *We*, tr. Clarence Brown. New York: Penguin.

Ziemer, Gregor. 1941. *Education for Death*. London: Oxford University Press.

Žižek, Slavoj. 1989. *The Sublime Object of Ideology*. London: Verso.

Žižek, Slavoj. 1991. *Looking Awry*. Cambridge: The MIT Press.

Žižek, Slavoj. 1993. *Tarrying with the Negative*. Durham: Duke University Press.

Žižek, Slavoj. 2000a. *The Fragile Absolute*. London: Verso.

Žižek, Slavoj. 2000b. *The Ticklish Subject*. London: Verso.

Žižek, Slavoj. 2000c. "From *History and Class Consciousness* to *The Dialectic of Enlightenment* ... and Back." *New German Critique* 81: 107–23.

Žižek, Slavoj. 2000d. *The Art of the Ridiculous Sublime*. Seattle: University of Washington Press.

Žižek, Slavoj. 2001. *Enjoy Your Symptom*, second edition. New York: Routledge.

Žižek, Slavoj. 2001b. *On Belief*. London: Routledge.

Žižek, Slavoj. 2002. *For They Know not What They Do*, second edition. London: Verso.

Žižek, Slavoj. 2003. *The Puppet and the Dwarf*. Cambridge: the MIT Press.

Žižek, Slavoj. 2005. *Interrogating the Real*. London: Continuum.

Žižek, Slavoj. 2006a. *How to Read Lacan*. New York: W.W. Norton.

Žižek, Slavoj. 2006b. *The Parallax View*. Cambridge: The MIT Press.

Žižek, Slavoj. 2008a. *In Defense of Lost Causes*. London and New York: Verso.

Žižek, Slavoj. 2008b. *Violence*. New York: Picador.

Žižek, Slavoj. 2010a. *Living in the End Times*. London and New York: Verso.

Žižek, Slavoj. 2010b. "Thinking Backward: Predestination and Apocalypse." Pp. 185–210 in *Paul's New Moment: Continental Philosophy and the Future of Christian Theology* by Milbank et al. Grand Rapids, MI: Brazos Press.

Žižek, Slavoj. 2012. *Less Than Nothing*. London: Verso.

Žižek, Slavoj. 2012b. "Don't Act. Just Think." *Big Think*. 3 July, 2010. Online: (https://bigthink.com/dont-act-just-think).

Žižek, Slavoj. 2012c. *The Year of Dreaming Dangerously*. London: Verso.

Žižek, Slavoj. 2014. *The Most Sublime Hysteric*, tr. Thomas Scott-Railton. Cambridge: Polity Press.

Žižek, Slavoj. 2014b. *Absolute Recoil*. London and New York: Verso.

Žižek, Slavoj, interviewed by Katie Forster. 2016. "Slavoj Žižek: We are all Basically Evil, Egotistical, Disgusting." *The Guardian*, 10 December. Online: (www.theguardian.com/lifeandstyle/2016/dec/10/slavoj-zizek-we-are-all-basically-evil-egotistical-disgusting).

Žižek, Slavoj. 2019. "Making use of Religion? No, Thanks!" *Los Angeles Review of Books*, 3 June. Online: (https://thephilosophicalsalon.com/making-use-of-religion-no-thanks/).

Žižek, Slavoj. 2019b. "Was I Right to Back Donald Trump Over Hillary Clinton? Absolutely." *The Independent*, 26 June. Online: (https://www.independent.co.uk/voices/trump-hillary-clinton-populist-right-left-democratic-party-civil-war-a8975121.html).

Zola, Emile. [1872] 2004. *The Kill*, tr. Brian Nelson. New York: Oxford University Press.

Zweig, Stefan. [1929] 2012. *Casanova, Stendhal, Tolstoy*. New Brunswick: Transaction Publishers.

Zweig, Stefan. [1943] 2013. "A Chess Story." Pp. 91–150 in *The Collected Novellas of Stefan Zweig*, tr. Anthea Bell. London: Pushkin Press.

Index

19th-century   21

absolute autonomy   67
absolute consciousness   181
absolute evil   98
absolute facts and representations   169
absolute Idea   158
absolute idealism   80, 82, 174, 181, 183, 204, 217, 227
absolute knowledge   162
absolute psychology   14–15
absolute sociology   1, 73, 159, 162, 174, 200, 223
Absolute Spirit   159
abyss   21, 45, 83, 86–87, 90, 99, 119, 146–47, 150, 162, 179
accumulation   4, 15, 50, 61, 188, 201, 207
alienation   13, 16, 32, 35, 55, 72, 75, 87, 91–92, 116–20, 125–27, 155, 157, 173–74
alterity   27
altruism   23, 28, 49, 54–55, 59–62, 87, 92, 95, 125, 128–29, 133, 135, 140
ambivalence   120
anarchy   10, 54, 63, 99, 102, 129, 131, 133, 137, 142, 150
anger   59, 91, 95, 107, 126, 129, 133–34, 138
anomie   48–49, 54, 59, 61, 66–67, 92, 95, 99, 120, 127–29, 133, 135, 137
   chronic   49
   extreme   63
   imperial   128
   positive   54
   regressive   82
anti-authoritarianism   5
anti-capitalism   7–8
anti-charisma   6
anti-drone protests   140
anti-hierarchy   5
anti-intellectualism   86
antinomianism   127
anti-reason   3–6, 18
antisemitic conspiracies   3, 4
antisemitism   25, 97, 98, 121
anxiety   94–95, 152, 176, 215
apriorism   213
aristocracy   75
Aristotelian realism   225
asceticism   42, 49, 60, 81, 94–95, 102–4, 107, 116, 130, 221–22

assemblage   21, 31, 35, 52, 53, 88, 114, 150, 152, 155, 169, 188, 191
Aufheben   174, 203
autarky   112
authoritarianism   5, 54, 96, 98, 103, 148
authority   5, 10, 13, 15, 17, 40, 44, 138, 142, 148–49, 166, 184, 195, 216, 221–22, 225
autocracy   82, 112
autonomy   1, 5, 49, 56, 63–67, 72, 74, 113, 116–17, 153, 180, 203
autothematicism   110, 112, 116
Autothematic-Rabelaisianism   115

being   10–11, 31–39, 52–53, 55–56, 61–62, 77–78, 83, 87, 89–92, 105–6, 125–26, 140–41, 158, 173–74, 182–83, 187–89, 202–3, 210–11, 222–23
   essential   182
   human   51, 55–56, 77, 80, 146, 202
   one-sided   8
   sacred   15, 192
   species   11
belief   21, 38, 50–51, 60, 101, 122, 174, 178, 208, 210, 219
bliss   51, 170
Bolshevism   124
bondage   27, 55, 72, 117, 127
boredom   14, 31, 90, 110, 140
bourgeoisie   18, 50, 79, 83, 113, 187, 194, 210

Caesar   44
callings   3, 19, 39, 103, 112–13, 132–33, 183, 208, 222
Calvinism   52, 75, 221
cannibalism   33, 35
capital   1–4, 15–16, 18, 25, 61, 73, 142–43, 154–55, 159–60, 162–64, 175–76, 181–82, 205, 208–10, 222
   accumulation   75, 127, 175
   constant   210
   dark   143
   fictional   143
   personifications of   15, 61
   variable   210
   virtual   143
capitalism   2, 4, 7–8, 12, 18, 21, 50, 74, 108–9, 123, 143, 155, 159, 221–22
capitalist spirit   158, 222

ceremonies   24, 102
chaos   51, 111, 129, 147, 157, 188, 226
charisma   3, 5, 17, 65, 97, 152, 178, 208, 215, 217
   negative   91
chimeras   72, 146
Christianity   52, 91, 98, 126, 162, 166, 183, 224
Christians   98, 224
church   3, 75, 98, 162, 165–66, 188, 192, 202, 209, 221, 225
circulation   50, 186, 201
clan   18, 39, 63, 207, 219
class conflict   76
class consciousnesses   187
classes   74–76, 80, 83, 86, 95–96, 121, 123, 184, 187, 200, 203, 206, 209
   middle   188
   radical   202
   revolutionary   210
   ruling   16, 56, 75
class exploitation   15
classifications   14, 55, 85, 109, 180, 206
coercion   195, 204, 214
collective consciousness   9, 47, 127, 161, 163, 179–80, 191, 193, 215–16
commodity   25–26, 32, 108–9, 143, 146, 149–50, 154–55, 159–60, 163, 174–76, 178, 205–9, 215
commodity fetishism   174, 210
commodity form   160
competition   22, 112–13, 118, 131, 176, 222
concept   5–6, 8–10, 13–14, 16–18, 23–25, 45, 86, 91–93, 110, 137, 153, 161–62, 167–68, 170–77, 179–81, 183–84, 186–88, 191, 196–200, 218
conceptualism   206–7
conflict   40, 47, 51, 65, 71, 199, 210, 220, 225
   ecstatic   112
   identity-based   4
consciousness   1, 13–15, 90, 92, 157, 159–62, 167, 171–72, 179, 181–84, 216, 218, 226–27
   false   120
   revolutionary   121
constructionism   205–6, 210
contracts   67, 71
contradictions   10, 46, 51, 56, 58, 65, 71, 81, 85, 149–50, 161, 185, 198–99
crime   17, 77, 97, 109, 124, 137, 141, 187
critical sociology   33, 201, 214
   contemporary   158, 191

critical theory   18, 22
   contemporary   187
critique   2, 7, 31, 77, 83, 117, 133, 159–60, 163, 182–83, 206
crusades   224
cult   22, 34, 85, 89, 95, 135, 141, 160, 165, 181, 183
cynicism   16, 22, 40, 107

death   11, 16–17, 33, 35, 50, 57, 90, 117, 119–20, 129, 133–37, 139, 141, 178, 185, 187
dehumanization   182
democracy   7, 10, 54, 96, 121, 123, 146, 148
demons   3, 6, 45, 98, 107, 153
deregulation   128, 131
derivatives   175
desacralization   20
despotism   54–55, 77, 114, 142
destiny   13, 33, 46, 62, 107, 109, 112, 123, 147, 153
destruction   4, 6, 12, 100–101, 103, 106, 129, 131, 139, 141, 143–44
destructiveness   103, 135
devaluation   213
dialectic   1, 5, 9, 25, 39, 53, 56, 59, 72, 132, 137, 149, 153, 158, 160, 174, 178, 180, 182, 186, 188, 198, 207–8
dialectical method   176, 194, 198, 207
disease of the infinite   54
disenchantment   3, 30
disequilibrium   74
disintegration   1–2, 4, 23, 25, 42, 48, 51–52, 71, 73, 79, 96, 103, 104, 111, 115, 150, 155
disobedience   17, 204, 222
diversity   30, 48, 51, 206, 218
domination   15, 68, 70, 76, 91, 149, 164
dreams   10, 13, 30, 34, 46, 48, 52, 66, 90, 125, 132–33
drones   127–28, 131, 140–41, 143–44
Durkheim, E.   1–4, 8–9, 14–17, 27–30, 53–55, 65–67, 83–86, 93–95, 103–4, 108–9, 157–59, 161–67, 177–82, 184–90, 192–96, 205–8, 212–13, 217–20, 222–23, 227
dyads   25–27, 33, 60, 151, 153
dynamism   160, 181

economy   70, 72, 160, 163, 175
   moral   125, 160

ecstasy   44, 49, 60, 83, 87–90, 92–93, 116, 125, 148, 152–53, 155
   apathetic   60
   negative   60
   passive   60
   revolutionary   188
effervescence   11, 148
   collective   85, 91, 160
egoism   7–8, 23, 48, 54–56, 59, 61, 81, 92, 112, 114–15, 118, 120, 125, 127, 137–38
   narcissistic   95
ekstasis   59, 87, 90–93, 104, 116, 148
   mechanized   141
   negative   92
emblems   39, 160, 207
   authoritative   85
   totemic   136, 207
emergence   23, 124, 126, 194, 218, 221
empire   17, 27, 89, 128, 143
   neoliberal   132
empiricism   171, 185–86, 195–96, 202, 213
emulation   27, 95, 103–4, 111
enchantment   59
enemies   4–5, 22, 36, 59–60, 97, 99, 112, 132, 143, 210, 220
energies   1, 4, 12, 15, 47, 49, 55–56, 59–60, 71, 73, 85, 92–93, 95, 152, 221
   collective   127
   moral   85, 146, 207, 226
   polar   72
   sacred   163
   social   85, 139, 207
ennui   23
Entäußerung   117
Entfremdung   117
enthusiasm   36, 88–89, 91, 129, 133, 168
Epicureanism   48, 79, 104, 107–8
equilibrium   35, 47, 74, 181, 193
   mechanical   79
   static   152
ergon   177, 182
estrangement   22, 55, 57, 93, 117, 120, 125, 136, 178
evil   6–8, 36, 49, 51, 53, 97, 136, 138, 140, 144, 147, 165, 203
exchange   2, 22, 91, 117, 135, 176–77, 207
exchange-value   4, 14, 25, 175–76, 205
expiation   103–4, 138
externality   6, 38, 45, 117, 157, 227

fanaticism   49, 60, 61, 79, 91, 106, 132, 133, 135, 140, 143, 148, 223
fanatics   60, 106, 133, 223
fantasy   31, 44, 92, 98, 121, 132, 169–70, 188, 191, 213
fascism   22, 76, 96, 114
fatalism   49, 54–55, 61–62, 72, 80–81, 112, 115, 118, 127, 154
fate   24, 33, 64, 67, 77, 92–93, 112, 150, 153, 187
fetishes   115, 136
fetishism   78, 110, 174, 202, 209, 216
fictions   25, 74, 141, 183, 186, 202, 214–15
Finitude Disease   62
fitna   129
freedom   35, 65–66, 74–75, 141, 145, 149, 151, 157, 176, 182, 223
   negative   6, 176
   positive   4, 10, 176

geometry   20, 23, 50, 154
   moral   16, 44, 150–51, 153, 155
   political   54
gift   32, 40, 65, 66, 102, 125
grace   3, 21, 38, 91, 111
grief   59, 92, 101, 138, 162
guns   134–37, 140, 188
gun violence   133

habitude   112
habitus   112
hate   15, 35, 44, 60, 91, 95, 98, 103, 107
hedonism   79
hegemony   4, 128, 166, 185
heterarchy   110, 112, 114, 116
heteronomous receptivity   72
heteronomy   8, 49, 63–64, 67, 71, 72, 74, 113, 116–17, 125, 153
hierarchy   5, 109, 161
historical constellations   219
historical individuals   219
historical materialism   123, 186, 196, 205–6, 208–9, 227
historicism   157
Homo duplex   16, 55
honor   26, 87, 90, 95, 100, 111, 136, 185
human sacrifice   135, 160
hyper-praxis   11, 79
hyper-production   77, 146, 182
hyper-rationality   3

hyper-spirituality 163, 187
hypo-rationality 4
hypo-repression 56
hypostatization 21, 204, 210

id 48–49, 115, 212
idealism 71, 80–83, 164, 166–68, 170–71, 173, 179, 185, 189–90, 198, 226–27
  critical 173
  dogmatic 80, 167
  empirical 81, 167, 179, 194
  formal 167
  magical 173–74
  pragmatic 173
  problematic 167
  realistic 173
  romantic 173
  skeptical 167
  speculative 171, 204, 218
  subjective 80, 167, 216, 228
identification 31, 33, 36, 42, 62, 67, 213
  introjection 41
  projective 41
  simple 32
  sublime 25
identity 30, 37, 40, 45–46, 50, 61, 72, 85, 120, 167, 169–70
identity-in-difference 30
identity philosophy 170, 179
ideologies 37, 80, 123, 137, 159, 202
idol worship 27
ilinx 154
imperial homunculi 128
impurity 2, 36, 38, 41, 46, 99, 138, 196, 223
indifference 93, 166, 190
individualism 8, 55, 56, 60, 63, 108, 217, 220–22, 227
individuality 40, 47, 55, 59, 65, 117–19, 126, 151, 159, 187–88, 210–12
infantilism 108, 110, 116
infinity 29, 36, 48–49, 61, 63, 72, 93, 108, 115, 132–33, 153
infinity disease 10, 48, 61, 66, 120, 132, 136
instincts 5, 21–22, 43, 111, 113–14
irony 86, 178
irrationalism 163, 186, 195, 212
isolation 3, 65, 87, 93, 106, 112, 133–34, 136, 199, 210, 223

Jesus 3–4, 16–17, 44, 91, 98
jihad 130, 139
joy 19, 101–2, 104, 106, 138, 149, 150
judgments 9, 33, 62–63, 66, 75, 84–85, 116, 170, 197–98, 221, 228
justice 45, 76, 109, 145, 187

Kantian autonomy 65
Kantian categories 172
Kantian idealism 81, 190
killing 6, 16, 70, 91, 102, 131, 134
knowledge 31, 53, 59, 66, 83, 165, 167, 169–72, 179, 193–94, 197–98
Krisis 74

labor 31, 70, 72, 117, 124, 131, 182, 186, 207–8, 209, 210
  concrete 186
  division of 63, 119, 154, 157, 163, 166, 181, 182, 185
  excess 4
  process 15, 117, 119
labor power 15, 39, 70–71, 117–18, 131, 160, 173–74, 182, 221
labor products 25, 30, 117, 186, 209
language 7, 18, 160, 162, 181, 192, 213, 226
laws 45, 47, 50, 56, 61, 63–67, 76, 80, 86, 110–11, 180–81, 211–13
leaders 22, 67, 76, 114, 123, 149, 185
  charismatic 17
  political 95
  totalitarian 67
leadership 22, 27, 115, 220
liberals 50, 131–32, 194
liberation 18, 19, 27, 195
limitations 14, 44, 50, 62–63, 75, 78, 93, 114, 163, 212, 227
limited slavery 71
limitlessness 10, 83, 132–33, 212
logic 15–16, 25–26, 93, 97, 100–101, 111–12, 143, 222, 133, 136, 140, 143, 149–51, 155, 161, 163, 169, 171, 196–97
logos 166, 177, 192, 208, 215
  a love of 166
lone wolf gunmen 143
looking glass self 27
love 14, 21, 34–35, 59–60, 62, 91, 95–96, 100, 107, 113, 129–30, 148, 166, 173

INDEX

loyalty 168
luck 13, 61, 188
lust 79, 140

madness 91–92, 104, 120, 126, 133
magic 2, 5, 12, 46, 49, 58, 60, 68, 73, 83, 85, 132, 145, 147, 174, 176
magical forces 98
magical thinking 2, 110
magicians 2, 46, 60, 174, 215
magic rites 61
magic tricks 86, 200
mana 3, 6, 53, 54, 152, 163, 181, 207–9
mana contamination 91
mania 67, 78–79, 110, 132, 151, 191, 203
Marines 40, 50
martyr 79, 90, 107, 130, 142
martyrdom 90, 103, 130, 148
Marx, K. 11, 30, 32–33, 50, 57–59, 72–73, 77, 108–9, 113–14, 117–24, 149, 157–60, 163, 176–77, 181–82, 186, 188–90, 205, 207–10, 222–23
Marxheimian Sociology 163
Marxism 2, 11, 22, 50, 73, 159, 203, 208–10
Marxist dialectics 207
Marxist materialism 33
mass death 42, 133, 149
masses 11, 15, 21–22, 27, 53, 89, 96, 123, 127, 149, 220–21
mass murderers and mass shootings 89, 131, 133, 134, 135, 144, 187
mass psychology 13
materialism 5, 30, 79, 85, 164, 171, 182–83, 185–86, 194, 208–9, 226–27
  dialectical 185–87, 205, 208–9, 227
mediation 15, 26, 38, 46, 77
medievalism 106
melancholia 24
melody 19, 65
metamorphosis 29
metaphor 8, 30, 79, 148, 153, 155, 165, 183, 214
methodological individualism 217, 220
methods
  individualist 202, 218
  speculative 218
  statistical 191
  stereoscopic 194
mimesis 27, 52, 112, 114

mind 13, 37, 59, 81–82, 84, 90–91, 106, 122, 126–28, 146–47, 166–67, 182, 184–85, 193, 195–96, 200–201, 203, 206–8, 216, 225–27
miracles 3, 6, 21, 49–51, 61, 105, 146, 174
Möbius bands 23, 48, 152
moderate realism 1, 200–201, 203–4, 206
molecularky 114
money 3–4, 160, 164, 173, 176, 191, 198, 201, 204, 213, 216, 218
money-price form 16
monsters 55, 71, 103, 113, 152
morality 65, 75, 178, 182, 212
mourning 101, 104, 138–40
murder rate 130
murders 5–6, 11, 47, 74, 129, 134, 137
murder-suicides 137
mystagogues 109, 215
mysteries 30, 90, 162, 168, 176, 179
mysticism 24, 49, 83, 87, 92, 104, 176, 186
  petit bourgeois 210
  primitive 24
mythologies 3, 52–53, 165, 202
myths 64, 114, 138, 140–41, 150, 165, 168, 174

narcissism 48, 61–63, 136, 140
Nazis 25, 50, 56, 67, 76, 95–96, 114–15, 133, 220
necessity 2–3, 7–8, 23–25, 64–66, 71, 73, 75, 77, 113, 116, 173, 184, 223
  dialectical 7
  irreducible 24
  negative 29
  physical 73, 125
  pragmatic 124
  pure 199
  transitory 64
necromancy 58–59
necrophilia 4, 110, 191
negation 2, 4–6, 13, 18, 28, 31, 32, 38, 141, 159, 162, 173, 176, 177, 183, 194–95, 200, 203
Negative Absolute 20–21, 23, 25, 27, 29, 31, 33, 35, 37, 39, 41, 43, 45, 47, 49
negative dialectics 146
negative ecstasy 92
negative love 91, 98
negative tetrarchy 119
negative unity 10, 53, 62, 82, 87, 110, 112

negativity   2, 4, 12, 29, 34, 36, 44, 79, 119, 145
neoliberal capitalism   55, 131, 144
nihilism   78, 80, 106, 139
nominalism   30, 164, 176, 198, 200–204, 206, 224–27
nomos   11, 64, 191
non-authoritarianism   5
norms   18, 28, 111, 171, 184, 195, 202, 204, 219–20

obedience   17, 72, 104, 127
object-choice   32, 42
object identity   173
objectification   117, 119, 152
objectivation   155
objective idealism   81, 167
objective spirit   79, 222
objectivism   80
objectivity   30, 157, 161–62, 168, 173–74, 193, 198–99, 211
  ontological   180
objects   21, 23, 29–30, 32, 62, 97–99, 128, 135–36, 146, 167–68, 170, 172, 178–79, 218, 225
octahedron   49, 54, 119, 146, 153
  moral   48, 54
conceptualism   207
ontology   55, 191–92, 220, 227
organicism   162, 180
organic social unity   114

pain   60, 93–95, 103–7, 140, 216
paranoia   41, 136, 212
particularities   18, 25, 31, 35, 39, 45, 73, 91, 151, 212, 214
  contingent   198
  historical   25
  institutional   76, 180
  mediating   23
  objective   32
  social-historical   23
party   93, 124, 142, 175, 187–88, 209
  communist   124
  corporate   67
  revolutionary   123
party system   7
passions   17, 51, 59–60, 88, 90, 113, 129
  destructive   93
  liberated   51
  sanguine   13
  ungovernable   54, 89
personality   7, 9, 83–85, 93, 107, 145, 150, 157, 187, 210, 212
personifications   64, 132, 135, 176, 200
perspectives and perspectivalism   36, 68, 80, 85–86, 158, 174, 176, 194, 198, 200, 221
perversions   2, 48, 124
phenomenology   16, 73, 179, 185, 191, 205, 207
physis   208
piacula   41, 60, 94, 95, 100, 102, 103–4, 128, 130, 137–40, 141, 143, 144
Platonic realism   190, 201, 204, 225
poiesis   11, 73
political economy   4, 14–15, 70, 159–60, 175, 177, 205
  critique of   159, 175
positivism   21, 171, 191, 195
  commercial   200
  empirical   169
possession (as a form of alienation)   3, 52, 55, 57, 59–60, 75, 78, 87, 97, 103–4, 124–25
poverty   11, 96, 104, 184
power   29–30, 63, 71–72, 75–76, 96–97, 103–4, 107, 122, 124–28, 165, 167–68, 178–79, 206, 209–10, 213–14
practical activity   11, 182
pragmatism   183, 204
praxis   11–12, 58, 73, 119, 160, 175, 178
predestination and predestinationism   49, 72, 93, 154, 182
predication   7, 29
prejudices   4, 7, 9, 159, 165–66, 190, 195
prestige   27, 76, 105, 121, 133, 208
prices   32, 34, 60, 62, 68, 89, 97, 131, 138, 203
primitivism   24, 71, 108, 116, 141, 183, 198, 226
  modern   110
a priori categories   84, 189, 196
profane and profanation   2, 12, 15, 20, 31, 46, 53, 113, 166, 182, 194, 196, 203, 209, 212–13
projections   37, 52, 67, 83, 161, 170, 173, 175, 196
proletariat, the   22, 75, 89, 101, 113, 124, 188
propaganda   124
  antisemitic   42, 98
  fascist   115

INDEX 277

property 68–69, 75, 77–78, 85, 201
   common 201
   private 183
property owners 176
Protestant ethos 154, 158
Protestantism 212, 218, 221
Protestant Reformation 49, 166, 227
psychoanalysis 22, 94, 159
psychodynamics 97
psychology 9, 14, 168, 180, 190, 193, 216, 227
   collective 180
   mainstream 13, 15
   object-relations 44
   personal 13, 15, 87, 168
psychosis 62, 133
   actual 166
   simulated 166
   inner 99, 148, 218
purity 2–3, 33, 40, 44, 52, 107, 196

quantification 28
quantum mechanics 82
quarks 163, 221
quatriads 151

Rabelaisianism 110, 116
race 4, 18, 36–37, 75, 121, 213
rage 7, 46, 60, 91–92, 98
rampage shooters 128, 130–31, 134, 136, 139, 144
rationalism 166, 172, 195, 203
rationality 3, 67, 101, 125
   instrumental 8
   negative 3
   technical 3
rationalizations 6, 92, 157
   infantile 100
   musical 18
   negative 3
realism 71, 164, 170–71, 173, 190, 192, 198, 200–204, 206–7, 223–28
reason 2–6, 8, 10–11, 31, 38–39, 81, 83, 90–94, 108, 121–22, 133, 146–47, 165, 169–72, 181–83, 196, 199–200, 212, 214–16, 224–25
   autonomy of 181
   concrete 3
   critical 51, 216
   religion of 165–66

recognition 29, 34, 74, 102, 114, 214
Reformation 20, 95, 159–60, 222
regulation 6, 11, 50, 63, 66, 68, 111, 119, 127
reification 205
relativism 158, 174
religion 63, 84, 87–88, 90, 131–32, 165–66, 175, 177, 181, 183, 185, 189, 197, 209–10, 218–19
repetition 150, 154, 189, 202
representations 11, 14, 31–32, 128, 157, 167, 169, 171–72, 181, 184, 187, 190, 192, 226–27
   collective 11, 17, 28, 31, 38, 135, 139–40, 172, 177, 187, 190, 192–93, 196–97
repression 4, 14, 17, 28, 31, 33–34, 56, 142
resignation 49, 60, 80–81, 87, 90, 92–93, 108, 113, 116, 153, 155
revenge 13, 46, 91–92, 95, 99–100, 104, 109, 140, 143, 148, 188
revolution 10–11, 17, 22, 24, 29, 58–59, 113, 147, 149, 162–63, 210
rights 73–77, 132
   abstract 77
   political 75
rites 11–12, 52, 64, 84, 95, 102, 138, 141, 177, 209, 212
rituals 53, 85, 102–3, 135, 137, 140, 187, 223
routinization 5–6

sacralization 31
sacred doubles 213
sacred pollution 36
sacrifice 11, 16–17, 32, 39, 50, 56, 130, 135, 137–38, 142, 173, 178
   expiatory 129
   obligatory 129
   voluntary 64
sadism 21, 103, 148
sadomasochism 96, 103
sages 27
salvation 3, 44, 166
Sandy Hook Elementary School 134, 135
Santana High School 131
scapegoats 12, 45, 91, 115, 148
schizophrenia 125–26, 166
Scholasticism 9, 190, 225
Schwärmerei 93–94, 102
self-alienation 28, 42, 142
self-consciousness 30, 81, 161, 171, 195

self-destruction 50, 91, 94, 101, 109, 118, 120, 128, 130–31, 139, 154–55
self-sacrifice 34, 56, 91, 114
self-torture 82, 97, 104, 107
servitude 28, 71, 83, 106, 111, 174
shooting sprees 139
signals 138, 194
signification 35, 39, 85
signifiers 4, 15, 130, 140, 176, 201, 203, 214, 221
  empty 1, 142, 201, 203, 215
sin 26, 63, 91, 93, 104, 106–7, 138, 224
singularities 9, 31, 38–39, 212, 219
skepticism 27, 51, 78, 80, 81, 93, 158, 166, 172, 179
slaves 56, 71, 96, 117, 182
social constructionism 18, 205, 210, 211
social cubes 150
social facts 10, 14, 162–63, 184, 190–95, 200, 206, 208, 212–13, 219–21, 227
social forces 13–14, 35, 168, 196, 207, 217
social forms 8, 89, 215
socialism 80, 121, 123, 124, 146, 187
social octahedron 23, 48–49, 53–54, 75, 116, 125, 153, 155
social organization 5, 9, 14, 99, 103, 134, 150, 157, 175, 182, 184, 189
social realism 190, 205, 210, 212, 216–17, 227
sociogony 10–11, 14, 27, 103, 120, 142, 150, 155, 180, 196
sociological heterarchy 110, 116, 133
sociological realism 205, 207, 210–11
solidarity 14, 21, 23, 28, 34–35, 50, 56, 62–63, 78, 209, 215
solitude 93
spirit 3, 6, 8, 15–16, 21, 79, 82, 90, 131–33, 135, 149, 158–60, 181, 197–98, 215–16
splitting 30, 32, 36, 55, 59–60, 65, 84, 87, 125, 173, 207
Stoicism 48, 54, 62, 93, 107
subjectivism 52, 67, 119, 173, 194, 210, 226–27
sublation 10, 25, 30, 34, 81–82, 85, 142, 158, 163, 174, 195
  positive 129
  productive 46
sublimation 33, 114, 209
submission 10, 35, 49, 60–61, 93, 102, 136, 138
subordination 32, 48
suicide 11, 13–14, 16, 34–35, 65, 80–81, 90–91, 119–20, 129–30, 134, 137, 139, 154, 180, 205
  anomic 129

intellectual 2, 51, 81, 83, 164, 199
moral 199
partial 45
political 168
suicide bombers 128–30, 139, 143–44
suicide rate 38, 177
superstition 3, 23, 49, 65, 120, 165, 176, 201, 210
surplus value 4, 15, 47, 77, 83, 127, 175, 187, 191, 207, 209
Sybaritism 79
syllogisms 1, 9, 16, 39, 116, 151, 153, 178, 186, 188, 190, 221
synthetic a priori judgments 23, 49, 153, 155

taboo 9, 18, 49, 53, 61–63, 125, 130, 135, 137, 176
teleological activity 1, 10, 178, 214
terror 4, 6, 12, 16–17, 45, 61, 89–90, 107, 120, 127–29, 136, 137, 142–44
theft 77, 187
Thélème 110–12
Themis 14, 112, 127, 150
totalitarianism 54, 67, 79
totality 30, 35, 78, 86, 151–52, 169, 174, 182, 200, 212, 219
  abstract 136
  concrete 184
  disaggregating 23, 47
totalization 43–44, 108
totemism 85, 160, 176, 219
totems 136, 159, 163, 189, 206–7
transcendental idealism 9, 81–82, 194
transcendentalism 169
triads 48, 151
Trumpism 53, 96–97, 99–101, 132, 168, 175

unconsciousnesses, collective 20, 180
understanding 21, 56, 59, 82, 84, 161, 171–72, 191, 193, 196–97, 211–14, 216, 221, 223
unfreedom 174
unhappiness 14
unions 22, 24, 70, 129, 131, 188
universal equivalent 38, 160
universality 25, 30, 39, 63–64, 82, 112, 117–18, 151, 182, 215, 219
universals 3, 24, 169, 191, 201, 204, 211–12, 224–26
Untergang 31, 42
uselessness-value 30

utopia   50, 110, 113, 142

value   1, 3–5, 15–16, 24–25, 30, 62, 146, 154, 159–60, 182–83, 200–201, 203, 207–10, 212, 215–16
value forms   25, 175, 181
value relativism   146
vengeance   99, 104, 109, 141
Vernunft   214
Verstehen   214
Verstehen sociology   162
victims   46, 101, 102–3, 115, 137–40, 210
victory disease   88
viewpoints   21, 85, 174, 176, 198, 221
violence   3, 77, 80, 102–3, 106, 133, 138, 140, 145, 152, 214
vocations   3, 19, 32, 56, 166, 188

wages   69, 117, 188, 221
   lower   131
   maximum   188
   minimum   188
   wage slavery   72, 187

war   20, 25, 45, 88–89, 103, 110, 124, 129, 133, 140, 149, 210
war charisma   89
war *ekstasis*   88
wealth   11, 12, 15, 50, 55, 57, 77, 89–90, 108, 175, 184, 188, 218
weapons   92, 131, 135, 140
Whitman, W.   51, 73, 148–49, 150, 181
workers   15, 22–23, 31, 70–71, 117–18, 122, 124, 209–10, 219
   antisemitic   42
   modern   15, 24
   revolutionary   209
   worker sentiment   22
Worrell, M.   4, 10, 13, 22, 27, 33, 42, 88–89, 128–29, 133, 136–37, 143

Young Hegelians   185

Zero-land   132
Zeus   46

www.ingramcontent.com/pod-product-compliance
Lightning Source LLC
Chambersburg PA
CBHW070913030426
42336CB00014BA/2393